READINGS IN THE MILITARY-INDUSTRIAL COMPLEX

SUPER ☆ STATE

READINGS IN THE MILITARY–INDUSTRIAL COMPLEX

Edited by
Herbert I. Schiller
and
Joseph D. Phillips

UNIVERSITY OF ILLINOIS PRESS
Urbana, Chicago, London

Manufactured in the United States of America
Library of Congress Catalog Card No. 73–104026

252 00096 X

To those Americans,
particularly the young,
who are challenging the Super-state

ACKNOWLEDGMENTS

A NUMBER OF PEOPLE contributed to the making of this book. Professor Robert Eisner of Northwestern University suggested the usefulness of such a collection of readings. Professor V. Lewis Bassie of the University of Illinois in Urbana read our introductory chapter and proposed a number of improvements in content and style. Charles Cooper, a graduate research assistant in the Bureau of Economic and Business Research of the University of Illinois helped to find relevant materials. Corinne Guntzel and Daniel Geraci, also graduate research assistants in the Bureau, contributed to the bibliography. Judith Halfman, Bette Kelley, Nancy Parrott, the able secretarial staff of the Bureau, typed the many manuscripts. Martha Bergland of the University of Illinois Press carefully edited the manuscript. To all of these we offer our thanks.

CONTENTS

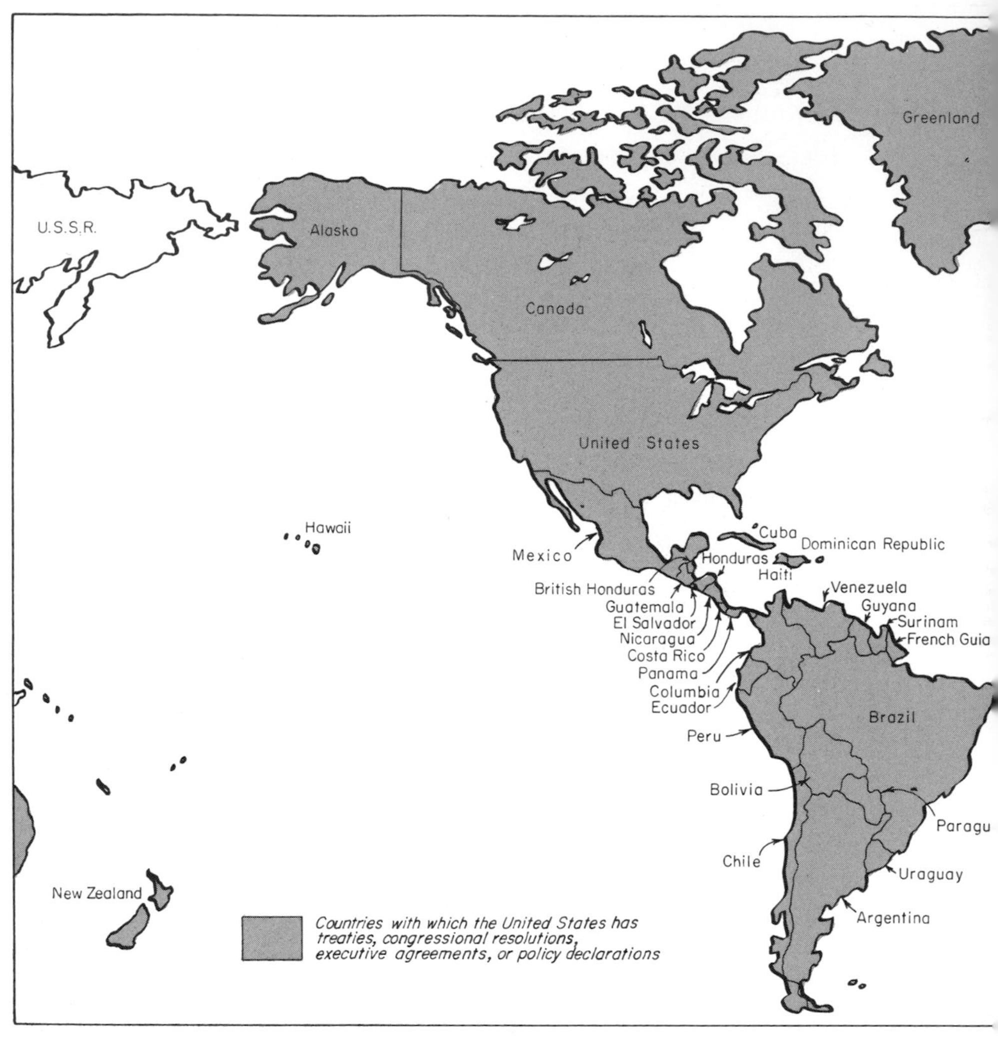
Greenland
U.S.S.R.
Alaska
Canada
United States
Hawaii
Mexico
Cuba
Dominican Republic
Honduras
Haiti
British Honduras
Guatemala
El Salvador
Nicaragua
Costa Rica
Panama
Columbia
Ecuador
Venezuela
Guyana
Surinam
French Guia
Brazil
Peru
Bolivia
Paragu
Chile
Uraguay
Argentina
New Zealand
Countries with which the United States has treaties, congressional resolutions, executive agreements, or policy declarations

Sweden
Iceland
Norway
Finland
Union of Soviet Socialist Republics
United Kingdom
Denm'k
Neth.
Poland
E.Ger.
W. Ger.
Ireland
Czech.
Hungary
Belgium
Aus.
Rum.
France
Sw.
Yug.
Bul.
Mongolia
N.Korea
Spain
Italy
Turkey
Afghanistan
Syria
Greece
Jammu &
Kashmir
Morocco
Tunis.
Leb.
Iraq
Iran
China
Israel
S. Korea
Japan
Nepal
Spanish
Algeria
Libya
U.A.R.
Jordan
Burma
Laos
Saudi Arabia
India
N.Vietnam
Taiwan
Pakistan
Mali
Niger
Chad
Pakistan
Thailand
Philippines
Sudan
Ethiopia
Cambodia
S.Vietnam
Nigeria
Somali Republic
Malaysia
Liberia
Ghana
Cam.
Ivory Coast
Dem. Rep. of the Congo
Gabon
Kenya
Congo
Indonesia
Tunzania
Angola
Zamb.
Rho.
Malagasy Republic
S.W. Africa
Bot.
Australia
Mozambique
Republic of South Africa

1 ☆ INTRODUCTION

THE MILITARY–INDUSTRIAL ESTABLISHMENT: COMPLEX OR SYSTEM?

Herbert I. Schiller and Joseph D. Phillips

In the early 1960s Americans rediscovered poverty. By the end of the sixties the military-industrial complex was uncovered. All told, this constituted quite a decade for finds that some observers felt had been quite visible and pervasive features of the national landscape for some time.

President Eisenhower delivered his farewell speech (see pp. 29–34) warning the nation against "undue concentrations of power" in the industrial and military sectors of the economy in January, 1961, but it was a long eight years later before *Time* took up as a cover-story the existence of such an alliance, and before *Newsweek* and *Look* reviewed the implications of this institutional development. Was this another instance of an idea whose time had come, at least as far as the mass media were concerned? Still, some may wonder with Senator Goldwater why there is such a "complex about a complex" (see pp. 234–241) at this time.

For certainly, the slightest exposure to the twentieth-century history of industrialized societies provides more than enough examples of predatory military-industrial partnerships. The appearance of still another case-history, if not yet routine, can scarcely arouse comment on its uniqueness. Military-industrial complexes are not, after all, as American as apple pie. To be sure, Germany still has an unmatchable modern record for fashioning business-grounded military juggernauts. Gas ovens, meticulously engineered by the world's most advanced scientific community, remain a testimonial to the efficient linkage of commercial objectives, technological know-how, and military conquest in the Third Reich.

Yet no less ambitious was the tandem driven by Japanese generals and industrial monopolies (Zaibatsu) in the Far East over Korea, across Manchuria into China, and eventually exploding into general Pacific warfare at Pearl Harbor in 1941. Moreover, Italian military and corporate elites had their short-lived dream of a Mediterranean basin restored to Roman hegemony in the 1930s. France, too, has teetered on the edge of military coups undertaken with the support of the industrial order since the days preceding the Popular Front in the early 1930s; it toppled into a semimilitary dictatorship under Petain during the second world war, and was taken over by a less unpopular and not quite so autocratic regime under De Gaulle in the 1950s. Of the *major* private enterprise, industrialized states, only the British have kept a continuous semblance of civilian order and decorum in the organization and performance of their state affairs.

The emergence of a powerful military-commercial component in the American system, therefore, is no exceptional event in the modern Western world. On the contrary, if generalizations can be made about cross-national organizational behavior in this period, the national business-military linkages have fairly uniform origins though obviously very specific national characteristics. In Germany, Italy, and Japan, at any rate, the efforts of leadership groups in those states to establish imperial systems of control beyond their national frontiers required substantial dependencies on their military sectors. In France, where an empire already existed, it was the rise of a united working-class challenge that stimulated the key elements in the established order, the industrial property-holders and the army, to open power-seeking initiatives to preserve the system-in-being.

It was entirely predictable therefore, that American economic expansionism during and since World War II should produce an ever-warmer association between economic operator and military protector, that is, between the principal agent and certainly the chief beneficiary of that expansion, U.S. corporate business, and the main instrument for protecting that expansion, the armed forces.

We have grown accustomed to self-justifying explanations of the origins of the cold war. Only recently have different perspectives of what occurred in the 1940s and early 1950s begun to appear.[1] Sam-

[1] One of the best examples of the reappraisal of the forties is Gabriel Kolko, *The Politics of War* (New York: Random House, 1969). See also William Appleman Williams, *The Roots of Modern American Empire* (New York: Random House, 1969).

uel P. Huntington, for instance, in 1967 wrote about this critical period:

By the year 2000 it should be clear retrospectively that the dominant feature of international politics during the thirty years after World War II was neither the East-West confrontation between the U.S. and the Sino-Soviet bloc nor the North-South conflict between the developed and the underdeveloped countries. Instead the crucial relationship was that between the United States and Western Europe, and the dominant feature of international politics during this period was the expansion of the power of the United States. A critical feature of this expansion was the extension of American power into the vacuums that were left after the decline of the European influence in Asia, Africa, and even Latin America. . . . Americans devoted much attention to the expansion of Communism (which, in fact, expanded very little after 1949), and in the process they tended to ignore the expansion of the United States influence and presence throughout much of the world.[2]

More recently, Walter Lippmann put it this way: ". . . we flowed beyond our natural limits. . . . That over-expansion in the nineteen fifties—beginning before the Korean War, beginning really with the Truman Doctrine—has been the cause of the distortion of our whole way of political life."[3]

The evidence of a United States global presence is no secret. American advertising messages now circle the world. U.S. television shows penetrate living rooms on all continents. Private United States–owned factories and industrial facilities comprise in Western Europe alone, a productive force which accounts for more goods than the output of any other national state excepting the U.S. itself and the Soviet Union. Americans, less than seven per cent of the world's population, drain the hemispheres for the raw material inputs that go into the celebrated U.S. standard of living, consuming thereby a wildly disproportionate share of the world's resource output. The U.S. Senate majority leader noted that American troops are stationed on 429 major and 2,297 minor bases which occupy 4,000 square miles of land around the world. The bases are located in 30 foreign countries and "altogether, counting

[2] Samuel P. Huntington, "Political Development and the Decline of the American System of World Order," *Daedalus* (Summer 1967), p. 927.

[3] Henry Brandon, "A Talk with Walter Lippmann at 80, About This 'Minor Dark Age,'" *The New York Times Magazine*, September 14, 1969, pp. 25–27.

service men, their dependents and foreign employees, the number of people encased in these bases number 1,750,000."[4]

This is a global presence indeed. In brief, the enormous penetration by American private and governmental interests in the last twenty-five years into hitherto inaccessible domains brings with it the inevitable necessities for policing, protecting, and overseeing the newly acquired, vital properties. Curiously, there is still considerable fuzziness about these relationships though they seem straightforward enough. For example, John Kenneth Galbraith, who is no inconsequential social analyst, is most uninformative on the international aspects of these matters. He inquired into the origins of the military-industrial complex (MIC) and found no single explanation, but was most taken with a line of reasoning which emphasized the bureaucratic organizational factor.

Galbraith offers six reasons for the powerful position that the military-industrial bureaucracy, as he terms it, now assumes in American life. Summarized briefly and perhaps not with full justice to the subtlety of the author's argument, these are: (1) the increasing bureaucratization throughout the economy at large because of specialization; (2) what Galbraith euphemistically calls the "circumstances and images of foreign policy in the late Forties, Fifties and early Sixties," by which he means the popular reaction to the carefully nurtured and widely distributed myth of communist aggression and imminent takeover—"a widely approved response to the seemingly fearsome forces that surrounded us"; (3) the climate of secrecy in the country, arising in large measure from the fear of communism; (4) personal fear, also emanating from point 2 above, which made potential critics of the social order apprehensive that they would sound "suspiciously like (a) Marxist(s)"; (5) domestic priorities had not yet asserted themselves, meaning the black revolts had not yet surfaced; (6) conservative and liberal criticism of the MIC was absent, again, as a result of point 2 above.[5]

Though six factors are offered only two are fundamental to the Galbraithian analysis: the "seemingly" fearful forces of communism were invoked to justify the heavy military build-up, and, once the structure was in being, the natural inclination of bureaucracy to expand carried on the process. We are left in this appraisal with an explanation for the

[4] Interview with Senator Mike Mansfield, *The New York Times,* April 27, 1969, "News of the Week" section.

[5] John Kenneth Galbraith, "How to Control the Military," *Harper's* 238, no. 1429 (1969): 31–46.

military-industrial complex which argues that this mighty construction was created on the basis of mistaken perceptions to begin with and thereafter expanded almost inadvertently according to its own bureaucratic dynamic. This is, if nothing else, a very reassuring accounting. If the pentagon-business alliance is the result of an initial "honest" error which has been extended by a more or less benign internal dynamic, its dismantling should require no herculean effort. Vexing and disagreeable as its demolition would be to some partisan special interests, the complex could not withstand rational assault. And so Galbraith believes: "Finally, all bureaucracy has a mortal weakness; it cannot respond effectively to attack. . . . A bureaucracy under attack is a fortress with thick walls but fixed guns." [6]

If, however, the complex is a symptom and not the source of the present disorder, we are in a very different situation indeed. If it is the functioning of the American economy that requires a massive protective-punitive instrument to maintain its privilege and to assert its authority on the global stage, the MIC is quite another beast than the almost pathetic, though autonomous, bureaucratic colossus described by Galbraith. If, instead, one must recognize the complex as an instrumental structure performing its chores (well or poorly) for a system whose objectives are its own maintenance and extension, the matter is more serious. Then, generals becoming corporate executives, monopolization of defense contracts, defense firms making excessive returns on capital investment, and the assorted evidence of the complex's activities and mechanics remain significant but reduced in scale to details on the section of a canvas which is itself only a corner of a larger picture.

The MIC in such an accounting is servant to, and not initiator of, policy. Of course this cannot be taken too literally or mechanically. Servants make errors. Sometimes they interpret their masters' wishes incorrectly. Occasionally they essay master roles on their own. But by and large, strategic policy is reserved for the legitimate order-givers. Post-World War II examples are amply illustrative: MacArthur, victorious and renowned general, was recalled from his command in Korea; the Cuban missile crisis was at all times a presidential exercise albeit based partly on biases and misjudgment of the CIA; the decision to plunge the nation's youth into the swamps and jungles of Vietnam was continuously a civilian, executive decision, though with advice and in-

[6] *Ibid.*, p. 43.

formation both at home and in the war theater from representatives of the MIC.

A limited view of the MIC as an entity unto itself feeds also simplistic notions of domestic conspiracy. The fact that a *portion* of American industry is heavily dependent on and intimately associated with the armed forces produces some odd economic-social relationships which are detailed further along in this chapter. Departures from competitive business practices, nepotism, flag-waving, lobbying, and psychological, as well as political, assaults on Congress are tried and tested means of commercial self-promotion. Influence peddling, congressional soft-soaping, and mutual interests interact and reinforce each other. These are standard "business methods" though perhaps a bit more expensively undertaken in the aerospace and communications industries.

If all American business is in that perspective a conspiracy, then the practices and performance of the arms-suppliers are certainly no exception. But it would be a mistake, we feel, to view the activities of this one sector, albeit a powerful one, as qualitatively different from the general behavior of the private economy at large. That the government is in most instances the sole purchaser of military output creates special opportunities for distorted business practices. Yet the industrial sector that caters to the military "requirements" of the state is behaving in a traditional manner, using its unique relationship to maximize its market position. To be singled out for behavior which is normal according to the system's own criteria leads to an understandable resentment and bewilderment in the defense-contracting community. If the spread of American interests overseas—the foreign investments, raw materials depots, PR-advertising-entertainment markets, bilateral licensing agreements and alliances—requires bases, troop deployments, materiel and equipment, why put special onus on the producers of the latter who are operating for the most part in the context of an enterprise system which has indicated it regards their outputs as essential?

If domestic needs have become so acute that the expenditures made in protecting and servicing the empire are increasingly questioned, the error of viewing the "defense" function as a cost imposed on the nation by a crafty sector of industry working closely with an ambitious military should be avoided. *It is the empire system itself that deserves the closest attention and criticism, not its subordinate though powerful agent of preservation.*

Vietnam is certainly no exercise undertaken originally by a restless military leadership. In fact, the bitterness engendered in the military services by the impending defeat in Vietnam, an engagement deliberately undertaken and periodically reviewed by the civilian leaders of the system-in-general, arises from an understandable feeling of being cast in the scapegoat role. The war produces, all the same, the growing domestic criticism of the armed forces. Its mindless and winless nature, the endless casualties, the long years of disappointment, the unfair draft system, and the economic dislocations arising out of a distorted economy are the visible consequences of the Vietnamese War. Accordingly, they serve to concentrate criticism on the most apparent principals in that undertaking—the armed forces. The willingness of the political leadership to move away from the policy it had quite carefully drafted and implemented feeds the fires of outrage in the instrumentality that has borne the brunt of the commitment. The political consequences are yet to be determined.

THE FUNCTIONING OF THE COMPLEX

Though the MIC is itself but a part of a larger complex, corporate capitalism—which deploys its capital and facilities on an international basis—its internal mechanics are still worthy of attention for the light they shed on the economy as a whole, revealing the general thrust of an enterprise system to concentration, monopoly, technological distortion, and giantism.

The term "military-industrial complex" does not imply the existence of a conspiracy. Conspiracy implies secrecy of a relationship established to contravene legal or social norms. Secrecy is not the essence of the relationship between the military and the large industrial corporations that are the principal contractors for the production of military equipment and services, although they may resort to it on occasion. In the main, the relationship between the military and industry is quite open. It is based on a general identity of interest in limitless production of weaponry.

The military may be regarded in this context as the selling agency for the whole group of corporations ready to produce military equipment. The Department of Defense makes the pitch for its budget within the administration and before the congressional committees. Seldom is there any indication that particular industrial corporations might have an interest in military appropriations. Occasionally a corporate military contractor may lobby for funds to keep a program in which it has a vested interest going when the program is threatened with elimination or reduction as a result of a decision by the Department of Defense (DOD) or Congress. More rarely, representatives of corporate military industry may try to drum up support for broad, new programs involving vast additions to funds for military procurement, such as the effort recounted in the selection on pp. 89–92. Generally, however, the military contractors leave these matters to the military and direct their efforts separately and in sharp competition with each other to getting as much business from the DOD as they can persuade that agency to give them.

The DOD, which does such an effective job of selling the administration, Congress, and the general public the products of the military industry, is in the position of parceling out the sales among the rival suppliers. The rivalry among the giant military contractors for orders from DOD and the necessity for the latter to allocate its funds among them rather than deal with a single, unified source of supply give rise to particular conflicts of interest—over who is to get what, over quality of performance of the product, etc.—but these are subordinate to the general identity of interest which is the basis of the complex.

THE MAJOR DEFENSE CONTRACTORS

The role of the industrialists engaged in military production in stimulating the expansion of military budgets can only be inferred from bits and pieces of evidence. Witnesses in behalf of DOD budgets before the Congressional Committees considering these are usually confined to military officers and civilian personnel of the agency. In other words, the major defense contractors let the military carry the ball when the game has reached that stage. Along with this and even well before, pressures have been exerted on individual senators and congressmen to support specific programs that affect the volume of business and the level of employment in their districts. Perhaps more important, defense contractors have gone to great expense in drawing up plans, conducting preliminary tests, and compiling scientific data to sell the DOD on the merits of their respective products and capabilities. This applies not only to bits and pieces of military hardware but to wholly new weapons systems. These outlays are often charged to existing contracts, since the same engineering and technical staff is employed on both activities.

Another form of industry sales effort involves the cultivation of military and civilian officials in the upper echelons of the Department of Defense and in the Congress. Major corporations engaged in military contracting provide high positions within their executive ranks to large numbers of generals and admirals on their retirement from military service. Senator Proxmire obtained a list of 2,072 retired military officers of the rank of colonel or Navy captain and above who were employed as of February, 1969, by the 100 companies with the largest volume of military prime contracts. Ten of these companies employed 1,065 and Lockheed alone had 210 on its payroll. A similar list for 1959 showed a total of 721 such retired officers employed by the top 100 defense contractors.

Corporate defense contractors also sponsor meetings with high military and civilian officials, such as the seminars conducted by the Allison Division of General Motors and those sponsored by General Electric. James Ling, head of Ling-Temco-Vought, another leading recipient of military contracts, has described how his company cultivates military officers who might be expected to rise to the exalted position of chief of staff within their service. By careful questioning, LTV officials obtain information about the type of weapon systems that each officer could be expected to push if he became a service chief. This information is a crucial element in LTV's future planning.

These efforts by corporations engaged in military work are largely self-promoting. They are motivated by the drive to secure profits from military contracts for the particular firm resorting to them and to some extent they cancel out in the rivalry for shares.

Another form of industry sales effort is of a more general character. It is directed to increasing total expenditures on armament without regard to their distribution among firms. The various trade associations of defense contractors and certain of the service and "patriotic" organizations pursue this more general approach, although most of them are advocates of particular types of armament expenditure. Thus the Aerospace Industries Association, which represents airplane and missile manufacturers, pushes increased spending for the products of these industries, while the Navy League presses for more aircraft carriers and submarines. It is also the approach taken in such general propaganda efforts as the Rockefeller Brothers' policy report on *International Se-*

curity: The Military Aspect. After citing various inadequacies in U.S. defense spending, the report stated: "The above deficiencies in our strategic positions can be removed only by substantially increased defense expenditures. These increases will run into billions of dollars and must rise substantially in each of the next few years." [7]

Even Frank Pace, Jr., then president of General Dynamics, a position to which he had advanced after serving as Secretary of the Army, in a speech before the American Bankers Association in September, 1957, phrased his support of armament expenditures in general terms, emphasizing its "continuous value to our survival. I refer to the civilian impact of military defense spending and its function as an economic growth stimulant in our society." Thomas G. Lanphier, Jr., a vice-president of Convair, after accusing Eisenhower of taking a "dangerous, dangerous gamble with the survival of our people," by holding down on spending for missiles, resigned from the company to campaign for an immediate boost of $4 billion to $5 billion in the military budget. At about the same time, Senator Henry M. Jackson, sometimes referred to as "the gentleman from Boeing," held hearings before a subcommittee of the Senate Government Operations Committee where an opportunity to demand larger defense expenditures and to criticize the views of President Eisenhower and others who had expressed concern over the impact of military spending on the economy was given to a number of defense contractors. These included Thomas J. Watson, Jr., head of IBM; Robert A. Lovett, a director of North American Aviation and a partner in Brown Brothers, Harriman & Co.; Robert C. Sprague, head of Sprague Electric and co-chairman of the Gaither Committee.[8]

Armaments manufacturers also place their representatives in the Department of Defense for varying periods of time. Often these are middle-rank management or technical personnel whose employment in DOD is ostensibly to make them familiar with the department's programs and procedures in case of a national mobilization. In some cases high arms-industry officials are offered top positions in DOD, a practice justified by all recent administrations on grounds that these men have demonstrated great managerial ability.

Specific knowledge of weapons and their manufacture may be a factor in the employment of "experts" by DOD. Thus Trevor Gardner,

[7] (New York: Rockefeller Brothers Fund, 1958), pp. 57–58.

[8] Cited in Victor Perlo, *Militarism and Industry* (New York: International Publishers, 1963), pp. 162–170.

then president of Hycon Manufacturing, a California munitions manufacturing firm, was appointed Special Assistant to the Secretary of the Air Force for Research and Development in 1953. He pressed for expansion of the missile program and resigned in 1955 in dissatisfaction with the Eisenhower administration's policies in this area. In the interval his firm, to which he returned as president and chairman of the board, had tripled its volume of business. More recently, David Packard, whose stockholdings in Hewlitt-Packard, West Coast electronics firm, were valued at $300 million, became Under-Secretary of Defense. Occasionally, appointments of industry officials lead to questions of conflict of interest, but these are usually settled in some *pro forma* manner.

MILITARY SPENDING AND GNP

The American economy has become heavily dependent upon military expenditures for its viability. As the one form of government spending that meets with little or no resistance, they have constituted the principal contribution of the federal government to effective demand. Defense outlays in World War II pulled the economy out of the Great Depression when all else had failed. The New Deal had increased federal government purchases of goods and services from $1.5 billion in 1932 to $5.1 billion in 1939 in the face of furious opposition from the Liberty League and other traditional opponents of government intervention, but 17 percent of the labor force were still unemployed in 1939. "The Great Depression of the thirties never came to an end. It merely disappeared in the great mobilization of the forties." [9] By 1944 federal government purchases of goods and services amounted to $89 billion, and unemployment was down to 1.2 percent of the labor force. All but $1.6 billion of $89 billion was for defense. (See Table 1.)

By 1946 defense spending was down to $14.7 billion, but the reduction was largely offset by a sharp expansion in consumer and business expenditures, reflecting the backlogs of demand built up during the war. The moderate decline in economic activity soon turned into a reconversion boom. The cold war brought a reversal of the cutback in military spending, which had reached a low of $9.1 billion in 1947, but

[9] John Kenneth Galbraith, *American Capitalism* (Boston: Houghton Mifflin, 1952), p. 69.

the initial increases were relatively small. These, even when coupled with larger increases in other federal government outlays and in state and local government spending that raised total government purchases of goods and services from $25.1 billion in 1947 to $37.8 billion in 1949, were not enough to prevent a decline in GNP and a sharp rise in the unemployment rate between 1948 and 1949. This minor decline was mainly a reaction to a high rate of inventory accumulation in 1948 and took place while other segments of the economy, particularly construction, remained strong.

The Korean War served to enhance greatly the amount of military spending and the percentage it represented of GNP. This expansion was associated with a sharp increase of GNP and a sharp decrease in the rate of unemployment. However, following the cutback in military spending in 1954, another minor recession was accompanied by a standstill in GNP and a near-doubling of the unemployment rate. Despite this adjustment, the total of military outlays remained above $40 billion and the percentage that they constituted of GNP stayed above 10 percent. After holding at about $40 billion from 1954 to 1956, there was a moderate increase after the Suez and Hungarian crises and then military spending held near $45 billion from 1957 to 1960, staying close to 10 percent of GNP throughout these years. Baran and Sweezy have contended that "the difference between the deep stagnation of the 1930's and the relative prosperity of the 1950's is fully accounted for by the vast military outlays of the 50's." [10] It would be difficult to disprove this contention, which has been made in substance by many other economists. It is clear, however, that these outlays have not eliminated the tendency for the U.S. economy to generate periods of expansion and contraction that are not closely related to changes in the military budget. The 10 percent increase in military spending in 1957 over 1956 did not prevent the contraction of 1957–58, and although the 7 percent increase between 1960 and 1961 may have helped halt the mild downturn of 1960, it was accompanied by a rise in unemployment to the postwar high of 1961.

The expansion of military expenditures by the Kennedy administration raised the total from $44.9 billion in 1960 to $51.6 billion in 1962. Military outlays remained close to that level during the following three years, but when the outlays on space research and technology (which

[10] Paul A. Baran and Paul M. Sweezy, *Monopoly Capital* (New York: Monthly Review Press, 1966), p. 176.

TABLE 1 U.S. Gross National Product, Military Expenditures, and Unemployment Rate, 1939–70

	GNP	MILITARY EXPENDITURES		RATE OF UNEMPLOYMENT
	Billions of dollars	*Billions of dollars*	*Percent of GNP*	
1939	90.5	1.2	1.3	17.2
1940	99.7	2.2	2.2	14.6
1941	124.5	13.8	11.1	9.9
1942	157.9	49.4	31.3	4.7
1943	191.6	79.7	41.6	1.9
1944	210.1	87.4	41.6	1.2
1945	211.9	73.5	34.7	1.9
1946	208.5	14.7	7.1	3.9
1947	231.3	9.1	3.9	3.9
1948	257.6	10.7	4.2	3.8
1949	256.5	13.3	5.2	5.9
1950	284.8	14.1	5.0	5.3
1951	328.4	33.6	10.2	3.3
1952	345.5	45.9	13.3	3.1
1953	364.6	48.7	13.4	2.9
1954	364.8	41.2	11.3	5.6
1955	398.0	38.6	9.7	4.4
1956	419.2	40.3	9.6	4.2
1957	441.1	44.2	10.0	4.3
1958	447.3	45.9	10.3	6.8
1959	483.6	46.0	9.5	5.5
1960	503.8	44.9	8.9	5.6
1961	520.1	47.8	9.2	5.7
1962	560.3	51.6	9.2	5.6
1963	590.5	50.8	8.6	5.7
1964	632.4	50.0	7.9	5.2
1965	684.9	50.1	7.3	4.6
1966	747.6	60.6	8.1	3.8
1967	793.5	72.4	9.1	3.8
1968	865.7	78.0	9.0	3.6
1969	932.1	79.2	8.5	3.5
1970–I	959.6	78.9	8.2	4.2

Source: Economic Report of the President, January 1969, pp. 227, 252; *Survey of Current Business*, May 1970, pp. 9, S–13.

are essentially military in nature) are added, a significant increase is evident. (In terms of the administrative budget these rose from $145 million in fiscal year 1959 to $5.1 billion in fiscal year 1965.) This combined $10 billion expansion contributed greatly to the rapid rise in GNP and the decline in unemployment in these years.

The sharp increases in military spending during 1966, 1967, and 1968 as a result of the escalation of the war in Vietnam not only have reduced the unemployment rate to the lowest level since the Korean war, but also have released strong inflationary pressures. The U.S. Department of Labor has estimated that the military build-up in Vietnam created more than one million jobs in the United States in the two years preceding mid-1967. These accounted for 23 percent of the total increase of more than four million jobs in the economy between 1965 and 1967. Defense work in fiscal year 1967 accounted for 4.1 million, or 5.9 percent, of the nation's total civilian employment compared with 3.0 million, or 4.7 percent, in fiscal year 1965. These estimates "do not include the income multiplier or accelerator effects which induce further consumption and investment purchases." Nor do they include the increase in military personnel from 2.7 million to 3.4 million. The increased civilian employment was the result of a rise from 2.1 million to 3.0 million in estimated private sector employment of wage and salary workers attributable to military procurement and an increase from 900,000 to 1.1 million in Department of Defense civilian employment in the United States for military functions. Each billion dollars of military purchases from the private sector was estimated to create 82,000 jobs in fiscal year 1965 and 73,000 jobs in fiscal year 1967, the decline being due to higher prices and increased productivity.[11]

INDUSTRY SHARES AND DEPENDENCY

Some industries are very dependent on military spending. The distribution of private employment attributable to DOD expenditures provides a measure of this dependency. Aircraft and parts manufacturing not surprisingly stands at the top: it accounted for 16 percent of the total in fiscal year 1967 and 59 percent of its total employment was attributable to military contracts. Ordnance accounted for only 6 percent

[11] Richard P. Oliver, "The Employment Effect of Defense Expenditures," *Monthly Labor Review* 90, no. 9 (1967): 9–16.

of total employment attributable to military spending, but it was even more dependent than the aircraft industry on large military budgets—65 percent of the industry's total employment was derived from military outlays. Radio, television, and communications equipment had a slightly larger share of the total, 7.5 percent, but was only about half as dependent. These were the industries with the largest shares of total employment attributable to DOD expenditures and with the greatest degree of dependency. Transportation and warehousing accounted for about 7 percent of the total and wholesale and retail trade for 5.6 percent, but their degree of dependency was much lower. A number of industries had high measures of dependency: electronic components and accessories, 26 percent; machine shop products, 23 percent; transportation equipment (other than aircraft), 22.5 percent; scientific and controlling instruments, 14 percent. But none of these accounted for as much as 4 percent of total DOD-generated employment.

In general, the employment generated by military spending is widely distributed over a broad range of industries. It accounted for 10.5 percent of total employment in manufacturing and 5 percent of total private employment in fiscal year 1967. The increase in private employment resulting from the Vietnam build-up was distributed in about the same proportions as the fiscal year 1967 totals, except that the shares of ordnance and transportation were somewhat higher and those of the other industry groups were slightly lower.[12]

THE CONCENTRATION OF MILITARY CONTRACTS

Military procurement is highly concentrated. As a consequence, it contributes to the further concentration of American industry as a whole, just as the concentration in the latter contributed to the concentration in military procurement.

The degree of this concentration is indicated in Table 2. The hundred corporations with the largest totals of military prime contracts accounted for nearly three-fourths of the total dollar amount of all such contracts in the fiscal years 1958 through 1964. The fifty corporations with the largest amounts received almost two-thirds of the total in those years. The higher degree of concentration beginning with fiscal year 1958 is attributed to the requirements of space technology and

[12] Oliver, *op. cit.*

sophisticated military systems; the lower degree beginning in fiscal year 1965 results from the strong rise in awards for more diversified military material, such as clothing and food, required by the Vietnam war.

TABLE 2 Distribution of U.S. Military Prime Contract Awards

Period	*Largest 100*	*Largest 50*
June 1940–Sept. 1944 (WWII)[a]	67.2	57.6
July 1950–June 1953 (Korean War)	64.0	56.3
Jan. 1955–June 1957	67.4	59.5
FY 1957	68.4	59.8
FY 1958	74.2	66.9
FY 1959	73.8	65.3
FY 1960	73.4	64.8
FY 1961	74.2	65.8
FY 1962	72.3	63.4
FY 1963	73.9	65.6
FY 1964	73.4	65.8
FY 1965	68.9	61.2
FY 1966	64.0	55.0
FY 1967	65.5	57.0
FY 1968	67.4	—

Source: William L. Baldwin, *The Structure of the Defense Market, 1955–1964* (Durham, N.C.: Duke University Press, 1967), p. 9; *The Economics of Military Procurement*, Report of the Subcommittee on Economy in Government, Joint Economic Committee, *Congressional Record*, 91st Cong., 1st Sess., 1969, p. 5.

[a] The figure for World War II is based on prime contracts of $50,000 or more and excludes procurement of food. The more recent series are based on contracts of $10,000 or more, including food procurement. Thus, the data are not strictly comparable, but since the latter are more inclusive, it might be expected that the percentages would be lower rather than higher.

Some turnover from year to year among the corporations in the lists of the recipients of the largest awards has, of course, occurred. Firms drop off the list of the 50 largest or the 100 largest for a given year, only to reappear in the list for a later year. After adjustment for mergers, joint ventures, and transfer of assets, only 13 of the firms of the 1957 list of the 50 largest contract recipients were not on the comparable list for 1964 and only four were not among the top 100 in 1964.[13] Table 3 shows the turnover between 1958 and 1967. It brings out the fact

[13] William L. Baldwin, *The Structure of the Defense Market, 1955–1964* (Durham, N.C.: Duke University Press, 1967), p. 21.

that the largest contract recipients have the most entrenched positions: 18 of the 25 largest in 1967 had been among the top in 1958 and only two were not in the top 100 at that time, but 41 of the next 75 on the 1967 list were not on the 1958 list of 100 largest contract recipients. Changes in both rank and dollar value of contract awards of the firms on the lists also occur. All these changes reflect primarily changes in the product mix demanded by the Department of Defense.

TABLE 3 Turnover Among Major Defense Contractors, 1958–67

	RANKING IN 1958					
Top 100 contractors, 1967	*1 to 25*	*26 to 50*	*51 to 75*	*76 to 100*	*Below 100*	*Total*
1 to 25	18	3	1	1	2	25
26 to 50	4	8	5	1	7	25
51 to 75	1	3	2	3	16	25
76 to 100	0	1	3	3	18	25
Total	23	15	11	8	43	100

Source: Murray L. Weidenbaum, Economics of Military Procurement, Hearings before the Subcommittee of the Joint Economic Committee, *Congressional Record*, 90th Cong., 2nd Sess., 1968, pt. 1, p. 53.

The measures of concentration and turnover cited above refer to military prime contracts. A considerable part of these is subcontracted by their recipients to other firms. Between 47 percent and 55 percent of military contract payments by reporting prime contractors were paid to their first-tier subcontractors in the fiscal years 1957 to 1963.[14] Data on the total amount of subcontracting have not been collected since 1963, but data for fiscal year 1968 from a sample of 886 large prime contractors indicate that the percentages were similar. However, subcontracting does not seem to alter the degree of concentration in military procurement awards: "Most of the major prime contractors are also substantial subcontractors."[15] A study conducted by the Department of Defense in 1966 revealed that 18 of the 26 leading subcontractors were also among the top 100 prime contractors. The top subcontractor for each prime contractor accounted for an average of 36 percent of all subcontracting by value and the top 10 subcontractors

[14] Baldwin, *op. cit.*, p. 28.
[15] Baldwin, *op. cit.*, p. 40.

for an average of 80 percent. (See p. 144.) Peck and Scherer found the concentration ratios for prime contracts received by 58 major contractors were similar to the concentration ratios for their net military business after adding subcontracts received and subtracting those given.[16]

PROFITS FROM MILITARY PROCUREMENTS CONTRACTS

The anticipation of profit is the principal motivation to business activity by corporations, and there can be little doubt that those who manage corporations try to maximize profits.[17] The eagerness with which many of the largest industrial corporations, as well as thousands of smaller firms, seek military contracts suggests that the profits from this business are generally greater than those from domestic civilian production, despite protestations to the contrary by those involved.

The evidence is hard to come by.[18] Most of the giant corporations that receive the bulk of the military prime contract awards are conglomerates engaged in a great variety of business activities. They usually make no attempt to separate the capital used in their military output from that used in their civilian production. As a consequence, profits on military contracts are usually expressed as a percentage of sales. This is a quite unsatisfactory measure of the rate of profit, particularly since in many cases much of the capital used in production is provided by the government in the form of facilities or cash advances (progress payments). However, it was this measure of profit that former Secretary of Defense Clark M. Clifford cited in a letter of June 13, 1968, to the chairmen of the Senate and House Armed Services Committees

[16] M. J. Peck and F. M. Scherer, *The Weapons Acquisition Process: An Economic Analysis* (Boston: Division of Research, Graduate School of Business Administration, Harvard University, 1962), pp. 150–152.

[17] Another motive for seeking military procurement contracts is to keep in the forefront of technical development. Discoveries can be used elsewhere in the operations of the corporation or sold to others, since the military contractor is permitted to obtain patents on inventions resulting from its DOD-financed research and development contracts.

[18] "Perhaps the most glaring fact about defense profits is that not enough is known about them." *The Economics of Military Procurement,* Report of the Subcommittee on Economy in Government, Joint Economic Committee, *Congressional Record,* 91st Cong., 1st Sess., 1969, p. 15.

and the House Appropriations Committee as indicating that there were "no grounds for concluding that a sharp increase in Defense profits has occurred." The data he reported showed that profits on all renegotiable contracts, which accounted for about three-quarters of all military procurement awards in fiscal year 1967, were down to 3.5 percent of sales in that year compared with 6.5 percent in fiscal year 1956. He added that "Department of Defense officials frequently have expressed concern with the steady decline in profit rates between 1956–1963." In response to this concern, the average negotiated "going-in" profit on noncompetitive contracts was raised from 7.7 percent on estimated cost in January 1964 to 9.4 percent in December 1967, but realized profits, Clifford reported, showed no improvement over the 1959 to 1963 level.[19]

The point to be made here is that these data do not reveal what the average rate of profit on capital invested by military contractors is or has been. The data are not inconsistent with a very high rate. Thus North American Aviation had contracts providing for a profit of 8 percent of costs, but in a 1962 tax court case the company was found to have realized profits of 612 percent and 802 percent on its investment in two successive years.[20] The 1956 Aircraft Production and Profits Hearings conducted by a subcommittee of the House Armed Services Committee revealed typical before-tax profits of aircraft manufacturers amounting to more than 50 percent of their net worth in the period from 1952 to 1955. Boeing obtained 68.3 percent and Lockheed 74.1 percent in 1953. Figures for the Allison Motors Division of General Motors indicate a return of more than 200 percent per year on fixed capital invested in the engine division over a five-year period.[21] Profits on investment in the Minuteman program from 1958 to 1966 amounted to 43 percent.[22]

Apparently someone in the Department of Defense realized that profits expressed as a percentage of sales or costs were an unsatisfactory measure of profit rate, for Secretary Clifford did note that "Two years ago, the Defense Department determined that more detailed information was required on profit trends related to sales, capital invested, and type of contract . . ." The Logistics Management Institute

[19] *Defense Management Journal* 4, no. 3 (1968): 35–37.

[20] *The Economics of Military Procurement, op. cit.*, p. 16.

[21] Cited in Victor Perlo, *Militarism and Industry: Arms Profiteering in the Missile Age* (New York: International Publishers, 1963), chap. 2.

[22] *The Economics of Military Procurement, op. cit.*, p. 17.

was employed to gather information from a number of medium-volume ($25–$200 million annually) and high-volume (over $200 million annually) military contractors. The survey covered 40 companies (23 high-volume and 17 medium-volume) with aggregate defense sales ranging between $13 billion and $15 billion annually since 1958. Table 4 compares the rate of profit to total capital invested for these 40 military contractors with that for 3,500 durable goods manufacturers reporting to the Federal Trade Commission and the Securities Exchange Commission. These data would seem to show that the average profit rate of the 40 military contractors tended to decline from 1958 to 1966, while that of the 3,500 durable goods manufacturers tended to rise. Furthermore, the rate of the latter was higher than that of the 40 military contractors in every year after 1960.

TABLE 4 Comparative Profit Rates of Defense and Nondefense Companies

	40 DEFENSE COMPANIES		3,500 FTC/SEC COMPANIES	
Year	*Profit to sales*	*Profit to total capital invested*	*Profit to sales*	*Profit to total capital invested*
	(*Percent*)	(*Percent*)	(*Percent*)	(*Percent*)
1958	5.4	20.4	7.1	14.1
1959	5.1	19.1	8.9	18.8
1960	4.5	17.0	7.8	15.9
1961	4.3	14.6	7.7	15.1
1962	4.2	14.3	8.9	18.5
1963	3.9	12.5	9.1	19.2
1964	4.0	12.2	9.5	20.4
1965	4.8	14.3	10.4	23.1
1966	4.5	13.0	10.0	22.6

Source: Defense Management Journal 4, no. 3 (1968): 36.

This study by the Logistics Management Institute (LMI) has been criticized by the Subcommittee on Economy in Government of the Joint Economic Committee of the U.S. Congress on the following grounds: (1) it used unverified, unaudited data; (2) the information was obtained on a voluntary basis—42 percent of those contacted provided no data—allowing contractors making high profits to choose not to participate; (3) no distinction between profits of the larger contractors and those of medium volume ones was made.[23] It should be added that there is nothing in Secretary Clifford's letter to indicate that the LMI made any attempt to separate the military from the civilian business of the 40 companies in the survey. If that was not done, the survey results reveal little about the rate of profit on military procurement of even the 40 companies. It also should be added that the LMI was created by the Department of Defense and has worked almost exclusively for DOD. Of the institute's 18 professional staff members, 6 had been employed by military contractors, 6 by research centers or consultant firms heavily oriented to military work, and one was a retired Air Force Reserve officer.[24]

Murray L. Weidenbaum compared six corporations whose contracts from the Department of Defense and the National Aeronautics and Space Administration were estimated to be in excess of three-quarters of their total sales volume in 1965 [25] with six corporations whose output went almost wholly into commercial channels.[26] Each of the latter "was chosen on the basis of similarity of sales volume in 1965 between it and one of the companies in the defense-space sample. (Generally, they were adjacent firms on the *Fortune* list of the 500 largest industrial corporations in 1965.) Each group reported an aggregate sales volume of $7.3 billion in 1965." As shown in Table 5, the return on net worth of the six corporations that are primarily producers for DOD and NASA was much higher in both the 1952 to 1955 period and in the 1962 to 1965 period than that of the six commercially oriented corporations despite smaller after-tax profit margins on sales. Large amounts of government-supplied capital, which are not reflected in the balance sheets of these corporations, permitted the defense-oriented six to obtain much higher rates of capital turnover (sales/net worth) than the commercially oriented six.[27]

[23] *The Economics of Military Procurement*, *op. cit.*, pp. 17–18.

[24] Richard F. Kaufman, "As Eisenhower Was Saying . . . 'We Must Guard against Unwarranted Influence by the Military-Industrial Complex,'" *New York Times Magazine*, June 22, 1969, p. 70.

[25] North American Aviation, Inc., Lockheed Aircraft Corp., General Dynamics Corp., McDonnell Corp., Grumman Aircraft Engineering Corp., and Thiokol Chemical Corp.

[26] National Dairy Products Corp., Firestone Tire and Rubber Corp., General Foods, Inc., Aluminum Company of America, Colgate-Palmolive Co., and Purex, Inc.

[27] Murray L. Weidenbaum, "Arms and the American Economy: A Domestic Convergence Hypothesis," *American Economic Review* 58, no. 2 (1968): 428–437.

The subcommittee of the Joint Economic Committee, after pointing out that "no complete and comprehensive study of this subject has ever been made by any agency of the executive branch or by the GAO," concluded that, "although our present knowledge is incomplete, there is evidence that profits on defense contracts are higher than in related nondefense activities, and higher for the defense industry than for the

TABLE 5[a] Comparison of Defense and Nondefense-Oriented Corporations

	AVERAGE OF SAMPLE OF DEFENSE FIRMS		AVERAGE OF SAMPLE OF INDUSTRIAL FIRMS	
	1952–55	*1962–65*	*1952–55*	*1962–65*
Financial Characteristics				
Profit margin on sales	3.0%	2.6%	4.5%	4.6%
Capital turnover	6.1X	6.8X	2.9X	2.3X
Return on net worth	18.6%	17.5%	13.0%	10.6%
Investor Evaluation				
Price/earnings multiple	7.3	10.9	10.7	20.6
Bond rating (Moody's)	Ba–Baa	Ba–Baa	A–Aa	A–Aa

Source: Moody's Industrial Manual, 1952–55 and 1962–65; company annual reports, 1952–55 and 1962–65.

[a] *American Economic Review* 58, no. 2 (1968): 434.

manufacturing industry as a whole. There is also evidence that this differential has been increasing. The arguments of the Department of Defense to the contrary are unconvincing."[28]

EXPORT SALES OF ARMAMENTS

One important area of close industry-DOD integration is that of U.S.-produced arms sales to foreign governments. This is an activity that was pressed most vigorously in the regime of Defense Secretary McNamara. He appointed Henry J. Kuss, Jr. as deputy assistant defense secretary for international logistics negotiations and instructed him to negotiate directly with other governments for the sale of American weapons. Earlier administrations had provided foreign governments with a large volume of U.S.-produced armament on a grant basis as a part of the

[28] *The Economics of Military Procurement, op. cit.*, pp. 16, 17.

military assistance program. By 1961 the U.S. was ready to collect on that earlier effort. During the seven years ended June 30, 1968, U.S. military export sales totaled $11.5 billion. Of this amount, 48 percent was the result of government-to-government sales. Thus, Kuss's office in the Department of Defense obtained nearly half of all the orders received by U.S. armament manufacturers for sales abroad.[29]

The DOD claimed that its program of encouraging such exports served three important needs: (1) to strengthen our allies militarily, consistent with our own political-economic objectives, (2) to promote cooperative logistics and standardization with our allies, and (3) to offset the current unfavorable balance of payments resulting largely from U.S. military deployments abroad.[30] In addition, Mr. Kuss claimed in 1966 that the orders, commitments, and options received since the end of fiscal year 1961, amounting to over $9 billion, would result in about 1.2 million man-years of employment, spread through all 50 states and the District of Columbia, and almost $1 billion in additional profits to U.S. industry.[31]

Corporations engaged in producing military hardware for foreign governments expect the same progress payments on this business as they receive when producing for the Pentagon's own account. About 70 percent of the military export orders are covered by such pay-as-you-go financing.

Another aspect of the DOD program is the provisions made for credit assistance to governments making purchases of military equipment from U.S. firms. About 30 percent of the export orders require such assistance from private banks or the U.S. government.

These developments were viewed as steps toward the development of a NATO common market for defense production.[32] Although it was recognized that a common market implied a two-way street, with foreign manufacturers of military products selling "less expensive but essential equipment" to the U.S. and participating in joint military research and production projects with U.S. firms, it is clear that U.S. producers are expected to continue to dominate the exchange.

[29] *Aviation Week and Space Technology*, June 2, 1969, p. 126.

[30] "American Business and U.S. Government Cooperate in $6 Billion Military Export Market," *Defense Industry Bulletin* 1, no. 4 (1965): 4.

[31] Henry J. Kuss, Jr., "Military Exports and World Affairs," *Defense Industry Bulletin* 2, no. 6 (1966): 6.

[32] Henry J. Kuss, Jr., "A NATO Common Defense Market," *Defense Industry Bulletin* 1, no. 11 (1965): 5.

In March 1969, Kuss's office was abolished and its responsibilities and some of its personnel were transferred to that of the deputy assistant secretary for military assistance and sales. This was expected to reduce the role of the government in the military export sales effort and to enhance that of the individual U.S. firms in the market.[33]

THE ROLE OF FOREIGN INVESTMENTS

Closely related to the corporations in the military-industrial complex are the corporations with large foreign investments in plant and equipment. In many cases they are the same. But in any case the giant international corporations with their extensive property interests abroad have a very strong motive for supporting the extension of U.S. military power throughout the world—it provides the best assurance against the capture of political power in foreign countries by radicals bent upon reforms that would affect adversely the interests of these corporations, the most extreme reform being the socialization of the economy with the concomitant confiscation of their property.

The enormous build-up of U.S. military power around the rim of the socialist bloc of countries and throughout the noncommunist part of the world has been a major factor in inducing U.S. corporations to invest in plant and equipment abroad, just as in the first place it was induced in large part by the existence of such investments and the felt need to protect them. It has been estimated that now nearly half of the 500 largest U.S. corporations have extensive foreign direct investments, representing an aggregate ownership interest of around $50 billion. "A score or two of these large companies now have a third or more of their total assets abroad; even a greater number derive a third or more of their total income from foreign sales through one channel or another."[34] Some of these companies had extensive foreign facilities before World War I, but the big expansion has come since World War II. The book value of U.S. direct investments abroad increased from $7.2 billion in 1946 to $64.8 billion in 1968.[35]

[33] *Aviation Week and Space Technology,* June 2, 1969, p. 126.

[34] Raymond Vernon, "Multinational Enterprise and National Sovereignty," *Harvard Business Review* 45, no. 2 (1967): 156.

[35] David T. Devlin and Frederick Cutler, "The International Investment Position of the United States: Developments in 1968," *Survey of Current Business* 49, no. 10 (1969): 28.

This expansion of U.S. direct investment abroad has been dominated by a relatively small number of giant firms. In 1957, the most recent year for which such information is available, 45 firms, each with direct investments valued at $100 million or more, accounted for 57 percent of the total value of all U.S. direct investments abroad. Only 2,812 corporate and noncorporate reporters of direct investment abroad were listed by the U.S. Department of Commerce. Clearly this segment of U.S. business wealth is highly concentrated.

These large and rapidly growing overseas investments of a relatively small number of giant U.S. corporations are highly dependent on the military-industrial complex. Their continued existence requires the continued existence of economies based on private property in the countries where they are located. Socialist revolutions must be prevented and, if possible, socialist countries must be converted to capitalism. To this end leading U.S. business circles have had a decisive part in the formulation of those policies on which the military-industrial complex is based.

CONCLUSION

Whither the military-industrial complex? If it is believed that the MIC is a bureaucratic colossus, an outgrowth of inadvertence rather than design, some specific recipes are available. John K. Galbraith has advanced some modest proposals on how to deal with the military.[36] In effect, he calls for getting "the military power under firm political control." The president, Congress, and the armed services committees of Congress must be tough-minded with the requests and programs of the armed forces. In this effort, independent scientific judgments must be available to the political power. Agreement on arms control and reduction with the Soviets is advocated, though unilateral disarmament has "no political future" in the Galbraithian formula. He does propose nationalization of the arms industry to eliminate what he regards as an unhealthy incestuous relationship between government and business.

In the same revisionist vein, Representative Jonathan Bingham (N.Y.) stresses also the necessity for firmer congressional participation

[36] Galbraith, "How to Control the Military." See note 5 above.

if military spending is to be controlled.[37] Bingham lays great emphasis on the internal checks and balances in the governmental structure that have been eroded in dealing with military expenditures. He calls for more representative and presumably critical congressional committees for the appropriations and armed services functions. Similarly, he advocates strengthened review powers for the Bureau of the Budget when it has its annual confrontation with the pentagon. Important also in Representative Bingham's view, though he is aware of the difficulties, is a decision at the highest national level between domestic needs and international commitments.

There are those also, quite numerous in fact, who believe that with the scaling down of the Vietnamese War, the swollen military budget will be deflated. They see a substantial reduction in the entire apparatus of the armed forces with the liquidation of the Southeast Asia venture and they claim that at such a time a return to a "normal" level of forces-in-being becomes inevitable. This optimism was shaken somewhat in the early months of the new Nixon Administration by the warning of presidential advisor Daniel P. Moynihan that the peace dividend accruing from the war's end might be much smaller than anticipated because other military needs had to be met. Recent accounts of widespread U.S. military activity in Cambodia, Laos, and Thailand limit further the expectations of a complete liquidation of the American involvement in that part of the world.

Charles Schultze, former budget director, also has pointed out that military programs already in existence and on drafting boards will eat up most, if not all, of the "savings" that the termination of the war may provide.[38] This leaves the dismantling of the MIC, even with the assumption of its dispensability to the economy accepted, a very uncertain possibility.

If, however, the MIC is regarded as organically inseparable from the politico-economic structure that has evolved in the United States, a nodal link in *a powerful imperial system still extending its influence globally,* a very different perspective unfolds.[39]

[37] Jonathan B. Bingham, "Can Military Spending Be Controlled," *Foreign Affairs* 48, no. 1 (1969).

[38] Charles L. Schultze, "The Military Budget and National Economic Priorities," Testimony before the Joint Economic Committee, Subcommittee on Economy in Government, 91st Cong., 1st Sess., June 3, 1969, pp. 57–70.

[39] In this regard, the description of Lt. General August Schomburg, former Commandant of the Industrial College of the Armed Forces, of his college's mis-

From this viewpoint, it is the future of advanced corporate capitalism that comes into question. The battle over the MIC widens into a struggle for the survival of the System itself, for the military component is hardly a frill if American capitalism expects to maintain its international position of dominance and its internal economic stability, such as it is. For example, what becomes of the multinational corporation, the public relations label for American companies operating in many national markets? Without the ever-present support of U.S. armed forces ready to intervene on the instant, what are the long run (say twenty years) chances for their unmolested operations? And what happens also, to the capital goods boom of quarter-century duration which has been fueled and supported by well over a trillion dollars (a thousand billions) of public funds poured into defense and ancillary industries? This is not to suggest the immediate onset of an economic slump when/if military spending is terminated or cut drastically. It is, however, a recognition of the enormous instabilities in the American economy which have been largely obscured and concealed by the almost institutionalized war budgets of recent decades. Any *significant* reduction in the annual military appropriations would reintroduce the probability of major cyclical activity in the production system, and what then?

Coming to grips with the MIC, in more ways than one, means going to the mat with the System itself. The interdependencies that characterize a modern economy may produce a remarkable number and variety of unanticipated consequences that could flow from a reduction in American militarism. Millions of young men of draft age would suddenly be thrust into a diminishing job market. The removal of pressure to be enrolled in a university once the threat of the draft was lifted could spill additional hundreds of thousands of youths into an already-shrunken employment scene. The strains on a sclerotic political system, visible in the 1968 elections, may well intensify as the claimants for shares in the goods economy multiply and press their demands. All this may be occurring simultaneously with the diminution of the

sion, is instructive: "Students are left in no doubt that American military power is rooted in American industry which develops and produces the sophisticated new military hardware, performs most of the applied research on which continued technological advance depends, and generates much of the enormous wealth that has enabled the United States to maintain a global military hegemony and support a considerable limited war effort with little disruption of normal economic life." *The Conference Board Record* (Sept. 1967), p. 14.

international safety valve of sales and investment in foreign markets and as the prop of domestic noncompetitive military production is yanked away.

Richard Barnet recommends the total reevaluation of the nation's foreign policy and urges the formulation of a national conversion program that would shift the country's entire production effort away from what he terms the Economy of Death to the Economy of Life.[40] This, in brief, is a recipe that requires a massive restructuring of the nation's industrial base, and, even more difficult, a different motivation for its operation. It suggests a fresh view of what life should be about in an electronic age. Where will the impetus for such imaginative and far-reaching changes come from? It is still too early to say with certainty but the battle is joined. In this or any other battle, the MIC will protect itself. In 1969, its efforts to suppress dissent grew apace. The vice-president attacked the mass media, never noted for their courage or vigorous criticism. The Attorney General extended governmental eavesdropping and legitimized political arrests. The increasingly popular slogan "law and order" bespeaks a willingness of national and local decision-makers to use law enforcement forces to maintain the order that their positions require. Perhaps the clamor of the National Guard patrolling America's streets, heard so often in recent months, may be a foretaste of the age upon which we are already embarked.

[40] Richard J. Barnet, *The Economy of Death* (New York: Atheneum, 1969).

2 ☆ THE PROBLEM STATED

LIBERTY IS AT STAKE

Dwight D. Eisenhower

GOOD EVENING, MY FELLOW AMERICANS: First, I should like to express my gratitude to the radio and television networks for the opportunities they have given me over the years to bring reports and messages to our nation. My special thanks go to them for the opportunity of addressing you this evening.

Three days from now, after half a century in the service of our country, I shall lay down the responsibilities of office as, in traditional and solemn ceremony, the authority of the Presidency is vested in my successor.

This evening I come to you with a message of leave-taking and farewell, and to share a few final thoughts with you, my countrymen.

Like every other citizen, I wish the new President, and all who will labor with him, Godspeed. I pray that the coming years will be blessed with peace and prosperity for all.

Our people expect their President and the Congress to find essential agreement on issues of great moment, and wise resolution of which will better shape the future of the nation.

My own relations with the Congress, which began on a remote and tenuous basis when, long ago, a member of the Senate appointed me to West Point, have since ranged to the intimate during the war and immediate postwar period, and finally to the mutually interdependent during these past eight years.

In this final relationship, the Congress and the Administration have, on most vital issues, cooperated well to serve the national good rather

Farewell address delivered to the nation, Washington, D.C., January 17, 1961, in Louis Filler, *The President Speaks: From William McKinley to Lyndon B. Johnson* (New York: G. P. Putnam, 1964), p. 365.

than mere partisanship, and so have assured that the business of the nation should go forward. So my official relationship with the Congress ends in a feeling on my part, of gratitude that we have been able to do so much together.

We now stand ten years past the midpoint of a century that has witnessed four major wars among great nations—three of these involved our own country.

Despite these holocausts America is today the strongest, the most influential, and most productive nation in the world. Understandably proud of this preeminence, we yet realize that America's leadership and prestige depend, not merely upon our unmatched material progress, riches, and military strength, but on how we use our power in the interests of world peace and human betterment.

Throughout America's adventure in free government, our basic purposes have been to keep the peace, to foster progress in human achievement, and to enhance liberty, dignity, and integrity among peoples and among nations.

To strive for less would be unworthy of a free and religious people.

Any failure traceable to arrogance or our lack of comprehension or readiness to sacrifice would inflict upon us grievous hurt, both at home and abroad.

Progress toward these noble goals is persistently threatened by the conflict now engulfing the world. It commands our whole attention, absorbs our very beings.

We face a hostile ideology—global in scope, atheistic in character, ruthless in purpose, and insidious in method. Unhappily the danger it poses promises to be of indefinite duration. To meet it successfully there is called for, not so much the emotional transitory sacrifices of crisis, but rather those which enable us to carry forward steadily, surely, and without complaint the burdens of a prolonged and complex struggle—with liberty at stake.

Only thus shall we remain, despite every provocation, on our charted course toward permanent peace and human betterment.

Crises there will continue to be. In meeting them, whether foreign or domestic, great or small, there is a recurring temptation to feel that some spectacular and costly action could become the miraculous solution to all current difficulties. A huge increase in newer elements of our defenses, development of unrealistic programs to cure every ill in agriculture, a dramatic expansion in basic and applied research—these and many other possibilities, each possibly promising in itself, may be suggested as the only way to the road we wish to travel.

But each proposal must be weighed in the light of a broader consideration: the need to maintain balance in and among national programs —balance between the private and public economy, balance between the cost and hoped for advantages—balance between the clearly necessary and the comfortably desirable; balance between our essential requirements as a nation and the duties imposed by the nation upon the individual; balance between actions of the moment and the national welfare of the future. Good judgment seeks balance and progress; lack of it eventually finds imbalance and frustration.

The record of many decades stands as proof that our people and their Government have, in the main, understood these truths and have responded to them well in the face of threat and stress.

But threats, new in kind or degree, constantly arise. Of these, I mention two only.

A vital element in keeping the peace is our military establishment. Our arms must be mighty, ready for instant action, so that no potential aggressor may be tempted to risk his own destruction.

Our military organization today bears little relation to that known of any of my predecessors in peacetime—or, indeed, by the fighting men of World War II or Korea.

Until the latest of our world conflicts, the United States had no armaments industry. American makers of plowshares could, with time and as required, make swords as well.

But we can no longer risk emergency improvisation of national defense. We have been compelled to create a permanent armaments industry of vast proportions. Added to this, three-and-a-half-million men and women are directly engaged in the defense establishment. We annually spend on military security alone more than the net income of all United States corporations.

Now this conjunction of an immense military establishment and a large arms industry is new in the American experience. The total influence—economic, political, even spiritual—is felt in every city, every state house, every office of the Federal Government. We recognize the imperative need for this development. Yet we must not fail to comprehend its grave implications. Our toil, resources, and livelihood are all involved; so is the very structure of our society.

In the councils of Government, we must guard against the acquisition of unwarranted influence, whether sought or unsought, by the military-industrial complex. The potential for the disastrous rise of misplaced power exists and will persist.

We must never let the weight of this combination endanger our liberties or democratic processes. We should take nothing for granted. Only an alert and knowledgeable citizenry can compel the proper meshing of the huge industrial and military machinery of defense with our peaceful methods and goals, so that security and liberty may prosper together.

Akin to, and largely responsible for, the sweeping changes in our industrial-military posture has been the technological revolution during recent decades.

In this revolution research has become central. It also becomes more formalized, complex, and costly. A steadily increasing share is conducted for, by, or at the direction of the Federal Government.

Today the solitary inventor, tinkering in his shop, has been overshadowed by task forces of scientists, in laboratories and testing fields. In the same fashion, the free university, historically the fountainhead of free ideas and scientific discovery, has experienced a revolution in the conduct of research. Partly because of the huge costs involved, a Government contract becomes virtually a substitute for intellectual curiosity.

For every old blackboard there are now hundreds of new electronic computers.

The prospect of domination of the nation's scholars by Federal employment, project allocations, and the power of money is ever present, and is gravely to be regarded.

Yet, in holding scientific research and discovery in respect, as we should, we must also be alert to the equal and opposite danger that public policy could itself become the captive of a scientific-technological elite.

It is the task of statesmanship to mold, to balance, and to integrate these and other forces, new and old, within the principles of our democratic system—ever aiming toward the supreme goals of our free society.

Another factor in maintaining balance involves the element of time. As we peer into society's future, we—you and I, and our Government—must avoid the impulse to live only for today, plundering, for our own ease and convenience, the precious resources of tomorrow.

We cannot mortgage the material assets of our grandchildren without risking the loss also of their political and spiritual heritage. We want democracy to survive for all generations to come, not to become the insolvent phantom of tomorrow.

During the long lane of the history yet to be written America knows that this world of ours, ever growing smaller, must avoid becoming a community of dreadful fear and hate, and be instead, a proud confederation of mutual trust and respect.

Such a confederation must be one of equals. The weakest must come to the conference table with the same confidence as do we, protected as we are by our moral, economic, and military strength. That table, though scarred by many past frustrations, cannot be abandoned for the certain agony of the battlefield.

Disarmament, with mutual honor and confidence, is a continuing imperative. Together, we must learn how to compose differences—not with arms, but with intellect and decent purpose. Because this need is so sharp and apparent, I confess that I lay down my official responsibilities in this field with a definite sense of disappointment. As one who has witnessed the horror and the lingering sadness of war, as one who knows that another war could utterly destroy this civilization which has been so slowly and painfully built over thousands of years, I wish I could say tonight that a lasting peace is in sight.

Happily, I can say that war has been avoided. Steady progress toward our ultimate goal has been made. But so much remains to be done. As a private citizen, I shall never cease to do what little I can to help the world advance along that road.

So, in this, my last good night to you as your President, I thank you for the many opportunities you have given me for public service in war and in peace.

I trust that, in that service, you find some things worthy. As for the rest of it, I know you will find ways to improve performance in the future.

You and I—my fellow citizens—need to be strong in our faith that all nations, under God, will reach the goal of peace with justice. May we be ever unswerving in devotion to principle, confident but humble with power, diligent in pursuit of the nation's great goals.

To all the peoples of the world, I once more give expression to America's prayerful and continuing aspiration:

We pray that peoples of all faiths, all races, all nations, may have their great human needs satisfied; that those now denied opportunity shall come to enjoy it to the full; that all who yearn for freedom may experience its spiritual blessings, those who have freedom will understand, also, its heavy responsibility; that all who are insensitive to the needs of others, will learn charity; and that the scourges of poverty, disease, and ignorance will be made to disappear from the earth; and that in the goodness of time, all peoples will come to live together in a peace guaranteed by the binding force of mutual respect and love.

Now, on Friday noon, I am to become a private citizen. I am proud to do so. I look forward to it.

Thank you, and good night.

3 ☆ THE ROLE OF INDUSTRY IN THE MILITARY-INDUSTRIAL COMPLEX

A CAUSERIE AT THE MILITARY-INDUSTRIAL

Paul Goodman

The National Security Industrial Association (NSIA) was founded in 1944 by James Forrestal, to maintain and enhance the beautiful wartime communication between the armament industries and the government. At present it comprises 400 members, including of course all the giant aircraft, electronics, motors, oil, and chemical corporations, but also many one would not expect: not only General Dynamics, General Motors, and General Telephone and Electronics, but General Foods and General Learning; not only Sperry Rand, RCA, and Lockheed, but Servco and Otis Elevators. It is a wealthy club. The military budget is $84 billion.

At the recent biennial symposium, held on October 18 and 19 in the State Department auditorium, the theme was "Research and Development in the 1970s." To my not unalloyed pleasure, I was invited to participate as one of the seventeen speakers and assigned the topic "Planning for the Socio-Economic Environment." Naturally I could make the usual speculations about why I was thus "co-opted." I doubt that they expected to pick my brains for any profitable ideas. But it is useful for feeders at the public trough to present an image of wide ranging discussion. It is comfortable to be able to say, "You see? these far-outniks are impractical." And business meetings are dull and I am notoriously stimulating. But the letter of invitation from Henri

New York Review 9, no. 9 (November 23, 1967): 14–19. Reprinted with permission from *The New York Review of Books*.

Busignies of ITT, the chairman of the symposium committee, said only, "Your accomplishments throughout your distinguished career eminently qualify you to speak with authority on the subject."

What is an intellectual man to do in such a case? I agree with the Gandhian principle, always cooperate within the limits of honor, truth, and justice. But how to cooperate with the military industrial club! during the Vietnam war 1967! It was certainly not the time to reason about basic premises, as is my usual approach, so I decided simply to confront them and soberly tell them off.

Fortunately it was the week of the demonstration at the Pentagon, when there would be thousands of my friends in Washington. So I tipped them off and thirty students from Cornell and Harpur drove down early to picket the auditorium, with a good leaflet about the evil environment for youth produced by the military corporations. When they came, the white helmets sprang up, plus the cameras and reporters. In the face of this dangerous invasion, the State Department of the United States was put under security, the doors were bolted, and the industrialists (and I) were not allowed to exit—on the 23rd Street side. Inside, I spoke as follows:

R & D FOR THE SOCIO-ECONOMIC ENVIRONMENT OF THE 1970s

"I am astonished that at a conference on planning for the future, you have not invited a single speaker under the age of thirty, the group that is going to live in that future. I am pleased that some of the young people have come to pound on the door anyway, but it is too bad that they aren't allowed to come in.

"This is a bad forum for this topic. Your program mentions the 'emerging national goals' of urban development, continuing education, and improving the quality of man's environment. I would add another essential goal, reviving American democracy; and at least two indispensable international goals, to rescue the majority of mankind from deepening poverty, and to insure the survival of mankind as a species. These goals indeed require research and experimentation of the highest sophistication, but not by you. You people are unfitted by your commitments, your experience, your customary methods, your recruitment, and your moral disposition. You are the military industrial of the United States, the most dangerous body of men at the present in the world, for you not only implement our disastrous policies but are an overwhelming lobby for them, and you expand and rigidify the wrong use of brains, resources, and labor so that change becomes difficult. Most likely the trends you represent will be interrupted by a shambles of riots, alienation, ecological catastrophes, wars, and revolutions, so that current long-range planning, including this conference, is irrelevant. But if we ask what *are* the technological needs and what ought to be researched in this coming period, in the six areas I have mentioned, the best service that you people could perform is rather rapidly to phase yourselves out, passing on your relevant knowledge to people better qualified, or reorganizing yourselves with entirely different sponsors and commitments, so that you learn to think and feel in a different way. Since you are most of the R & D that there is, we cannot do without you as people, but we cannot do with you as you are.

"In aiding technically underdeveloped regions, the need in the foreseeable future is for an intermediate technology, scientifically sophisticated but tailored to their local skills, tribal or other local social organization, plentiful labor force, and available raw materials. The aim is to help them out of starvation, disease, and drudgery without involving them in an international cash nexus of an entirely different order of magnitude. Let them take off at their own pace and in their own style. For models of appropriate technical analyses, I recommend you to E. F. Schumacher, of the British Coal Board, and his associates. Instead, you people—and your counterparts in Europe and Russia—have been imposing your technology, seducing native elites mostly corrupted by Western education, arming them, indeed often using them as a dumping ground for obsolete weapons. As Dr. Busignies pointed out yesterday, your aim must be, while maintaining leadership, to allow very little technical gap, in order to do business. Thus, you have involved these people in a wildly inflationary economy, have driven them into instant urbanization, and increased the amount of disease and destitution. You have disrupted ancient social patterns, debauched their cultures, fomented tribal and other wars, and in Vietnam yourselves engaged in genocide. You have systematically entangled them in Great Power struggles. It is not in your interest, and you do not have the minds or the methods, to take these peoples seriously as people.

"The survival of the human species, at least in a civilized state, demands radical disarmament, and there are several feasible political means to achieve this if we willed it. By the same token, we must drastically de-energize the archaic system of nation-states, e.g. by internationalizing space exploration, expanding operations like the International Geophysical Year, de-nationalizing Peace Corps and aid programs, opening scientific information and travel. Instead, you—and your counterparts in Europe, Russia, and China—have rigidified and aggrandized the states with a Maginotline kind of policy called Deterrence, which has continually escalated rather than stabilized. As Jerome Wiesner has demonstrated, past a certain point your operations have increased insecurity rather than diminished it. But this has been to your interest. Even in the present condition of national rivalry, it has been estimated, by Marc Raskin who sat in on the National Security Council, that the real needs of our defense should cost less than a fourth of the budget you have pork-barreled. You tried, unsuccessfully, to saddle us with the scientifically ludicrous Civil Defense program. You have sabotaged the technology of inspection for disarmament. Now you are saddling us with the anti-missile missiles and the multi-warhead missiles (MIRV). You have corrupted the human adventure of space with programs for armed platforms in orbit. Although we are the most heavily armed and the most naturally protected of the Great Powers, you have seen to it that we spend a vastly greater amount and perhaps a higher proportion of our wealth on armaments than any other nation.

"This brings me to your effect on the climate of the economy. The wealth of a nation is to provide useful goods and services, with an emphasis first on necessities and broad-spread comforts, simply as a decent background for un-economic life and culture; an indefinitely expanding economy is a rat-race. There ought to be an even spread regionally, and no group must be allowed to fall outside of society. At present, thanks to the scientific ingenuity and hard work of previous generations, we could in America allow a modest livelihood to everyone as a constitutional right. And on the other hand, as the young have been saying by their style and actions, there is an imperative need to simplify the standard of living, since the affluent standard has become frivolous, tawdry, and distracting from life itself. But you people have distorted the structure of a rational economy. Since 1945, half of new investment has gone into your products, not subject to the market nor even to Congressional check. This year, 86 percent of money for research is for your arms and rockets. You push through the colossally useless Super-Sonic Transport. At least 20 percent of the economy is directly dependent on your enterprises. The profits and salaries of these enterprises are not normally distributed but go heavily to certain groups while others are excluded to the point of being outcaste. Your system is a major factor in producing the riots in Newark. [*At this remark there were indignant protests.*]

"Some regions of the country are heavily favored—especially Pasadena and Dallas—and others disadvantaged. Public goods have been neglected. A disproportionate share of brains has been drained from more useful invention and development. And worst of all, you have enthusiastically supported an essentially mercantilist economics that measures economic health in terms of abstract Gross National Product and rate of growth, instead of concrete human well-being. Both domestically and internationally, you have been the bellwether of meaningless expansion, and this has sharpened poverty in our own slums and rural regions and for the majority of mankind. It has been argued that military expenditure, precisely because it is isolated and wasteful, is a stabilizer of an economy, providing employment and investment opportunities when necessary; but your unbridled expansion has been the chief factor of social instability.

"Dramatically intervening in education, you have again disrupted the normal structure. Great universities have come to be financed largely for your programs. Faculties have become unbalanced; your kind of people do not fit into the community of scholars. The wandering dialogue of science with the unknown is straitjacketed for petty military projects. You speak increasingly of the need for personal creativity, but this is not to listen to the Creator Spirit for ideas, but to harness it to your ideas. This is blasphemous. There has been secrecy, which is intolerable to true academics and scientists. The political, and morally dubious co-opting of science, engineering, and social science has disgusted and alienated many of the best students. Further, you have warped the method of education, beginning with the primary grades. Your need for narrowly expert personnel has led to processing the young to be test-passers, with a gross exaggeration of credits and grading. You have used the wealth of public and parents to train apprentices for yourselves. Your electronics companies have gone into the 'education industries' and tried to palm off teaching machines, audio-visual aids, and programmed lessons in excess of the evidence for their utility. But the educational requirements of our society in the foreseeable future demand a very different spirit and method. Rather than processing the young, the problem is how to help the young grow up free and inventive in a highly scientific and socially complicated world. We do not need professional personnel so much as autonomous professionals who can criticize the programs handed to them and be ethically responsible. Do you encourage criticism of your programs by either the subsidized professors or the students? [*At this, Mr. Charles Herzfeld, the chairman of the session, shouted "Yes!" and there was loud applause for the interruption, yet I doubt that there is much such encouragement.*] We need fewer lessons and tests, and there ought to be much less necessity and prestige attached to mandarin requirements.

"Let us turn to urbanism. *Prima facie,* there are parts of urban planning—construction, depollution, the logistics of transportation—where your talents ought to be peculiarly useful. Unfortunately, it is your companies who have oversold the planes and the cars, polluted the air and water, and balked at even trivial remedies, so that I do not see how you can be morally trusted with the job. The chief present and future problems in this field, however, are of a different kind. They are two. The long-range problem is to diminish the urbanization and suburban sprawl altogether, for they are economically unviable and socially harmful. For this, the most direct means, and the one I favor, is to cut down rural emigration and encourage rural return, by means of rural reconstruction and regional cultural development. The aim should be a 20 percent rural ratio instead of the present 5 percent. This is an aspect of using high technology for simplification, increasing real goods but probably diminishing the Gross National Product measured in cash. Such a program is not for you. Your thinking is never to simplify and retrench, but always to devise new equipment to alleviate the mess that you have helped to make with your previous equipment.

"Secondly, the immediately urgent urban problem is how to diminish powerlessness, anomie, alienation, and mental disease. For this the best strategy is to decentralize urban administration, in policing, schooling, social welfare, neighborhood renewal, and real-estate and business ownership. Such community development often requires heightening conflict and risking technical inefficiency for intangible gains of initiative and solidarity. This also is obviously not your style. You want to concentrate capital and power. Your systems analyses of social problems always tend toward standardization, centralization, and bureaucratic control, although these are not necessary in the method. You do not like to feed your computers indefinite factors and unknown parameters where spirit, spite, enthusiasm, revenge, invention, etc., will make the difference. To be frank, your programs are usually grounded in puerile theories of social psychology, political science, and moral philosophy. There is a great need for research and trying out in this field, but the likely cast of characters might be small farmers, Negro matriarchs, political activists, long-haired students, and assorted sages. Not you. Let's face it. You are essentially producers of exquisite hardware and good at the logistics of moving objects around, but mostly with the crude aim of destroying things rather than reconstructing or creating anything, which is a harder task. Yet you boldly enter into fields like penology, pedagogy, hospital management, domestic architecture, and planning the next decade—wherever there is a likely budget.

"I will use the last heading, improving the quality of man's environment, as a catch-all for some general remarks. In a society that is cluttered, overcentralized, and overadministered, we should aim at simplification, decentralization, and decontrol. These require highly sophisticated research to determine where, how, and how much. Further, for the first time in history, the scale of the artificial and technological has dwarfed the natural landscape. In prudence, we must begin to think of a principled limitation on artifice and to cut back on some of our present gigantic impositions, if only to insure that we do not commit some terrible ecological blunder. But as Dr. Smelt of Lockheed explained to us yesterday, it is the genius of American technology to go very rapidly from R & D to application; in this context, he said, prudence is not a virtue. A particular case is automation: which human functions should be computerized or automated, which should not? This question—it is both an analytic and an empirical one —ought to be critical in the next decade, but I would not trust IBM salesmen to solve it. Another problem is how man can feel free and at home within the technological environment itself. For instance, comprehending a machine and being able to repair it is one thing; being a mere user and in bondage to service systems is another. Also, to feel free, a man must have a rather strong say in the close environment that he must deal with. But these requirements of a technology are not taken into account by you. Despite Dr. Smelt, technology *is* a branch of moral philosophy, subordinate to criteria like prudence, modesty, safety, amenity, flexibility, cheapness, easy comprehension, repairability, and so forth. If such moral criteria became paramount in the work of technologists, the quality of the environment would be more livable.

"Still a further problem is how to raise the scientific and technical culture of the whole people, and here your imperialistic grab of the R & D money and of the system of education has done immeasurable damage. You have seen to it that the lion's share has gone to your few giant firms and a few giant universities, although in fact very many, perhaps more than half of, important innovations still come from independents and tiny firms. I was pleased that Dr. Dessauer of Xerox pointed this out this morning. If the money were distributed more widely, there would probably be more discovery and invention, and what is more important, there would be a larger pool of scientific and competent people. You make a fanfare about the spinoff of a few socially useful items, but your whole enterprise is notoriously wasteful —for instance, five billions go down the drain when after a couple of years you change the design of a submarine, sorry about that. When you talk about spinoff, you people remind me of the TV networks who, after twenty years of nothing, boast that they did broadcast the McCarthy hearings and the Kennedy funeral. [*This remark led to free and friendly laughter; I do not know whether at the other industry or at their own hoax.*] Finally, concentrating the grants, you narrow the field of discovery and innovation, creating an illusion of technological determinism, as if we *had* to develop in a certain style. But if we had put our brains and money into electric cars, we would now have electric cars; if we had concentrated on intensive agriculture, we would now find that this is the most efficient, and so forth. And in grabbing the funds, you are not even honest; 90 percent of the R & D money goes in fact to shaping up for production, which as entrepreneurs you should pay out of your own pockets.

"No doubt some of these remarks have been unfair and ignorant. [*Frantic applause.*] By and large they are undeniable, and I have not been picking nits.

"These remarks have certainly been harsh and moralistic. We are none of us saints, and ordinarily I would be ashamed to use such a tone. But you are the manufacturers of napalm, fragmentation bombs, the planes that destroy rice. Your weapons have killed hundreds of thousands in Vietnam and you will kill other hundreds of thousands in other Vietnams. I am sure that most of you would concede that much of what you do is ugly and harmful, at home and abroad. But you would say that it is necessary for the American way of life, at home and abroad, and therefore you cannot do otherwise. Since we believe, however, that that way of life itself is unnecessary, ugly, and un-American [*Shouts of "Who are we?"*]—we are I and those people outside—we cannot condone your present operations; they should be wiped off the slate."

Most of the 300 in the audience did not applaud these remarks, but there was quite strong applause from a couple of dozen. Afterward these sought me out singly and explained, "Thanks for having the courage" or more significantly, "Those kids outside are right. My son is doing the same thing in Boston—Ohio State—etc."

The chairman of the session, Charles Herzfeld of ITT, felt obliged to exclaim, "The remark about our committing genocide in Vietnam is obscene. He does not say what is really intolerable there, the Viet Cong single out college graduates for extermination." !!

More poignantly, the director of the symposium, a courteous and intelligent man, apologized to the gathering for having exposed them to me, which must have been a wrench for him to say. He had of course seen my text beforehand.

We went out by the exit onto the other avenue, and I was able to rejoin the more amiable company of the young people, who were now sitting with their backs pressed against the auditorium doors, still among the white helmets. I answered their questions about the proceedings and we dispersed. That night NBC–TV showed a picture of the pickets, and next morning I got a story in the Post.

"Where is it at? Unquestionably the week of Resistance demonstrations was successful and made its point, that thousands and probably tens of thousands are now willing to go to jail or get their heads broken to stop the Vietnam war. There were no disappointments: Turning in the draft-cards, resistance at the induction centers and staging areas and against the Dow and Navy recruiters, the crowd in Washington and the melee at the Pentagon, all proved strong enough.

"We are witnessing a test of legitimacy, and in my opinion the government position is now untenable. Despite a few exotic slogans, there is a groundswell of American populism, including sporadic populist violence as in 1890 or 1933, but mainly solidly secure in the belief that it is itself the democratic voice and LBJ is a usurper. As was not reported in the press, the night vigil on the Pentagon steps on October 22 sang *The Star-Spangled Banner*. It was probably a mistake for the President to have exposed so many troops to the young resisters who were mostly peaceful but obviously spunky and sometimes persuasive.

"The climate is beginning to feel like the eve of the French withdrawal from Algeria, including the same coalition of the young, the intellectuals, and the Algerians (Negroes). The question remains, is the American structure so rich and technologically powerful that its government can dispense with legitimacy? I don't know. And while the NLF and the North Vietnamese have been hanging on and continuing to counter-attack (and their people and our people are dying), American opinion has finally begun to veer sharply toward getting out. The hawk spokesmen have become divided and confused.

"There is a persistent rumor in Washington that the President (or the hidden government) is about to cast the die and approve the prepared invasion of North Vietnam in December. If so, a hundred thousand youth and many many others will resist non-violently or violently and there will be martial law and concentration camps. I will not speculate further along this atomic line.

"But there is evidence that shrewder counsel might prevail; to write off this odious war, adopt a somewhat less adventurous foreign policy, put a little more money into the cities, divert some of the military industrial enterprise into Outer Space and 'long-range planning,' and come to a solid understanding with the Russians. I think this is the meaning of the rapidly increasing dovishness in Congress and the sudden conversion of the Republicans who threaten to nominate Percy or Gavin. The strategy is similar to the New Deal: when the going gets too rough domestically, accommodate and go on to build a grander corporate structure that is, in some respects, better—temporarily. For this plan, however, Johnson would have to go, since it now seems impossible for him to sound a retreat from Vietnam without getting shot by the irate father of a young man who died in vain. Whether we would then get Robert Kennedy or a moderate Republican is probably unimportant.

"Needless to say, this is not the outcome that the radical young are after. They fear, justifiedly, that if we stop the war, most of the Americans will again fall morally and politically asleep. Yet they, like the rest of us, do want to stop the Vietnam war; there are few indeed who are so fanatical for world upheaval as to want that particular evil to continue so that good may come. In my opinion, also, they will have to learn that one is not going to re-structure modern society with a fraction of the 10 percent Negro population, nor even with the 'Third World' ruled by Ben Bellas, Nassers, Maos, Nkrumahs, Sukarnos, or their successors. This is not the stuff of new humanism. For instance, those who objected to being processed at Berkeley will have to think seriously about Chairman Mao's little red book. And those who want to make love not war but who also want to imitate Che Guevara in American cities, must ask themselves what adequate guerrilla tactics would be in a high technology, namely to poison the water, wreck the subways, and cause power failures in New York and Chicago; is this what they intend?

"But I do not think the young themselves will fall asleep. They have been through remarkable experiences and have found one another. There is the potentiality of a kind of youth international. Most important, the present power-systems of the world are indeed unfit for modern conditions, and this will become increasingly apparent. If the young continue to be in conflict, to try out innovations, and to study professionally what ought to be done with our technology and ecology, mores and authority-structure, and the fact of one world, they will gradually shape for themselves a good inheritance to come into. Considering the tremendous power and complexity of the systems they want to displace, twenty years is a short time to devise something better."

BLANK CHECK FOR THE MILITARY

William Proxmire

BLANK CHECK FOR THE MILITARY

Mr. PROXMIRE. Mr. President, I rise today to speak on a most serious matter. In my judgment the President and the Congress and, indeed, the country, have lost control over military spending.

No Adequate Critical Review

There is now no sufficiently critical review of what we spend or how we spend it. There is no adequate machinery either in the executive or legislative branch to control the total amount spent or the way in which military funds are disbursed. This is especially the case with respect to contracting for major weapons systems. The results are vast inefficiencies in procurement, waste in supply, and less security for the country than we could get by spending smaller amounts more efficiently.

When former President Eisenhower left office, he warned against the danger of "unwarranted influences, whether sought or unsought, by the military-industrial complex."

Danger Is Here

I speak today not to warn against some future danger of this influence. I assert that, whether sought or unsought, there is today unwar-

Congressional Record, 91st Cong., 1st Sess., March 10, 1969, vol. 115, no. 42, pp. S2518–S2522.

ranted influence by the military-industrial complex resulting in excessive costs, burgeoning military budgets, and scandalous performances. The danger has long since materialized with a ravaging effect on our nation's spending priorities.

In the first place, we are paying far too much for the military hardware we buy.

But, in addition, and perhaps even more shocking, we often do not get the weapons and products we pay the excessive prices for.

Major components of our weapons systems, for example, routinely do not meet the contract standards and specifications established for them when they are bought.

All of this puts the country in a most ironic position. On the one hand, we have a supply of missiles and weapons which could literally destroy the world. There is little doubt about that.

On the other hand, we find ourselves unable to defend ourselves even against military incidents where relatively minor amounts of force are involved. The *Pueblo* incident is a case in point.

While it is not my purpose to argue what action we should or should not have taken during that incident, I do say that it was shocking that apparently we were unable to take appropriate action at all, even if we had determined to do so.

Supposedly, forces to protect the *Pueblo* were on alert and ready to defend the ship if necessary. They were allegedly "on call." But in the case of the *Pueblo,* as the testimony at the inquiry clearly showed, the forces supposed to be on call were not on call. For a period of about 24 hours after the initial attack took place, we were unable to bring to bear, even if we had desired to do so, the relatively small force from the vast military might of this country needed to protect that ship.

Thus, while we have sufficient military might to create an atomic holocaust and blow up the world, we are at times incapable of countering even a relatively small military force. There are times when we are like the giant Gulliver who was tied down and made immobile by the Lilliputian dwarfs.

This example from this military side is symptomatic of the general situation we face with respect to procurement and contracting. It epitomizes our dilemma.

Situation Out of Control

The problem of defense spending is out of control. The system is top heavy. The military-industrial complex now writes its own budgetary ticket.

This situation is, in part, a result of the highly ambivalent attitudes the country has taken toward our defense over the years. Looking at the long view we seem to have a roller coaster policy. During the 1930's when the threat from Germany, Italy, and Japan was obvious for all to see if only they would look, we starved our military services and placed the security of our country in deadly peril.

Then, after World War II, we overreacted with respect to contracts for weapons systems. Nothing was too good for the military. We have followed a policy of "gold plating." It might even be called "All This and Heaven Too." Americans, in general, have even felt slightly guilty about raising the question of excessive defense spending and whether we were getting our money's worth. The military has had a blank check. It could be said that we have had over two decades of "carte blanche for defense."

Surfeited with Excesses

The result is a system not unlike the medieval knight who was so encased in armor that he was unable to move. We are now so surfeited with excesses that we are almost unable to fight.

This uncritical policy should end. It should end because it is wasteful and costs too much money. It should end because it reduces the real security of the United States.

The military should lighten its pack. It should get into fighting trim.

We Pay Too Much for What We Buy

But whatever mistakes we have made in the past and whatever warnings we may make about the future, at the present time we face a condition and not a theory.

That condition, first of all, is that we pay too much for what we buy.

The evidence that this is true is overwhelming. This is particularly the case on contracts for large weapons systems. Let me cite some of the evidence.

Mr. Robert S. Benson, formerly in the Office of the Assistant Secretary of Defense, Comptroller, has just written in the March issue of the *Washington Monthly* that—"Few Americans are aware that about 90 percent of the major weapons systems that the Defense Department procures end up costing at least twice as much as was originally estimated."

The services from time to time admit this as well. In the official Air Force Guidebook for May of 1966, the Air Force stated, in arguing for a new concept of total package procurement, that—"Thus, the history of defense procurement was replete with cost overruns, less than promised performance which were at least in part the result of intentional buy-in bidding, and this has been the case even in the situation where there has been no substantial increase in the then state of the art."

This was not only true in 1966, but it continues, believe me, to be true today. We have just held a series of hearings on this matter under the auspices of the Subcommittee on Economy in Government of the Joint Economic Committee, of which I am chairman. The C-5 airplane is a major example of a weapon system or plane secured under the concept of "total package procurement." This was a method introduced, it was said, to overcome the terrible inefficiencies.

But our hearings established that the C-5A will probably cost the American taxpayer $2 billion more than the original contract ceiling of $3 billion. The Air Force itself admits that the cost overrun will amount to at least $1.2 billion. And they would admit, I am sure, it would cost $2 billion if they included the cost of spares, which are essential, which would be in the neighborhood of $800 million more.

Delayed Delivery

And, as we have seen in the past few days, delivery is to be delayed now from June until next December. So we face the same old problems of cost overruns and late delivery that the total package concept was supposed to cure.

Profits Up

Let me cite more evidence. When Admiral Rickover testified before our committee, he stated that the Pentagon's "weighted guideline" system of profit determination had resulted in an increase of about 25 percent in profits on defense contracts without regard to the contractor's performance.

He stated that the suppliers of propulsion turbines are now insisting on a 20 to 25 percent profit as a percent of cost as compared with 10 percent a few years ago.

He testified that profits on shipbuilding contracts based on cost had doubled in the last 2 years.

Cost Reimbursement Contracts

Assistant Secretary of the Air Force Robert Charles, in his testimony before the Economy in Government Subcommittee in January, quoted with approval a study by C. H. Danhof for the Brookings Institution on "Government Contracting and Technological Change," which said: "During the 1950's virtually all large military contracts reflected an acceptance by the military agencies of contractor estimates which proved highly optimistic. Such contracts ultimately involved costs in excess of original contractual estimates of from 300 to 700 percent."

Secretary Charles further stated that—"A substantial amount, however, was due to the fact that most contracts for major systems were of a cost reimbursement type which provided little, if any, motivation for economy, and were not awarded on a price competitive basis."

From the evidence we have from a wide variety of sources, there is no question whatsoever that we have routinely paid more than double the original price for the procurement of major weapons systems.

There is no convincing evidence that the use of "total contract packaging" or other devices has changed this at all. In fact, the specific evidence on the C-5A, where that method was used, shows an overrun of some $2 billion. The testimony of Admiral Rickover is equally convincing. This situation continues and, in my judgment, has been intensified during the last 2 years because of the buildup of procurement for the Vietnam war.

Funds Could Be Cut

Mr. Benson, a former official of the Office of the Assistant Secretary of Defense, comptroller, whom I quoted earlier, believes that $9 billion can be cut from the Pentagon budget; and I quote this Defense Department expert: "without reducing our national security or touching those funds earmarked for the war in Vietnam."

He says even under those circumstances spending can be cut $9 billion.

Admiral Rickover testified that by establishing uniform standards of accounting for recording costs and profits—which, of course, would be entirely separate from the Benson concept—we could save "at least 5 percent" of the defense procurement budget. That is $2 billion for that item of waste alone.

The editors of Congressional Quarterly recently interviewed highly placed sources in the Pentagon and in industry about the 1969 defense budget. Those sources agreed that the 1969 budget was loaded with "fat" and said that $10.8 billion could have been cut from the fiscal 1969 budget without in the slightest way impairing our level of national defense.

There are other items as well. We spend a disproportionate amount of our resources on marginal items such as post exchanges, commissaries, and ship's stores. Vast funds are spent for military public relations.

The Congressional Quarterly recently pointed out how topheavy we were in the field. It pointed out that we had 20 officers in Vietnam for every command post.

Excess Supplies

I will cite just one further example. On June 30, 1968, the value of the excess and long supply in our military supply pipeline was $12.7 billion. This was 28 percent of the $45.8 billion value of the supply system stocks on hand. This is the excess.

While the proportion of excess and surplus items has dropped considerably since 1961, it is still correct to ask, "What kind of a supply system do we have when 28 percent of the value of the supply system stocks are in excess of requirements? What kind of supply system is it that generates such vast surpluses and excesses?

Contracts Fail to Meet Standards

Not only are we paying too much for what we buy, but often we do not get what we pay for.

This, it seems to me, should shock all of those who are concerned about our defense, whether they support enthusiastically the amount we are spending, and feel we should have more in national defense, or whether they are critical of it. We do not get what we pay for.

A most shocking example of this is to be found in a paper by a Budget Bureau specialist, a very distinguished and able man, Mr. Richard Stubbings, entitled "Improving the Acquisition Process for High Risk Electronics Systems."

Mr. Stubbings shows that in the procurement of some two dozen major weapons systems costing tens of billions of dollars during the 1950's and 1960's, the performance standards of the electronic systems of these weapons seldom met the specifications established for them.

How far they fell below their specifications is a real shock.

Of 11 major weapons systems begun during the 1960's, only two of the 11 electronic components of them performed up to standard. One performed at a 75-percent level and two at a 50-percent level. But six—a majority of them—of the 11 performed at a level 25 percent or less than the standards and specifications set for them.

But that is not all.

Excessive Costs—Late Delivery—High Profits

These systems typically cost 200 to 300 percent more than the Pentagon estimated.

They were and are delivered 2 years later than expected.

The after-tax profits of the aerospace industry, of which these contractors were the major companies, were 12.5 percent higher than for American industry as a whole.

Those firms with the worst records appeared to receive the highest profits. One firm, with failures on five of seven systems, earned 40 percent more than the rest of the aerospace industry, and 50 percent more than industry as a whole.

One other company, none of whose seven weapons systems measured up to the performance specifications, had earnings in excess of the industry average.

Think of that, Mr. President (Mr. HUGHES in the chair). A company not one of whose weapons systems measured up to performance specifications still had earnings in excess of the industry average.

This is a shocking situation. We are talking about the computers, radar, and gyroscopes—the key to performance—in our major weapons systems.

No Bang for a Buck?

In the past, the system managers and efficiency experts have talked about "more bang for a buck." But the analysis of Mr. Stubbings raises the question "Are we not approaching the time when there will be 'No bang for a buck'?"

These revelations raise the most serious questions.

We have high profits without performance.

Rewards are in inverse relationship to the time taken and the funds spent.

Failures are rewarded and minimum standards seldom met. Prices soar. Profits rise. Contracts continue.

This is what I mean when I say that military spending is out of control. This is what I mean when I refer to the "unwarranted influence by the military-industrial complex." This is what I mean when I assert that we face a condition of excessive costs, burgeoning military budgets, and scandalous performance.

This is why we could get more security for the country by spending smaller amounts, but spending them more effectively.

Same Dangers Ahead

The conditions I have cited above are not only a condition of the 1950's and 1960's. The same dangers lie ahead. There are numerous additional huge weapons systems for the future. Some of them are already authorized. Some have begun to be funded. We may wake up some morning soon and find that we are committed to billions upon billions of future expenditures where costs will burgeon and performance will be substandard. The fact is that things may soon become a great deal worse.

One of the ablest men we have had on the financial side of the Government in recent years is Charles Schultze, who was Budget Director under President Johnson for a number of years. Mr. Schultze recently wrote an excellent article in the Brookings Agenda papers, which lists some of the programs now contemplated, authorized, or funded. Among them are:

Minuteman II, which is being improved, and Minuteman III, which is in the offing. Estimated cost: $4.6 billion.

Thirty-one Polaris submarines to be converted to carry 496 Poseidon missiles. Estimated cost: $80 million per submarine, or almost $2.5 billion.

Two hundred and fifty-three new FB-111 bombers. Mr. Schultze does not give the cost estimate.

The thin Sentinel system—the ABM system. Estimated cost was $5 billion. I am now told on excellent authority that it is $10 billion and that this figure does not include funds for the Sprint missiles. If the thin system becomes a "thick" system, the total estimated cost is said to be in the neighborhood of $50 billion. And in a very fascinating analysis the other day by one of the real authorities in Congress on defense, the former Secretary of the Air Force, the Senator from Missouri (Mr. SYMINGTON), he estimated that the cost could go as high as $400 billion.

Incidentally, this is a system that even its supporters agree would protect the country for only a limited period of time, perhaps a decade. So that would mean spending $40 billion a year, or half of the total military budget as of now.

Four nuclear-powered carriers. These cost $540 million each, or $2.16 billion.

A new destroyer program. Mr. Schultze does not give the original estimated cost.

Five nuclear-powered escort ships. The cost is estimated at $625 million.

An advanced nuclear attack submarine. Again no cost estimate.

A new Navy fighter—VFX-1—to replace the F-111.

Mr. Schultze, and he should know—as I say, he was Budget Director for a number of years, and an outstanding, and brilliant young man—concludes that: "One fairly predictable feature of most of these weapons systems is that their ultimate cost will be substantially higher than their currently estimated cost."

Mr. President, that is the understatement of the year. We have seen a doubling in the estimated cost of the Sentinel system alone in a period of 1 year. And we all know that what the military has hoped to do is to convert it into a "thick" system as a defense against a Soviet as well as a Chinese attack.

Mr. SYMINGTON. Mr. President, will the Senator yield:

Mr. PROXMIRE. I am happy to yield to the distinguished Senator from Missouri, to whom, incidentally, I made reference just before he came on the floor. I referred to his interesting analysis of the ABM and its possible potential cost.

Mr. SYMINGTON. Mr. President, I have had the privilege of reading the text of the address that the distinguished Senator from Wisconsin is giving today and am much impressed. I would hope every Member of the Senate reads it also. As we face unprecedented fiscal and monetary problems it would appear most timely, so I congratulate the Senator, and with his permission, would ask him several questions which I have drawn up as a result of reading his address.

Mr. PROXMIRE. I should be delighted.

Mr. SYMINGTON. Inasmuch as the Senator is one of the two or three foremost experts in the Congress on matters that have to do with our financial stability, does he not agree that it is vitally important for us to look ever more closely at these gigantic expenditures of the military?

Mr. PROXMIRE. I agree with the distinguished Senator from Missouri. We now give it only the most superficial kind of a look. I believe we give it no detailed scrutiny, to speak of.

I do not blame those in the Congress who are charged with this responsibility. They are the most able people we have. But the Bureau of the Budget itself gives very little attention to the matter, compared to the relative size of the military budget. There is no question in my mind but that we must do better.

Mr. SYMINGTON. Does not the able Senator agree that, in addition to the ABM which has created so much interest lately, there are other weapons systems, such as the SRAM—short range attack missile—and the Mark II avionics which now heavily exceed their originally estimated costs; that these, too, should receive careful scrutiny by the Congress?

Mr. PROXMIRE. The Senator is absolutely correct. I am delighted that he phrased his question the way he did, because I think there is a tendency for Congress to be very deeply concerned, as we should be, about the ABM, because it is the most spectacular item, and the one that has received public attention; but there is no question that in these other areas, we have exactly the same kind of problems or much the same kind of problems, such as the problem of very great cost overruns and the problem of inadequate consideration of whether or not these particular weapons deserve a priority that would warrant our spending billions of dollars on them. Certainly the Senator has touched, in the SRAM and the Mark II, on two weapons of which this is particularly true.

Mr. SYMINGTON. My able colleague notes that the situation with respect to the weapons acquisition process is getting worse instead of better. In this connection, does he believe that part of the problem is related to the fact that military procurement officers are not properly trained, particularly in view of the gigantic amounts of money they control, and, in addition, the fact that most of these officers are constantly being shifted from one duty station to another?

Mr. PROXMIRE. I agree wholeheartedly with the distinguished Senator from Missouri. This is a point that has been brought up in our hearings. I am sure that the Senator from Missouri is a much greater expert in this area than I ever could hope to be. As a former Secretary of the Air Force, he is a man who has had as one of his prime responsibilities in Congress oversight of defense matters, and he speaks with great authority.

There is no question in my mind that these men who have this very heavy responsibility do not have the kind of training or background which would be in many cases essential to hold down expenditures.

Mr. SYMINGTON. I thank the distinguished Senator, and again emphasize that he is making an important contribution to the security and well-being of this country.

Mr. PROXMIRE. Mr. President, I thank the distinguished Senator from Missouri very much.

Uncritical Approach

What is so discouraging about both the past and the future is the cavalier way in which increases and overruns are shrugged off by the military.

Two billion dollars is a very great amount of money. That is the estimated overrun for only one plane—the C-5A.

Five billion dollars is a tremendous amount of money. But that is the increase in the estimated cost of the thin Sentinel system in less than a year.

It is virtually impossible to get such funds for housing, jobs, or poverty programs. But the examples I have given are merely the increases and overruns for only two of the many defense weapons systems.

An article published not too long ago in the Washington Post indicated the dimensions involved in the matter. It was pointed out that $5 billion, the overrun on the military system, is more than we spend in a year in the entire foreign aid program plus everything we put into housing and urban development. The Pentagon handles it as if it were small change.

What appals us is the uncritical way in which these increases are accepted by the military. To be consistently wrong on these estimates of cost, as the military has been consistently wrong, should bring the entire system of contracting under the most detailed scrutiny. But there is not the slightest indication that this is being done by the military. In fact, when such questions are raised, we find the services far more defensive than they are eager to improve the system.

But let me give this solemn warning. The time has come when many of those willing to provide this country with the defense it needs are unwilling to vote funds or authorize new weapons systems or accept the military justifications for them except after the most critical review.

The time of the blank check is over.

The military should make its case and compete for funds equally with other programs.

Why is the situation so bad. Why is military spending now out of control? Let me give some of the reasons:

Need for Zero-Base Budgeting

First of all, there is far too little critical review at the Pentagon itself. Apart from the natural bias of the military services and their effort to increase their budgets, there is an inherent flaw in the Defense Department's budgetary process. I refer to what Mr. Benson, a Defense Department official, calls the lack of "zero base" budgeting.

According to Mr. Benson: "The Defense Department budgeting process virtually concedes last year's amount and focuses on whatever incremental changes have been requested. The result, of course, is higher budgets, with past errors compounded year after year."

What we need, Mr. President, both at the Pentagon and elsewhere is "zero-base" budgeting. The reviews should be made each year from the ground up. We should no longer accept uncritically last year's budget for any item and then merely examine with some slight critical sense the added increment for the new year.

Let us move to "zero-base" budgeting at all levels.

Inadequate Budget Bureau Scrutiny

Now, second, we must have a much sterner and more critical review of the military budget by the Budget Bureau itself.

On January 17, 1969, a few weeks ago, I asked the then Director of the Budget, Mr. Zwick, the following question: "I am asking you . . . whether or not the Defense budget is scrutinized as carefully, for example, dollar for dollar as the OEO budget and the HUD budget, and so forth."

Mr. Zwick answered by saying: "We obviously do not get into as great detail in that Department as we do in some other departments."

When the new Director of the Budget, Mr. Mayo, was before the Joint Economic Committee on February 18, I pursued the same subject with him.

The Defense Budget is about $80 billion. Of the remaining budget, according to the Budget Bureau's own analysis, only some $20 billion are "controllable items," that is, items other than interest on the debt, pension and social security payments, and so forth, which are relatively fixed and not possible to cut except by major changes in legislation. The military budget of $80 billion, plus that part of the "controllable civilian" budget of $20 billion, together compose about $100 billion which can be critically reviewed. But of the 500 or so personnel in the Budget Buréau, only about 50, according to Mr. Mayo, are assigned to scrutinize the Defense budget. This is only 10 percent of the personnel assigned to the Defense budget.

When I asked Mr. Mayo if at least two to three times as much attention is concentrated on the nondefense, as opposed to the defense dollars, he said that judged by the allocation of personnel he would not quarrel with the point.

I think it is fair to say, therefore, that the Budget Bureau makes no adequate review of the military budget.

Mr. PEARSON. Mr. President, will the Senator yield?

Mr. PROXMIRE. I yield.

The PRESIDING OFFICER (Mr. Packwood in the chair). The Senator from Wisconsin yields to the Senator from Kansas.

Mr. PEARSON. Mr. President, I share the concern expressed in the address of the distinguished senior Senator from Wisconsin today.

I recall that during World War II, a committee of the Senate—and perhaps of the entire Congress—addressed itself to a constant review of contracts, costs, and perhaps performance. The committee was headed by the former Senator from Missouri and former President of the United States, Harry Truman.

That committee served a great and useful purpose at that time. I later learned that the committee became the Preparedness Subcommittee of the Armed Services Committee. With all of the responsibilities they have today, they are no longer really performing this oversight function.

I ask the Senator if, among the suggestions he is making today, he has considered the possibility of reinstituting that kind of committee to address itself primarily to contracts and costs.

Mr. PROXMIRE. Mr. President, I think the suggestion of the Senator from Kansas is excellent. There is not any question that President Truman made an excellent contribution to the economy and security of the country because of his chairmanship of that committee. As the Senator said so well, it should be devoted primarily, perhaps exclusively, to the matter of contracts and costs.

The members of that committee have the heaviest authorization burden by far of any of our committees. The committee is very ably headed by the distinguished Senator from Mississippi (Mr. Stennis). It was formerly very ably headed by the distinguished Senator from Georgia (Mr. Russell).

I think they would agree that they are immersed, and so properly immersed, in strategy and tactics and many other problems in regard to this enormous sum that if we can zero in on this matter, it would be a great contribution.

Mr. PEARSON. Mr. President, I thank the Senator.

Mr. PROXMIRE. Mr. President, I thank the Senator for his very helpful and constructive suggestions.

Congress Is Last Defense

Since the military departments are self-seeking, push their own requests, and have little or no "zero-base" budgeting, and as the Budget Bureau itself does not scrutinize military spending in anything like the same degree as it examines the budgets of most other departments, this leaves only the Congress and the review we give to military spending as a last defense against excesses and overruns. I think that the remarks of the distinguished Senator from Kansas are most appropriate and helpful.

I think we would all agree that, while we have very competent and knowledgeable members of both the Armed Services and Appropriation Committees, and while they spend a great amount of time and effort on the Defense Department requests, and give as much scrutiny to these matters as it is possible for very busy men and women to give, it is just not possible for Congress to do the detailed job which the Department of Defense and the Budget Bureau should do. At best, Congress is the safety man on the football team and gets only one chance to stop the runner after everyone else has failed. But Congress cannot act as a fearsome foursome, a front-line defense or even as the linebackers or corner-backs. We are rather inadequate safety men. We do not have the personnel. We do not have the knowledge. We do not have the time. Under the most difficult circumstances we do a reasonably good job, but it is obvious that Congress cannot review the military budget with the kind of critical review it should have. We are not and should not be an operating agency.

This is not meant as a criticism of my colleagues. In the nature of things and given the size of the Defense budget, they do a Herculean job.

Problem of Sheer Size

There are other reasons why military spending is out of control apart from the lack of adequate review at the Pentagon, the Budget Bureau, and by Congress. Foremost among these is its sheer size. It is almost impossible for any man or bureau or agency to comprehend, let alone control, $80 billion in funds.

Lack of Competitive Bidding

The next most important reason is the lack of competitive bidding and the system of negotiated contracts. This problem is getting worse rather than better.

We have the Defense Department's competitive military contract awards dropped from a far too small 13.4 percent of total military procurement in fiscal year 1967, to a pathetic 11.5 percent in fiscal year 1968, or the lowest level since adequate records have been kept.

In addition, the cost plus fixed fee contract has once again increased. It has gone up from a level of about 9 percent of awards to about 11 percent, and the Defense Department states that this level may be too low.

Since Secretary McNamara instituted his major reforms in defense contracting, the Department has made very strong claims that it has made dollar savings over what would otherwise have been spent by shifting from noncompetitive to more competitive contracts. Savings of as much as 25 cents on the dollar has been claimed for shifting from noncompetitive to competitive procurement.

But now we see a return to some of the old methods. In any case, the amount of real competition in defense procurement is very low.

Furthermore, given the routine 200 to 300 percent overrun on most major defense systems, the practice of "buying-in" by firms is promoted and has become notorious.

By "buying-in" I mean a situation where there may be a so-called negotiated procurement in which there are two possible producers at the research and development level. The one who buys in is the one who bids below what he knows it will cost to produce and perhaps takes the business away from the more efficient firm. Once the firm gets it, then watch out, because the overruns, as we have documented again and again, occur. As Secretary Charles testified, those overruns averaged in the past 300 to 700 percent, so that they have been three to seven times as much as the original bid.

Secrecy and Audits

There are a variety of other reasons why expenditures are so excessive.

As Admiral Rickover told us, we have no uniform accounting system for defense procurement.

There is an unwillingness of any Department ever to admit a mistake.

There is an excessive amount of secrecy which, at times, prevents serious public scrutiny of matters which would benefit from critical review.

There is no really good system of audits while work is underway. Much of the excellent work of the General Accounting Office, by its very nature, is focused on a post-audit review.

Military-Industrial Connections

But more than all of this, there is what we have come to know as the military-industrial complex and its many ramifications.

The connections between the military, on the one hand, and the major industries which supply it, on the other, are very close and very cooperative. Some of the major companies have dozens of high ranking retired military personnel on their payrolls.

The major civilian appointive positions at the Department of Defense—the Secretaries, Under Secretaries, and Assistant Secretaries—are routinely filled by those whose private careers have been with defense industries, key investment houses or banks, or with major law firms which represent the huge industrial complex.

Representatives and Senators know only too well the way industry and the military can reach back into States and districts from the howls that go up when any attempt is made to close down even a very inefficient military base in their State or district. We all know the pressures that come upon us to help direct defense projects into our States or districts and the efforts made to keep them there once they have arrived.

The result of all this is a system which is not only inefficient but is now literally out of control. Excessive amounts are spent on overhead and supplies. Huge cost overruns are standard occurrences. Weapons systems routinely do not meet the standards and specifications set for them. Now is the time to call a halt to these excesses. To do so will not harm us. It will make the country stronger and more secure.

Much like the middle-aged boxer who has grown obese from overindulgence, we need to get our Military Establishment and its contracting and financial systems back into fighting trim.

What to Do

Let me summarize specific items which should be put into effect immediately:

First. A system of zero-base budgeting by the individual services—the Defense Department and the Budget Bureau—should be instituted.

Second. The Budget Bureau itself must set up the procedures and hire the personnel to make a separate, highly competent, highly skeptical, and penetrating review of the Defense budget in a way in which it has never before been done. There are highly competent analysts already there, but 10 percent of the personnel cannot examine critically 80 percent of the "controllable" budget.

Third. Immediate steps should be taken to reverse the increase in nonnegotiated contracts and increase the amount of truly competitive bidding.

Fourth. The "buy in" bidding system must be stopped. Firms which make a low bid to gain contracts knowing that the military will later approve increases of 100 to 200 percent or more, must not be rewarded. I urge a system of severe penalties and loss of future status to bid for those companies where cost overruns and huge increases occur.

Fifth. We need to institute immediately an effective and uniform system of accounting for military contractors.

Sixth. Serious penalties need to be instituted for contractors whose delivery dates are not met. The fact that the greatest profits have gone to those electronic weapon system contractors who were routinely 2 years late meeting their deadlines, as Mr. Stubbings pointed out, is scandalous.

Seventh. While major improvement has been made in the supply systems and a great decrease in the number of items stored and bought, under the unified Defense Supply Agency, we must attack the problem of excesses and surpluses. Surpluses of as much as 28 percent of the total amount of supplies is an appalling and unwarranted figure, even though it represents a major improvement over previous periods.

Eighth. We must find some method of monitoring and auditing contracts while they are in process in order to avoid the huge cost overruns. The General Accounting Office, which is an arm of Congress, should do this job in the obvious absence of an adequate job now done by the individual military services. I believe that the Air Force, the Navy, and the Army are so involved in defending the weapon system they initiate that they are really incapable of reviewing the work in process, using a critical eye when things are going wrong, and cutting off the contractors when they are inefficient. The individual services are too closely tied to their pet projects to do this properly.

The GAO is an arm of Congress. It saves many dollars for every dollar it spends. Now, much of its effort is concentrated on postaudit reviews. I think they should play a much larger role at the time the contracts are in process.

Mr. President, these are some of the things which might be done.

Finally, Congress must be ready to demand that the military services prove that their demands are as important and have as high a priority as do major civilian needs. Some system must be devised, hopefully by the President and the Budget Bureau, to make an intelligent judgment as to whether the $2 billion overrun on the C-5A airplane should have as high a priority as $2 billion for jobs and housing in the central cities.

At the moment, no such real test for priorities is required.

Congress must demand that it be done. The day of the blank check for military spending must end.

The military budget must be brought under control.

RETIRED HIGH-RANKING MILITARY OFFICERS EMPLOYED BY LARGE CONTRACTORS

William Proxmire

Mr. PROXMIRE. Mr. President, recently I asked the Department of Defense for a list of certain high-ranking retired military officers employed by the 100 companies who had the largest volume of military prime contracts. I did this in connection with the hearings of the Subcommittee on Economy in Government of the Joint Economic Committee.

In fiscal year 1968 these 100 companies held 67.4 percent of the $38.8 billion of prime military contracts, or $26.2 billion.

The Defense Department has now supplied to me the list of high-ranking military officers who work for these 100 companies. They include the subsidiaries. In one case, that of the 35th ranking contractor, four firms were involved in a joint venture.

I asked only for the names of those retired military officers of the rank of Army, Air Force, Marine Corps colonel or Navy captain and above. Excluded are all officers below those ranks. I asked for only retired regular officers and not reserve officers, although in a very few cases the reserve officers may be included.

Top 100 Companies Employ Over 2,000 Retired Officers

The facts are that as of February, 1969, some 2,072 retired military officers of the rank of colonel or Navy captain and above were em-

Congressional Record, 91st Cong., 1st Sess., March 24, 1969, vol. 115, no. 50, pp. S3072–S3081.

ployed by the 100 contractors who reported. This is an average of almost 22 per firm. I shall ask to have printed in the *Record* as exhibit A of my statement a list of the 100 companies, ranked according to the dollar volume of their prime military contracts, and the number of high-ranking retired officers they employ.

Ten Companies Employ Over 1,000

The 10 companies with the largest number on their payrolls employed 1,065 retired officers. This is an average of 106 per firm. These 10 companies employed over half the total number of high-ranking former officers employed by all the top 100 defense contractors. These companies, listed according to the number of retired officers employed by them, are given in table 1, as follows:

TABLE 1 Ten Military Prime Contractors Employing Largest Number of High-Ranking Retired Military Officers, and Value of Their Fiscal Year 1968 Contracts

Company and rank by number of high-ranking retired officers employed	*Number employed February 1, 1969*	*Net dollar value of defense contracts fiscal year 1968*
1. Lockheed Aircraft Corporation	210	$1,870,000,000
2. Boeing Company	169	762,000,000
3. McDonnell Douglas Corporation	141	1,101,000,000
4. General Dynamics	113	2,239,000,000
5. North American Rockwell Corporation	104	669,000,000
6. General Electric Company	89	1,489,000,000
7. Ling Temco Vought, Inc.	69	758,000,000
8. Westinghouse Electric Corporation	59	251,000,000
9. TRW, Inc.	56	127,000,000
10. Hughes Aircraft Company	55	286,000,000
	1,065	4,552,000,000

Key ABM Contractors Employ 22 Percent of Total

Among the major defense contractors involved in producing the key components of the anti-ballistic-missile system—ABM—nine of them employ 465 retired officers. This is an average of 51 each.

In 1968 they held contracts valued at $5.78 billion and, of course, will receive many billions more if the ABM system is deployed. These companies and the number of retired officers they employ are given in table 2, as follows:

TABLE 2 Major Prime Contractors Involved in ABM System and Number of High-Ranking Retired Military Officers Employed by Them

1. McDonnell Douglas	141
2. General Electric	89
3. Hughes Aircraft	55
4. Martin Marietta	40
5. Raytheon	37
6. Sperry Rand	36
7. RCA	35
8. AVCO	23
9. A.T. & T.	9
Total	465

Comparison of 1969 with 1959

Mr. President, almost 10 years ago in connection with hearings before the Senate Finance Committee on the extension of the Renegotiation Act, former Senator Paul H. Douglas asked for and received a similar list from the Pentagon. We can, therefore, make comparisons over a decade as to what has happened with respect to the employment of high-ranking retired military officers by the top 100 defense contractors.

In 1959, the total number employed was only 721—88 of 100 companies reporting—or an average of slightly more than eight per company.

In 1969, the 100 largest defense contractors—95 of the 100 companies reporting—employed 2,072 former high military officers, or an average of almost 22 per company.

In 1959, the 10 companies with the highest number of former officers employed 372 of them.

In 1969 the top 10 had 1,065, or about three times as many.

Some 43 companies which reported were on both the 1959 and 1969 list of the top 100 largest contractors. There were several more who were on the list in both years but failed to report in one or the other year. But we can compare the 43 companies. These 43 companies employed 588 high-ranking former officers in 1959. In 1969 these same companies employed 1,642 retired high-ranking officers.

In each case where a comparison can be made; namely, in the total number of former high-ranking officers employed by the top 100 contractors, the top 10 contractors employing the largest number, and the number employed by firms reporting in both 1959 and 1969, the number employed has tripled. It has increased threefold.

Roughly three times the number of retired high-ranking military officers are employed by the top 100 companies in 1969 as compared with 1959.

Significance

What is the significance of this situation? What does it mean and what are some of its implications?

First of all, it bears out the statement I made on March 10 when I spoke on the "blank check for the military," that the warning by former President Eisenhower against the danger of "unwarranted influence, whether sought or unsought, by the military-industrial complex," is not just some future danger.

That danger is here. Whether sought or unsought there is today unwarranted influence by the military-industrial complex which results in excessive costs, burgeoning military budgets, and scandalous performances. The danger has long since materialized. The 2,072 retired high-ranking officers employed by the top 100 military contractors is one major facet of this influence.

No Conspiracy or Wrongdoing

Second, I do not claim nor even suggest that any conspiracy exists between the military and the 100 largest defense contractors. I do not believe in the conspiracy theory of history. I charge no general wrongdoing on the part of either group.

In the past many of the officers have performed valiant and even heroic service on behalf of the United States. The country is indeed grateful to them for their past service and for their patriotic endeavors.

We should eschew even the slightest suggestion of any conspiracy between the Pentagon, on the one hand, and the companies who hire former employees, on the other. There is not a scintilla of evidence that it exists.

Community of Interest

But what can be said, and should properly be said, is that there is a continuing community of interest between the military, on the one hand, and these industries on the other.

What we have here is almost a classic example of how the military-industrial complex works.

It is not a question of wrongdoing. It is a question of what can be called the "old boy network" or the "old school tie."

This is a most dangerous and shocking situation. It indicates the increasing influence of the big contractors with the military and the military with the big contractors. It shows an intensification of the problem and the growing community of interest which exists between the two. It makes it imperative that new weapon systems receive the most critical review and that defense contracts be examined in microscopic detail.

I am alarmed about this trend not because I question the integrity or the good will of the retired officers who have found employment with military contractors but because I believe that the trend itself represents a distinct threat to the public interest.

Dangers When Coupled with Negotiated Contracts

Third, this matter is particularly dangerous in a situation where only 11.5 percent of military contracts are awarded on a formally advertised competitive bid basis. It lends itself to major abuse when almost 90 percent of all military contracts are negotiated, and where a very high proportion of them are negotiated with only one, or one or two, contractors.

Former high-ranking military officers have an entree to the Pentagon that others do not have. I am not charging that is necessarily wrong. I am saying that it is true.

Former high-ranking officers have personal friendships with those still at the Pentagon which most people do not have. Again, I charge no specific wrongdoing. But it is a fact.

In some cases former officers may even negotiate contracts with their former fellow officers. Or they may be involved in developing plans and specifications, making proposals, drawing up blueprints, or taking part in the planning process or proposing prospective weapons systems. And they may be doing this in cooperation with their former fellow officers with whom they served and by whom, in some cases, even promoted.

With such a high proportion of negotiated contracts there is a great danger of abuse.

In addition, there is the subtle or unconscious temptation to the officer still on active duty. After all, he can see that over 2,000 of his fellow officers work for the big companies. How hard a bargain does he drive with them when he is 1 or 2 years away from retirement?

This danger does not come from corruption. Except in rare circumstances this is no more prevalent among military officers than among those with comparable civilian responsibilities.

Mutual Interests—Uncritical Views

The danger to the public interest is that these firms and the former officers they employ have a community of interest with the military itself. They hold a narrow view of public priorities based on self-interest. They have a largely uncritical view of military spending.

As a group they have what has been termed "tunnelvision." But in this case their narrow training can be fortified by self-interest. In too many cases they may see only military answers to exceedingly complex diplomatic and political problems. A military response, or the ability to make one, may seem to them to be the most appropriate answer to every international threat.

Summary

When the bulk of the budget goes for military purposes; when 100 companies get 67 percent of the defense contract dollars; when cost overruns are routine and prime military weapon system contracts normally exceed their estimates by 100 to 200 percent; when these contracts are let by negotiation and not by competitive bidding; and when the top contractors have over 2,000 retired high-ranking military officers on their payrolls; there are very real questions as to how critically these matters are reviewed and how well the public interest is served.

That, Mr. President, is the point. That is why I think it important that there be public disclosure of these facts so that the American public can know more about the community of interests involved in our huge defense contract spending.

I ask unanimous consent that a list of the 100 largest defense contractors and the number of high-ranking officers they employed in early 1969 be printed in the *Record* as exhibit A;

That a similar list of the 100 largest military contractors and the number of high-ranking former officers they employed in 1959 be printed in the *Record* as exhibit B;

That a list of the 100 largest military contractors for fiscal year 1968, and the dollar value and percent of military contracts each held, be printed as exhibit C; and

That a list of the names of the former high-ranking officers employed by the 100 largest defense contractors in February 1969 be printed as exhibit D.

There being no objection, the exhibits were ordered to be printed in the *Record* as follows:

EXHIBIT A A List of the 100 Largest Companies Ranked by 1968 Value of Prime Military Contracts and Number of Retired Colonels or Navy Captains and Above Employed by Them, February 1969

1.	General Dynamics Corporation	113
2.	Lockheed Aircraft Corporation	210
3.	General Electric Company	89
4.	United Aircraft Corp.	48
5.	McDonnell Douglas Corp.	141
6.	American Telephone & Telegraph	9
7.	Boeing Corporation	169
8.	Ling-Temco-Vought, Inc.	69
9.	North American Rockwell Corp.	104
10.	General Motors Corp.	17
11.	Grumman Aircraft Engineering Corp.	31
12.	AVCO Corp.	23
13.	Textron, Inc.	28
14.	Litton Industries, Inc.	49
15.	Raytheon Co.	37
16.	Sperry-Rand Corp.	36
17.	Martin Marietta Corp.	40
18.	Kaiser Industries Corp.	11
19.	Ford Motor Co.	43
20.	Honeywell, Inc.	26
21.	Olin Mathieson Chemical Corp.	3
22.	Northrop Corp.	48
23.	Ryan Aeronautical Co.	25
24.	Hughes Aircraft Co.	55
25.	Standard Oil of New Jersey	2
26.	Radio Corp. of America	35
27.	Westinghouse Electric Corp.	59
28.	General Tire & Rubber Co.	32
29.	International Telephone & Telegraph Corp.	[1]
30.	IBM	35
31.	Bendix Corp.	25
32.	Pan American World Airways	24
33.	FMC Corp.	6

[1] Not yet reported.

34. Newport News Shipbuilding	6
35. Raymond/Morrison, etc.[2]	6
36. Signal Companies, Inc. (The)	9
37. Hercules, Inc.	13
38. Du Pont, E. I. de Nemours, & Co.	3
39. Texas Instruments, Inc.	7
40. Day & Zimmerman, Inc.	1
41. General Telephone & Electronics Corp.	35
42. Uniroyal, Inc.	6
43. Chrysler Corp.	11
44. Standard Oil of California	6
45. Norris Industries	2
46. Texaco, Inc.	4
47. Collins Radio Co.	3
48. Goodyear Tire & Rubber Co.	6
49. Asiatic Petroleum Corp.	0
50. Sanders Associates, Inc.	17
51. Mobil Oil Corp.	([1])
52. TRW, Inc.	56
53. Mason & Hanger Silas Mason	5
54. Massachusetts Institute of Technology	5
55. Magnavox Co.	3
56. Fairchild Hiller Corp.	7
57. Pacific Architects & Engineering	16
58. Thiokol Chemical Corp.	3
59. Eastman Kodak Co.	15
60. United States Steel Corp.	([1])
61. American Machine & Foundry	7
62. Chamberlain Corp.	3
63. General Precision Equipment	23
64. Lear Siegler, Inc.	4
65. Harvey Aluminum, Inc.	4
66. National Presto Industrial, Inc.	0
67. Teledyne, Inc.	8
68. City Investing Co.	4
69. Colt Industries, Inc.	4
70. Western Union Telegraph Co.	5
71. American Manufacturing Co. of Texas	0
72. Curtiss Wright Corp.	1
73. White Motor Co.	([1])
74. Aerospace Corp.	6
75. Cessna Aircraft Co.	0
76. Emerson Electric Co.	3
77. Seastrain Lines, Inc.	4
78. Gulf Oil Corp.	1
79. Condec Corp.	1
80. Motorola, Inc.	3
81. Continental Air Lines, Inc.	4
82. Federal Cartridge Corp.	1
83. Hughes Tool Co.	13
84. Vitro Corp. of America	25
85. Johns Hopkins Univ.	([1])
86. Control Data Corp.	14
87. Lykes Corp.	0
88. McLean Industries, Inc.	2
89. Aerodex, Inc.	5
90. Susquehanna Corp.	7
91. Sverdrup & Parcel Assoc., Inc.	9
92. States Marine Lines, Inc.	0
93. Hazeltine Corp.	7
94. Atlas Chemical Industrial, Inc.	0
95. Vinnell Corp.	0
96. Harris-Intertype Corp.	4
97. World Airways, Inc.	4
98. International Harvester Co.	6
99. Automatic Sprinkler Corp.	3
100. Smith Investment Co.	0
Total	2,072

[1] Not yet reported.

[2] Raymond Int'l, Inc.; Morrison-Knudsen Co., Inc.; Brown & Root, Inc.; and J. A. Jones Construction Co.

EXHIBIT B The 100 Largest Companies Ranked by 1958 Value of Prime Military Contracts and Number of Retired Colonels or Navy Captains and Above Employed by Them, June 1959

1. American Bosch Arma Corp. 0
2. American Telephone & Telegraph Co. 1
3. Asiatic Petroleum Corp. 0
4. Avco Corp. 4
5. Bath Iron Works Corp. 2
6. Beech Aircraft: Not available
7. Bell Aircraft Corp. 3
8. Bendix Aviation Corp. 14
9. Bethlehem Steel Co. 8
10. Blue Cross Association 0
11. Boeing Airplane Co. 30
12. Brown-Raymond-Walsh 0
13. California Institute of Technology 0
14. Cessna Aircraft Co. 1
15. Chance Vought Aircraft, Inc. 6
16. Chrysler Corp. 11
17. Cities Service Co. 4
18. Collins Radio Co. 5
19. Continental Motors Corp. 2
20. Continental Oil Co. 2
21. Curtiss-Wright Corp. 4
22. Defoe Shipbuilding Co. 0
23. Douglas Aircraft Co., Inc. 15
24. E. I. du Pont de Nemours & Co. 1
25. Eastman Kodak Co. 12
26. Fairchild Engine & Airplane Corp. 7
27. Fairbanks Whitney Corp. 4
28. Firestone Tire & Rubber Corp. 3
29. Food Machinery & Chemical Corp. 6
30. Ford Motor Company 5
31. The Garrett Corp. 2
32. General Dynamics Corp. 54
33. General Electric Co. 35
34. General Motors: Survey being taken.
35. General Precision Equipment Corp.: Not available
36. General Tire & Rubber Co. 28
37. Gilfillan Brothers, Inc. 0
38. B. F. Goodrich Co. 1
39. Goodyear Tire & Rubber Co. 2
40. Greenland Contractors: Not available
41. Grumman Aircraft Engineering Corp. 1
42. Hayes Aircraft Corp. 3
43. Joshua Hendy Corp. 0
44. Hercules Powder Co., Inc. 1
45. Hughes Aircraft Co. 7
46. International Business Machine Corp. 3
47. International Telephone & Telegraph Corp. 24
48. The Johns Hopkins University 16
49. The Kaman Aircraft Corp. 1
50. Peter Kiewit Sons Co. 1
51. Lear, Inc. 2
52. Lockheed Aircraft Corp. 60
53. Marine Transport Lines, Inc. 1
54. Marquardt Aircraft Co. 2
55. The Martin Co. 15
56. Massachusetts Institute of Technology: Not available
57. Mathiasen's Tanker Industries, Inc. 1
58. McDonnell Aircraft Corp. 4
59. Minneapolis Honeywell Regulator Co. 0
60. Motorola, Inc.: Not available

61. Newport News Shipbuilding and Dry Dock Co. 6
62. North American Aviation, Inc. 27
63. Northrop Aircraft, Inc. 16
64. Olin Mathieson Chemical Corp. 6
65. Oman-Farnsworth-Wright 0
66. Morrison-Knudsen Co., Inc. 1
67. Pan American World Airways, Inc. Not available
68. Philco Corp. 17
69. Radio Corp. of America 39
70. The Rand Corp. 14
71. Raytheon Mfg. Co. 17
72. Republic Aviation Corp. 9
73. Richfield Oil Corp. 4
74. Ryan Aeronautics Co. 9
75. Shell Oil Corp. 0
76. Sinclair Oil Corp. 1
77. Socony Mobil Oil Co. 1
78. Sperry Rand Corp. (Gen. Douglas MacArthur not included) 12
79. Standard Oil Company of California: Not available
80. Standard Oil Company of Indiana: Not available
81. Standard Oil of New Jersey 1
82. States Marine Corp. 0
83. Sundstrand Machine Tool Co.: Not available
84. Sunray Mid-Continent Oil Co. 0
85. Sylvania Electric Products, Inc. 6
86. Temco Aircraft Corp. 6
87. Texaco, Inc. 0
88. Thiokol Chemical Corp. 8
89. Thompson Ramo Wooldridge, Inc. 6
90. Tidewater Oil Company 3
91. Tishman (Paul) Company, Inc. 0
92. Todds Shipyards Company 2
93. Union Carbide Corp. 4
94. Union Oil Company of California 0
95. United States Lines Co. 0
96. United Aircraft Corp. 15
97. Westinghouse Air Brake Co. 42
98. Westinghouse Electric Corp. 33
99. The White Motor Co. 0
100. System Development Corp. 2

Total 721

Source: Congressional Record, June 17, 1959, pp. 11044–45. Statement by former Senator Paul H. Douglas.

EXHIBT C

100 COMPANIES AND THEIR SUBSIDIARIES LISTED ACCORDING TO NET VALUE OF MILITARY PRIME CONTRACT AWARDS

[Fiscal year 1968 (July 1, 1967 to June 30, 1968)]

Rank and name	Thousands of dollars	Percent of U.S. total	Cumulative percent of U.S. total
U.S. total[1]	38,826,625	100.00	100.00
Total, 100 companies and their subsidiaries[2]	26,171,192	67.41	67.41
1. General Dynamics Corp	2,231,488		
Dynatronics, Inc	27		
Stromberg Carlson Corp	7,782		
United Electric Coal Co	42		
Total	2,239,339	5.77	5.77
2. Lockheed Aircraft Corp	1,858,363		
Lockheed Shipbuilding Construction	11,834		
Total	1,870,197	4.82	10.59
3. General Electric Co	1,485,096		
General Electric Supply Co	3,611		
Total	1,488,707	3.83	14.42
4. United Aircraft Corp	1,320,991	3.40	17.82
5. McDonnell Douglas Corp	1,087,660		
Conductron Corp	5,372		
Hycon Manufacturing Co	7,805		
Total	1,100,837	2.84	20.66
6. American Telephone & Telegraph Co	161,405		
Chesapeake & Potomac Telephone Co	13,018		
Illinois Bell Telephone Co	38		
Mountain States Telephone and Telegraph Co	1,872		
New England Telephone & Telegraph Co	549		
New Jersey Bell Telephone Co	529		
New York Telephone Co	152		
Northwestern Bell Telephone Co	235		
Ohio Bell Telephone Co	601		
Pacific Northwest Bell Telephone	160		
Pacific Telephone & Telegraph Co	225		
Southern Bell Telephone & Telegraph	2,178		
Southwestern Bell Telephone	1,197		
Teletype Corp	22,591		
Western Electric Co., Inc	571,177		
Total	775,927	2.00	22.66
7. Boeing Co	762,141	1.96	24.62
8. Ling Temco Vought Inc	50,011		
Altec Services Co	58		
Braniff Airways Inc	46,304		
Continental Electronics Manufacturing Co	4,238		
Jefferson Wire & Cable Corp	151		
Jones & Laughlin Steel Corp	695		
Kentron Hawaii, Ltd	8,549		
L T V Electro systems	123,592		
L T V Aerospace Corp	487,762		
L T V Ling Altec, Inc	886		
Memcor, Inc	25,883		
National Car Rental System	11		
8. Ling Temco Vought Inc.—Continued			
Okonite Co	1,656		
Wilson & Co., Inc	8,299		
Wilson Pharmaceutical & Chemical Corp	16		
Wilson Sporting Goods Co	150		
Total	758,261	1.95	26.57
9. North American Rockwell Corp	668,482		
Remmert-Werner, Inc	159		
Total	668,641	1.72	28.29
10. General Motors Corp	629,515		
Frigidaire Sales Corp	95		
Total	629,610	1.62	29.91
11. Grumman Aircraft Engineering Corp	629,197	1.62	31.53
12. Avco Corp	583,648	1.50	33.03
13. Textron, Inc	18,438		
Accessory Products Co	133		
Bell Aerospace Corp	478,691		
Bell Aerosystems Co	100		
Bostitch, Inc	14		
Camcar Screw Manufacturing Co	80		
Fafnir Bearing Co	1,501		
Fanner Manufacturing Co	66		
Talon, Inc	332		
Textron Electronics, Inc	993		
Townsend Co	297		
Waterbury Farrel	102		
Total	500,747	1.29	34.32
14. Litton Industries, Inc	28,752		
Aero Service Corp	822		
Allis (Louis) Co	1,318		
Alvey Ferguson Co	130		
Clifton Precision Products Co	27		
Eureka X-Ray Tube Corp	33		
Ingalls Shipbuilding Corp	277,289		
Kimball Systems, Inc	22		
Litton Precision Products, Inc	6,829		
Litton Systems, Inc	150,386		
Monroe International, Inc	43		
Profexray, Inc	27		
Royal Typewriter Co., Inc	13		
Total	465,691	1.20	35.52
15. Raytheon Co	431,241		
Amana Refrigeration, Inc	18		
Machlett Laboratories, Inc	19,350		
Micro State Electronics Corp	125		
Raytheon Education Co	926		
Seismograph Service Corp	94		
Total	451,754	1.16	36.68
16. Sperry Rand Corp	447,197	1.15	37.83

EXHIBIT C—Continued

100 COMPANIES AND THEIR SUBSIDIARIES LISTED ACCORDING TO NET VALUE OF MILITARY PRIME CONTRACT AWARDS—Continued

[Fiscal year 1968 (July 1, 1967 to June 30, 1968)]

Rank and name	Thousands of dollars	Percent of U.S. total	Cumulative percent of U.S. total
17. Martin Marietta Corp	357, 642		
Amphenol-Borg Electronics, GMBH	286		
Bunker Ramo Corp	35, 526		
Total	393, 454	1. 01	38. 84
18. Kaiser Industries Corp	97		
Kaiser Aerospace & Electronics Co	5, 615		
Kaiser Jeep Corp	295, 803		
Kaiser Steel Corp	52, 836		
National Steel & Shipbuilding Co	31, 983		
Total	386, 334	1. 00	39. 84
19. Ford Motor Co	76, 771		
General Micro-Electronics, Inc	170		
Philco Ford Corp	304, 403		
Total	381, 344	.98	40. 82
20. Honeywell, Inc	351, 625		
Computer Control Co., Inc	57		
Total	351, 682	.91	41. 73
21. Olin Mathieson Chemical Corp	329, 415	.85	42. 58
22. Northrop Corp	182, 150		
Hallicrafters Co	33, 467		
Northrop Carolina, Inc	26, 183		
Page Communications Engineers, Inc	67, 934		
Secda, Inc	493		
Warnecke Electron Tubes, Inc	29		
Total	310, 256	.80	43. 38
23. Ryan Aeronautical Co	133, 751		
Continental Aviation & Engineering Corp	39, 142		
Continental Motors Corp	111, 891		
Wisconsin Motor Corp	8, 374		
Total	293, 158	.76	44. 14
24. Hughes Aircraft Co	285, 858		
Meva Corp	251		
Total	286, 109	.74	44. 88

Rank and name	Thousands of dollars	Percent of U.S. total	Cumulative percent of U.S. total
30. International Business Machines Co	223, 023		
Science Research Associates, Inc	199		
Service Bureau Corp	439		
Total	223, 661	0. 58	48. 74
31. Bendix Corp	214, 398		
Bendix Field Engineering Corp	7, 426		
Bendix Westinghouse Automotive	175		
Dage Electric Co., Inc	13		
Fram Corp	1, 017		
Mosaic Fabrications, Inc	195		
P & D Manufacturing Co., Inc	331		
Total	223, 555	.58	49. 32
32. Pan American World Airways, Inc	205, 652	.53	49. 85
33. FMC Corp	175, 860		
Gunderson Bros. Engineering Corp	9, 406		
Total	185, 266	.48	50. 33
34. Newport News Shipbuilding & Dry Dock Co	181, 248		
Nuclear Service & Construction Co., Inc	61		
Total	181, 309	.47	50. 80
35. Raymond Morrison Knudsen (JV)	176, 000	.45	51. 25
36. Signal Cos., Inc.:			
Dunham Bush, Inc	465		
Garrett Corp	114, 620		
Mack Trucks, Inc	48, 407		
Signal Oil & Gas Co	5, 792		
Southland Oil Corp	2, 287		
Total	171, 571	.44	51. 69
37. Hercules, Inc	170, 242		
Haveg Industries, Inc	1, 119		
Total	171, 361	.44	52. 13
38. du Pont, E. I. de Nemours & Co	30, 662		
Remington Arms Co	193, 907		
Total	170, 569	.44	52. 57
39. Texas Instruments, Inc	169, 271	.44	53. 01

American Cryogenics, Inc	251		
Enjay Chemical Co	93		
Esso A.G	1,310		
Esso International Corp	114,905		
Esso Ptrol Co., Ltd	92		
Esso Research & Engineering Co	1,164		
Esso Standard Eastern, Inc	340		
Esso Standard Italiana	2,035		
Esso Standard Oil Co., S.A	2,584		
Esso Standard S.A.F	119		
Esso Standard Thialand, Ltd	124		
Humble Oil & Refining Co	121,212		
Total	274.377	.71	45.59
26. Radio Corp. of America	254,961		
RCA Defense Electronics Corp	39		
RCA Institutes, Inc	12		
Total	255,012	.66	46.25
27. Westinghouse Electric Corp	247,664		
Thermo King Corp	1,466		
Thermo King Sales & Service	66		
Westinghouse Electric Supply Co	1,319		
Westinghouse Learning Corp	524		
Total	251,039	.65	46.90
28. General Tire & Rubber Co	11,636		
Aerojet-Delft Corp	979		
Aerojet-General Corp	210,232		
Batesville Manufacturing Co	24,182		
Fleetwood Corp	10		
Frontier Airlines, Inc	21		
General Tire International Co	996		
Total	248,056	.64	27.54
29. International Telephone & Tel Corp	135,713		
Amplex Corp	67		
Barton Instrument Corp	37		
Consolidated Electric Lamp Co	11		
Continental Baking Co	2,194		
Federal Electric Corp	65,499		
ITT Electro Physics Laboratories	2,715		
ITT Gilfillan, Inc	34,809		
ITT Technical Services, Inc	521		
Total	241,566	.62	48.16

Footnotes at end of table.

41. General Telephone & Electronics Corp	93		
Automatic Electric Co	9,682		
Automatic Electric Sales Corp	1,829		
General Telephone and Electronic Lab	273		
General Telephone Co., of Southeast	151		
Hawaiian Telephone Co	4,626		
Lenkurt Electric Co., Inc	8,650		
Sylvania Electric Products, Inc	133,706		
Total	159,010	.41	53.85
42. Uniroyal, Inc	154,163		
Uniroyal International Corp	136		
Total	154,299	.40	54.25
43. Chrysler Corp	146,586		
Factory Motor Parts Co	14		
Total	146,600	.38	54.63
44. Standard Oil Co. of Calif	71,462		
Caltex Asia, Ltd.[3]	1,853		
Caltex Oil Products Co.[3]	61,766		
Caltex Oil Thailand, Ltd.[3]	1,995		
Caltex Overseas, Ltd.[3]	379		
Caltex Philippines, Inc.[3]	436		
Chevron Asphalt Co	50		
Chevron Chemical Co	797		
Chevron Oil Co	2,153		
Chevron Oil Co. of Venezuela	1,610		
Chevron Shipping Co	1,297		
Standard Oil Co., Kentucky	2,297		
Standard Oil Co., Texas	122		
Total	146,217	.38	55.01
45. Norris Industries	139,064		
Fyr Fyter Co	202		
Total	139,266	.36	55.37
46. Texaco, Inc	45,404		
Caltex Asia, Ltd.[3]	1,853		
Caltex Oil Products Co.[3]	61,766		
Caltex Oil Thailand, Ltd.[3]	1,995		
Caltex Overseas, Ltd.[3]	379		
Caltex Philippines, Inc.[3]	436		
Jefferson Chemical Co., Inc	105		
Texaco Antilles, Ltd	88		
Texaco Export, Inc	22,561		

EXHIBIT C—Continued

100 COMPANIES AND THEIR SUBSIDIARIES LISTED ACCORDING TO NET VALUE OF MILITARY PRIME CONTRACT AWARDS—Continued

[Fiscal year 1968 (July 1, 1967 to June 30, 1968)]

Rank and name	Thousands of dollars	Percent of U.S. total	Cumulative percent of U.S. total
46. Texaco, Inc.—Continued			
Texaco Puerto Rico, Inc	2,451		
White Fuel Co., Inc	984		
Total	138,022	0.36	55.73
47. Collins Radio Co	134,754	.35	56.08
48. Goodyear Tire & Rubber Co	55,358		
Goodyear Aerospace Corp	76,201		
Motor Wheel Corp	2,046		
Total	133,605	.34	56.42
49. Asiatic Petroleum Corp	132,796	.34	56.76
50. Sanders Associates, Inc	130,830		
Mithras, Inc	481		
Total	131,311	.34	57.10
51. Mobil Oil Corp	128,065	.33	57.43
52. TRW Inc	126,363		
Globe Industries, Inc	348		
International Controls Corp	672		
Ramsey Corp	14		
United-Carr, Inc	70		
Total	127,467	.33	57.76
53. Mason & Hanger Slas Mason Co	127,064	.33	58.09
54. Massachusetts Institute of Technology (N)	124,143	.32	58.41
55. Magnavox Co	123,100	.32	58.73
56. Fairchild Hiller Corp	121,165		
Burns Areo Seat Co., Inc	94		
Total	121,159	.31	59.04
57. Pacific Architects & Engineers, Inc	120,895	.31	59.35
58. Thiokol Chemical Corp	119,363	.31	59.66
59. Eastman Kodak Co	117,566		
Eastman Chemical Products Corp	51		
Eastman Kodak Stores, Inc	706		
Total	118,323	.30	59.96
60. United States Steel Corp	108,322		

Rank and name	Thousands of dollars	Percent of U.S. total	Cumulative percent of U.S. total
67. Teledyne, Inc.—Continued			
Milliken, D. B., Co., Inc	1,024		
National Geophysical Co., Inc	92		
Ordnance Specialties, Inc	24		
Packard Bell Electronics Corp	6,504		
Penn Union Electric Corp	11		
Pines Engineering Co., Inc	158		
Rodney Metals, Inc	11		
Wah Chang Corp	26		
Total	92,514	0.24	62.09
68. City Investing Co.:			
American Electric Co	35,966		
Hayes Holding Co	49,002		
Rheem Manufacturing Co	1,857		
Wilson Shipyard, Inc	164		
Total	86,989	.22	62.31
69. Colt Industries, Inc	2,258		
Chandler Evans, Inc	10,087		
Colts, Inc	68,989		
Elox Corp	194		
Fairbanks Morse, Inc	4,582		
Pratt & Whitney, Inc	436		
Total	86,546	.22	62.53
70. Western Union Telegraph Co	79,299	.20	62.73
71. American Manufacturing Co. of Texas	76,552	.20	62.93
72. Curtiss Wright Corp	74,799		
Comet Tool & Die Co	350		
Zarkin Machine Co	275		
Total	75,424	.19	63.12
73. White Motor Co	15,976		
Hercules Engines, Inc	58,610		
Minneapolis Moline, Inc	394		
Total	74,980	.19	63.31
74. Aerospace Corp. (N)	73,541	.19	63.50
75. Cessna Aircraft Co	71,834		
Aircraft Radio Corp	1,076		

61. American Machine & Foundry Co.	108,871		
Cuno Engineering Corp.	1,052		
Total	109,923	.28	60.54
62. Chamberlain Corp.	104,441	.27	60.81
63. General Precision Equipment Corp.:			
American Meter Controls, Inc.	29		
Controls Co. of America	377		
General Precision Decca Systems	90		
General Precision Systems, Inc.	86,361		
Graflex, Inc.	1,571		
Industrial Timer Corp.	15		
National Theatre Supply	16		
Strong Electrical Corp.	3,605		
Tele-Signal Corp.	9,686		
Vapor Corp.	2,194		
Total	103,944	.27	61.08
64. Lear-Siegler, Inc.	74,000		
American Avitron	43		
L S I Service Corp.	27,526		
Transport Dynamics, Inc.	685		
Verd A Ray Corp.	18		
Total	102,272	.26	61.34
65. Harvey Aluminum, Inc.	25,048		
Harvey Aluminum Sales	74,045		
Total	99,093	.26	61.60
66. National Presto Industries, Inc.	96,886	.25	61.85
67. Teledyne, Inc.	77,173		
Adcom, Inc.	309		
Amelco, Inc.	4,146		
Continental Device Corp.	27		
Crystalonics, Inc.	13		
Electro Development Co.	50		
Geotechnical Corp.	25		
Getz William Corp.	128		
Gill Electric Manufacturing Corp.	517		
Hydra Power Corp.	1,017		
Irby Steel Co.	59		
Isotopes, Inc.	802		
Landis Machine Co.	22		
Micronetics, Inc.	346		
Microwave Electronics Corp.	30		

Footnotes at end of table.

Pace, Inc.	[illegible]		
Rantec Corp.	31		
Ridge Tool Co.	26		
Supreme Products Corp.	8,807		
Wiegand (Edwin L.) Co.	134		
Total	72,842	.19	63.88
77. Seatrain Lines, Inc.	42,039		
Commodity Chartering Corp.	1,667		
Hudson Waterways Corp.	22,547		
Transeastern Shipping Corp.	4,348		
Total	70,601	.18	64.06
78. Gulf Oil Corp.	66,934		
Goodrich Gulf Chemicals Inc.	81		
Gulf Oil Trading Co.	259		
Pittsburgh Midway Coal Mining Co.	104		
Total	67,378	.17	64.23
79. Condec Corp.	65,162		
Consolidated Controls Corp.	1,587		
N J E Corp.	155		
Total	66,904	.17	64.40
88. Motorola Inc.	65,715		
Motorola Overseas Corp.	218		
Total	65,933	.17	64.57
81. Continental Air Lines Inc.	64,523	.17	64.74
82. Federal Cartridge Corp.	64,519	.17	64.91
83. Hughes Tool Co.	62,353	.16	65.07
84. Vitro Corp of America	59,674		
Vitro Minerals Corp.	1,471		
Total	61,145	.16	65.23
85. Johns Hopkins University (N)	57,674	.15	65.38
86. Control Data Corp.	50,225		
Associated Aero Science Labs, Inc.	1,891		
CEIR, Inc.	852		
Control Corp.	142		
Electronic Accounting Card Corp.	723		
Pacific Technical Analysts, Inc.	1,705		

EXHIBIT C—Continued

100 COMPANIES AND THEIR SUBSIDIARIES LISTED ACCORDING TO NET VALUE OF MILITARY PRIME CONTRACT AWARDS—Continued

[Fiscal year 1968 (July 1, 1967 to June 30, 1968)]

Rank and name	Thousands of dollars	Percent of U.S. total	Cumulative percent of U.S. total
86. Control Data Corp.—Continued			
TRG, Inc.	1,264		
Total	56,802	0.15	65.53
87. Lykes Corp.	55,247		
Gulf South American Steamship Co.	683		
Total	55,930	.14	65.67
88. McLean Industries, Inc.	•		
Equipment, Inc.	5,902		
Gulf Puerto Rico Lines, Inc.	259		
Sea-Land Service, Inc.	49,751		
Total	55,912	.14	65.81
89. Aerodex, Inc.	55,345	.14	65.95
90. Susquehanna Corp.	2,415		
Atlantic research Corp.	51,452		
Xebec Corp.	886		
Total	54,753	.14	66.09
91. Sverdrup Parcel Association Inc.	1,396		
Aro, Inc.	53,165		
Total	54,561	.14	66.23
92. States Marine Lines, Inc.	54,015	0.14	66.37
93. Hazeltine Corp.	53,781	.14	66.51
94. Atlas Chemical Industries, Inc.	53,574	.14	66.65
95. Vinnell Corp.	51,609	.13	66.78
96. Harris-Intertype Corp.	913		
Gates Radio Co.	796		
PRD Electronics, Inc.	20,613		
Radiation, Inc.	29,156		
Total	51,478	.13	66.01
97. World Airways, Inc.	51,358	.13	67.04
98. International Harvester Co.	51,271	.13	57.17
99. Automatic Sprinkler Corp. of America	50,395		
Badger Fire Extinguisher Co.	38		
Total	50,433	.13	67.30
100. Smith Investment Co.:			
Smith, A. O. Corp.	40,323		
Smith, A. O. of Texas	9,998		
Total	50,321	.13	[4] 67.43

[1] Net value of new procurement actions minus cancellations, terminations, and other credit transactions. The data include debit and credit procurement actions of $10,000 or more, under military supply, service and construction contracts for work in the United States plus awards to listed companies and other U.S. companies for work overseas. Procurement actions include definitive contracts, the obligated portions of letter contracts, purchase orders, job orders, task orders, delivery orders, and any other orders against existing contracts. The data do not include that part of indefinite quantity contracts that have not been translated into specific orders on business firms, nor do they include purchase commitments or pending cancellations that have not yet become mutually binding agreements between the Government and the company.

[2] The assignment of subsidiaries to parent companies is based on stock ownership of 50 percent or more by the parent company, as indicated by data published in standard industrial reference sources. The company totals do not include contracts made by other U.S. Government agencies and financed with Department of Defense funds, or contracts awarded in foreign nations through their respective governments. The company names and corporate structures are those in effect as of June 30, 1968, and for purposes of this report company names have been retained unless specific knowledge was available that a company had been merged into the parent or absorbed as a division with loss of company identity. Only those subsidiaries are shown for which procurement actions have been reported.

[3] Stock ownership is equally divided between Standard Oil Co. of California and Texaco, Inc; half of the total of military awards is shown under each of the parent companies.

[4] Does not agree with percentage shown on 2d line at beginning of table due to rounding.

Exhibit D

Retired Officers at or Above the Rank of Colonel, or the Equivalent, who are Officials or Employees of the Named Companies

Aerodex Inc. (5): Randolph E. Churchill, Burl B. Davenport, Harold V. Pletts, Clare Bunch, Roy Z. Peck.

Aerospace Corp. (6): Charles A. Brown; James H. Cox, Jr.; Lawrence D. Ely; Manley C. Osborne; John G. Urban; Curtis F. Vossler.

American Machine & Foundry Co. (7): Carl J. Baldick, John A. Bartol, R. Q. Brown, Leonard T. Coupland, John R. Leeds, George A. Roll, Allan W. Stephens.

American Manufacturing Co. of Texas: none.

American Telephone & Telegraph Co. (9): B. E. Shumate; Forrest M. Price; William C. Bishop; C. Unnevehr; R. E. Van Liew, John H. Schulte, M.D.; James H. Weiner; E. A. Kenny; W. W. Sturdy.

Asiatic Petroleum Corp.: none.

Atlas Chemical Industries Inc.: none.

Automatic Sprinkler Corp. America (3): Allen W. Glienke, Preston J. Hundley, L. T. Shuler.

AVCO Corp. (23): James R. Kerr, Lawrence B. Ocamb; Jackson Dew; Ben Legare; Beverly Warren; Elmer T. Dorsey; Arthur C. Cox; George A. Tuttle; John D. Edmunds; Loran J. Anderson; E. David Reynolds; John M. Ferris; John A. Anderson.

David W. Stonecliffe; Yale H. Wolfe; Edward J. Cleary; Edgar R. Kay; D. McAneney; John E. Heath; Evan F. Bourne, Jr.; Ted Hodgkins; Gordon Newell; T. Kirkpatrick.

Bendix Corp. (25): Emery E. Bellonby; Dr. Laurence J. Legere; Frederick Kenneth Nichols; Jack D. Koser; John M. Chapman; Donald Kirkpatrick, Jr.; Raymond H. Bass; Eugene I. Malone; Herbert K. Anderson; Winfred A. Ross; Andrew M. Sinclair; John F. Miller, Jr.

George A. Dugas; Charles F. H. Begg; John W. Wise; C. W. Stelle, M.D.; C. F. Watkins; E. E. Matchett; L. F. Mathison; Donald A. Briola; Franklyn E. Moffitt; Lucius A. Perry; William R. Poindexter; Frederick N. Russell; Richard C. Shangraw.

Boeing Co. (169): Donald C. Almy; George L. Bennett; Eugene A. Blue; Charles W. Boedeker; Robert V. Bowler; Loyd W. Brenneman; Harvey S. Browne; Thomas W. Brundage; Roy T. Bucy; Edward S. Burns.

Elbert S. Churchill; William A. Clark; Peter V. Colmar; Emmett V. Conkling; Leslie W. Cowan; John W. Crosby; Henry Cushman; John H. Dacus; Stanley A. Dallas; Frederick E. Dally.

Lorin R. Dedrickson; Francis R. Delaney; Nicholan S. Detolly; Donald B. Diehl; Leonard F. Dow; Gordon R. Egbert; Donald A. Elliott; Richard M. Fernbaugh; Earl R. Finney, Jr.; Joseph O. Fitzgerald.

Oscar F. Fowler; Gilbert F. Friederichs; Max S. George; Ritchie B. Gooch; Donald E. Good; Timothy J. Guinan; Charles H. Haase; Robert H. Hahnemann; George W. Haney; Felix M. Hardison.

Richard D. Harwood; William P. Hawley; Harold T. Henderickson; Max W. Henney; Jesse G. Henry; Joseph M. Hermanson; Theodore R. Hikel; Lauri J. Hillberg; Francis R. Hoehl; Robert Irvine.

Albert W. James; Ervin L. Keener; John G. Kneeland; Sanford Knotts; Donald F. Krick; Nathan L. Krisberg; Raymond J. Lacombe; Porter Lewis; Stanley C. Lewis.

Edwin Loberg; John N. Longfield; Henry M. Marshall; Frederick W. Maxwell, Jr.; James L. McCallum; William F. McLaren; Howard E. Michelet; John R. Middleton; Frank J. Muller; Edmund E. Novotny.

Homer R. Oldfield; John Palowez; Robert R. Perry; Daniel A. Ranney; Orville H. Rehmann; Robert H. Richard; William E. Ruark; Mills S. Savage; William Scarpino; F. D. Schwartz.

John D. Seaberg; John R. Smith; Houck Spencer; Raymond M. Staley; Clyde B. Stevens, Jr.; Robert R. Stewart; Roy A. Tate; Paul Van Leunen, Jr.; Thomas R. Waddleton; Paul E. Wallace.

Floyd Wikstrom; Sherman Wilkins; David M. Williams; Robert J. Wilson; Richard A. Zais; Heber J. Badger; Louis K. Bliss; Clingmon E. Bowman; Merle C. Brown; Gerald L. Cameron.

Thomas J. Colley; Joseph A. Coppola; Ercla De Tenley; John M. Devane, Jr.; Frank H. Drake; Robert G. Ellis; Jack Fitzgerald; Louis W. Ford; Robert F. Harris; Paul F. Helmick.

Donald E. Hillman; James L. Jacobson; Lionel F. Johnson; Albert L. Jones; George A. Kirsch; Arthur M. Lien; Tyler R. Matthew; Anthony J. Maurel; David W. McFarland; Kenneth G. Miles.

Robert W. Millar; Arthur J. Mills; James S. Muzzy; Marshall W. Nicholson; Guy E. Oneil, Jr.; Samuel P. Parsons; Jesse C. Peaslee; Howard B. Seim; Gordon K. Sherman; Robert W. Siegismund.

Gregory J. Skinner; Donald D. Steele; Charles B. Stewart; Raymond D. Swett; David A. Tate; Raymond S. Thompson; Harlan C. Wilder; Robert M. Wray; James B. Burrow; Weston H. Price.

Phillip G. Cobb; Joe G. Duvall; Frank J. Malloy; James F. McRoberts; Reginald W. Wagner; Hugh D. Wallace; Victor W. Alden; Ira K. Blough, Jr.; John F. Carey; Robert L. Cochran.

William M. Davis; Glen O. Goodhand; David W. Hassemer; Orville Hegseth; Leroy P. Hunt, Jr.; Bruce K. Lloyd; James R. Locher, Jr.; John H. Martin; Harold Mitchener; Edward L. Nielsen.

John T. Pierce, III; Barclay T. Resler; Robert T. Simpson; Charles S. Tanner; Clyde D. Gasser; Robert A. Hartnett; William J. McGinty; G. L. Meyers; E. M. Parker; J. S. Russell.

Cessna Aircraft Co.: None.

Chamberlain Corp. (3): John M. Ulrich; William G. Kussmaul; O. D. Moore.

Chrysler Corp. (11): Arthur J. Schultz, Jr.; Parnag Adamian; John W. Guerin, M.D.; William J. Parsons; Joseph J. Schmidt; Gerald E. Moore; Frederick O. Rudesill; John L. Hornor, Jr., William T. Weissinger; William G. Johnson; James M. Nifong.

City Investing Co. (4): Russell B. Sell; George B. Hooker, Jr.; I. R. Mollen; R. W. VanWert.

Collins Radio Co. (3): R. G. Bounds, Jr.; Richard A. Hansen; J. B. Yakeley, Jr.

Colt Industries, Inc. (4): Edward J. Hale, Thomas E. Bass, Gilbert Schumacher, Joseph Rinehart.

Condec Corp. (1): Lucas V. Beau.

Continental Air Lines Inc. (4): George P. Caldwell, Phil Parrott, M. P. Barnwell, F. W. Scheible.

Control Data Corp. (14): Stanley W. Phillips, C. A. Ousley, S. P. Steffes, Joseph Hannah, Frederick J. Karch, Ward T. Shields, Ralph F. Bishop, Cleland Early, Francis J. Berry, Charles W. Turner, Edgar Doleman, W. H. Fleming, Merlin Olson, Earle L. Lerette.

Curtiss Wright Corp. (1): John Condon.

Day & Zimmerman Inc. (1): Augustus M. Minton.

Dupont, E. I. De Nemours & Co. (3): Philip J. Smith, Charles K. Morris, Thomas J. Sharpe.

Eastman Kodak Co. (15): K. C. Raynor, H. D. Parmelee, W. Herrington, R. E. O'Neill, J. F. Reinhard, D. L. Willis, C. LaPorte, E. K. Smith, W. M. Steele, G. P. Carter, K. D. Gallinger, H. Hickman, J. R. Hoff, R. Koch, J. A. Newton.

Emerson Electric Co. (3): Ralph J. Nunziato, Lester Personeus, Robert L. Morris.

Fairchild Hiller Corp. (7): C. G. Botsford; T. M. Ashton; J. C. Stockett, Jr.; J. Pfaff; J. W. Gurnow; C. Bussey; J. Colovin.

Federal Cartridge Corp. (1): Howard L. Bartholomew.

F. M. C. Corp. (6): Wood B. Kyle, W. Paul Johnson, Barney D. White, Michael J. Sisul, Henry H. Wishart, Millard B. Hodges.

Ford Motor Co. (53): Dr. Carroll Hungate; R. C. Hyder; P. N. Gillon; A. Whitley; G. O. Hackett; E. Dreiss; S. S. Jack; B. O. Norman; C. E. Rankin; Dr. R. L. Weir.

D. H. Yielding; J. W. Bensen; W. R. Ewing; E. S. Garner; G. G. Getz; E. G. Kar; W. E. Kooken; Dr. C. E. Mack; W. Minton; G. D. R. H. Prothero; Harold A. Radetsky; A. W. Reed; Henry G. Reed; Vendor H. Reeder; Arthur C. Reinhart; H. Reiter; James Reynolds; Elmer W. Richardson; J. B. Robinson, III.

C. I. Ross, Jr.; Columbus Savage; Fred C. Schmidt; John Schmidt; T. S. Sedaker; R. M. Sewall; L. E. Shea; W. M. Shewbart; Shyrock, W. H.; Peter Smenton.

George Smith; R. E. Soper; I. Sykes, Jr.; M. Tremaine; Russell F. Trudeau; S. J. Veneziano; Willima Weisert; Harold A. Wilging; R. L. Wolf; John F. Yoder; M. R. Yunk.

General Motors Corp. (17): Francis Box; L. R. Braswell, M.D.; W. C. Chapman; E. H. Eddy; L. C. Freeman, Jr.; G. G. Garton; E. Gray; T. W. Howell, M.D.; R. P. Klein; E. L. Knapp; A. E. Lancaster; C. Momsen, Jr.; W. Moore; W. F. Patient, M.D.; A. J. Shower; J. L. Wagner; G. H. Minor.

General Precision Equipment Corp. (23): George Le Breche; Robert J. Lynch; Guy B. Richardson, Jr.; Russell Gardinier; George J. Keithley; Robert Wilson; Thomas Dickens; J. A. Scott; Raymond Du Bois; Scott Lathrop; John O'Halloran.

Donald Olson; H. F. Duffey; Williard W. Smith; Wayne O'Hern; William Romberger; Richard Horridge; Edward Penneybaker; Ward Witter; Frank Mears; Norman Jungers; A. E. Kraps; H .E. Fry.

General Telephone & Electronics Corp. (35): A. B. Newhouse; George W. Carrington, Jr.; Harold E. Bieau; Cecil V. Broadway; Martin E. Wilson; John Becker; Harry Jost; Carl D. Broein, Jr.; Dr. William L. Smith; James Cochran; George Newton.

Elliot Wilson; Alexander G. Evanoff; William C. Golladay; Dave O. Sprankle; C. M. Christensen; G. W. England; L. E. Swope; O. W. Miller; W. C. Newbauer; P. A. Gugliotta; T. H. McKenzie; C. H. Bowen.

S. Trusso; P. E. Greenlee; F. N. Miller; E. D. Vaughan; L. Loken; M. L. Cripe; J. R. Blackburn; G. R. Trimble; Norbert Miller; William Scandrett; Francis D. Walker; Robert B. Keagy.

General Electric Co. (89): Names not yet Jones; Frank C. Tyrrell; Homer H. Nielsen; Jay V. Chase; Kenneth J. Latimer.

Honeywell Inc. (26): W. C. Bergstedt; G. E. Chalmers; J. W. Cunnick, III; C. L. Davis; M. Esch; H. Gorman; J. Hardy; B. Harris; W. T. Herring; K. C. Houston; B. Jones; J. Jones; F. H. LaMurre.

J. P. Laurin; W. D. McDowell; J. G. Merz; A. Poehler; C. Putman; L. J. Rasmussen; D. Schweitzer; L. Sherman; C. F. Spencer; E. B. Stansbury; J. J. Wermuth; J. L. Wilson, Jr.; P. Wyman.

Hughes Aircraft Co. (55): J. A. Barrett; F. W. Coleman, III; G. E. Erb; C. H. McKinney; M. L. Martin; J. H. Allen; L. V. Barr; J. L. DeBoer; G. Guy; V. Hayes.

J. E. Holligan; M. W. Kernkamp; W. L. Schreiber; W. R. Shanahan; L. Tamanian; E. R. Vanderburg; R. W. Worthington; R. R. Yeaman; W. H. Baynes; H. J. Blanchard; R. L. Bothwell; M. W. Boyer.

J. R. Brown; R. H. Caldwell; E. S. Davis; J. E. Davoli; J. L. Dickson; G. A. Doersch; C. B. Downer; J. G. Foster; C. H. Gerlach; G. P. Gibons; J. F. Greco; S. W. Heinonen.

R. S. Hill; J. W. Hiney; B. H. Hinton; R. Hogg; J. W. Hough; W. G. Jackson, Jr.; S. W. Josephson; D. F. Logan; G. E. Marcus, Jr.; H. Reich; R. W. Rood.

C. U. Ruzek, Jr.; J. G. Sliney; R. M. Smith; P. Sowa, Jr.; L. F. Upson, Jr.; P. B. Woodward; H. H. Green; R. W. Lindgren; E. H. Beverly; V. R. Woodward.

Hughes Tool Co. (13): E. R. Eastwold, G. H. Whisler, A. G. Russell, C. C. Bliss, N. R. Hoskot, R. W. Hanson, Clark W. Ecton, John R. McQueen, William F. Borellis, Merle G. Coombs, L. T. Ryhlick, E. H. Nigro, Jerome Triolo.

International Business Machine Co. (35): R. W. Arthur, S. F. Balaban, R. M. Brewer, J. S. Carpenter, D. M. Clark, J. T. Cockrill, E. M. Collins, E. F. Comstock, R. W. Curtis, T. A. Daffron, J. E. Dyar.

H. B. Ferrill, C. W., Glassen, H. H. Greer, R. Hatch, W. Hussey, M. M. Kovar, H. A. Lazott, T. H. Lewis, IV, M. Lind, H. T. Neal, E. O'Con-

Wilcox; W. P. Ennis; W. G. Hipps; R. T. Herget; N. B. Gibson; J. D. Luse; R. W. McNamee, Jr.; R. E. Smith.

C. W. Abbitt; N. D. Burnside; V. F. Creighton; E. E. Crowell; C. L. Elder; W. Hagin; A. A. Kurz; A. Martin; T. N. Natt; H. L. Norwood; A. R. St. Angelo.

General Dynamics Corp. (113): R. P. Alexander; Charles F. Alfano; Stanley E. Allen; H. T. Alness; E. Arentzen; L. C. Baldauf; Roger Banner; George E. Botswick; P. Branson; Willima Budding, Jr.

Berton H. Burns; Luther W. Burns; William R. Calhoun; Walter E. Chambers; C. W. Cecil; Ovle D. Clark; E. P. Coffey; Charles Cushman; L. P. Daniels; Charles Daval, Jr.

J. P. Dawley; Alfred J. Diehl; Donald G. Dockum; R. Evans; J. S. Fahy; H. Field; Lawrence G. Forbes; A. E. Freedman; Terrence A. Freeman; A. P. Gandy.

Philip Glennon; G. P. Gould; Edward Hamby; Otha B. Hardy, Jr.; J. T. Hayward; Charles E. Healy; J. B. Hess; Blish Hills; Florian A. Holm; C. F. Horne.

W. Jeancon; James K. Johnson; W. M. Kasper; H. Kay; J. W. Kelly; G. S. Kingston; S. B. Keonig; R. V. Laney; D. L. Lassell; C. P. Lessig.

E. M. Link, Jr.; William A. Looney; Frank Lynch; J. M. MacInnes; Herbert Mandel; W. J. Mang; W. C. Manicom; William Marchesi; William H. Markos; Wallace S. Martin; F. N. Masuen.

J. P. McCann; B. J. McCarrol; C. C. McCutoheon; F. A. McGee; Howard J. McIntire; R. E. L. Michie; Leo C. Moon; H. W. Moore; H. E. Moose; Robert E. Morris; Lawrence Mowell.

Daniel C. Mulloney; James R. Munro; C. B. Nelson; P. Niekum; James D. Nutt; Frank L. O'Brien; J. Oldfield; Robert Page; C. Palmer; A. C. Perry.

Ayres, F. N. Lebershall, W. J. Robinson, L. H. Schofield, James M. Farrin, William Willman, John A. Martin, Francis F. Parry, Douglas S. Barker, Sam Burno, George N. Eisenhart.

Arthur Bouvier, John E. Hausman, Arron L. Johnson, George Y. Jumper, Warren E. Oliver, Harry C. Smith, Robert A. Thompson, Ed Hribar, Albert C. Wells, Walter W. Woodard, Solomon J. Zoller.

Arthur J. Barrett, Donald J. Iddins, Robert L. Kelly, W. F. Raborn, R. B. Pirie, B. A. Schriever, Clyde Eddleman, Ed O'Neil, Fred Hayden, F. F. Everest.

Goodyear Tire & Rubber Co. (6): F. G. Selby, W. F. Cassidy, P. L. Dixon, P. S. Peca, M. E. Galusha, H. H. McIntosh.

Grumman Aircraft Engineering Corp. (31): John Breehl; Herbert Mosca; Paul Hoeper; Emerson Fawkes; Francis Gabreski; Richard Centner; John Courtney, Jr.; Charles Michaels; Alan Strock; James Moore.

Dave Dillard; Jack Nicholas; John Shinkle; Gus Macri; Tom Meritt; Dean Swain; Widmer Hansen; Roy Voris; William Spiegel; Frank Edwards; Boyd McElhany.

William Ditch; Loys Satterfield; Elbert Stever; Ross Mickey; Fred Schroeder; Joseph Rees; Fred Oliver; John Koch; William Clampet; Arthur Warner, Jr.

Gulf Oil Corp. (1): H. W. Blackwood.

Harris-Intertype Corp. (4): A. W. Sissom, M. F. Skinner, Grayson Merrill, F. A. Escobar.

Harvey Aluminum Inc.: Joseph Metzger, Homer G. Barber, Alfred Kaufman, Ed Miller.

Hazeltine Corp. (7): N. K. Dietrich, R. I. Olson, A. J. Stanziano, S. M. Thomas, Oswald S. Colclough, Jennings B. Dow, John Slezak.

Hercules Inc. (13): Charles E. Jordan; Leland S. McCants, Jr.; Robert S. Kittel; John W. Sevareid; Walter J. Fellenz; James H. Traul; W. M. Pierce; Joel W. Salter; Lewis A.

W. B. Stubbs, R. W. Swanson, T. M. Taylor, H. C. Weadler, F. J. Wesley, R. C. Whittman, S. C. Wilson, B. H. Witham, J. F. Wood.

International Harvester Co. (6): Donald I. Thomas, Bud K. Beaver, Richard K. Margetts, Roger E. Strasburg, A. J. Norris Hill, Robert Etzkorn.

International Telephone & Telegraph Corp.: Not available at the time of preparation.

Johns Hopkins University (11): Not available at the time of preparation.

Kaiser Industries Corp. (11): Stanley J. Benkoski, Stirling S. Cook, M.D., J. G. Capka, F. W. Hastings, F. T. Matthias, E. G. Peacock, E. J. Stann, D. C. Christensen, F. A. Gunn, A. K. Romberg, J. B. Conners.

Lear Siegler Inc. (4): John K. Gerhart, Charles A. Roberts, V. L. Anderson, Frank A. Koszarek.

Ling Temco Vought Inc. (69): Herbert George Bench; Chester Arthur Briggs; George Budway; Francis Taylor Cooper; Marshall Pierce Deputy, Jr.; L. R. Bell; G. B. Kaiser; George Hundt, Jr.; F. S. Grutze, Jr.; E. S. Hartshorn, Jr.

H. B. Hardin, Jr.; D. F. Starr; R. P. Brett; G. P. Disosway; Alex Wilding; A. H. Perry; W. B. Taylor; J. E. Arnold; C. R. Eldredge; E. C. Ethell; G. E. Frency; Jr.

P. D. Green; C. B. Grimm; G. W. Jackson; C. C. Kennedy; H. E. Lucas; W. B. Packard; R. W. Priest; M. E. Riley; A. E. Shook; T. E. Stewart.

H. A. Templeton; O. O. Turner; P. H. Van Sickle; E. F. Klinck; G. B. Lotridge, M. Blaylock; J. B. Cline; A. B. Conner; D. E. Dressendorfer; R. P. Field.

W. C. Gammon; A. C. Holt; W. W. Kitts; C. A. Knight; R. W. Windsor; C. A. Yontz; J. K. Dill; A. B. Galatian; E. M. Hargrave.

H. G. Russell; F. R. Ulrich; M. J. Piatnitza; O. S. Kincannon; D. R. Schultze; B. D. Wood; M. G. Haines; R. E. Baker; F. B. Frost; R. W. Stanley.

V. Kellan; R. C. Gales; H. W. Russell; B. K. Sams; W. J. McIntyre; E. B. Gladding; Hermah Rumsey; Claude Duke; R. C. Drum.

Litton Industries, Inc. (49): Albert B. Scoles; Norman F. Garton; Rue Green; John B. Rawlings; H. S. Isaacson; Richard D. Dick; Donovan P. Yeuell, Jr.; James H. Courtney; Ben Wade.

G. L. McKee; Millard J. Smith; Roy W. Ballard; Earl Paules; A. Barney Oldfield; John D. Prodgers; Harry C. Cox; John W. Gilluly; Olav Njus; Carl H. Stober.

Richard R. Bradley, Jr.; Leonard Erb; Francis P. Cuccias; G. M. McHaney; Van Beck; Alfred Gallant; J. R. Reeves; J. L. Reed; Philip R. Deubler; David McIntosh.

Robert F. Pope; Charles J. Schroder; Joseph L. Brack; Everett M. Glenn; Arthur W. Johnsen; Dr. F. D. Minerva; Peter E. Romo; Thomas C. Gurley; Floyd B. Schultz, Ken Huff; P. L. Freeman.

Kenneth C. Boyce; C. B. Curtis; Lawrence Vivian; Lewis O. Smith; H. L. Kubel; W. O. Roemer; T. Melusky; Kenneth M. Beyer; Edgar B. Gravett.

Lockheed Aircraft Corp. (210): L. C. Craigie; L. I. Davis; W. W. Dick, Jr.; D. L. Lay; E. M. Lightfoot; E. L. Robbins; J. H. Sides; B. E. Steadman; R. A. Trennert; W. R. Tuck.

W. P. Abdallah; J. Y. Adams; R. C. Anderson; J. O. Appleyard; N. C. Appold; C. F. Bailey; F. E. Bardwell; J. A. Barker; R. O. Beer; J. E. Bennett.

J. S. Blais; J. M. Bowers; G. M. Boyd; C. W. Brigham; N. S. Brooks; K. E. Brown; P. Brown; R. F. Buckley, Jr.; C. C. Cain; D. C. Campbell.

E. A. Carter; J. W. Chapman; S. E. Clark; W. A. Cloman, Jr.; R. L. Colligan, Jr.; T. L. Conroy; G. S. Curtis, Jr.; H. E. Day, Jr.; H. O. Deakin; V. Deitchman.

R. L. Denig, Jr.; A. W. Dill; J. C. Dillow; N. G. Doukas; W. Dubyk; J. M. Elliott; C. L. Geant; R. A. Shane; R. Steinbach; J. H. Voyles, Jr.

E. Watts, Jr.; J. Arnold, Jr.; J. F. Brewer; G. K. Crain; H. C. Krim, Jr.; L. W. Congdon; R. N. Davie; R. A. Erdin; E. F. Estrumse; W. A. Harmon.

C. E. Harris; H. B. Heyer; C. C. Hoffman; L. R. Hopper; R. P. Loughrey; W. M. Massengale; R. K. McDonough; B. H. Meyer; W. L. Moore, Jr.; H. L. Parris.

J. W. Perry; O. K. Reynolds; W. W. Riser, Jr.; H. S. Sabatier; R. C. Sears; L. G. Sidwell; L. A. Tenold; J. W. Tooley; E. A. Waterfill; K. S. Wilson.

D. H. Christensen; R. H. Fagan; J. M. Jones; G. E. Price; E. C. Wittenbach; C. L. Clay; A. J. De Angelis; F. C. Forsberg; W. S. Kohlhagen; K. W. Mitchim.

D. T. Morse; Ralph A. Smith; H. F. Bunze; G. Cechmanek; F. V. Genetti; R. Hundevadt; H. W. Robbins; M. L. Shumaker; Walter Weddle; R. F. Toliver.

Lykes Corp.: None.

Magnavox Co. (3): James H. Schofield, Jr.; R. Bruce Crane; George F. Smith.

Martin Marietta Corp. (40): Allen Abt; Harry Cruver; William Norton; B. J. Reilly; J. S. Reynaud; Gerald Brockman; R. H. Foltz; C. J. Odendhal; T. W. Ackert; L. R. Anderson.

H. V. Bastin, Jr.; H. F. Boone; F. X. Bradley; M. B. Chandler; D. A. Clark; R. H. Cooke; P. R. Cornwall; H. E. Davidson, Jr.; C. E. Dunlap, Jr.; D. W. Forbes, Jr.

W. R. George; F. N. Green; S. A. Hall; N. M. Hadenick; J. M. Henschke; B. B. Hovell; V. W. Harvard; C. D. Lang; M. G. Megica; W. W. Quinn.

J. B. Sanders; F. D. Selbie, Jr.; R. F. Sellars; J. G. Sheridan; D. M. Simpson; W. A. Stellenwerf; A. J. Walker; H. B. Wells; D. K. Yost; V. L. Zoller.

Mason & Hanger Silas Mason Co. (5): Joel G. Holmes; Lawrence H. Prather; Foster L. Furphy; George E. Davis; Jesse L. Pennell

Massachusetts Institute of Technology (5): James Gormley; Robert F. Scofield; C. Warren Smalzel; Lewis Larson; Robert Mil-

David E. Honodle; A. L. Hopwood; K. H. Houghton; E. F. Hutchins; R. K. Jacobson; C. R. Johnson; William R. Jones; D. Klein; B. A. Miles; Wilton B. Moats.

R. L. Neyman; W. C. Nielsen; Paul A. Noel, Jr.; R. Nudenberg; J. A. O'Leary; C. W. Pangburn; Joseph A. Patalive; J. R. Penland; C. A. Peterson; J. Pietz.

Richard S. Quiggins; R. C. Randall; E. S. Rice; G. M. Rice; O. J. Ritland; J. M. Rouse; G. J. Schaffer; M. C. Smith; S. D. Stooksberry; R. D. Stowell.

R. B. Sullivan; A. J. Walden; P. S. Walker; L. Q. Westmoreland; R. V. Wheeler; S. Yarchin; William B Taylor; William C. Armstrong; Edward J. Gujer; L. Boyd Kendall; Phillip O. Robertson.

McLean Industries, Inc. (2): John E. Terrell, Leon A. Michaelis.

Mobil Oil Corp.: (Not available at time of preparation.)

Motorola Inc. (3): Bradford Smith, John Parham, Jr., Roy Klein.

National Presto Industries Inc.: None.

Newport News Ship Building & Dry Dock Co. (6) J. S. Bethea, P. K. Taylor, J. H. Lofland, Jr., L. D. Bellinger, L. G. Richards, D. E. Fairchild.

Norris Industries (2): Fred A. Wheeler, Melvyn H. McCoy.

North American Rockwell Corp. (104): W. A. Davis; R. E. Greer; C. W. Schott; E. B. Gallant; W. M. Garland; H. W. Powell; W. W. Wilcox; C. G. Allen; W. A. Anderson; J. E. Andres.

J. L. Armstrong; R. E. Barton; J. E. Bicknell; E. L. Bishop; R. W. W. Booth; W. B. Cannon; Armando Caseria; R. E. Cathcart; C. A. Culpepper; B. C. Dunn.

S. E. Ellis; M. E. Fields; C. D. Fisher; S. G. Fisher; W. S. Ford; J. H. Foster; J. M. Foxx; W. H. Frederick; C. R. Gregg; W. B. Henderson.

H. D. Hewett; W. K. Horrigan; C. Houck; B. W. Humphries; H. E. Johnson, Jr.; J. H. Kellerman; C. D. Kester; I. F. Larkey; D. R. Longino, Jr.; J. Maddalena, Jr.

H. C. May; J. B. Miller; R. S. Nye; V. R.

F. E. Gorman; J. B. Green; H. J. Halberstadt; F. L. Harris.

W. A. Hasler, Jr.; B. W. Heckemeyer; F. G. Henry; P. J. Heran; H. J. Heuer; S. W. Hickey; J. B. Honan; E. F. Hoover; D. A. Hornby; M. H. Hubbard.

J. F. Johnston; R. D. King; J. F. Kinney; E. F. Klinke; J. B. Koenig; C. H. Kretz, Jr.; B. A. Lawhon; B. L. Lubelsky; J. H. Mackin; R. H. Maynard.

R. C. McGlashan; R. B. McLaughlin; F. J. Mee; R. M. Metcalf; E. W. Miles; G. C. Moore; L. W. Morefield, Jr.; W. E. Moring; J. F. Mullen, Jr.; E. G. Mulling, Jr.

S. Neman; J. R. Nickel; F. C. E. Oder; E. G. Osborn; G. L. Ottinger; W. B. Parham; R. A. Paton; P. B. Peabody; R. W. Peterson; J. J. Preston.

K. J. Prim; J. J. Randazzo; Q. A. Riepe; W. H. Rowen; E. A. Sandor; L. Saxton; M. S. Schmidling; M. J. Senn; M. W. Shea; W. A. Sheppard.

J. L. Shoenhair; J. E. Shuck; C. C. Smith; H. J. Smith, Jr.; V. C. Smith; W. R. Smith, III; B. F. Such; W. A. Sullivan; P. E. Summers; W. L. Tagg.

J. H. Terry; H. F. Thompson; R. C. Thorburn; P. E. Villars; A. H. Walton; V. E. Warford; I. E. Wetmore; E. R. White; R. K. Worthington; N. C. Anderson.

C. H. Andrews; M. H. Austin; B. Battino; J. Beyer; H. G. Bradshaw; J. R. Brown; F. D. Buckley; L. K. Carson; R. F. Cassidy; R. R. Catterlin.

L. D. Coates; V. J. Coley, Jr.; S. H. Dodge; D. J. Gehri; D. Gordon; M. B. Hammond; D. E. Huey; L. E. Ireland; K. J. Kirk, Jr.; A. L. Logan.

J. Lynn; T. L. Macleod; R. McMillan; M. W. Munk; R. A. Neale; J. L. Neefus; J. A. Sear-

B. Sloan; Clyde H. Parmelee; R. W. Fellows; M. Kauffman; Joseph W. Antonides; E. M. Beauchamp; William D. Cavness; Edward M. Day.

John G. Glover; Laverne F. Houston; Richard F. Kane; William C. Lemke; Haydon L. Leon; Arthur A. McCartan; Richard S. McConnell; Thomas W. Ownby; Arnold T. Phillips; Eugene W. Phillips.

Charles C. Sanders; Robert W. Shick; Siegfried H. Spillner; Robert C. Starkey; Vernon E. Teig; Frank T. Watrous; J. D. Blanchard; R. L. Cormier; R. E. Cutts; J. Desmond.

J. G. Hedrick; A. N. Jones; R. J. Lavery; R. A. Lowcock; W. T. Luce; T. B. Payne; R. V. Porter; R. E. Schleeh; J. A. Thomas; J. A. Sullivan.

J. F. Daniels, Jr.; A. S. Pitts; K. W. Longnecker; J. Morrissey; J. J. Davis; F. D. Turnbull; F. M. Goode; N. Garrett; R. L. Towne; L. L. Sailor.

K. K. Kelley; G. M. Clarke; H. W. Heber; K. A. Harcos; M. F. O'Donnell; W. W. Waters; K. Herman; R. D. Coffee; K. K. Lewis; L. C. Rochte.

R. L. Baseler; A. J. Walden; R. M. Tunnell; W. C. Adams; Ford E. Alcorn; Carl Arnold; L. R. Ash; P. H. Best; H. H. Bowe; R. H. Bowen.

W. D. Brady; R. S. Buchanan; R. H. Bull; W. C. Bumm, F. B. Carlson, M. B. Chatfield; R. A. Clendenin; E. L. Cole; M. R. Collins, Jr.; W. J. Collum, Jr.

H. D. Courtney; C. D. Dalton; S. P. Dillon; R. C. Dineen; J. G. Duncan; C. B. Evans; G. B. Felton; P. L. Fishburne; R. W. Fletter; C. H. Greene, Jr.

S. Greene; Jack Guy; L. R. Hall; K. T. Hanson; Robert J. Hanson; B. T. Hemphill; R. M. Herrington; J. B. Herweg; J. A. Hewitt; P. L. Hill.

G. T. Smith; J. J. Smith; O. W. Snodgrass; P. W. Toomey; H. E. Wardon; R. J. Watson; W. T. Wilborn; D. J. Yockey; E. B. Young; G. Crum.

G. A. Aubrey; W. P. Brooks; E. R. Gillespie; H. R. Greenlee; J. B. Jeffords; R. M. Kelly; J. H. Lattin; W. M. Smith; J. E. Stone; J. P. Condon.

W. V. Crockett; H. Hansen, Jr.; F. E. Hollar; J. S. Holmberg; E. W. Johnston; A. C. Lowell; W. D. Roberson; L. E. Roberts; J. L. Smith; E. H. Vaughn.

S. W. Carpenter; R. N. Clark; J. L. Melgaard; K. A. Aho; F. P. Anderson; R. S. Chandler; T. W. Collins, Jr.; L. E. Flint, Jr.; R. E. Harris; F. E. Hayler.

J. S. Hill; F. Larsen; H. N. Larson; W. L. Nyburg; J. F. Parker; F. D. Pfotenhauer; E. S. Quilter; C. E. Robertson; W. M. Shifflette; J. Steinberger; F. Turner; D. S. Walton; H. C. Weart; R. M. Wilson.

Northrop Corp. (48): J. T. Bradley; R. M. Elder; W. H. Gurnee, Jr., H. J. Jablonsky; M. C. Johansen; W. C. Mahoney; Y. A. Pitts, Jr.; L. Shapiro; J. R. Anderson; M. M. Coons.

M. M. Dupre; J. L. Fisher; R. W. Fox; C. R. Heffner; J. H. Jennette; D. M. Lynch; R. W. Parks; J. C. Schofield; R. C. Works; R. Carlson.

N. A. Severson; G. A. Barclay; V. A. Cherbak, Jr.; D. K. Dean; J. F. Enright; A. Herron; J. W. Koletty; J. Duganne; H. Haszard; A. Jackson.

K. Buchak; A. Burke; J. A. Buzzell; R. Canny; T. F. Collins; R. S. Drake; W. A. Haycock; W. M. Hodges; H. Hughes; E. Lavier.

N. Misenheimer; F. T. Pomeroy; R. Sansone; A. Sullivan; K. M. Welborn; F. T. West; R. M. Bell; G. A. Peters.

Olin Mathieson Chemical Corp. (3): Richard E. Johnson, E. A. Lovingood, Kenneth W. Brewer.

Pacific Architects & Engineers Inc. (16): William J. New, John Francis Wolf, Robert H. Calahan, William A. Cunningham, James S. Greene, Hugh B. Grundvig, Charles E. Houston, Frederic G. Miller, Richard L. Moody, George O. Pearson, Louis P. Pressler, Cecil P. Rice, Harry G. Roller, Tolson A. Smoak, John H. White, Edwin F. Woodhead.

Pan American World Airways Inc. (24): S. G. Ashdown; J. C. Grain; R. D. Dean; A. V. Dishman; V. J. Donohue; G. C. Fleming; R. Lamoreaux; W. L. Leverette; L. Lipscomb, Jr.; R. B. Madden; C. E. McClure; O. G. Quanrud.

F. P. Stainback, Jr.; R. L. Stell; R. S. Van Benschoten; H. P. Wagner; K. Withington; Robert Bell; Lawrence Kuter; C. A. Lindbergh; Maurice Fitzgerald; Robert Sandford; Dr. J. K. Cullen; Leland Johnson.

Radio Corp. of America (35): Z. R. Glocheski, E. W. Fuller, P. B. Foote, B. D. Hale, G. E. Pinkston, R. S. Maloney, J. E. Stevens, M. Williamson, G. Dawson, C. V. Johnson, J. Brandt, L. W. Van Antwerp, J. H. Brockway, S. L. Miller, H. Harnly, H. C. Henry, W. Heard.

L. W. Pflanz, T. P. Ross, F. K. Smith, G. P. Williams, T. N. Chavis, F. P. Henderson, W. H. Kreamer, B. F. McMahon, M. L. Ogden, P. T. Preuss, E. E. Roberts, P. N. Shamer, J. H. Wergen, J. Boning, A. C. Gay, R. E. Hogan, L. J. McNulty, R. K. Saxe.

Raymond Morrison Knudsen—Raymond International, Inc.; Morrison-Knudsen Co., Inc.; Brown & Root, Inc.; & J. A. Jones Construction Co. (Joint venture) (6): Jean E. Bush, Robert R. Helen, Kenneth Kermit Anderson, Luther E. Bell, L. B. Wilby, Andrew D. Chaffin, Jr.

Raytheon Co. (37): Rolland D. Appleton; Alfred R. Bauch; William V. Beach; John B. Bond; Ernest V. Cameron; Charles E. Collins, Jr.; Erling J. Foss; Albert P. Hilar; Archie T. Madsen; Francis G. McBride; Charles R. Moulder; Charles C. Roberts; Eldon W. Schmid; Eldon D. Sewell; John B. Maher; Benjamin E. Moore; Gill M. Richardson; Henry E. Bernstein.

Lynn, H. W. Maw, S. D. B. Merrill, R. Mugg, J. R. Payne, K. Pryor, J. A. Rice, J. M. Richardson, I. Robinson, O. L. Robinson, A. B. Roby, S. Schesinger, R. F. Sladek.

Standard Oil Co. of California (6): C. M. Clifford, J. E. Fratis, A. C. Bonnycastle, W. T. Kelly, R. E. Morandes, G. R. Deits.

Standard Oil of New Jersey (2): Eric Barr, J. H. Bowell.

States Marine Lines Inc. None.

Susquehanna Corp. (7): W. O. Blandford; W. M. Burgess; J. Carter; J. B. Cochran; D. L. Evans, III; H. W. Norton; N. Schramm, Jr.

Sverdrup & Parcel & Associates, Inc. (9): L. J. Sverdrup; E. J. Peltier; W. J. Ely; P. Z. Michener; Samuel T. Wallace; Lowell W. Shallenberg; Samuel F. Miller; Charles B. Alexander; George M. Gans.

T.R.W. Inc. (56): Richard C. Snyder; John Kooken; Richard Broberg; James Foster; E. J. Arakelian; J. J. Baranowski; Edward Blum; George W. Bollinger; E. L. Brady; M. C. Brennan.

C. T. Campbell; H. B. Chrissinger; Howard Cook; H. S. Croyts; T. B. Dabney; J. O. Davenport; H. H. Eichel; L. A. Franz; H. K. Gilbert; J. J. Gilchrist; G. A. Gilliland; C. W. Griffing.

Lacey C. Hall; H. B. Hansell; Bruce B. Hammond; J. F. Harris; Carson Hitler; R. L. Huber; L. J. Hutton; Cam Knox; W. A. Kruge; C. J. Lemmon; Stan R. Mason; R. M. McMahon.

C. Medinnis; J. O'Connor; R. E. O'Denning; D. Pilliod; Elmer G. Prohaska; E. C. Pruett; J. Ruebel; Oliver M. Scott; James S. Seay; S. L. Siler; R. P. Sims; S. H. Sherrill, Jr.

J. W. Smith; R. J. Speaks; Lester L. Stone; J. B. Summers; R. Trauger; J. A. Urban; L. E. Vandeveer; H. E. Walters; R. W. Yundt; John E. Zink; Andrew J. Kelley.

Teledyne Inc. (8): Dr. Kenneth C. DeGon; Dr. George Stead; Herman J. Mecklenburg; Elby D. Martin; John Hyerle; Robert Williams; Joseph Neely; Roy Nelson.

Texaco Inc. (4): Violas Bishop, Henry F. Bell, Albert Benjamin, J. A. Obermeyer.

Texas Instrument Inc. (73): Harlan Free-

Vinnell Corp.: None.

Vitro Corp. of America (25): Paul C. Murphy; L. E. Andre; H. H. Miller, Jr.; W. F. Keating; W. E. Antle, Jr.; N. B. Atkins; H. G. Doyle; S. E. Ellison; L. S. Eubanks; J. B. Gay, Jr.; R. J. Ramsbotham; G. A. Reaves, III.

R. J. Rudolph; P. S. Savidge; J. B. Wallace; J. K. Fyfe; N. S. Chase; D. J. Freund; S. Gassett; C. J. Harrison; J. B. Jacob; S. J. Mancuso; C. A. Merkle; E. J. Quashnoch; H. W. Swan.

Western Union Telegraph Co. (5): J. W. Davis, H. Dorfman, R. F. Flynn, J. A. Moore, R. M. Perry.

Westinghouse Electric Corp. (59): T. S. Bond; C. F. Burch; F. W. Campbell; W. D. Coyne; A. Creal; P. W. Crutchfield; R. K. Cunningham; P. C. Davis; R. W. Dickerson; J. L. Dickey.

D. K. Ela; S. W. Fitzgerald; W. J. Foley, Jr.; J. A. Garath; T. E. Harper; J. W. Henry; M. E. Hinden; J. E. Hoker; H. J. Islev-Peterson; C. D. Jeffcoat.

M. Kadick; E. S. Keats; T. K. Kimmel; C. B. Lindstrand; R. B. Linnenkin; J. E. Mahon; J. E. Miller; R. T. Miller; J. E. Mills; C. H. Morrison, Jr.

J. Munholland; E. D. Northrop; P. L. M. Packard; H. J. Pence; H. E. Skinner; W. M. Smith; R. W. Soderberg; J. K. Sun; J. T. Traylor; W. E. Underwood.

K. O. Vandayburg; G. W. Albin; W. M. Braley; V. P. Carlson; W. J. Germershausen; J. E. Hammerstone; C. J. Heath; J. W. Losch; C. Wiedman; W. L. Kabler.

W. A. Dolan, Jr.; R. S. Froude; J. D. Frye; J. C. McCawley; A. M. Prentiss; Roy G. Moore; William T. Shealy; A. Wermuth; J. A. Woodbury.

White Motor Co.: Not available at time of preparation.

World Airways Inc. (4): Harry G. Adam; Herbert E. Greuter; Jack Reiter; Robert I. Johnson.

Lange; James T. Lay; Francis R. O'Brien; James G. Prout, Jr.; Leslie S. Robinson; Poyntell C. Staley; Donald N. Yates; Harry L. Evans; Alan R. K. Burton; David M. Crabtree; John D. Crisp; Henry M. Harlow; Bernard R. Muldoon; Joseph J. Pellegrini; Walter H. Williamson.

Ryan Aeronautical Co. (25): C. Bogner; T. A. Ahola; D. C. Emrich; W. W. Forehand; J. N. Highley; J. H. Owens; R. Pollack; L. M. Ryan; H. L. Wood; W. E. Clasen; A. D. Gomez; V. M. Bennett.

N. B. Davis, Jr.; W. R. Harman; R. S. Johnson; W. Mercer; O. F. Meyer; J. H. Tripp; G. T. Peterson; H. Cox; W. L. Drennen; W. E. King; J. T. Shephard; J. F. Thorlin; J. G. Cornett.

Sanders Associates Inc. (17): Barry Atkins; James Casler; William J. Caspari; Donald A. Detwiler; John Doll; Stephen H. Gimber; Rolland A. Helsel; Ralph Lamond; Douglas B. Lapierre; Brainard Macomber; Ralph J. Mattus; Jesse P. Moorefield; John G. Palo; Raymond W. Raines; Charles Register; Ferrer Regni; Orville J. Schulte.

Seatrain Lines Inc. (4): F. T. Voorhies; C. P. Bellican; W. Savidge; C. R. Hamblett.

Signal Companies Inc. (The) (9): Mark E. Bradley, James R. Cumberpatch, William Barnes, Raymond Deitsch, Keith G. Lindell, Aubrey Lyons, James J. Treacy, Innes Robert Lee White, Ray J. Sherry.

Smith Investment Co. None.

Sperry Rand Corp. (36): L. Armstrong, A. Baker, D. H. Baker, J. J. Benshoff, R. J. Billado, R. L. Brown, D. Buntine, W. Campbell, V. H. Castle, M. A. Connor, H. Cowart, F. H. Cunnare, P. C. Droz, P. Folsom, H. S. Foote, T. L. Gaines, R. P. Gentry, J. A. Gloriod.

G. Gunderman, C. A. Heath, G. C. Higginbotham, F. R. Kaspereen, J. Keiper, R. R. er, J. Baxter.

Textron Inc. (28): J. A. C. Andrews; J. Clapper; J. F. Gill; J. V. Hearn; B. J. L. Hirshorn; R. M. Hurst; D. McKee; H. C. Newcomer; D. R. Ostrander; J. Otts; J. M. Schweizer, Jr.; W. B. Stevens; D. Wilson; H. R. Archibald.

S. J. Clark; C. Coates; E. McGrane; C. A. Mette; A. Niemi; H. R. Smith; W. Tetley; W. M. Boyd; H. H. Howze; J .W. Oswalt; R. W. Van Orne; W. J. Yates; R. L. Ramsey; Roy Southworth.

Thiokol Chemical Corp. (3): Harry M. Murray, Willard L. Nielsen, Paul C. Trammell.

Uniroyal Inc. (6): W. M. Coy, George P. Nichols, Edward A. Nunn, S. A. Meyer, Karl F. Moessner, A. C. Hamilton.

United Aircraft Corp. (48): R. L. Duncan; H. W. Everett; J. P. Keegan; G. A. Palmer; T. A. Sims, Jr.; Strouther B. Hardwick; Albert R. Weldon; Joseph M. Silk; Marc M. Ducote; John F. Quinn; Donald N. Alexander; L. V. Marchbanks, Jr.

Paul Steinle; Milton Waltcher; Harold J. Larson; George A. Linko; Eugene Tatom; Richard L. Long; Herbert S. Brown; Robert R. Corey; E. C. Dyer; Alexander Rankin; Allen C. Miller; James G. J. Kellis.

William E. Kenna; Murlin W. Alley; Clarence R. Easter; Robert D. Dearth; Robert D. Bowers; George P. Gould; Herbert G. Hoover; Norair M. Lulejian; Arthur Pfeiffer; Frederick B. Tucker; W. C. Erlenbusch; E. T. B. Sullivan.

W. J. Corcoran; C. R. Doerflinger; J. H. Mallett; Robert Morris; E. A. Swanke; John Amann; George Kronmiller; E. S. Ligon; D. L. Putt; E. N. Hall; H. A. Arnold; R. B. Laning.

United States Steel Corp.: Not available at time of preparation.

INDUSTRIES LINKED TO AN AD FOR ABM

Neil Sheehan

WASHINGTON, AUG. 3—The defense industries were well represented among the signers of a prominently circulated newspaper advertisement promoting the Nixon Administration's antiballistic missile defense proposal.

An analysis of the business connections of 344 persons who signed a full-page advertisement that appeared in several newspapers at the end of June showed that about 55 had defense industry associations.

Fourteen were directors, officers or lawyers for companies that are already doing ABM work under the more than $1-billion in contracts awarded by the Defense Department from funds appropriated by Congress in previous fiscal years for missile defense system development.

Group Formed in May

Another 20 signers had similar connections with companies that rank among the top 100 defense contractors in volume of business, while 21 more were associated with companies that do some defense business or are potential subcontractors if the Administration's $10.8-billion ABM project is approved by Congress. Unofficial cost estimates run as high as $13-billion.

New York Times, August 4, 1969, pp. 1 and 21.

A large number of other signers were men with banking and insurance interests, such as George Champion, the chairman of the Chase Manhattan Bank.

The advertisement, which contends that "84 per cent of all Americans support an ABM system" according to a poll by the Opinion Research Corporation of Princeton, was placed by the Citizens Committee for Peace with Security. The committee was organized in May by William J. Casey, a well-known New York Republican, who is a law partner of Leonard Hall, a past chairman of the Republican National Committee.

It and a similar advertisement appeared in 25 newspapers throughout the country in June and July. Opinion Research has publicly disavowed the use to which its poll was put on the ground that the advertisement misrepresented the findings.

There have been persistent reports that the White House encouraged the formation of the committee and that Charles West, a White House staff assistant who has been coordinating ABM correspondence and information for Kenneth E. Belieu, the Administration's chief of congressional liaison on the missile defense plan, helped organize the group.

Mr. Casey has denied these reports.

The advertisement made no mention that any of the 344 signers, who appeared as members of the committee, had any defense business connections.

In a telephone interview last week, Mr. Casey said, "I didn't feel any responsibility to do that."

He said he did not believe that any conflict of interest was involved. "These people were all individuals speaking as citizens. That's how they were presented and that's how they were acting, in my opinion."

When the committee was formed, he said, "I laid down a rule that we don't want this committee to be labeled an arm of the military-industrial complex as we tried to stay away from people who were heavy in defense."

The appearance of 55 persons with defense associations was "purely accidental," he said.

Among those companies with ABM contracts, directors of the International Business Machines Corporation, which has received $7-million in ABM work, were particularly evident. Four signed, including

George Hinman, a lawyer from Binghamton, N.Y., whose firm also represents I.B.M.

Former Defense Chief

Neil McElroy, a Secretary of Defense during the Eisenhower Administration and now a director of the General Electric Company, which has obtained $75.2-million in ABM business, also signed.

Other signatories in this group included Robert W. Galvin, the chairman of Motorola, Inc., and president of the Electronic Industries Association; Mansfield Sprague, a former Assistant Secretary of Defense, who is now a vice president of the American Machine and Foundry Company, and B. Edward Bensinger, the chairman and director of the Brunswick Corporation. Motorola has been awarded $9.4-million in ABM contracts, while American Machine and Foundry and Brunswick hold amounts of $1.6-million each.

"Hell," Mr. Casey said, "I didn't know that George Hinman is a director of I.B.M. George Hinman is a lawyer."

"Neil McElroy," Mr. Casey continued, "He's a soap manufacturer." Mr. McElroy is the president of Procter & Gamble Company. "His primary interest is not C.E."

Refers to a Signer

Asked about three men associated with Olin-Mathieson who have signed, Mr. Casey said, "I wouldn't think of Olin-Mathieson as a defense contractor. That's a chemical company."

Olin-Mathieson ranks among the leading 50 defense contractors in the country and has been the principal source for army small arms powder since World War II.

"If they make powder, I didn't know," Mr. Casey said. "They make pesticides."

Mr. Casey said that one of the three signers, John Olin, past chairman of the company, was "an old friend" and that he knew Keith G. Funston, the present chairman, who also signed, as "a former president of the New York Stock Exchange."

When the committee was formed, individuals with prominent defense associations were "eliminated," Mr. Casey said. He refused, however, to give any names.

Letter to Stockholder

"One thing I resent here is the implication that just because a guy makes parts, he's going to subvert his views of what is best for the country to his best economic interests," he said. "I'll say his view might be colored . . . he might be so close he has trouble differentiating. But that they would sell something just to make money out of it, I don't think these guys do that."

One of the signers of the advertisement was William C. Croft, the president of the Pyle National Company of Chicago, which does some defense business.

In a letter to the stockholders in the company's annual report this April, Mr. Croft said the company was expanding its sale of electrical parts to the aerospace industry.

"Another recently developed line of connectors has been selected for use in the Lockheed L-1011 airbus. Still other product lines have been selected for use in applications in the Lockheed L-1011, the jumbo jet and the Sentinel antiballistic missile system," he wrote.

Mr. Casey said he did not know Mr. Croft and had never heard of the Pyle National Company.

Earlier this year, Mr. Casey was nominated by President Nixon to the Advisory Council of the United States Arms Control and Disarmament Agency.

4 ☆ THE ARMED FORCES IN THE MILITARY-INDUSTRIAL COMPLEX

THE NEW AMERICAN MILITARISM

David M. Shoup

AMERICA HAS BECOME a militaristic and aggressive nation. Our massive and swift invasion of the Dominican Republic in 1965, concurrent with the rapid buildup of U.S. military power in Vietnam, constituted an impressive demonstration of America's readiness to execute military contingency plans and to seek military solutions to problems of political disorder and potential Communist threats in the areas of our interest.

This "military task force" type of diplomacy is in the tradition of our more primitive preWorld War II "gunboat diplomacy" in which we landed small forces of Marines to protect American lives and property from the perils of native bandits and revolutionaries. In those days the U.S. Navy and its Marine landing forces were our chief means short of war, for showing the flag, exercising American power, and protecting U.S. interests abroad. The Navy, enjoying the freedom of the seas, was a visible and effective representative of the nation's sovereign power. The Marines could be employed ashore "on such other duties as the President might direct" without congressional approval or a declaration of war. The U.S. Army was not then used so freely because it was rarely ready for expeditionary service without some degree of mobilization, and its use overseas normally required

Atlantic 223, no. 4 (April 1969: 51–56. The opinions contained herein are the private ones of the author and are not to be construed as official or reflecting the views of the Navy Department or the naval service at large.

a declaration of emergency or war. Now, however, we have numerous contingency plans involving large joint Air Force-Army-Navy-Marine task forces to defend U.S. interests and to safeguard our allies wherever and whenever we suspect Communist aggression. We maintain more than 1,517,000 Americans in uniform overseas in 119 countries. We have 8 treaties to help defend 48 nations if they ask us to—or if we choose to intervene in their affairs. We have an immense and expensive military establishment, fueled by a gigantic defense industry, and millions of proud, patriotic, and frequently bellicose and militaristic citizens. How did this militarist culture evolve? How did this militarism steer us into the tragic military and political morass of Vietnam?

Prior to World War II, American attitudes were typically isolationist, pacifist, and generally anti-military. The regular peacetime military establishment enjoyed small prestige and limited influence upon national affairs. The public knew little about the armed forces, and only a few thousand men were attracted to military service and careers. In 1940 there were but 428,000 officers and enlisted men in the Army and Navy. The scale of the war, and the world's power relationships which resulted, created the American military giant. Today the active armed forces contain over 3.4 million men and women, with an additional 1.6 million ready reserves and National Guardsmen.

America's vastly expanded world role after World War II hinged upon military power. The voice and views of the professional military people became increasingly prominent. During the post-war period, distinguished military leaders from the war years filled many top positions in government. Generals Marshall, Eisenhower, MacArthur, Taylor, Ridgway, LeMay, and others were not only popular heroes but respected opinion-makers. It was a time of international readjustment; military minds offered the benefits of firm views and problem-solving experience to the management of the nation's affairs. Military procedures—including the general staff system, briefings, estimates of the situation, and the organizational and operational techniques of the highly schooled, confident military professionals—spread throughout American culture.

World War II had been a long war. Millions of young American men had matured, been educated, and gained rank and stature during their years in uniform. In spite of themselves, many returned to civilian life as indoctrinated, combat-experienced military professionals. They were veterans, and for better or worse would never be the same again. America will never be the same either. We are now a nation of veterans. To the 14.9 million veterans of World War II, Korea added another 5.7 million five years later, and ever since, the large peacetime military establishment has been training and releasing draftees, enlistees, and short-term reservists by the hundreds of thousands each year. In 1968 the total living veterans of U.S. military service numbered over 23 million, or about 20 percent of the adult population.

Today most middle-aged men, most business, government, civic, and professional leaders, have served some time in uniform. Whether they liked it or not, their military training and experience have affected them, for the creeds and attitudes of the armed forces are powerful medicine, and can become habit-forming. The military codes include all the virtues and beliefs used to motivate men of high principle: patriotism, duty and service to country, honor among fellowmen, courage in the face of danger, loyalty to organization and leaders, self-sacrifice for comrades, leadership, discipline, and physical fitness. For many veterans the military's efforts to train and indoctrinate them may well be the most impressive and influential experience they have ever had—especially so for the young and less educated.

In addition, each of the armed forces has its own special doctrinal beliefs and well-catalogued customs, traditions, rituals, and folklore upon which it strives to build a fiercely loyal military character and esprit de corps. All ranks are taught that their unit and their branch of the military service are the most elite, important, efficient, or effective in the military establishment. By believing in the superiority and importance of their own service they also provide themselves a degree of personal status, pride, and self-confidence.

As they get older, many veterans seem to romanticize and exaggerate their own military experience and loyalties. The policies, attitudes, and positions of the powerful veterans' organizations such as the American Legion, Veterans of Foreign Wars, and AMVETS, totaling over 4 million men, frequently reflect this pugnacious and chauvinistic tendency. Their memberships generally favor military solutions to world problems in the pattern of their own earlier experience, and often assert that their military service and sacrifice should be repeated by the younger generations.

Closely related to the attitudes and influence of America's millions of veterans is the vast and powerful complex of the defense industries, which have been described in detail many times in the eight years since General Eisenhower first warned of the military-industrial power complex in his farewell address as President. The relationship between the defense industry and the military establishment is closer than many citizens realize. Together they form a powerful public opinion lobby. The several military service associations provide both a forum and a meeting ground for the military and its industries. The associations also provide each of the armed services with a means of fostering their respective roles, objectives, and propaganda.

Each of the four services has its own association, and there are also additional military function associations, for ordnance, management, defense industry, and defense transportation, to name some of the more prominent. The Air Force Association and the Association of the U.S. Army are the largest, best organized, and most effective of the service associations. The Navy League, typical of the "silent service" traditions, is not as well coordinated in its public relations efforts, and the small Marine Corps Association is not even in the same arena with the other contenders, the Marine Association's main activity being the publication of a semi-official monthly magazine. Actually, the service associations' respective magazines, with an estimated combined circulation of over 270,000, are the primary medium serving the several associations' purposes.

Air Force and Space Digest, to cite one example, is the magazine of the Air Force Association and the unofficial mouthpiece of the U.S. Air Force doctrine, "party line," and propaganda. It frequently promotes Air Force policy that has been officially frustrated or suppressed within the Department of Defense. It beats the tub for strength through aerospace power, interprets diplomatic, strategic, and tactical problems in terms of air power, stresses the requirements for quantities of every type of aircraft, and frequently perpetuates the extravagant fictions about the effectiveness of bombing. This, of course, is well coordinated with and supported by the multibillion-dollar aerospace industry, which thrives upon the boundless desires of the Air Force. They reciprocate with lavish and expensive ads in every issue of *Air Force.* Over 96,000 members of the Air Force Association receive the magazine. Members include active, reserve, retired personnel, and veterans of the U.S. Air Force. Additional thousands of copies go to people engaged in the defense industry. The thick mixture of advertising, propaganda, and Air Force doctrine continuously repeated in this publication provides its readers and writers with a form of intellectual hypnosis, and they are prone to believe their own propaganda because they read it in *Air Force.*

The American people have also become more and more accustomed to militarism, to uniforms, to the cult of the gun, and to the violence of combat. Whole generations have been brought up on war news and wartime propaganda; the few years of peace since 1939 have seen a steady stream of war novels, war movies, comic strips, and television programs with war or military settings. To many Americans, military training, expeditionary service, and warfare are merely extensions of the entertainment and games of childhood. Even the weaponry and hardware they use at war are similar to the highly realistic toys of their youth. Soldiering loses appeal for some of the relatively few who experience the blood, terror, and filth of battle; for many, however, including far too many senior professional officers, war and combat are an exciting adventure, a competitive game, and an escape from the dull routines of peacetime.

It is this influential nucleus of aggressive, ambitious professional military leaders who are the root of America's evolving militarism. There are over 410,000 commissioned officers on active duty in the four armed services. Of these, well over half are junior ranking reserve officers on temporary active duty. Of the 150,000 or so regular career officers, only a portion are senior ranking colonels, generals, and admirals, but it is they who constitute the elite core of the military establishment. It is these few thousand top-ranking professionals who command and manage the armed forces and plan and formulate military policy and opinion. How is it, then, that in spite of civilian controls and the national desire for peace, this small group of men exert so much martial influence upon the government and life of the American people?

The military will disclaim any excess of power or influence on their part. They will point to their small numbers, low pay, and subordination to civilian masters as proof of their modest status and innocence. Nevertheless, the professional military, as a group, is probably one of the best organized and most influential of the various segments of the American scene. Three wars and six major contingencies since 1940 have forced the American people to become abnormally aware of the armed forces and their leaders. In turn the military services have produced an unending supply of distinguished, capable, articulate, and effective leaders. The sheer skill, energy, and dedication of America's military officers make them dominant in almost every government or civic organization they may inhabit, from the federal Cabinet to the local PTA.

The hard core of high-ranking professionals are, first of all, mostly service academy graduates: they had to be physically and intellectually above average among their peers just to gain entrance to an academy. Thereafter for the rest of their careers they are exposed to constant competition for selection and promotion. Attrition is high, and only the most capable survive to reach the elite senior ranks. Few other professions have such rigorous selection systems; as a result, the top military leaders are top-caliber men.

Not many industries, institutions, or civilian branches of government have the resources, techniques, or experience in training leaders such as are now employed by the armed forces in their excellent and elaborate school systems. Military leaders are taught to command large organizations and to plan big operations. They learn the techniques of influencing others. Their education is not, however, liberal or cultural. It stresses the tactics, doctrines, traditions, and codes of the military trade. It produces technicians and disciples, not philosophers.

The men who rise to the top of the military hierarchy have usually demonstrated their effectiveness as leaders, planners, and organization managers. They have perhaps performed heroically in combat, but most of all they have demonstrated their loyalty as proponents of their own service's doctrine and their dedication to the defense establishment. The paramount sense of duty to follow orders is at the root of the military professional's performance. As a result the military often operate more efficiently and effectively in the arena of defense policy planning than do their civilian counterparts in the State Department. The military planners have their doctrinal beliefs, their loyalties, their discipline—and their typical desire to compete and win. The civilians in government can scarcely play the same policy-planning game. In general the military are better organized, they work harder, they think straighter, and they keep their eyes on the objective, which is to be instantly ready to solve the problem through military action while ensuring that their respective service gets its proper mission, role, and recognition in the operation. In an emergency the military usually have a ready plan; if not, their numerous doctrinal manuals provide firm guidelines for action. Politicians, civilian appointees, and diplomats do not normally have the same confidence about how to react to threats and violence as do the military.

The motivations behind these endeavors are difficult for civilians to understand. For example, military professionals cannot measure the success of their individual efforts in terms of personal financial gain. The armed forces are not profit-making organizations, and the rewards for excellence in the military profession are acquired in less tangible forms. Thus it is that promotion and the responsibilities of higher command, with the related fringe benefits of quarters, servants, privileges, and prestige, motivate most career officers. Promotions and choice job opportunities are attained by constantly performing well, conforming to the expected patterns, and pleasing the senior officers. Promotions and awards also frequently result from heroic and distinguished performance in combat, and it takes a war to become a military hero. Civilians can scarcely understand or even believe that many ambitious military professionals truly yearn for wars and the opportunities for glory and distinction afforded only in combat. A career of peacetime duty is a dull and frustrating prospect for the normal regular officer to contemplate.

The professional military leaders of the U.S. Armed Forces have some additional motivations which influence their readiness to involve their country in military ventures. Unlike some of the civilian policy-makers, the military has not been obsessed with the threat of Communism per se. Most military people know very little about Communism either as a doctrine or as a form of government. But they have been given reason enough to presume that it is bad and represents the force of evil. When they can identify "Communist aggression," however, the matter then becomes of direct concern to the armed forces. Aggressors are the enemy in the war games, the "bad guys," the "Reds." Defeating aggression is a gigantic combat-area competition rather than a crusade to save the world from Communism. In the military view, all "Communist aggression" is certain to be interpreted as a threat to the United States.

The armed forces' role in performing its part of the national security policy—in addition to defense against actual direct attack on the United States and to maintaining the strategic atomic deterrent forces—is to be prepared to employ its *General Purpose Forces* in support of our collective security policy and the related treaties and alliances. To do this it deploys certain forces to forward zones in the Unified Commands, and maintains an up-to-date file of scores of detailed contingency plans which have been thrashed out and approved by the Joint Chiefs of Staff. Important features of these are the movement or deployment schedules of task forces assigned to each plan. The various details of these plans continue to create intense rivalries between the Navy-Marine sea-lift forces and the Army-Air Force team of air-mobility proponents. At the senior command levels parochial pride in service, personal ambitions, and old Army-Navy game rivalry stemming back to academy loyalties can influence strategic planning far more than most civilians would care to believe. The game is to be ready for deployment sooner than the other elements of the joint task force and to be so disposed as to be the "first to fight." The danger presented by this practice is that readiness and deployment speed become ends in themselves. This was clearly revealed in the massive and rapid intervention in the Dominican Republic in 1965 when the contingency plans and interservice rivalry appeared to supersede diplomacy. Before the world realized what was happening, the momentum and velocity of the military plans propelled almost 20,000 U.S. soldiers and Marines into the small turbulent republic in an impressive race to test the respective mobility of the Army and the Marines and to attain overall command of "U.S. Forces Dom. Rep." Only a fraction of the force deployed was needed or justified. A small 1935-model Marine landing force could probably have handled the situation. But the Army airlifted much of the 82nd Airborne Division to the scene, included a lieutenant general, and took charge of the operation.

Simultaneously, in Vietnam during 1965 the four services were racing to build up combat strength in that hapless country. This effort was ostensibly to save South Vietnam from Viet Cong and North Vietnamese aggression. It should also be noted that it was motivated in part by the same old interservice rivalry to demonstrate respective importance and combat effectiveness.

The punitive air strikes immediately following the Tonkin Gulf incident in late 1964 revealed the readiness of naval air forces to bomb North Vietnam. (It now appears that the Navy actually had attack plans ready even before the alleged incident took place!) So by early 1965 the Navy carrier people and the Air Force initiated a contest of comparative strikes, sorties, tonnages dropped, "Killed by Air" claims, and target grabbing which continued up to the 1968 bombing pause. Much of the reporting on air action has consisted of misleading data or propaganda to serve Air Force and Navy purposes. In fact, it became increasingly apparent that the U.S. bombing effort in both North and South Vietnam has been one of the most wasteful and expensive hoaxes ever to be put over on the American people. Tactical and close air support of ground operations is essential, but air power use in general has to a large degree been a contest for the operations planners, "fine experience" for young pilots, and opportunity for career officers.

The highly trained professional and aggressive career officers of the Army and Marine Corps played a similar game. Prior to the decision to send combat units to South Vietnam in early 1965, both services were striving to increase their involvement. The Army already had over 16,000 military aid personnel serving in South Vietnam in the military adviser role, in training missions, logistic services supporting helicopter companies, and in Special Forces teams. This investment of men and matériel justified a requirement for additional U.S. combat units to provide local security and to help protect our growing commitment of aid to the South Vietnam regime.

There were also top-ranking Army officers who wanted to project Army ground combat units into the Vietnam struggle for a variety of other reasons; to test plans and new equipment, to test the new air-mobile theories and tactics, to try the tactics and techniques of counter-insurgency, and to gain combat experience for young officers and non-commissioned officers. It also appeared to be a case of the military's duty to stop "Communist aggression" in Vietnam.

The Marines had somewhat similar motivations, the least of which was any real concern about the political or social problems of the Vietnamese people. In early 1965 there was a shooting war going on and the Marines were being left out of it, contrary to all their traditions. The Army's military advisory people were hogging American participation—except for a Marine Corps transport helicopter squadron at Danang which was helping the Army of the Republic of Vietnam. For several years young Marine officers had been going to South Vietnam from the 3rd Marine Division on Okinawa for short tours of "on-the-job training" with the small South Vietnam Marine Corps. There was a growing concern, however, among some senior Marines that the Corps should get involved on a larger scale and be the "first to fight" in keeping with the Corps's traditions. This would help justify the Corps's continued existence, which many Marines seem to consider to be in constant jeopardy.

The Corps had also spent several years exploring the theories of counterinsurgency and as early as 1961 had developed an elaborate lecture-demonstration called OPERATION CORMORANT, for school and Marine Corps promotion purposes, which depicted the Marines conducting a large-scale amphibious operation on the coast of Vietnam and thereby helping resolve a hypothetical aggressor-insurgency problem. As always it was important to Marine planners and doctrinaires to apply an amphibious operation to the Vietnam situation and provide justification for this special Marine functional responsibility. So Marine planners were seeking an acceptable excuse to thrust a landing force over the beaches of Vietnam when the Viet Cong attacked the U.S. Army Special Forces camp at Pleiku in February, 1965. It was considered unacceptable aggression, and the President was thereby prompted to put U.S. ground combat units into the war. Elements of the 3rd Marine Division at Okinawa were already aboard ship and eager to go, for the Marines also intended to get to Vietnam before their neighbor on Okinawa, the Army's 173rd Airborne Brigade, arrived. (Actually the initial Marine unit to deploy was an airlifted antiaircraft missile battalion which arrived to protect the Danang air base.) With these initial deployments the Army-Marine race to build forces in Vietnam began in earnest and did not slow down until both became overextended, overcommitted, and depleted at home.

For years up to 1964 the chiefs of the armed services, of whom the author was then one, deemed it unnecessary and unwise for U.S. forces to become involved in any ground war in Southeast Asia. In 1964 there were changes in the composition of the Joint Chiefs of Staff, and in a matter of a few months the Johnson Administration, encouraged by the aggressive military, hastened into what has become the quagmire of Vietnam. The intention at the time was that the war effort be kept small and "limited." But as the momentum and involvement built up, the military leaders rationalized a case that this was not a limited-objective exercise, but was a proper war in defense of the United States against "Communist aggression" and in honor of our area commitments.

The battle successes and heroic exploits of America's fine young fighting men have added to the military's traditions which extol service, bravery, and sacrifice, and so it has somehow become unpatriotic to question our military strategy and tactics or the motives of military leaders. Actually, however, the military commanders have directed the war in Vietnam, they have managed the details of its conduct; and more than most civilian officials, the top military planners were initially ready to become involved in Vietnam combat and have the opportunity to practice their trade. It has been popular to blame the civilian administration for the conduct and failures of the war rather than to question the motives of the military. But some of the generals and admirals are by no means without responsibility for the Vietnam miscalculations.

Some of the credibility difficulties experienced by the Johnson Administration over its war situation reports and Vietnam policy can also be blamed in part upon the military advisers. By its very nature most military activity falls under various degrees of security classification. Much that the military plans or does must be kept from the enemy. Thus the military is indoctrinated to be secretive, devious, and misleading in its plans and operations. It does not, however, always confine its security restrictions to purely military operations. Each of the services and all of the major commands practice techniques of controlling the news and the release of self-serving propaganda: in "the interests of national defense," to make the service look good, to cover up mistakes, to build up and publicize a distinguished military personality, or to win a round in the continuous gamesmanship of the interservice contest. If the Johnson Administration suffered from lack of credibility in its reporting of the war, the truth would reveal that much of the hocus-pocus stemmed from schemers in the military services, both at home and abroad.

Our militaristic culture was born of the necessities of World War II, nurtured by the Korean War, and became an accepted aspect of American life during the years of cold war emergencies and real or imagined threats from the Communist bloc. Both the philosophy and the institutions of militarism grew during these years because of the momentum of their own dynamism, the vigor of their ideas, their large size and scope, and because of the dedicated concentration of the emergent military leaders upon their doctrinal objectives. The dynamism of the defense establishment and its culture is also inspired and stimulated by vast amounts of money, by the new creations of military research and matériel development, and by the concepts of the Defense Department-supported "think factories." These latter are extravagantly funded civilian organizations of scientists, analysts, and retired military strategists who feed new militaristic philosophies into the Defense Department to help broaden the views of the single service doctrinaires, to create fresh policies and new requirements for ever larger, more expensive defense forces.

Somewhat like a religion, the basic appeals of anti-Communism, national defense, and patriotism provide the foundation for a powerful creed upon which the defense establishment can build, grow, and justify its cost. More so than many large bureaucratic organizations, the defense establishment now devotes a large share of its efforts to self-perpetuation, to justifying its organizations, to preaching its doctrines, and to self-maintenance and management. Warfare becomes an extension of war games and field tests. War justifies the existence of the establishment, provides experience for the military novice and challenges for the senior officer. Wars and emergencies put the military and their leaders on the front pages and give status and prestige to the professionals. Wars add to the military traditions, the self-nourishment of heroic deeds, and provide a new crop of military leaders who become the rededicated disciples of the code of service and military action. Being recognized public figures in a nation always seeking folk heroes, the military leaders have been largely exempt from the criticism experienced by the more plebeian politician. Flag officers are considered "experts," and their views are often accepted by press and Congress as the gospel. In turn, the distinguished military leader feels obliged not only to perpetuate loyally the doctrine of his service but to comply with the stereotyped military characteristics by being tough, aggressive, and firm in his resistance to Communist aggression and his belief in the military solutions to world problems. Standing closely behind these leaders, encouraging and prompting them, are the rich and powerful defense industries. Standing in front, adorned with service caps, ribbons, and lapel emblems, is a nation of veterans—patriotic, belligerent, romantic, and well intentioned, finding a certain sublimation and excitement in their country's latest military venture. Militarism in America is in full bloom and promises a future of vigorous self-pollination—unless the blight of Vietnam reveals that militarism is more a poisonous weed than a glorious blossom.

PENTAGONISM OR IMPERIALISM?

Richard B. DuBoff

For the socialist Left, this book raises one issue, suggested by its title. Is "pentagonism" a substitute for imperialism or a means for carrying it out?

Juan Bosch's view, shared in many left-wing circles these days, is the first, and he makes his case as follows. The old, classical imperialism, defined in terms recalling the Hobson-Lenin economics of surplus capital and a colonialist search for investment outlets and markets, is now extinct, "a shadow of the past." It has been "replaced by a superior force . . . by pentagonism." The reason for this shift is that America today must be understood as an outgrowth of "mass society" and "overdeveloped capitalism." Spiraling productivity in the economy, combined with a receptive social environment—a class structure built upon faceless blue- and white-collar workers whose culture is super-consumption, nothing else—has opened the gates for a sort of post-imperialist power elite. The new ruling class comprises military managers, corporate executives, and government bureaucrats who don't need "colonial territories in order to accumulate profits." They reap them in an easier way at the expense of their own nation. They appropriate and exploit the resources of their own people by brainwashing, overtaxing, drafting them; anything to sustain the pentagonist juggernaut. However, to keep their citizen-subjects in the required state of submissiveness, the pentagonists continually have to justify their power. In other words, they have to be able to put it to use from time to time, even

Monthly Review 20, no. 11 (April 1969): 25–36.

without any legitimate reasons. This is accomplished by uncovering foreign "threats" to American security. (Bosch refers to the "need to establish the [pentagonist] doctrine of defensive wars waged outside the country.") Every effort at revolutionary change anywhere in the world is immediately taken as a "war of aggression against the United States which must be answered by the military power of the country, just as if it were an armed invasion coming from outside the national territory." (p. 92)

One summary is worth quoting at length:

> The fact is that the use of military power has not changed; what has changed is the purpose for which it is used. The military forces of a pentagonist country are not sent out to conquer colonial territories. War has another purpose . . . to conquer positions of power in the pentagonist country, not in some far-off land. What is being sought is not a place to invest surplus capital for profit; what is being sought is access to the generous economic resources being mobilized for industrial war production . . . profits where arms are manufactured, not where they are employed, and these profits are obtained in the pentagonist mother country, not in the country that is being attacked. A contract for bombers brings in several times more profit, in a much shorter time, than the conquest of the richest mining territory. The planes are built at home, and this is where the fabulous sums produced by the contract are earned. These sums come out of the pockets of the pentagonized people, who are at the same time the mother country and the seat of pentagonized power. The pentagonized people are exploited as colonies were since they are the ones who pay . . . The mother country thus turns its own people into its best colony. (pp. 21–22)

How and when was this pentagonist leviathan born? Suddenly and, in historical terms, discretely, according to Bosch. Until the 1930's the United States was an "individualist, juridical" society where power lay in bourgeois-democratic hands, in parliamentary bodies. The next decade brought a radical transformation. Because of the Second World War "imperialism entered its death throes," and the 1941–1945 mobilization and Cold War that followed opened up the possibility—unparalleled in American history—for a military-industrial complex to fill the vacuum left by the collapse of imperialism and its social pillars. Dynamic pressures now had to be turned inward, not outward. Thus, *domestic* exploitation became the one source of political power available to the emergent pentagonists, and they made the most of their opportunity. As already pointed out, they maintain the control they were able to seize by externalizing threats to the status quo; hence the foreign wars and interventions, which in turn provide them their *raison d'être,* and so on. A tight feedback mechanism, one so compelling that its beneficiaries "can plan, and carry out, a long-range policy that allows [them] to come into possession of the effective command structures in national life in the field of non-military administration." (p. 125)

Just a few years ago, in 1961–1962, words like these would have seemed fantastic coming from Juan Bosch. At that time Trujillo had just been assassinated, and Bosch, a liberal reformer, had returned to the Dominican Republic to triumph in the first free elections held there in thirty-eight years. With that, the Kennedy administration in Washington hitched its own wagon to the Bosch star. The newly elected Dominican President became a Free World savior, a "democratic alternative" to Fidel Castro in Latin America. Then, in September 1963, the Bosch government was overthrown by a conservative, landlord-supported military coup, recognized three months later by the United States. Bosch went into exile in Puerto Rico until April 1965, when a popular uprising in his favor came close to restoring him to power, only to be brutally smashed at the last moment by 24,000 U.S. troops. In 1966, after this "Inter-American Peace Force" had cleaned out the "Communists and subversives," elections were carried out under the eyes of the Organization of American States and planeloads of American observers. Bosch was defeated by Joaquín Balaguer, a conservative with links to international finance and a "go-between" whose conciliatory role was sweetened by massive U.S. aid: dollars and food for the good guys and a CIA reign of terror for the bad guys.

Such experiences would leave a scar on any man; their impact upon Bosch has been increasingly evident since 1965. *Pentagonism,* in this perspective, marks one more step in a personal metamorphosis which is carrying the author further away from his earlier Social Democratic, anti-Communist moorings (reflected, for example, in his 1964 book, *The Unfinished Experiment: Democracy in the Dominican Republic*). By late 1967, in a series of articles published from his new exile in Spain, Bosch was calling for "popular dictatorships" established by force as the only answer for the economic and social miseries of Latin America. He saw these dictatorships as the sole alternative to Communist-led revolutions, but nonetheless added that between an American and a Communist solution, his own choice would be clear: "I'd rather die a Communist than die being pro-Yankee." [1]

So another political figure comes full circle. He joins the ranks of those the world over who have learned the hard way, by discovering first-hand what it means to try to oppose, or negotiate with, or for that matter reason with, a star-spangled colossus bent on domination. This, in stark relief, is what U.S. power does to *moderate* leaders who desire little more than some measure of political and economic independence for their own people. It crushes and humiliates them; it leaves them with no choice but to become revolutionaries.

Latin America isn't the only region where this holds true. Greece, a good bet to become the next Vietnam, represents another case history where U.S. power and influence were used to destroy moderate, even anti-Communist, leaders who attempted to defy Washington (that is, to chart an independent path of their own choosing). Significantly, in the wake of similar experiences suffered at American hands, Andreas Papandreou shares Bosch's views on U.S. foreign policy and the way it imposes its own militarized processes on satellite nations. Recently he wrote that the April 21, 1967 military coup in Greece, in which the American Ambassador and CIA were intimately involved, "represents a new phenomenon. . . . The colonels did not have the support of any political party, *any class interest,* or any region of the nation. . . . Thus the Greek coup belongs to a new species of coups. It is the outgrowth of the enhancement of the power of the military-intelligence complex in the context of the Cold War, and it constitutes a warning to the countries of the West. For it is no longer true that 'it can't happen here.'" [2]

If it is easy to understand, then, why Bosch feels as he does, and why similar views are held by so many left-liberals, it may be less easy to accept *Pentagonism.* For as I see it, there is one absolutely essential point of departure for books that deal with any aspect of America's relations with the rest of the world: American foreign policy as a factor in international politics is at least seven decades old. It follows that it

[1] Robert Berrellez, Associated Press, October 1, 1967. See also Bosch's review of Régis Debray and the preesnt situation in Latin America in *The New York Review of Books,* October 26, 1967, reprinted in *Régis Debray and the Latin American Revolution,* Leo Huberman and Paul Sweezy, eds. (New York: Monthly Review Press, 1968).

[2] *Columbia University Forum* (Winter 1968), italics added.

is the first task of the serious writer to find out whether there is a pattern to it, against which any departures or unusual features might be compared or measured.

Here Bosch stumbles. His historical analysis is badly flawed, and it leads him into a number of political and economic misconceptions, all of which point in one direction: that in general pentagonism *hasn't replaced* imperialism, it *has been serving* it. The pentagonist story begins many decades before Bosch picks it up in the 1950's and 1960's; and if its theme, an aggressive and militarized set of foreign policy institutions, has grown more strident and frightening since the Second World War, the reason appears to be that American ruling circles consider these changes necessary to undergird imperial expansion in a world full of new dangers and challenges. A higher level of "military security" is required to carry out in today's world what have long been the cornerstones of U.S. foreign policy—expansion and counterrevolution.

First, however, a brief digression, apart from the American case. Why does Bosch think that pentagonist-type institutions are so unique in Western history and that only post-Second World War United States has produced them? Before the First World War, well before America's military-industrial complex, they were already in evidence in imperialist nations, notably Germany. Nearly everything Bosch observes in the United States today had its rough counterpart in the 1871–1918 Reich: an aggressive, integral nationalism imbued with a sense of mission; close links among finance, industry, and the military; "Great Society" welfare sops thrown to the working class to undercut the growth of socialism; a bloated state bureaucracy staffed by mandarins; a surly impatience with international legalities and world opinion; the violation of Belgian neutrality in 1914, later matched by the U.S. subversion of the 1954 and 1962 Geneva Accords. Yet an even more apt historical example might be the Reich of 1933–1945, the Nazi Germany that created the first "permanent war economy." This is certainly what the United States represents at present, and Bosch deserves credit for emphasizing that fact in any way he can. In this light, though, pentagonism doesn't turn out to be a new phenomenon, even in its underdeveloped and highly lethal American variety.

As for the United States itself, this is a nation with a long and consistent history of expansionism, both within and outside continental North America. It had a "Vietnam" from 1898 to 1913 in the Philippines and a "Dominican Republic" several times in the past throughout Central America and the Caribbean. Bosch, himself Latin American, must be familiar with this history, but presumably he would dismiss it as irrelevant on the grounds that during these earlier times the United States was steering a classical, traditional imperialist course (which, as he argues, faded out with the Second World War). The trouble with this line of thought is that even then, before the 1920's, American imperialism defied the classical model, as it does today. Its expansionist policies were always fundamentally different from British, French, and German. Commercial and financial penetration—the "Open Door"—stood out then, and still stands out, as the chief American stratagem, with outright territorial occupation playing a secondary role. "Informal empire," to borrow William Appleman Williams' label, was the vision of American statesmen beginning in the 1890's; [3] and it well describes the modern version known as the "free world" or *Pax Americana.*

Furthermore, if American imperialism failed to conform to the classical model from 1890 to 1914, it can scarcely be expected to have conformed to it in the years following, in face of the upheavals in world politics, economics, and finance which have ceaselessly thrown new challenges at the United States, the leading imperialist power of the twentieth century. Three successful anti-capitalist revolutions (Russia, China, Cuba) and their unfolding into a rival social system, two world wars, a catastrophic depression and several recessions, one collapse of the international financial system and three or four close calls, persistent social crises which produce fascist regimes at worst and unrelenting poverty, inequality, and public-sector squalor at best—in our lifetime events like these have made Western capitalism something less than irresistibly attractive for the underdeveloped "third world" nations. Confronted with this precarious state of affairs, this ominous drift of history (John F. Kennedy was obsessed by that), imperialist powers have naturally tried to develop a new and enlarged range of responses. More flexible methods of penetration, control, and domination are tested out; their mix varies and their emphasis shifts, from the economic to the political to—enter Bosch, Papandreou and company—the military or proxy-military (support for junta regimes). But through all these variations in the forms of imperialism, its substance has to be kept clearly in focus, for there is no evidence that it has changed in any

[3] The definitive account of this critical period is Walter LaFeber, *The New Empire: An Interpretation of American Expansion 1860–1898* (Ithaca, N.Y.: Cornell, 1963).

material way. Whether its most striking external characteristic at any moment happens to be economic or political or military, its almost instinctive goal remains the building up of a network of rewards and compulsions ("carrots and sticks") to help it direct the internal affairs of foreign nations enough (1) to guarantee key profit-makers at home continued access to "resource areas" (to use the current State Department jargon); (2) to furnish some assurance that future expansion in these areas won't be closed off by the rise of hostile or "Communist" governments; and (3) to protect against the spread of revolutions that might set bad examples for other nations.

For me, this formula offers the only way to reconcile otherwise contradictory behavior on the part of the American ruling class—unless it is assumed that its behavior is essentially planless and just happens to fit a mold artificially imposed upon it. If its most prominent features since 1945 have been "pentagonist," the reason would be that the American empire is far bigger—maybe overextended—and harder to defend without recourse to war. But here too the decisions to deploy such a gigantic war machine were made by civilians, not soldiers. The civilians were the first to define the world in military terms and the first to call in the military, before 1941. And I find no evidence that they have lost *ultimate* control over their offspring, a la Frankenstein. The public statements, speeches, and acts of men like Dean Acheson, Robert Lovett, James Forrestal, George C. Marshall, John Foster Dulles, Douglas Dillon, John J. McCloy, George Ball, Dean Rusk, the brothers Bundy and Rostow, and others at the center of U.S. policy-making indicate very emphatically that the expansion of American military power around the globe was undertaken by the civilian leadership,[4] to secure the Free Enterprise World against all threats, external and—especially—internal. This military-intelligence establishment was created to serve a preconceived function; aside from the blunders typical of any mili-

[4] Another prime example of the civilians behind the military is Nelson Rockefeller, who, although on the margin of the formal policy-making apparatus, has still had as much influence as any other single individual. See the review of his long and hawkish career, in *I. F. Stone's Weekly,* July 22, 1968. On the general question of civilians promoting the military buildup, see William A. Williams, *The Tragedy of American Diplomacy* (New York: Dell, 1962), pp. 184–186; and on the background of these decisions, which were tied up with the origins of the Cold War, David Horowitz, *The Free World Colossus* (New York: Hill and Wang, 1965); Walter LaFeber, *America, Russia, and the Cold War 1945–1966* (New York: Wiley, 1967) (both in paperback); and Gabriel Kolko, *The Politics of War, 1943–1945* (New York: Random House, 1969).

tary establishment, it has done its job fairly well, and in a greater variety of ways than could have been imagined twenty years ago. Thus, while Marxists talk about "unity of theory and practice," capitalists achieve it.

Of course at this advanced stage of American imperialism, it really doesn't pay to make a neat and tidy distinction between means and ends (let alone between Boschian "pentagonism" and "imperialism"). They feed on each other, they interlock and reinforce. There is, as Harry Magdoff has put it, an "underlying unity. . . . Economic control, military control, and political control mutually support and stimulate each other" (MR, November 1968). As the military blazes paths for the economic, the economic aids and profits from the military. In 1961, for instance, the Kennedy administration set up a special Defense Department office to increase export sales of arms, as one means to reduce the balance of payments deficit. Later, the Export-Import Bank, supposedly an "aid" agency, was brought in to extend credits to underdeveloped countries to assist them in purchasing U.S. arms. Through mid-1967, $12.6 billion of sales were rung up. "These sales," stated the then Secretary of Defense Robert McNamara, "are employing American labor and they are providing profits to American business. I think we should be encouraged and congratulated on making these arrangements" (*New York Times,* July 23, 1967).

The same intertwined relationships exist in the actual sites of American intervention as well. Direct economic interests in Vietnam were small in 1953 when Dulles and Eisenhower began to worry about losing its potential "tin and tungsten" resources to the native Communists. A dozen years later, with escalation and (attempted) pacification, money and entrepreneurial energy started to follow the troops in. Eugene Black of the World Bank and, after him, David Lilienthal of the Development and Resources Corporation, got busy programming "postwar development . . . a general economic strategy for the postwar period" to be linked to the United States and Japan (*New York Times,* November 14, 1966; October 29, 1967; and Lilienthal in *Foreign Affairs,* January, 1969). Laos, the tortured stepchild of the Vietnam war, also finds itself being pulled into this "development" mill. American spending at present accounts for "virtually all of the national income of Laos, including a 50 percent subsidy of the National budget. . . . One highly placed American official recently estimated that the United States last year contributed at least $100 for every man, woman, and child in Laos" (*New York Times*, January 17, 1969). Now forty miles north of Vientiane, the World Bank, headed by McNamara, is financing a $33-million hydropower project which will eventually generate electricity for export to Thailand, a notorious U.S. client state.

Turning to Bosch's own country, the same mutually reinforcing factors are again conspicuous. U.S. investment had taken root there long before the April 1965 invasion (and in part explains it: Ellsworth Bunker and the sugar lobby). But since the invasion the environment has become still safer for free enterprise, and a renewed wave of expansion is under way. An "international consortium to develop agriculture and industry in the Dominican Republic" was launched last year and supported by the Balaguer government, which is providing 200,000 acres of its own land and $15 million of initial funds, the latter a loan from the U.S. Agency for International Development. The developers in this case include Dow Chemical, International Harvester, and Studebaker-Worthington (*New York Times*, April 16, 1968).

Any book that helps draw world attention to the dangerous, pathological tendencies in American society today has to be welcomed on that account alone. For a treatment of the sheer militarism that has eaten its way into virtually all corners of American life since 1945, it would be hard to improve upon the insights offered by Bosch. Moreover, nobody can dismiss out of hand the possibility of some wild aberration or some bizarre turn of events leading to a "final solution," with our Strangeloves in the Pentagon and CIA fully in command of a ticking Doomsday Machine of one kind or another.

Perhaps. But outside chances are not what social analysis is all about. Thus, *Pentagonism* earns our sympathy, but our criticism as well. It misses the mark in describing U.S. imperialism as one thing prior to the Second World War and something entirely different after it. America's aims abroad have been remarkably consistent through the years; and the means employed to attain them have been a blend of classic Western-capitalist and vintage Yankee. Also, and this may be the key point, Bosch appears to err in claiming that the pentagonist tail now wags the imperialist dog. With that thesis, how would he explain why this country is trying to wriggle its way out of Vietnam? Surely the pentagonist complex would prefer to continue, and the new Washington guard of Nixon-Laird-Kissinger, with its ties to the Prussians and geopoliticians of the *arriviste* Right, might like to accommodate them. The elders of the system, however, have clearly had enough.

Wall Street, the multinational corporations, the foundation technocrats, the major news media, the international bankers all understand that the Vietnam intervention was essentially "correct," but that the tenacity of Vietnamese resistance was disastrously underestimated. The military and its civilian spokesmen sold them a bill of goods, and its cost has become unbearably high. The enterprise has got to be liquidated—and it probably will be. It remains to be seen whether pentagonist pressure can hold out for long against that.

WEAPONS AND SOCIETY

Ralph E. Lapp

"Priorities are reflected in the things we spend money on. Far from being a dry accounting of bookkeepers, a nation's budget is full of moral implications; it tells what a society cares about and what it does not care about; it tells what its values are."

Senator J. William Fulbright
August 8, 1967

ANY ACCOUNTANT going over the postwar books of the United States would find some rather discouraging facts. Over seven tenths of federal expenditures have been for national security. In the vital area of federally funded research and development, almost nine tenths of this work was directed to defense-atomic-space activities. Less than one tenth of one percent of these funds went to support research in problems of urban development. Naturally, a nation must look to its security, but the material developed in previous chapters suggests that the United States overreacted to foreign threats. Furthermore, in view of the recent decision to build up ballistic defenses, it appears that this country is stepping up the tempo of the arms race.

Robert L. Heilbroner, in his *Limits of American Capitalism,* states: "No attempt to speak of the long-run prospects for American capitalism can overlook the central fact that it is now a semimilitarized economy and that it will probably become even more so during the next decade." Gradually the U.S. involvement with defense industry has

The Weapons Culture (New York: Norton, 1968), chap. 7. Reprinted from *The Weapons Culture* by Ralph E. Lapp. By permission of W. W. Norton & Company, Inc.

proceeded to the point where weapons-making begins to dominate our society. This protracted dedication of American effort to devising and manufacturing new arms has created a techno-military establishment that threatens to make greater inroads upon our economy. A central problem for democracy is the control of this military-industrial complex that has grown in influence as its political connections have ramified.

No nation can devote so much of its ingenuity, manpower, and resources to the works of war without at the same time being deeply changed in the process. Many of the changes are subtle, slow to surface, and hard to trace as to origin. There is a certain aseptic and detached quality to our techno-militarization which insulates people from its impact. The Long Island housewife who assembles tiny electronic components for a bomb mechanism does not associate herself with the weapons that may bring death to some victim. She lives in her own microcosm and, if queried about her occupation, may shrug off the questioner with the reply, "A job is a job." The scholarly professor who probes the chemical secrets of certain compounds may fail to associate his research with destructive defoliants. The senator who champions a $40 billion Nike-X defense will reject the charge that he is his own lobbyist, asserting that his only concern is with national security. The industrialist who mass-produces napalm may brush aside any qualms he may have with the contention that he simply fulfills orders given to him by his Government.

This is a deteriorating situation that contributes to allowing the arms race to run out of control, for if all are compliant and feel no responsibility, then our democracy is in jeopardy. A new order of discourse is called for—linking the American people to major national decisions in which their security is intimately involved. It needs to be a spirited dialogue, marked by the sharpest questioning of techno-military issues. Those who criticize or seek to examine the wisdom of national decisions need not have the answers; it is sufficient if they phrase the questions properly and publicly. Any operations analyst knows that half the problem is finding the right questions to ask.

Here are some of the key questions that need expression:

1. How does the nation arrive at a rational determination of the strategic forces adequate for a policy of nuclear deterrence?

2. Given the decision on a "thin" ballistic-missile defense, how does a democracy prevent automatic escalation to a "thick" defense system?

3. What constitutes an effective mechanism for objectively evaluating whether or not a "megaton gap" poses a real threat to U.S. security?

4. What should be done about future defense contracting with firms fully committed to having the U.S. Government as a single customer?

5. How should the nation's scientific and technical resources, so preponderantly oriented to atomic-space-defense, be converted to a larger share of peaceful missions?

6. What can the United States do to arrest the momentum of the runaway arms race and start on the road to arms controls?

7. How does a democracy go about applying restraints to the military-industrial-political complex, which fuels the arms race?

This list of questions does not end here; it is merely a beginning, but it may serve to suggest the dimensions of the debate needed if democracy is not to be tyrannized by defense technology.

There has been so much recent publicity about the peacetime benefits of federal technology, especially with regard to civilian space programs like Project Apollo, that this "technological fallout" or spinoff needs to be put in perspective. It is true that certain wartime developments like radar and jet aircraft development did feed through to the civilian economy. But as atomic-space-defense technology has extrapolated to such requirements as the ICBM, lunar rockets, and space weapons, it has gotten farther and farther from the civilian marketplace.

There is a deeply held conviction among many people that technology advances in lock step with war—and that this is the only feasible avenue for technological innovation. But the farm tractor came long before the armored tank and the Wright brothers enjoyed no military subsidy.

When the Supersonic Transport (SST) reached the development stage, the aircraft companies found that they could not borrow military technology to take shortcuts and save money on the new plane. In the case of the work undertaken for manned lunar flight, a program costing some $30 billion, much of the effort went to huge boosters, enormous tanks, pumps, and "freak out" engineering with little relevance to the civilian economy. While the National Aeronautics and

Space Administration concentrated on getting men to the moon, metropolitan surface travel and city-to-city air travel clogged the available traffic lanes. The safety of air passengers was jeopardized as NASA spent less than one percent of its funds on aeronautics.

One of the underlying reasons for the massive NASA space activity, it must be recalled, was the image of military proficiency that this technology projected. A number of air-power enthusiasts were quick to seize upon the notion that the control of space would grant a nation supremacy in military power. Even the moon's surface was not too remote a rendezvous for some military men—Gen. James M. Gavin, for example, testified before a Senate committee investigating the U.S. space potential: "If I, as a soldier, were asked by my superiors in this country, is the moon of any significance to us, if the Soviets for example, are occupying it, I would say absolutely, yes. We have got to get out there. We have got to get out there first, and if they are out there, we have got to have some understanding of who is going to occupy the moon."

The success of Project Apollo involved the efforts of a million aerospace workers, half of whom will be out of jobs in 1968. Presumably the decision on Nike-X will reemploy many of these workers, but the build-up of specialized work forces like that engaged in making the Apollo craft imposes a constraint upon the economy. Companies like Boeing and North American Aviation promoted huge post-Apollo programs, amounting to $6 billion or $7 billion per year. Such activity would help to sustain the upward thrust of the aerospace industry. This very rapidly growing segment of the economy aims at a total of $30 billion in sales for 1970. Even if sales of commercial aircraft increase sharply, this still leaves the bulk of the money to be provided by the Federal Government.

If the U.S. aerospace industry—by all odds, the most rambunctious component of the military-industrial complex—is to fit into the national economy without depending primarily on defense contracts, then the means must be found to convert it to new objectives. This is an especially acute problem for companies like Lockheed, which are so top-heavy in arms sales. The state of California, anticipating conversion problems in the event of defense or space cutbacks, let four study contracts to aerospace companies for analysis of certain problems, such as transportation. The results were widely advertised but added little to California's knowledge of how to solve its transportation problem. The fact is that aerospace industries are quite specialized in their know-how and lack experience in diversifying to invade the civilian market for consumer products on a competitive basis. Much of the aerospace technical talent lies in the field of engineering which is not easily adapted to new endeavors. Furthermore, lack of dollar consciousness in the artificial aerospace business hamstrings companies when they try to penetrate fields already served by experienced corporations. Here the Federal Government, long the exclusive patron of many of the aerospace firms, has a responsibility to help in converting the defense contractors to enter the free play of the marketplace.

The author is no dreamer who thinks that the United States can abandon its commitment to arms overnight. He does not recommend giving up a policy of nuclear deterrence that has been the mainstay of our national security for so many years. It would be foolish in the extreme to believe that peace will break out on this planet in a great wave of international understanding. Therefore, we must be reconciled to large defense budgets for some years to come, but we must also avoid too great extremes in defense, which provoke equal reactions from hostile powers. Since it is the U.S. Congress that controls defense purse strings, it is imperative that this legislative body be equipped with some better and more objective means of analyzing the nation's security needs.

Recently, the Science Policy Research Division of the Legislative Reference Service of the Library of Congress has demonstrated a high quality of objectivity in analyzing certain technical issues, especially for the U.S. Senate. If this activity could be broadened to include a mandate to study defense policy, it might be very useful to the Congress. One of the faults of the committee operations of the Congress is that staff members are often ex-military or federal agency personnel on loan to the committees. Since the committee staff is a vital part of setting up hearings or defining congressional interest in a technical area, a defense-oriented staff in effect becomes an arm of the Pentagon. One does not find pacifists or disarmament-minded men on the staffs of the armed-services committees. Instead there are weapons sub-cultures so lodged that the normal checks and balances of the democratic process are blocked.

If the Congress becomes the obedient handmaiden of the Pentagon, where will our democracy find the means of opposing constant escalation of the defense budget? Or how will it begin to think about and take action on arms controls? Here I believe that scientists have a special responsibility to take the lead in public discussion because many of the issues involve complex technology. Furthermore, over the past two decades many of the nation's scientists have shown that they are capable of stimulating national debate on topics like radioactive fallout, nuclear testing, and arms controls.

Dr. Linus Pauling, for example, demonstrated an ability to pioneer in public discussion of a major issue—namely, that of a nuclear test ban. His famous 1957 petition urging a test ban was signed by 2,875 scientists. Only a dozen scientists working at Atomic Energy Commission facilities, including the Los Alamos weapons laboratory, placed their signatures on the petition. One may conclude that people working for the AEC felt that it would be unhealthful for them to associate their names with Dr. Pauling's cause.

In connection with the Pauling petition, two additional comments are worth making. First, the entire effort was made by a very few individuals working on their own; no scientific organization like the American Chemical Society aided in circulating the petition. In general the professional organizations concerned with science steer clear of any political action. Second, Dr. Pauling was vigorously attacked in the press and on Capitol Hill on the basis that he was aiding the Communist cause and that he had Communist affiliations. Although pilloried at home, Dr. Pauling won the Nobel Peace Prize in 1963.

Since Dr. Pauling took his responsibility as a scientist-citizen to heart in 1957, it has become more difficult for people like him to act as modern Paul Reveres to alert their fellow citizens to the dangers of the arms race. For one thing, scientists are less free than they were a decade ago. More scientists work for and are implicated in the military-industrial complex and, in addition, thousands more on campus are intimidated by the fact that research funds for most colleges and universities come from the Federal Government. Rightly or wrongly, many scientists feel it is safer to remain aloof from controversy. For another, the scientist faces a dilemma when he comes to speaking out on a controversial issue. If he has access to classified data, he runs the risk of violating security when he breaks into print; if he does not know the secret data, he has to find some means of generating an authoritative grasp of the subject matter. The nuclear test ban issue was relatively simple compared to current problems like ballistic-missile defense. On the other hand, the issues have become more acute and much is at stake—scientists should be motivated to do the hard work necessary to understand current defense issues.

Another hurdle facing the dissenting scientist is that he is often paired off against a weapons scientist, who has the advantage of official position and the backing of the Military Establishment. The scientific community, like any other, has its various kinds of characters—left wing and rightist, hawks and doves, emotional and cold-blooded—so it is not surprising that some scientists in the weapons business should be as militant as the most swashbuckling general. Nor should it be looked upon as unusual when a man like Dr. Edward Teller takes to the national stage to promote ballistic-missile defense or some new weapons system. Scientists may seem unlike the military, but as sociologist Hans H. Gerth and C. Wright Mills foresaw in 1942: "Precisely because of their specialization and knowledge, the scientist and technician are among the most easily used and coordinated of groups in modern society . . . the very rigor of their training typically makes them the easy dupes of men wise in political ways."

The public may be confused when experts disagree on a national issue, but it is essential that opposing viewpoints be aired; otherwise policy will be determined by a technological elite. It is not proper that Americans should bow their heads before the altar of technology, averting their eyes as did ancient multitudes when high priests sought auguries in animal entrails. As Robert Oppenheimer has remarked: "We do not operate well when the important facts, the essential conditions, which limit and determine our choices are unknown. We do not operate well when they are known, in secrecy and in fear, only to a few men."

The fundamental issue of nuclear superiority as opposed to nuclear parity has never been fully exposed to the public view. In general the news is leaked from the Pentagon or via Capitol Hill that the Soviets have developed or are about to produce a new weapons system. Then there is a clamor for the United States to "catch up" and surpass the Soviets. Most recently this sequence of events was illustrated for ballistic-missile defense. Now an attempt is being made to have the United States "match" the orbital-eject bomb delivery system of the Soviet Union, even though its military value for the Soviets is highly dubious and is even more so for the United States. There is the automatic assumption that any Soviet military development represents a margin of superiority and that it must be offset by a corresponding counterdevelopment. In this manner the arms race escalates and provokes corresponding reactions by the Soviets, which in turn set off new cycles of armament.

If there is ever to be any stability in arming, people must recognize that there is a point in armament beyond which no additional security is purchased. By the same token, an enemy may achieve the same degree of security—that is, nuclear parity by fashioning his strategic deterrent forces to the lethal point. But when either side attempts to multiply its killing power, it invites duplication. In effect, a nation signs its own death certificate in multiple copies.

The concept of nuclear sufficiency—of the military ever having enough of anything—is still so novel that it has not yet gained acceptance in some military and political quarters. Defense Secretary McNamara understood and adopted the principle of nuclear parity as applied to the U.S. missile force, only to be overruled by President Kennedy. The latter, having campaigned on a missile-gap platform, apparently found it politically necessary to commit the nation to more missiles than Mr. McNamara believed to be enough for strategic deterrence. The full consequences of this missile escalation will have to be assessed by historians, but one thing seems clear: If the politics of defense dominates national security, then the world may never disengage from a spiraling arms race. When defense decisions are taken for political reasons—and domestic ones at that—a democracy may become an escalator in the arms race.

On November 6, 1967, the Joint Committee on Atomic Energy began investigating the nation's nuclear defenses in hearings headed up by Sen. Henry M. Jackson. Ostensibly the hearings were designed to explore the nature of the anti-ballistic missile defense problem, but in the course of the investigation it became clear that the committee was concerned with nuclear parity. Senators expressed their alarm over the increasing number of Soviet ICBM's, while the United States did not attempt to add more ICBM's to its own strike force. As I listened to the committee members question witnesses, I could not help but reflect that many of the committee members had served for many years on the Joint Committee; they had heard much testimony in previous years about the catastrophic nature of nuclear war. These men were granted access to data denied the great majority of Congress. Yet it seemed as though the most elemental arithmetic of the nuclear age had not been absorbed. If these men with access and with so much exposure to the facts about nuclear weapons could not accept the principle of nuclear sufficiency, then how could the other members of Congress be expected to do so?

If a U.S. President authorizes a $5 billion Sentinel system to protect himself from Republican charges of failing to insure the nation's security, then one might just as well junk all the elaborate systems of defense analysis that we possess. If our representative form of government gives disproportionate influence to the military-industrial constituency, we had better seek out checks and balances to offset this menace. If our legislators act as promotional lobbyists for the military-industrial complex, then reforms must be enacted. Needless to say, corrective measures will not be easy because the disease of our weapons culture has metastasized itself into the lymphatic system of our society.

On December 13, 1967, Senator J. W. Fulbright surveyed the impact of the "military-industrial complex" in a Senate speech. "More and more our economy, our Government and our universities are adapting themselves to the requirements of the continuing war—total war, limited war, and cold war." Warning that this adaptation was "making ourselves into a militarized society," Senator Fulbright described the "military-industrial complex" as forming "a giant concentration of socialism in our otherwise free enterprise economy."

Moreover, we have exported our weapons culture. Our Military Establishment has deployed its forces on a global basis. U.S. military forces bulked in groups of more than 3,000 uniformed personnel are to be found in each of 17 foreign countries. We have 132 major installations in foreign countries, some of which have been negotiated at a loss of our prestige. For example, to secure air-base rights in Spain we had to make a deal with Generalissimo Franco. While these foreign military bases are meant to increase our national security, some become liabilities—as in the case of Jupiter missile bases in Turkey.

Not only has the United States stationed its own troops abroad; it has engaged in advising, supervising and training armed forces in 35 foreign nations. This activity includes bringing officers from other countries to the United States for training at our military schools. In 1967, some 12,000 Americans were engaged in military-training operations overseas, not counting the U.S. commitment to Vietnam.

The major U.S. military and foreign-assistance programs, covering most of the postwar years have involved over $102 billion. . . . In some cases, as for India, Austria, and a few others, the extent of military aid is kept secret. Sen. J. W. Fulbright, chairman of the Senate Foreign Relations Committee, has maintained that much of this foreign aid is dangerous in that it may backfire and encourage conditions that lead to war. Again, there is the action-reaction principle about which Defense Secretary McNamara has warned—the U.S. initiative may be followed by enemy-supported countermoves, and the United States then has to pour in more aid to offset these. This could well have been the case in Vietnam and, if so, the tragedy of our position there was that we boxed ourselves into a situation which our own action magnified into a commitment out of proportion to its strategic significance. Then face-saving, traditionally an Oriental monomania, became critical to the United States.

The U.S. military-industrial complex has profited from contracts for arms that foreign assistance made possible. There is little doubt that the political support for these foreign programs was linked to this domestic tie-in. At one time (1963) the United States was engaged in the sale of armaments to no fewer than 63 foreign governments. As *Business Week* magazine commented: "'Buy American' is becoming an increasingly prevalent slogan in the world arms market." Considering the diffusion of modern arms across national borders, it is inevitable that American arms become weapons used against us or nations whose cause we support.

The redemption of our weapons-oriented society is a monumental undertaking; armaments have acquired such momentum that they dictate their own policy. As Konrad Lorenz wrote in *On Aggression:* "An unprejudiced observer from another planet, looking upon man as he is today, in his hand the atom bomb, the product of his intelligence, in his heart the aggression drive inherited from his anthropoid ancestors, which this same intelligence cannot control, would not prophesy long life for the species." The separate worlds of Darwin and Einstein are nearing collision. Man, the twig-tip of the fabulous evolutionary tree, is in danger of nuclear blight—a disease of his own making. All too quickly Einstein's ideas have become arsenal items; all too sluggishly do men forget the ways of war.

America is now a land of incredible violence—in many forms and in many places—

A thousand sleek missiles, deadly warheads pretargeted at Soviet cities, stud our western prairies, once solely a source of life-giving grain.

Sunny California slopes, once orange-blossomed and fruitful, now sprout cavernous plants where engineers design orbital weapons.

Boston's Route 128 is festooned with mushrooming research laboratories, a Cold War–financed necklace of industrial innovation.

In Maryland's richest farmland, a few miles west of Frederick, biologists at the highly secret Fort Detrick perfect virulent weapons of biological warfare.

Not far away, at the Pennsylvania border, lies the subterranean command post to which the President will be spirited in time of national emergency.

—America, the beautiful; now America, arms-maker and arms merchant to the world.

THE COLD WAR IS DEAD, BUT THE ARMS RACE RUMBLES ON

Jerome B. Wiesner

. . . WHO ARE THE PROPONENTS of the ABM system, and why do they want it?

President Eisenhower in his valedictory speech to the nation issued an urgent warning about the danger of a military-industrial-technological coalition whose pernicious pressures he had felt to be almost overwhelming. In issuing this warning, he did his successor, President Kennedy, a great service; forewarned, Kennedy was braced to withstand the enormous, well-coordinated campaigns that were waged to force him into large procurement programs for new weapons systems of tremendous cost and little value, such as the B–70, the Nike Zeus, the nuclear-powered aircraft, and space-based attack weapons. The campaigns in favor of the B–70 and the Nike Zeus were particularly vigorous and included very large and effective advertising campaigns in the national periodicals peddling a mixture of military security and economic benefit. Ironically, investigation brought out the fact that most of these expensive advertisements were charged to the government contracts of the companies involved, contracts which supported the development of the weapons systems being considered.

Today there is general agreement that Kennedy made the correct decisions. The Nike Zeus would have provided essentially no protection; the B–70 was an inadequate bomber; and space-based nuclear weap-

Bulletin of the Atomic Scientists 23, no. 6 (June 1967): 7–9. Reprinted with permission from the June, 1967, issue of the *Bulletin of Atomic Scientists.*

ons still make no sense. Today, the same groups that pressed Kennedy to build those weapons are leading the fight for the new ABM system and using most of the same arguments. While the fact that they were so completely wrong does not automatically insure that they are wrong today, it does mean that their emotional entreaties should be viewed with some suspicion.

It is important, however, that the country know what its options are. The military leaders, for example, have a responsibility to insure that the President and the Congress are fully informed about their views and how these may differ from those of the civilian leadership. The danger to the nation stems not from actions of responsible military leaders, but rather from the distortions which arise because vested interests have a great stake in selling their point of view. Scientists and engineers from companies and governmental laboratories having a special stake in the decisions being made take their views to the Congress and mass media. Unfortunately, too often there are not equally well-informed and dedicated spokesmen to present the reasons for not procuring a new weapons system.

It is interesting to note that President Eisenhower failed to mention congressional pressure in his warning. Possibly Eisenhower was not subjected to pressures by members of Congress because the Democratic Party controlled the legislative branch of the government during much of the time of his administration. President Kennedy found congressional pressure the most difficult to deal with because it came from former colleagues. Not only was President Kennedy subjected to extremely heavy congressional pressure; so was the Secretary of Defense.

The legislative proponents of the Nike Zeus and the B–70 were the most outspoken public proponents of these programs. Congressional leaders who are involved are obviously confronted with a dilemma too. It is important to maintain a vigorous and strong national defense until better security arrangements can be devised, but it is also necessary to formulate independent judgments about both the need for various weapons systems and their effectiveness. Admittedly, this is extremely difficult to do. Too often, the armed services committees and the other committees dealing with national security problems, such as the Joint Committee on Atomic Energy, have allied themselves with the military-industrial complex and against the President. This is, in part, because it is the safest, most popular course, but it is also because these committees attract legislators from those areas that have industries and laboratories involved in military activities, so they hear much more about the arguments in favor of a given military procurement than they do about a weapon's shortcomings or about the dangers inherent in an unlimited arms race. Inevitably, serious conflicts develop here, and in general, the broader and longer range considerations are not given adequate weight in the decisions.

Surprisingly, some elements of the press corps, too, present a strong bias in favor of military procurements of all kinds. This is largely because writers who specialize in military affairs are dependent upon officers and civilians in the Department of Defense and upon Congressmen who sit on the committees dealing with defense matters for most of their information. Fortunately, not all journalists reporting the Washington scene reflect the viewpoint of the weapons advocates. Most journalists have sufficient initiative and independence to dig in deeply, but a distressing number survive and, in fact, thrive by being conduits for their Pentagon contacts.

The ABM decision will have a major effect on the mood and direction of international relations for years to come. If the U.S. and USSR decide that a strategic weapons race is the best way to insure their survival, there can be little hope of effective arms limitation agreements, and conflict—military and political—will be our continuing diet.

It is likely that the efforts to achieve a nonproliferation treaty will succeed in spite of the current hard bargaining by some nations and the hesitancy based on the genuine concerns of others. Success with the nonproliferation treaty could set the stage for serious negotiation of arms control steps that would stop the present, dangerously escalating weapons races among large and small nations. Many additional steps appear sensible: agreements to halt the production of nuclear materials, to reduce nuclear armaments in Europe, to halt the conventional arms race everywhere, to reduce strategic force levels and, most important of all, to build up the U.N. peacekeeping capabilities. Whether or not anything can be done will depend to a large extent upon the ABM decision. The rest of the world, having taken the nonnuclear vows, will be waiting eagerly to see if the United States and the Soviet Union are willing to practice what they preach. They will be waiting for a clear clue to U.S.–USSR intentions, objectives, and commitments.

If, in the face of the clear-cut mutual advantage of avoiding a strategic weapons race, the leaders of the world's two dominant nations cannot resist the pressures on them to deploy an ABM, the others will have to conclude that eliminating the arms race is not a serious agenda item in either country.

Surprisingly, there seems to be little public concern about the ABM issue, either pro or con. This may be proof of the demise of the Cold War and the reduction of tensions, suspicions, and fears on both sides. It is probably also due to the lack of appreciation of the long-term consequences of a decision to deploy a missile defense system. But it is also a consequence of the fact that disarmament and rational international security arrangements have no effective lobby. Lacking vested interests, concern about disarmament will never come about unless the general public becomes involved enough to understand and support it. Everything possible should be done to stimulate a widespread public discussion of the alternatives.

Responsible citizens who lack technical training and specialized knowledge about military technology are reluctant to make judgments about armament issues; they undoubtedly would be more willing to participate in debating these important issues if more comprehensible technological information were available to them. Scientists and engineers, such as those contributing to this discussion, can help increase public awareness and widen participation in national debate by speaking and writing on the broad range of issues involved in making decisions affecting the national security.

5 ☆ THE MILITARY-INDUSTRIAL COMPLEX AND THE ECONOMY

THE DEFENSE SECTOR: ITS IMPACT ON AMERICAN BUSINESS

Charles J. Hitch

FOUR CHARACTERISTICS combine to give today's defense sector an impact upon American business which is unique in the history of our nation. These characteristics are the substantially high level of defense spending, its continuing nature, the growth of defense industries, and the constant push to extend the frontiers of military technology. Operating together, these factors have given much of American business a new and different look since the early 1950's.

HISTORICAL CHANGES

Present United States expenditures for national defense (including military assistance, AEC, and NASA) constitute approximately 10 per cent of our gross national product. This figure is, of course, far lower than peak wartime rates—during World War II the proportion soared to about 40 per cent. But the present 10 per cent is considerably above the levels of approximately 4 to 5 per cent in the years immediately following World War II. More important, defense spending has contin-

Jacob J. Javits, Charles J. Hitch, and Arthur F. Burns, *The Defense Sector and the American Economy* (New York: New York University Press, 1968), pp. 19–56. Reprinted by permission from *The Defense Sector and the American Economy,* by Jacob J. Javits, Charles J. Hitch, and Arthur F. Burns.

ued at a relatively high level for a decade and a half and shows no likelihood of significant reduction in the foreseeable future. Thus defense income has become a substantial and more-or-less normal factor in the economic reckoning of many American businesses.

The economic scene of the past few years is distinguished also by the emergence of a new phenomenon, the defense industry. Prior to World War II, defense industries as such were virtually nonexistent. American business directed its productive capacity almost exclusively to civilian markets in time of peace. When the nation found itself at war, business converted as quickly as possible to production of the tools of war. And when war ended, it reconverted as quickly to its normal civilian products. Today there are many industries whose defense production constitutes a relatively minor part of their operations, and whose defense products are closely related to their civilian products. But there are other industries, and a number of individual firms, whose major production effort is specifically directed to defense items and whose products bear little or no resemblance to those in the civilian sector.

These defense industries grow out of the increasing gap between civilian and military technology, the growing specialization and sophistication of the tools of war, and the pressure to extend the state of the art as a major means of maintaining military ascendancy. Throughout most of our history as a nation, military technology was sufficiently similar to civilian technology so that conversion from one to the other presented few problems. The gunsmiths who made the muskets for the hunting and household protection needs of the early settlers could turn out arms for military use during colonial times. Powder manufacturers who were making blasting powder for the westward expansion of the railroads could produce gunpowder for Civil War armament. The First World War found some industries momentarily adapting their normal civilian products to military needs. When the Germans surrendered, these industries returned to the output of peace time products. This same pattern—temporary conversion to military output, with innovation in weaponry dependent primarily on advances in civilian technology—continued well into World War II. The one exception was ship-building, where the development of armor plate, naval gunnery, the submarine, and the torpedo gave rise to what could truly be called a specialized defense industry.

World War II saw the first extensive effort to extend military technology well beyond the levels achieved in peacetime industrial production.

The conscious scientific effort to develop new military tools resulted in rapid achievements in electronics and rocketry, and culminated in the development of the atom bomb.

Scientific work in military technology and in the military and civilian uses of atomic energy continued after World War II, but on a relatively small scale. It took the growing tensions of the Cold War and the outbreak of Korean hostilities to push new developments in military technology and to translate them into operational readiness. Increasingly, these developments led in directions totally different from civilian technology and markets. In other countries where similar advances in military technology were also taking place, the governments assumed much of the responsibility for both design and production. The United States, however, is unique in the degree to which we rely upon private enterprise for the provision of defense materiel, and for defense research and development as well. Accordingly, new firms quickly sprang into existence and some totally new industries evolved to produce the specialized innovations of the new military technology.

I shall not dwell on the underlying reasons for the high continuing levels and the directions of our defense spending. The two fundamental causes are obvious. The first, of course, is the current division of a substantial portion of the world between two basically opposing forces. In defense of our own nation and in support of our allies abroad, we must stand ready at all times to meet the military threat from Communist Russia in Europe and from Communist China in Asia. Russia is powerful now. China with its developing industrial base and its millions of people is steadily acquiring power. While we must hope that the military threat from these nations will eventually abate, we cannot realistically expect that to happen in the near future.

The second fundamental cause is the status of modern military technology. Weapons are now global in their reach, unprecedented in their destructiveness, and almost instant in their delivery. A nation under major attack no longer has the time to mobilize its industry, to convert its peacetime business to wartime production, to update its military technology. Its potential retaliatory time is cut to hours and even to minutes. On the other hand, tremendous lead-time is now required for development of the sophisticated weaponry of modern defense. Key weapon systems may take five, or ten, or even more years from initial design to construction of prototypes to actual production and deployment. This revolution in military technology is irreversible: never again can we resume our historical pattern of converting our factories to military production after the need arises. Defense thus appears destined to exert a significant and more or less permanent impact on American business, at least until the world turns a not-yet-foreseeable corner toward lasting peace.

THE NEED FOR BETTER DATA

The relative novelty of the American defense sector makes a review of its impact on business difficult at this time. One reason is that economists have not yet had, or taken, the time to study the subject in definitive detail. Another is that systematic and comparable data in the field are seriously lacking. As Jacoby and Stockfish point out, official economic statistics are based on a classification system that reflects the problems and concerns of an earlier day. "For this reason," they state, "there is no 'defense sector' now identified in official, standard industrial classifications. Yet one clearly exists, insofar as a substantial portion of the nation's economic activity and resources are devoted to performing a function that differs markedly from the functions of other resource-using activities." [1]

In the absence of systematic data, various government and private agencies and scholars have made studies of one or another aspect of the defense sector. Many of these differ in years covered, breakdowns by industry or by defense product, and definitions of defense spending —they may or may not include military assistance or AEC or NASA, or they may simply fail to specify precisely what is covered. The resulting data are generally noncomparable, and their use is highly frustrating to students of the economics of defense, or at least to one Moskowitz lecturer.

In 1963 President Johnson appointed a Committee on the Economic Impact of Defense and Disarmament. In his memorandum of appointment he said: "The Committee will be responsible for the review and coordination of activities in the various departments and agencies designed to improve our understanding of the economic impact of de-

[1] Neil H. Jacoby and J. A. Stockfish, "The Scope and Nature of the Defense Sector of the U.S. Economy," in *Planning and Forecasting in the Defense Industries*, ed. J. A. Stockfish (Belmont, Calif.: Wadsworth Publishing Company, 1962), p. 2.

fense expenditures and of changes either in the composition or in the total level of such expenditures." [2] In its first report to the President in 1965, the Committee stated: ". . . there is vital need for more adequate, comprehensive, and accurate *information and analysis* of the impact of defense programs on the U.S. economy." [3]

The Committee cited a number of studies underway at various departments but warned that their completion "will still leave numerous gaps to be filled if the most intelligent choices of private and public policies are to be available." [4]

Among the major research programs undertaken after the Committee's establishment was the Economic Impact Project initiated by the Department of Defense in early 1964. Studies completed to date under that program have provided us with some of the best current data.

Using these and other available materials, I should like now to offer what must of necessity be a highly impressionistic view of various aspects of the defense impact on American business.

SHIFTS IN THE DEFENSE "MIX"

While the total level of defense spending as a percentage of national product has remained more or less stable for the past decade or so, broad shifts have occurred in the composition of the overall program. This shifting pattern will undoubtedly continue to be an important feature of the defense sector. The year-to-year allocation of the defense budget must respond to the constantly changing international situation, the Communist bloc's military innovations, and our own technological breakthroughs. Thus the late 1950's and early 1960's brought a heavy concentration on missiles and other items of the strategic retaliatory force buildup, reflecting both technological advances and the necessity to match Russian strategic strength and maintain the "balance of terror." Expenditures in this area leveled off as the major systems were brought to readiness in the early 1960's. Defense spending then began to show the effects of the growing Vietnam action. Impacts were shifting from aerospace and electronics and missile industries and toward

[2] Memorandum of the President to the Hon. Robert S. McNamara *et al.*, December 21, 1963.

[3] *Report of the Committee on the Economic Impact of Defense and Disarmament* (Washington, D.C.: U.S. Government Printing Office, July, 1965), p. 56.

[4] *Ibid.*, p. 65.

the industries producing the more "conventional" weapons of limited war: field and hand weapons, planes and helicopters, tanks, uniforms, and the array of material needed to support troops in the field. A substantial portion of defense spending today is going to the producers of these defense requirements—producers that in many instances are not classified among the defense industries.

Meantime, a new round of strategic and global defense buildup appears to be underway, as indicated by recent announcements of plans for a thin anti-missile umbrella and for new multiple-warhead missiles. The anti-missile program responds to Communist China's developing nuclear and missile technology. The multiple-warhead missiles reflect a new technological breakthrough and a move to update the missile systems completed in the early 1960's.

THE MAJOR POINTS OF IMPACT

Each of these shifts changes the impact of defense spending on various industries, firms, and geographic regions. Let us now look at the impact in terms of these classifications.

The Industries Involved

Industrial involvement in the defense sector needs to be examined from two different viewpoints. The first is each industry's share of the total government outlay for defense spending. The second is the degree of each industry's reliance on defense income. Some large industries may rank very high in their share of total defense production and yet rank relatively low in their reliance on defense income—that is to say, they may ship a much smaller part of their total output to defense purchasers than to civilian purchasers. Other industries may rank lower in their share of total defense production and yet be very highly dependent on defense income, i.e., they ship most of their output to the government rather than to civilian purchasers. A few industries, notably aircraft, missiles, communications equipment, and shipbuilding and ordnance, rank high on both scales. These latter groups comprise the major "defense industries."

Industry Shares of Defense Activity

A general picture of the distribution of defense spending among American industries may be derived from a breakdown of the military prime contract procurement program. The most detailed study to date —available, unfortunately, only for fiscal year 1963—breaks down the entire military prime contract procurement program by the traditional industrial classification, the SIC Product Code, at the four-digit level.[5] The resulting table shows that the procurement program is spread over seventy-eight different industries, but that seven industrial categories account for more than three-fourths of the total military prime contracts. Three of those categories are concerned with aircraft (aircraft, aircraft engines and parts, other aircraft equipment), and they together account for 34 per cent of the entire procurement program. In second place is the "Radio, TV communication equipment" industry, with 20 per cent of the total. Shipbuilding and repairing ranks third, complete guided missiles fourth, and ammunition not elsewhere classified fifth.

A new study has just been published which uses 1967 figures and, more importantly, a much broader measure of defense spending impact, not restricted to prime contractors. Richard P. Oliver, in the September, 1967, issue of the *Monthly Labor Review,* reports the distribution of defense-generated employment among industries in 1967, as calculated by the processing of data on military purchases through an interindustry model.[6] The model, developed as part of the Interagency Growth Project, estimates the direct and indirect effects of purchases, tracing chains of input requirements from prime contractors back through the more basic stages of production, distribution, and transportation.

While most of the other available interindustry data focus primarily on manufacturing, Oliver's information shows that 26 per cent of defense-generated employment in 1967 actually fell in the category of services, particularly transportation and warehousing, with 7 per cent, and wholesale and retail trade, with 6 per cent. Sixty-eight per cent of defense-generated employment was in manufacturing, and here the

[5] Research Analysis Corporation, *Economic Impact Analysis: A Military Procurement Final-Demand Vector* (Study for Department of Defense, 1967), vol. 1, pp. 9–10, 15, 36.

[6] Richard P. Oliver, "The Employment Effect of Defense Expenditures," *Monthly Labor Review* (September 1967), pp. 9–16.

leading industries were aircraft and parts, with 16 per cent, radio, television, and communications equipment, with 8 per cent, and ordnance (including missiles), with 6 per cent. No other industry exceeded 3 per cent. Oliver's study helps to correct the tendency to overemphasize the importance of the big weapons manufacturers and to underrate the effects of defense spending on other sectors of American business.

Industry Reliance on Defense Income

One measure of each industry's reliance on defense income is its government shipments. Information on shipments was collected by the Bureau of the Census in 1963 and again in 1965 for six major "defense-oriented" industry groups, some of them covering as many as five SIC-coded individual industries at the four-digit level. These figures include major sub-contracting. In 1963, 68 per cent of the total shipments for these six industry groups went to the government. By 1965 the total figure for the six groups had dropped substantially, to 54 per cent. The percentage of government shipments by individual groups differed considerably in each year, ranging from 80 per cent for aircraft and missile products to 9 per cent for machinery in 1965. All six industries showed a decline in percentage of government shipments from 1963 to 1965.[7]

These industry groups, except for shipbuilding, are heavily involved in procurement for strategic retaliatory forces, and the declines in the percentage of their shipments going to the government undoubtedly reflect the cutback in funds for strategic retaliatory forces between 1963 and 1965 as programs initiated earlier reached required levels of strength. They also reflect the beginning effects of the shift in defense allocations toward general purpose forces and general support in response to Vietnam hostilities, programs in which these industry groups play a less concentrated part.

Percentage changes in government shipments do not necessarily indicate absolute declines in either defense shipments or total shipments. Expanding civilian purchases may also account for percentage reductions in defense shipments. Actually, both causes were in operation in this instance: total defense shipments for the six groups de-

[7] *1963 Census of Manufacturers* and *Shipments of Defense-Oriented Industries 1965,* U.S. Department of Commerce, Bureau of the Census.

clined somewhat while nondefense shipments rose substantially from 1963 to 1965.

The Oliver article mentioned earlier also reports defense-generated employment for each industry in 1967 as a percentage of the industry's total employment. The two industries most dependent on defense spending by this measure are ordnance (including missiles) and aircraft and parts. Also ranking high in defense dependence are radio, television, and communications equipment, electronic components and accessories, machine shop products, and "other transportation equipment" (including shipbuilding). Defense-generated employment as a percentage of total employment for these six groups ranges from 65 per cent for ordnance to 23 per cent for other transportation equipment. While the services account for 26 per cent of total defense employment, less than 3 per cent of employment in the services is defense-generated.[8]

The Firms Involved

Most of the important defense firms are big businesses, and some are among the biggest in the United States. A recent study prepared for the Department of Defense points out: "Of the 100 largest defense prime contractors in fiscal year 1963, 39 were among the largest 100 U.S. industrial corporations, 2 were among the 50 largest U.S. utility companies, and 2 were among the 50 largest U.S. transportation companies. Sixty-nine of the largest 100 defense contractors were included among the largest 500 industrial corporations for 1963." [9]

The one hundred top companies in dollar volume of military prime contracts in fiscal year 1966 accounted for 64 per cent of the total dollar volume, and the top five companies accounted for 18 per cent.[10] The top company, Lockheed Aircraft Corporation, received awards of just over $1.5 billion, and three other companies received awards of over $1.0 billion each. The company in one-hundredth place received awards totaling $40 million. The heavy concentration of awards to the

[8] Oliver, *op. cit.*, pp. 9–11.

[9] Research Analysis Corporation, *Industrial Classification and Economic-Impact Analysis* (Study for Department of Defense, 1966), pp. 27–28.

[10] "100 Companies and Their Subsidiary Corporations Listed According to Net Value of Military Prime Contract Awards, Fiscal Year 1966," Office of the Secretary of Defense, 1966.

leading companies has, however, been declining slowly but steadily in recent years.

Some changes in the list of one hundred top companies occur from year to year because of mergers and other corporate changes. One new joint venture in 1966, a merger of construction companies making military bases and installations, is in ninth place with contracts exceeding a half billion dollars.

Other changes reflect shifts in procurement patterns. The 1966 list contains companies in four new industrial categories—weapons, textiles and clothing, construction equipment, and building supplies—and a substantial increase in the number of ammunition companies. These shifts obviously reflect the rising demands for conventional materiel for Vietnam.

Awards to small business concerns, generally defined as those with five hundred or fewer employees, comprise about one-fifth of the dollar volume of prime contracts. The percentage has fluctuated from a peak of 25 per cent in 1954 to a low of 16 per cent in 1963, rising since then to 21 per cent in 1966.[11]

Small business concerns are more likely to receive awards for textiles and clothing, weapons, construction, and miscellaneous equipment—the more conventional defense items. Not surprisingly, they receive very few prime contracts for work in aircraft or missiles. The current shift toward more conventional defense purchases for the Vietnam action improves the economic outlook for the small businesses, whereas likely future shifts toward strategic retaliatory weapons and intercontinental missile defenses would cause a decline in defense opportunities for small businesses.

Like industries, individual companies differ both according to their share of defense income and their reliance on defense income. A study by Murray Weidenbaum classified the top thirty-five companies in dollar volume of defense awards in 1962 according to the percentage those awards constituted of each firm's total sales.[12] Seven of these companies, all aircraft firms, received awards amounting to more than 75 per cent of their total sales, whereas nine companies received awards amounting to less than 25 per cent of their total sales. Some companies

[11] *Military Prime Contract Awards*, July–December, 1966, Office of the Secretary of Defense, pp. 11–13, 21.

[12] Cited in Research Analysis Corporation, *Industrial Classification and Economic-Impact Analysis, op. cit.*, p. 27.

received very substantial shares of the total defense program but were nevertheless little dependent upon defense income in relation to civilian sales. General Motors, for example, ranked tenth in dollar volume of defense awards,[13] but these awards constituted only 3 per cent of the company's total sales. Near the other extreme was Lockheed, ranking first in volume of awards and making 81 per cent of its total sales to defense purchasers. The differences in degree of military versus civilian diversification indicate the complexities in attributing major roles to the defense firms. One does not think of General Motors as a defense firm; yet it is a considerably heavier contributor to the defense program in dollar volume than, for example, Grumman Aircraft, which most people do think of as a defense firm.

The Regions Involved

For various reasons of climate, geography, economic history, and accident, defense spending is unevenly distributed throughout the country. Shipbuilding takes place in coastal locations, much aircraft and missile work where climate permits all-year testing and launching. Large manufacturing firms are in dense population areas, and large military installations are in outpost areas like Alaska and Hawaii.

The most common, but not the most accurate, measure of geographic distribution of defense spending is the Defense Department's annual report of military prime contract awards by region and state. The distribution for fiscal year 1966 ranges from 20.0 per cent for the Pacific Region down to only 0.4 per cent for Alaska and Hawaii. The Middle Atlantic Region is next highest, and the Mountain region next lowest. By states, California is far in the lead, followed by New York, Texas, Connecticut, and Pennsylvania.[14]

Data on dollar distribution of prime contracts alone do not give a clear picture of the actual impact of defense spending upon an area. The total size of the area's labor force, the number employed on contract awards, and the number in other defense-generated employment such as the servicing of large military bases all play an important role. A recent Department of Defense study attempted to measure the total

[13] Data on 1962 dollar volume of awards is from "100 Companies and Their Subsidiary Corporations Listed According to Net Value of Military Prime Contract Awards, Fiscal Year 1962," Office of the Secretary of Defense, 1962.

[14] *Military Prime Contract Awards by Region and State,* Fiscal Years 1962–1966, Office of the Secretary of Defense, 1967, pp. 1–2.

impact by state more accurately by developing a "defense dependency ratio"—the ratio of total defense-generated employment to a state's total work force.[15] Results for mid-1966 showed that Alaska is the most dependent on defense spending, with 9.7 per cent of its work force engaged in defense-generated employment, mainly through military bases. Alaska ranked forty-fourth among the states in prime contract awards in 1966. California, which ranked first in prime contract awards, is rated eighth in defense dependency, and New York, which ranked second in prime contract awards, drops all the way down to thirty-first place in defense dependency.

This study also surveyed the distribution of defense employment by state and region for major defense product groups. Results showed aircraft employment to be the most widely distributed among regions, with all except two getting at least 10 per cent of total aircraft employment. Missile and space employment, by contrast, is concentrated heavily in the three Pacific Coast states and the South Atlantic states. The Pacific states account for 26 per cent of all surveyed defense employment, and the region is unique in its substantial employment in every product group.

In a study published in 1966 by the Brookings Institution, Roger E. Bolton takes a somewhat different approach to the determination of defense impact by state and region.[16] He assumes that local income—income developed from within a state or region—is passive and that exogenous income—income from outside the state—is the primary determinant in the economic growth of an area. He classifies all defense purchases as exogenous income, and determines what percentage defense income represents of the total exogenous income of an area, and what the rate of growth of defense income has been in the area over a ten-year period. His findings indicate that the contribution of defense income to regional growth for the period 1952–1962 was greatest for the Mountain region, closely followed by the Pacific region. More modest growth impacts were found for five other regions, and two regions, Middle Atlantic and East North Central, suffered negative growth effects, primarily as a result of post-Korean War cutbacks. Unfortunately, as Bolton emphasizes, his conclusions are only estimates because of the

[15] Col. Vernon M. Buehler, USA, "Economic Impact of Defense Programs," *Defense Industry Bulletin* (March 1967), pp. 1–12.

[16] Roger E. Bolton, *Defense Purchases and Regional Growth* (Washington, D.C.: The Brookings Institution, 1966).

unavailability of complete data, and the necessity for reliance solely upon prime contract figures. And, of course, his conclusions are already somewhat dated. But his model looks sufficiently promising that one might hope it will be brought up to date with the use of the more reliable data now becoming available.

Bolton also studies the concentration of various specific types of programs in certain geographical areas, and observes:

> Not only are some states heavily dependent on one or two programs, but in several cases this amounts to dependence on one or two companies. Examples are the Martin-Marietta Company in Colorado; United Aircraft and General Dynamics (Electric Boat Division) in Connecticut; Lockheed in Georgia; Boeing Company in Kansas and Washington; Bath Iron Works in Maine; Ingalls Shipbuilding Company in Mississippi; McDonnell Aircraft in Missouri; and Newport News Shipbuilding and Dry Dock Company in Virginia. In such cases, apprehension about the effects of dependence of certain states and metropolitan areas on defense business is understandable, for these areas may suffer a great loss in demand even if the total defense budget is not cut.[17]

Effects of Subcontracting

Most of the foregoing data are based on first-order or prime contract distribution and do not reflect the impact of subcontracting. For some years various critics have expressed concern about the economic effects of the heavy concentration of prime contracts in relatively few industries and firms and in certain geographic areas. The standard reply has been that the prime contract figures exaggerate this apparent concentration and that figures on subcontracts, if only they were available, would show that subcontracting suffuses the impact broadly through other industries, smaller firms, different geographic areas.

Late in 1966 the Department of Defense completed its first detailed study of subcontracting procurement patterns.[18] Although the study had a number of limitations, it was certainly indicative of general trends. And it turned up some surprising results, results that overturned so many assumptions about subcontracting that one reliable

[17] *Ibid.*, p. 117.

[18] CEIR, Inc., *Economic Impact Analysis of Subcontracting Procurement Patterns* (Study for Department of Defense, 1966).

business publication headed its account of the findings "End of a myth."[19] Some of the key findings were these:

—For all prime contractors, their top subcontractor accounts for an average of 36 per cent of all subcontract value and their top ten subcontractors account for an average of 80 per cent of all subcontract value.

—Many of the leading subcontractors are also important prime contractors. Eighteen of the twenty-six leading subcontractors are also among the top one hundred Department of Defense prime contractors.

—Subcontracting concentration by industry awaits further study, but a small sample study shows subcontracting concentration to be particularly heavy in missile and space programs, where the top ten subcontractors account for 92 per cent of the total subcontract value. By contrast, the top ten subcontractors in the aircraft and airframe program account for only 50 per cent of the total subcontract value.

—Perhaps most startling of all, geographic concentration appears to be even heavier for subcontract than for prime contract awards. The leading ten states in the prime contract series account for 67 per cent of total prime contract procurement, whereas the ten top states in the subcontract series receive over 75 per cent of all subcontract awards. Furthermore, eight of the top ten states appear on both lists. And California and New York, which rank first and second in both series, together account for over 40 per cent of the total value of subcontract awards.

These findings point up the need for much more sophisticated data and analysis in the field of economic impact of defense spending, and the pitfalls of operating on assumptions—however logical they might appear to be—rather than on hard facts.

OTHER DEFENSE EFFECTS ON BUSINESS

Now I should like to comment briefly on several other ways in which the defense sector affects business.

Research and Development

As was noted earlier, a major characteristic of the present defense effort is its concentration on extending the frontiers of military technol-

[19] *Business Week*, April 8, 1967.

ogy. As a result, funds for so-called "research and development" have for the past fifteen years constituted a very substantial part of the total defense budget.

In contrast, with a few notable industrial exceptions, private industry in the United States spends very little on research and development of a fundamental sort. Civilian efforts are more likely to go into styling and minor product improvements rather than into basic advances in technology. This occurs, in part, because research costs are high and it is hard to protect property rights to successful innovations.

The large military expenditures for research and development help to make up in some measure and in some areas this deficit in civilian research spending. Military research and development, as Murray Weidenbaum points out, constitute one of the major growth areas of the American economy.[20] While military technology is the direct beneficiary of these expenditures, their results spread indirectly into many areas of non-defense output. Transport aircraft, cheap nuclear power, exploration of space, high speed computers, and other electronic developments are just a few examples of the benefits of military research and development to the nation's general technological progress.

A precise measure of the impact of military research and development is impossible to determine, in part because definitions differ widely among the different sectors of the economy. In defense budgets, the research and development category includes not only basic and applied research, but the actual construction and testing of numbers of prototypes. Thus comparative data may give a misleading picture of the actual role of military research and development.

According to figures developed by the Bureau of the Budget and the National Science Foundation, two-thirds of all the research and development work in the entire nation is presently financed by the Department of Defense, NASA, and the AEC.[21] Defense-supported R and D was 57 per cent of the United States total in 1954 and had climbed to 65 per cent in the U.S. total by 1963. By 1965 the dollar amount had risen to almost $15 billion.

Most of this total goes directly for development of military hard goods. A breakdown of military prime contract awards for research and

[20] Murray L. Weidenbaum, "The Impact of Military Procurement on American Industry," in Jacoby and Stockfish, *Planning and Forecasting in the Defense Industries,* p. 150.

[21] *Report of the Committee on the Economic Impact of Defense and Disarmament, op. cit.,* Appendix Table 16, p. 87.

development in 1966 shows only 6 per cent allocated to basic research, a decline from 9 per cent in 1965 and 11 per cent in 1964.[22]

The largest military R and D contracts go, of course, to those industries which are closest to the frontiers of weapon development. By far the largest allocation presently goes to programs concerned with missile and space systems, followed by electronics and communications equipment and aircraft. R and D allocations as a percentage of total allocations have been falling for aircraft and electronics and communications programs in recent years, but climbing for missile and space programs.

Employment Patterns

The most notable defense impact upon employment patterns is the shift away from production workers and toward the technical, scientific, and managerial ranks. In 1960, production workers constituted 75 per cent of total employment in U.S. manufacturing. But the percentage of production workers to total employees in five major defense-oriented industries stood at 60 per cent. By 1964, production workers in these five industries had dropped to 57 per cent. Production workers by individual industry ranged from 84 per cent in ship and boat building and repairing to 41 per cent in ordnance and accessories (including missiles and space vehicles). A major manufacturer of aircraft and missiles has estimated that his employment requirements for production workers will have dropped to 29 per cent by 1970.

This shift, of course, reflects the growth of research and development allocations and the resulting increase in technical and scientific employment in defense work, as well as the automation of many production processes. It has been estimated that the number of engineers and scientists employed in five major defense-oriented industries in 1962 constituted 31 per cent of the total of all scientists and engineers employed in all U.S. industries. The five industries employed 48 per cent of all physicists in U.S. industries.[23]

To help fill in gaps in the data on defense impact, the Department of Defense and NASA have jointly undertaken the collection of em-

[22] *Military Prime Contract Awards by Service Category and Federal Supply Classification,* Fiscal Years 1963–1966, Office of the Secretary of Defense, 1967, p. 2.

[23] *Report of the Committee on the Economic Impact of Defense and Disarmament, op. cit.,* Appendix Table 19, p. 89.

ployment and other information from large defense contractors in a program called the Economic Information System (EIS). Data on defense-generated industrial employment trends from 1963 to 1966 for 150 EIS-surveyed plants were published in March, 1967.[24] They show that total defense-generated employment in these plants declined from 1963 to 1965 but began to rise again in 1966. Among product groups, the biggest decreases occurred in missiles (40 per cent) and electronics and communications (28 per cent). Significant percentage gains were shown by ships and by ammunition, although both of these product groups involved much smaller absolute numbers of employees.

The Oliver article cited earlier analyzes trends in defense-generated employment in several heavily defense-oriented industries from 1965 to 1967. The percentage of defense-generated employment dropped very slightly for aircraft and for communications equipment, and rose substantially for ordnance. Oliver points out that while defense purchases of aircraft and communications equipment rose during the period, civilian purchases in both fields rose even faster to produce the slight decline in percentages of defense employment.[25]

Changes in Procurement Policies

During the years immediately following the Korean War, at a time when major new weapons systems were being developed, there was increasing reliance by the Department of Defense on the cost-plus-fixed-fee contract. This type of contract rose from 20 per cent to a high of 38 per cent of all contract awards during the period of 1956 to 1961. The argument for its use was that contractors venturing into relatively new weapons fields could not reasonably anticipate their costs and so should be reimbursed for actual costs incurred in the development and production of new military products.

The trouble with this type of contract, as Defense Secretary McNamara has pointed out, is that it "offers neither reward for good performance nor penalty for bad." [26] In 1961 the Defense Department undertook a program to reduce use of this type of contract and to replace it with firm fixed price or incentive contracts and the widest possible

[24] Buehler, *op. cit.*, pp. 10–12.

[25] Oliver, *op. cit.*, pp. 9–11.

[26] Memorandum to the President from the Secretary of Defense, "Department of Defense Cost Reduction Program—Annual Progress Report," July 5, 1967, p. 7.

price competition. The results have been notable. "Cost-plus" contracts declined from the high of 38 per cent in 1961 to 9.4 per cent in 1966 and have been held to 10.0 per cent thus far in 1967, even under the exigencies of procurement for the Vietnam war. Contracts awarded on the basis of competitive bidding have increased from 33 per cent to 47 per cent for the period from 1961 to 1967. Fixed price awards have increased from 44 per cent to 60 per cent, and incentive contracts have increased from 17 per cent to 28 per cent for the period.[27]

The actual economic effects of these changing procurement policies are difficult to measure. The Department of Defense claims that shifting the risk to the contractor and then compensating him fairly for that risk does indeed reward good performance and penalize bad, and saves the taxpayers many millions of dollars annually. Some industry representatives, on the other hand, claim that contractors are being forced to assume unwarranted risks, with the results that profits on defense contracts have dropped from 4.0 per cent in 1960 to 3.0 per cent in 1965 and 1966 and that the quality of military hardware is declining.

I might note that the risks contractors assume under the current procurement policies are generally the same they assume in any nondefense sector of the economy. The effect of "cost-plus" contracting tended to remove rewards for initiative and ingenuity and to place many of management's normal decisions and prerogatives with service contracting officers, so that the contracting firms were halfway nationalized. The new policies return these contractors to the same economic basis of operations as that of any other kind of business activity in America.

A LOOK TO THE FUTURE

Predicting future trends is a risky undertaking at best, and I am no better qualified at soothsaying than the next man. I recall giving a speech in 1960 in which I remarked that a defense budget higher than $45 billion or lower than $40 billion in the near future was hard to imagine. Today, as we pass the $70 billion mark, I am comforted to recollect that I did add to that speech the qualification that greatly

[27] Office of the Assistant Secretary of Defense, Installation and Logistics, August, 1967.

changed military budget levels were not only possible but likely since the defense sector was full of surprises.

It was, and it still is and will continue to be. Much depends, of course, on those totally unpredictable technological breakthroughs that can cause such major shifts in direction in so short a time. Even more depends on the state of the world around us—relations with Russia, developments in Red China, the state of affairs in Vietnam. Ruling out for the moment any momentous changes in these factors, are there any educated guesses we can make about the impact of the defense sector on American business over the next few years? I think there are a few worth attempting.

Strategic Retaliatory Forces

Expenditures for these forces declined in the early 1960's as major missile systems initiated earlier were brought to required levels of strength. My guess is that this trend will be reversed as we enter a new round of improvements. The recent news stories about new missiles with multiple warheads lend credence to this assumption. As I remarked earlier, the revolution in military technology is irreversible. So long as an external threat exists, we have no alternative but to attempt to maintain superiority over advances in military technology by the Communist nations. Improvements in our retaliatory weapons are now possible, and some are likely to be put into production.

Intercontinental Defense Forces

These are definitely slated for buildup, with Defense Secretary McNamara's announcement of the development of a thin anti-ballistic missile defense against possible attack from Red China. The real question is whether it will remain "thin" or whether it will have some tendency to become thicker with time. Other things remaining relatively equal, my guess is that some very gradual and limited thickening is likely to take place. Once a system is in operation, it is only natural to want to incorporate at least minor improvements, to build up some obvious weak spots. But a major expansion of the program should not occur unless other things do become unequal and Russia, for example, undertakes a heavy anti-missile defense program.

Conventional Weaponry

These levels would, of course, decline substantially if the Vietnam war comes to an end. But I would guess that we will continue a low-level program to keep these materiel modernized and to maintain a sound base for quick expansion of production should the need arise for their use in any other limited actions. The very ultimate nature of the destructive power of the new global weapons enforces limited military actions with conventional weapons as the only alternative to holocaust.

These several major trends would mean for business:

—Expanding shares of defense income for the aircraft and missile industries, both heavily involved in retaliatory and anti-missile defense programs. Future declines in manned aircraft would be offset by the aircraft industries' substantial involvement in missile production.

—Expanding shares of defense income for the electronics and communications industries. These manufacturers are involved not only in the so-called "flyaway" products—the planes and missiles—but they are heavily involved in the increasingly important "ground environment" —the warning systems, the landing and launch sites, the guidance control and communications centers.

—When Vietnam hostilities cease, a sharp decrease in shares of defense income for industries producing conventional weapons, but then a leveling-off to maintain an immediately available general purpose force.

Expanding shares of defense spending for research and development. These shares leveled off somewhat in recent years as major new weapons systems were brought from exploratory stages to actual production and operational readiness. A new round of technological advances will involve increases once more in R and D allocations.

A continuation of the shift in employment patterns from production to technical and scientific workers. The increasing automation of all of American industry will support this trend, and growing R and D allocations will continue to accentuate it in defense-oriented industries.

Continuing concentration of major contracts among a relatively small number of very large business firms. Global weapons and defense systems are necessarily limited in number and gigantic in size and complexity. If the government itself is not to assume major responsibility for weapons production, then major responsibility must be assigned to a relatively few firms for overall management of individual weapons systems. Some important subsections may be broken out for separate contracting. Much of the actual work will be subcontracted. But firms with annual contracts above the $1 billion level will continue as a highly significant part of the defense picture.

Continuing geographic concentration. Aircraft work is fairly evenly spread throughout the major regions of the country, but the other growth programs—missiles, electronics and communications, and research and development—are much more concentrated geographically. The Pacific region, ranking high already in most of these growth areas, may even increase its dominance. Relative gains will occur for the Middle and South Atlantic regions. The Mountain region may hold its own because of its missile work. Relative losses will be sharpest for the four Central regions (East and West, North and South.)

The Problem of Cutbacks

The specter of drastic future cutbacks in the defense sector is one that I think is somewhat exaggerated, although it is certainly a subject for sober study. We managed to survive a huge cutback after World War II and a significant cutback after the Korean War, not without many instances of severe dislocation but certainly without dire harm to the economy as a whole. Hostilities in Vietnam do not appear likely to terminate with precipitate withdrawal of American forces. A more likely eventuality is more or less gradual decrease in spending for Vietnam. These gradual cutbacks will affect primarily those industries which are not "defense industries"—that is, industries which have large non-defense markets—clothing, fuel and lubricants, vehicles, machinery. Most of them diverted production to defense needs as the Vietnam action expanded, and could probably redirect their output to civilian markets without major dislocations. One exception which may suffer serious cutback problems is the ammunition industry.

The heavily defense-oriented industries are those involved with the major global weapons and defense systems. Here the possibilities of cutbacks center on new disarmament agreements or on the shift to new weapon developments because of technological breakthroughs. Disarmament agreements are slow in coming and are likely to involve only one type of weapon system at a time. Shifts from one to another weapon system are likely to occur from time to time, but the same industries may be equipped to play at least some continuing roles in the newer systems. The obvious answer for defense-oriented industries is diversification—diversification both in the area of military products and in the direction of adapting their technological advances for civilian products. The defense industries are well aware of this. Lockheed, for example, currently has contracts for three military transport planes and a patrol bomber, is the principal prime contractor for the Polaris and Poseidon Missiles, and receives additional contracts for space vehicles, satellite control research, electronics, and shipbuilding—all this in addition to a substantial nondefense output.

Defense Department officials believe that the change in procurement policies from "cost-plus" to fixed price contracts following price competition has encouraged diversification—a firm which may lose a competition will be aggressive about developing other markets as a cushion. And a recent change in procurement regulations allows companies to charge to defense contracts certain costs associated with planning for diversification. While it does not permit research and development costs for new nondefense products, it does permit "costs of generalized long-range management planning which is concerned with the future overall development of the contractor's business and which may take into account the eventual possibility of economic dislocations or fundamental alterations in those markets in which the contractor currently does business." [28]

TWO POLICY QUESTIONS

I should like to conclude with a brief consideration of two important policy questions concerning the defense impact on American business.

Defense Procurement Policy

The general policy guiding defense purchases, simply stated, is to obtain the most for a given budget. No one argues with this as a general rule, but the question does arise as to whether there ought to be some exceptions, and on what grounds. Two other considerations are sometimes put forward to compete with the "least cost" policy. They are the "fair share" and the "social cost" considerations.

The "fair share" proponents are concerned about the heavy concen-

[28] Armed Services Procurement Regulation, revised, March 6, 1964.

tration of defense spending in some geographic regions, some industries, and some firms—usually not their own. A Senate bill cosponsored in 1959 by my distinguished predecessor in this lecture series proposed a policy declaration by Congress that: ". . . the security of the Nation requires that its economy, and the economy of each section of the country, be maintained at a level which can support its programs for defense and sustain the private economic system. . . . In placing purchases under this chapter the procuring agency shall consider the strategic and economic desirability of allocating purchases to different geographical areas of the Nation and to eligible suppliers from whom relatively small proportions of procurement have been purchased. . . ."

Although Congress did not adopt this bill, it has enacted one measure under the "fair share" criterion—the special defense program to aid small business.

If the concentration of defense work increases, and if the country's general economic health should dip, so that alternative markets and employment sources are not so readily available, the pressure for at least some concessions to the "fair share" criterion is certain to increase.

The "social cost" argument runs that some contracts ought to be directed to economically distressed or labor surplus areas as a means of keeping all parts of the economy in sound health and as a means of saving other and greater government costs in unemployment insurance, relief and welfare measures, and loss of taxes on earned income. Congress has provided for some use of the "social cost" criterion by a policy of special consideration to labor surplus areas—certain preferences are given to contractors who will have part of their work performed in these areas. To date, however, this program has had only very limited success. A major problem is that many labor surplus areas simply do not have the kind of capacity needed to produce defense items.

Certainly the defense budget is a large and powerful economic tool for the government, and one is tempted to seek its uses to solve an array of problems. But, other, more direct means are or can be made available to aid distressed areas. And sound economic principles would argue that those industries not getting their "fair share" of defense spending should develop markets where they can compete successfully rather than through artificial supports. Generally speaking, I think we are better off to stick close to the "least cost" policy in defense purchases. In the long run, the cost to the nation will be less if monies are used for direct rather than indirect purposes, and the public will be better informed of the actual costs of the programs among which it must allocate its support.

The "Military-industrial Complex"

In his farewell speech to the nation in 1961, President Eisenhower warned against "the acquisition of unwarranted influence, whether sought or unsought, by the military-industrial complex." Has there been such influence exercised by an alliance of military and industrial interests against the general interests of the broader public?

Certainly the large defense budget carries enormous potentials for such influence. A recent Associated Press survey of defense spending spoke of the "Pentagon's awesome power" and described the Department of Defense as "the mightiest concentration of economic power in the world today."

Suspicions of improper relationships between the military and some large defense firms are heightened by the frequency with which retired military officers once active in procurement areas or choices among weapons systems accept high positions with defense firms.

If I might speak half—but only half—facetiously, I sometimes think a truer picture is not of one giant military-industrial complex but of a whole array of little military-industrial complexes, each promoting its own service or branch of the service, its favored weapon, and its own firm, each cheerfully attempting to cut down all the competing little military-industrial complexes. The mutual backscratching that goes on among them is more likely to be outdone by the backstabbing. I think it likely that the safety of the general interest lies in large part in the fierce competition among the many special interests that comprise the supposedly monolithic military-industrial complex.

One way or another, we must produce the defense products essential to our survival in today's world. The only alternative to our present system would be the nationalization of weapons production. Then we might be faced with the "military complex, period" or perhaps with the "military-bureaucratic complex." I for one would not choose either of those alternatives.

But there are some things we can do to lessen the possible threats to the public interest from the military-industrial complex or complexes. We can continue and extend the current shift toward price competition in defense contracting. We might adopt a policy to discourage former military or Defense Department personnel from accepting positions with firms over which they had exercised some power of decision in weapon selection or other procurement activities. We should insist on continuing our strong Constitutionally-based civilian control over military affairs, with the maximum number of budgetary decisions based on the disinterested results of systems analysis rather than on the special pleadings of any alliance of military and industrial groups.

The defense sector today is large and continuing. Its impact on American business is substantial. Properly regulated, it will continue to provide for the nation's military might without undermining either our economic strength or our democratic institutions in the years to come.

THE WAR INDUSTRY AND ITS EFFECTS

Kenneth E. Boulding

I HAVE BEEN CONCERNED for a good many years with the problem of the "war industry" and its effects. I use the term "war industry" to describe that segment of the economy which is financed by the military budget and which produces whatever is purchased by the expenditure of the military budget. In the United States, this is now between 9 and 10 per cent of the gross national product. The world war industry, according to the estimates of the United States Arms Control and Disarmament Agency, amounted last year to about 182 billion dollars, which is approximately the total income of the poorest half of the human race.

The economic burden of the war industry falls partly on the present generation and partly on future generations. In the present generation it clearly represents a withdrawal from potential household purchases on consumption. Thus, in 1929, when the war industry was only about 1 per cent of the American economy, household consumption was about 75 per cent; today with the war industry nearly 10 per cent, household consumption is down to 62 per cent of the gross national product. This means in effect that the rise of the war industry in the last generation now deprives the average American household of something like 15–20 per cent of his total potential purchases.

It may be thought that this is a relatively small burden, but averages are misleading, and at certain points the war industry bites much more severely into the American economy than it does on the average. This

Testimony before the Joint Economic Committee, Subcommittee on Economy in Government, 91st Cong., 1st Sess., June 4, 1969, pp. 137–141.

is because the war industry is part of what I have been calling the "grants economy," rather than the market or exchange sector, the grants economy being that part of the economic system in which allocations of resources or income are determined by one-way transfers, rather than by exchange, which is a two-way transfer. Thus, the grants economy includes most of the government tax and expenditure system outside of what might be called "government business," like the post office, and it includes the greater part of private charitable grants and foundation grants. The grants sector of the economy is an "economy" in the sense that the total of grants is not indefinitely expansible, but depends on the general willingness of the society to make one-way transfers. Even though the grants sector of the economy has been expanding substantially in the last fifty years, at any one time it is subject to quite sharp limitations.

The war industry is now more than half the grants sector of the economy, so it is clear that it bites much more severely into this sector than it does into the economy as a whole. Thus, the segments of the economy which are most affected by the war industry are those which are competitive with it in the structure of one-way transfers. Professor Bruce Russett of Yale has suggested that of these education is the most vulnerable. The problem here is "what goes down when the war industry goes up a dollar?" Even though the answer to this question may vary from time to time, it seems clear from the evidence of the last thirty years that the main thing which goes down is expenditure on education, though all other civilian sectors of the grants economy may be expected to suffer.

The adverse effect of the war industry on the future generation comes about mainly in two ways; the first is the effect on education mentioned above. This is likely to be an increasingly serious problem simply because education as an industry and as a proportion of the gross national product needs to expand very rapidly in the coming years. There are two reasons for this. One is that as the total stock of knowledge increases, the resources that have to be put into transmitting it to the next generation likewise must increase. The second reason is that as the productivity of education rises slowly, if at all, the relative price of education continually rises in the form of rising wages and salaries for those engaged in it, who must get their share of the generally increasing per capita product of the society. Education, however, is mainly financed through the grants economy, especially through the tax system, and it is even now running into severe resistance to expansion, as evidenced in the failure of school bonds and millage increases, and the failure of central city school systems to cope with the flood of rural migrants. Even though the decline in the birthrate is likely to make this problem somewhat easier in the future, the increasing burden of the transmission of knowledge is something which will accelerate rather than decline.

The other point at which the war industry may be costly to future generations is in its absorption of a very large proportion (some have estimated 60 per cent) of research and development expenditures. There is a great deal of evidence to suggest that civilian industry is starved of able research scientists and engineers because of the "internal brain drain" into the war industry. By far the most important resource of any society from the point of its future is the innovative capacity of its ablest minds, and if these are absorbed into the war industry they will clearly not be available elsewhere. Furthermore, the spillovers from the war industry into the civilian sector seem to have been declining, and are quite inadequate to compensate for the drain of problem-solving capacity. Because of the obsessive expansion of the war industry many vital sectors of the civilian economy are failing to solve their technical problems. We see this in transportation, in building, even in many of the areas of general manufacturing. Shipbuilding is a case where the domination of an industry by the war industry has itself resulted in technical backwardness because even within the war industry itself certain areas, such as the aerospace complex, have absorbed problem-solving capacity at the expense of others.

The final cost of the war industry is the probability of destruction which it creates. If we were to assess the real costs of the war industry we would have to add to its budget an insurance premium expressing the probability of the destruction which may result from it. How high this would be nobody knows. My own guess is that the probability of nuclear war may well be of the order of 1 per cent per annum. Below this would seem to be below the level of "just noticeable difference" at which its decisions would be affected. This may not seem to be very much, but accumulated for a hundred years it becomes rather frightening. In assessing the insurance premium for war destruction we also have to make an estimate of how much destruction there would be. This again has to be a wild guess. If we suppose, however, that nuclear war would destroy half the population and capital in the United States and that recovery would be very slow simply because the survivors would all be sick and disorganized, the income equivalent of this capital loss could easily be of the same order of magnitude as half the gross national product itself, or $450 billion per annum. If what we are buying with the military budget is a positive probability of irretrievable disaster, this seems expensive at any price.

On all these grounds, the case for sharp reductions in the military budget is very strong. The military budget, however, is a function of our own image of ourselves as a nation and our image of the international environment. The military budget is a function of two things—the desire for power and the sense of threat. Of these, the first is considerably under our control, and the second may be controlled in part by a shift in policy. One of the things we must learn if we are to survive is that the national interest is a variable of the system and not a constant. The national interest is what the nation is interested in. Within wide limits this is a subjective variable. If we have an image of ourselves as *the* great power, making everyone else conform with our wishes, we will tend to have a large war industry. If we visualize ourselves in a more modest role in the international system, even perhaps as first among equals, we can get along with a war industry which is much smaller.

From a strictly economic point of view, being a great power is extremely unrewarding. The Swedes discovered this a hundred years ago, the British and the French have just discovered it in this generation, but we do not yet understand this. There is little doubt that the economic development of Britain and France, for instance, was seriously hampered by their imperial and great power positions in the hundred years after 1850. The development of the United States in this period was unquestionably assisted by the fact that it did not visualize itself as a great power and hence devoted a very small proportion of its resources to the war industry. In the next generation or so, if we persist in our image of ourselves as not only a great power, but the greatest power, we not only greatly increase the risk of mutual destruction, but we will seriously hamper our own internal development and the quality of our internal life.

External threats are not unreal, but they tend to loom much larger in the popular imagination than they really are. Furthermore, our own almost exclusive reliance on the threat system in our international relations increases rather than decreases the external threat. Our external relations now are fantastically unbalanced on the side of threat. We may ourselves visualize our armed forces merely as counterthreat, but the world outside does not see it in these terms. We need to move towards much more balanced foreign policy which would be quite consciously directed towards the establishment of stable peace, and which would place much greater stress on the development of integrative and trade relationships, rather than on the use of threat.

The American eagle is portrayed as holding an olive branch in one claw and a sheaf of arrows in the other. What kind of policy is it that weights down the one claw with 90 billion dollars worth of arrows and provides the other with a minute, wilted, olive branch on which we spend practically nothing? The restoration of a balanced posture is a critical need of the day. Without this we are in grave danger of failing to solve our internal problems, and we are increasing rather than diminishing the threat of nuclear disaster.

The war industry is a cancer within the body of American society. It has its own mode of growth, it represents a system which is virtually independent and indeed objectively inimical to the welfare of the American people, in spite of the fact that it still visualizes itself as their protector. We have not yet lost civilian control over the war industry, but if this control is not reasserted we are in grave danger of going the way of Japan—a country conquered by its own war industry in the middle thirties, with eventually catastrophic consequences.

6 ☆ THE MILITARY-INDUSTRIAL COMPLEX AND COMMUNICATIONS

THE DOMESTIC COMMUNICATIONS COMPLEX: THE MILITARY-INDUSTRIAL TEAM

Herbert I. Schiller

CONSIDERED BY ITSELF, the military encirclement of governmental communications could be minimized, perhaps, as a temporary consequence of a continuing international emergency. What has been happening, though, gives little support to the notion that this is a transient condition, an interlude that will eventually disappear in a not-too-distant, more settled time. The same forces that have produced the military-industrial complex in American society-at-large have accounted for the rise of a powerful sub-sector, but by no means miniature, complex in communications.

The growth of the electronics industry has been phenomenal. The heavy governmental research and developmental expenditures, under the stimulus of anticipated military advantage, have been concentrated especially in the communications field. As reported in *Business Week* in 1967, "More than half the total R & D done by profit-making corporations this year will be concentrated in two industries—aerospace, and electrical machinery and communications. And these are the two industries in which the National Aeronautics and Space Administration and the Defense Department sink huge sums of research and development money." [1]

[1] "R & D Looms Big in Fiscal Budget," *Business Week*, May 13, 1967, p. 69.

Mass Communications and American Empire (New York: A. Kelley, 1969), chap. 4, pp. 51–62.

In addition to the massive governmental expenditures for technological improvement that have promoted growth in the big private companies, there is also the enormous guaranteed market made available to these same concerns by the continuing military purchases of hardware and systems. Eighteen electronics and communications corporations are represented among the top fifty industrial defense contractors in 1967. More would be included if transport, aircraft and missile-producing companies with substantial electronics productions were included.

Finally, the dynamics of industrial growth have produced a concentration in the electronics industry, in both its hardware and broadcasting sides, that affords an economic leverage difficult to assess but not wise to underestimate. Along with their major manufacturing activities, the electronics equipment producers have been deeply involved in the informational broadcast field as well. The Radio Corporation of America (RCA), for example, was an offshoot in the early 1920s of the Westinghouse, General Electric and American Telephone and Telegraph companies. Since then it has grown into a two billion dollar-plus electronics manufacturer including the ownership of the National Broadcasting Company. NBC, in turn, is a mammoth radio and television concern that owns some of the most influential television and radio stations in the major cities of the country. It operates the second largest TV network in the nation over which its programming reaches into practically every home.

In 1965, the International Telephone and Telegraph Company (ITT), another two billion dollar producer of communications equipment, announced its intention to merge with the American Broadcasting Company (ABC), the nation's third largest radio-television corporation. Though this merger was not consummated, it served to alert whoever chooses to pay attention to the far-reaching pyramiding of information control that is taking place. It is not only a matter of large-scale economic power blocs that exclude competitors in critically sensitive areas. The three national broadcasting companies, CBS, NBC, and ABC, for example, exercise "an almost complete concentration of economic and cultural control—a virtual 'monopoly' or 'triopoly,' if you will, of production and procurement of television programs." [2]

[2] Second Interim Report of the Office of Network Study, *Television Network Procurement Part II* (Washington, D.C.: Federal Communications Commission, 1965), p. 13.

Still more significant, though certainly related, is the emergence of a monopolized informational apparatus which is tightly bound up with an industrial producer interest, itself inseparably connected to the military establishment. In this interlock of powerful interests, the objectivity and reliability of the output of the entire communications machine comes increasingly into doubt. No one seems to know to what extent the military-industrial "partnership" affects the public's access to and the quality of information. One of the chief issues of the contested ITT–ABC merger was the almost disregarded subject of the control and objectivity of electronically-provided news. One pertinent question, asked by the Chairman of the Senate monopoly subcommittee, Senator Gaylord Nelson, touched on this vital matter. "Is it possible," Nelson queried, "that ITT, in view of its large foreign investment in so many nations, will tailor its news commentary and reporting so as to minimize any conflict with local governments?" [3]

Senator Wayne Morse saw another aspect of the problem: "The assurances of ITT that its foreign interests would not in any way interfere with ABC's news coverage is pretty hard for any realistic person to swallow, when the television industry is well known for its very prompt response to the economic pressure of its advertisers." [4]

And, FCC Commissioner Nicholas Johnson, in his dissenting opinion against the merger cut through the legal niceties and took up the jugular issue. He wrote: ". . . scarcely a day can be found in which ITT's economic interests are not affected by some big news event at home or abroad . . . there is only one example of a licensee whose business interests and broadcast properties present a situation in any way comparable to that which we create by this merger. That is the case of RCA's ownership of NBC. That ownership, however, antedated this Commission's existence. It certainly cannot be cited as excuse for allowing a second network to come under the control of a similar company. To say that, since RCA owns NBC, ITT must be allowed to acquire ABC, is to say that things are so bad now there is no point in doing anything now to stop them from getting worse. *I, for one, can see great virtue in having only one-third rather than two-thirds of the major networks owned by corporations heavily engaged in domestic de-*

[3] Gaylord Nelson, letter to Rosel H. Hyde, Chairman, Federal Communications Commission, September 22, 1966.

[4] Senator Wayne Morse, Senate, *Congressional Record,* 90th Cong., 1st Sess., Jan. 19, 1967, p. 572.

fense and space work and in foreign countries. Perhaps we should consider requiring RCA to divest itself of NBC, but nothing could be more absurd than the majority's suggestion that 'We could not in good conscience forbid ABC to merge with ITT without instituting proceedings to separate NBC from RCA.'"[5]

The pressures and interest groups involved in the military-industrial communications complex are stronger than the conventional business biases of advertising sponsors. *Variety* too, has touched on the roots of the danger in a few reportorial commentaries. Headlining the problem on its first page in one issue, the paper declared: "There is a deep undercurrent of concern among critical observers of broadcasting over the strong profit allegiance between the Government and broadcasters through multi-million dollar defense contracts—How, observers are asking, can such special interests be justified when radio and TV stations have become the most important force in mass media news; and especially at so critical a point in history when discerning assessment of Government news is essential . . . ?"[6] Some months later, returning to the same subject, another *Variety* reporter wrote: "Today's broadcast titans, by virtue of parental ties, are simply too enmeshed in war contracting and national-international business."[7] And again, in a comment titled "War Contracts and News Objectivity," the weekly paper of show biz flatly asserted: ". . . it's not unreasonable to conclude that none of the broadcast subsidiaries of war-contracting corporations acquitted its news obligations in a way upsetting to the contractor, the Defense Department."[8]

The web of connections that constitute the communications military-industrial coalition is at the same time formal and unstructured, individual and institutional. Consider, for example, the composition of the Committee on Communications of the National Citizens' Commission on International Cooperation.[9] This ad hoc body of five members, appointed by the President in 1965, to review and report on the role of communications in international cooperation, included three representa-

[5] *The ITT–ABC Merger Case,* Federal Communication Commission, Docket No. 16828, Dissenting Opinion of Commissioner Nicholas Johnson, December 21, 1966. Italics added.

[6] *Variety,* February 23, 1966, p. 1.

[7] *Ibid.,* Dec. 28, 1966, p. 1.

[8] *Ibid.,* June 7, 1967, p. 29.

[9] National Citizens' Commission, *Report of the Committee on Communications,* November 28–December 1, 1965, Washington, D.C.

tives of the most powerful industrial triumvirate in electronics: Harold Geneen, Chairman of the Board and President of the International Telephone and Telegraph Corporation, Frederick R. Kappel, at the time Chairman of the Board of the American Telephone and Telegraph Company, and General David Sarnoff, Chairman of the Board of the Radio Corporation of America. These were very special citizens indeed to be advising the nation about the future of international communications.

As another instance of the concentration of influence that has emerged in the communications structure of the country, the situation of Mr. Frank Stanton, president of the Columbia Broadcasting System (CBS) is instructive. Until very recently, Mr. Stanton wore, all at once, some very intriguing hats. In addition to being president of the nation's most powerful broadcasting system with network connections and radio-tv station-ownership, Mr. Stanton served also as the Chairman of the United States Advisory Commission on Information. The Commission comprises a four-man panel, which, under congressional authorization and presidential appointment, assesses the operations of the United States Information Agency (USIA), the propaganda arm of the American Government overseas, and proposes recommendations for its future.[10]

For ten years, and until early 1967, Mr. Stanton was also the Chairman of the Board of the Rand Corporation, a non-profit California research organization funded almost entirely with Air Force money. The Rand "think-tank" has occupied itself over the years with such questions as "the best way to drop an H-bomb," and "classified counterinsurgency research" among other esoteric subjects.[11]

A fourth hat, still donned by Stanton, is his chairmanship of the Executive Committee of Radio Free Europe. RFE is a private organization which operates broadcasting facilities in Western Europe which are used to transmit programs, for inspiration and "liberation," to Eastern Europe and the Soviet Union. In 1967, Radio Free Europe was uncovered as a conduit for the Central Intelligence Agency and a brief flurry arose in the CBS command about continuing to donate time for RFE's spot announcements and its requests for contributions.

[10] See, for example, *Twenty-Second Report of the U.S. Advisory Commission on Information, 90th Congress, 1st Session,* House Document No. 74, Washington, D.C., 1967.

[11] Richard Reeves, "U.S. Think Tanks: $2-Billion Induction," *The New York Times,* June 12, 1967, pp. 1, 48.

What do Mr. Stanton's activities as president of a great broadcasting system, as well as chairman of a governmental propaganda agency review panel, a Department of Defense-financed research organization, and an unabashed anti-communist broadcast intelligence service signify? No one can be sure and misinterpretation is always possible. But who can feel confident of the character and direction of information transmission in the United States when such conflict-of-interest assignments are simultaneously undertaken by one individual, so influential in the nation's communications structure? Fred Friendly, in reviewing his sixteen years at CBS, the last two of which were as president of CBS News, mentions often Stanton's interventions and his reservations about CBS News programs and reports. Referring to a half-hour interview with Senator Fulbright about the war in Vietnam, Friendly quotes Stanton as saying: "What a dirty trick that was to play on the President of the United States . . . I didn't know about it until I saw the news release." About CBS coverage of Vietnam in general, Friendly reports that Stanton objected to such broadcasts because of "his concern that too much 'dove-hawk' talk unsteadied the hand of the Commander-in-Chief." [12]

More illuminating, perhaps, is Friendly's admission of the constraints under which *he* worked and which were internalized in his own decision-making. Writing of his reactions to management's unceasing interventions, he concludes: "Looking back now, I suppose I was subtly influenced to do controversial subjects in a non-controversial manner." And, ". . . I must confess that in my almost two years as the head of CBS News I tempered my news judgment and tailored my conscience more than once." [13]

Stanton's assignments, conflicting as they were and are, are still the duties of a single individual, and men come and go. Accordingly, only the *flavor* of enormous concentrated influence can be extracted from a single biography, however important the subject may be. More difficult to minimize is the evidence of *structural organization* designed to influence the character and the content of American communications. The existence of permanent, organizational forms with clearly stated objectives introduces us to the visible world of pressure and influence.

[12] Fred W. Friendly, *Due to Circumstances Beyond Our Control* (New York: Random House, 1967), pp. 216–217.

[13] *Ibid.*, pp. 135 and 265.

The organic fusion of the American electronics industry and the military establishment is realized as well as symbolized in a very special organization, the Armed Forces Communications and Electronics Association (AFCEA). David Sarnoff, board chairman of one of the giants of the electronics industry, the Radio Corporation of America, member of the Citizen's Committee on Communications for International Cooperation, and a former president as well as a permanent director of AFCEA, in an address to the Association remarked on ". . . the working alliance of industrial and military leadership represented in this organization." He observed that "it took nearly two centuries and several prolonged conflicts to teach us that the absence of this vital alliance in time of peace could be costly in time of war." Furthermore, Sarnoff noted: "AFCEA has fashioned a community of interest so closely interwoven that whatever affects the progress of one partner is reflected in the progress of the other."[14]

General Sarnoff was not overstating the case. *Signal Magazine*, the organ of the Association, claims that it "serves the industry military team." Founded in 1946, AFCEA is dedicated, in its own words, "to the military-civilian partnership concept." The Association, according to a recent statement of its aims and organization, includes over 60 chapters located throughout the United States, with some overseas chapters as well. A local chapter's primary purpose "is to promote closer personal relationship between its military and industry members and thereby cultivate a more intimate understanding of their mutual problems."

Membership in the Association is open to individuals in the Armed Services as well as individual citizens interested in the objectives of the organization. Although individual annual dues are quite modest ($5.00), the Association apparently relies for most of its financial support on corporate sustaining memberships offered at $1,000 each and on corporate group memberships, each available at $500. Sustaining memberships currently are held by the American Telephone and Telegraph Co. (Long Lines Department, General Dynamics Corporation, International Telephone and Telegraph Co., Litton Industries, Inc., New York Telephone Co., North American Philips Co., Radio Corporation of America, the Western Electric Co., and Western Union Tele-

[14] Address by David Sarnoff at the Annual Convention Banquet, Armed Forces Communications and Electronics Association, Washington, D.C., May 26, 1965.

graph Co. Group memberships number well over 150 United States corporations, most of whom, but by no means all, are engaged in the electronics and communications business.[15]

Not unexpectedly, the officers and directors of the Armed Forces Communications and Electronics Association represent the highest corporate and military echelons and occupy as well the most important governmental posts in these areas. Amongst the directors of the Association are: Lt. General Gordon A. Blake, formerly director of the National Security Agency; Clovis E. Byers, Vice-President of General Telephone and Electronics Corporation; Lt. General Harold W. Grant, USAF, Director of Telecommunications Policy in the Department of Defense; David Sarnoff, Chairman of the Board, RCA; James R. McNitt, President of ITT World Communications; Frederick R. Lack, former vice-president of the Western Electric Company; and Lowell F. Wingert, Vice-president of AT&T. The current president of AFCEA is Dr. John T. Planje, vice-president of North American Philips Co. Amongst the six vice-presidents of the Association is Lt. General R. P. Klocko, who is also the director of the Defense Communications Agency and, at the same time, the manager of the National Communications System.

The recent work experience of a current AFCEA director, Lt. General Gordon A. Blake, USAF (ret.) illustrates the interlocks that so characterize the Association's connections with the many layers and segments of the American communications community. General Blake, before his retirement from the military establishment, was head of the National Security Agency. Coincident with his departure from this post, he was made director of a study, undertaken by the Stanford Research Institute, to review all the aspects of international communications. The Stanford project was commissioned by General O'Connell of the Office of Telecommunications Management in the Office of Emergency Planning. It was financed largely by the Department of Defense.[16] Upon completion of this report, General Blake was named a consultant to Comsat, the communications satellite corporation,[17] half

[15] *Signal*, August, 1966, pp. 67–68.

[16] *Government Use of Satellite Communications*, Hearings before a Subcommittee of the Committee on Government Operations, House of Representatives, *Congressional Record*, 89th Cong., 2nd Sess., Aug. and Sept. 1966, pp. 90, 266.

[17] *Telecommunications Report* (Washington, D.C.: Telecommunications Publishing Co., October 3, 1966), p. 14.

of whose stock is owned by AT&T, RCA, ITT and a couple of other electronics concerns.

In calling the attention of prospective exhibitors to its annual convention in the nation's capital, which is also an electronics show, AFCEA points out that "For the exhibitor, here is where industry really meets the men who know—prominent government and military leaders who have the power of decision. In other words, industry brings its products to the doorway of defense."

The voluntary symbiosis visible in AFCEA, of the military establishment and the electronics industry evolved and is sustained in the market-place. Here the nation's electronics producers find a continuously growing outlet for their wares, provided in large part by an obliging military demand that is seemingly insatiable. The industry sold well over 60% ($12.2 billions) of its output of approximately $23 billion in 1967 to the national government, the overwhelming share of which went to the Armed Forces. It is predictable that one would find that "The great majority of companies manufacturing electronic products are involved in some phase of work for the military" [18] though the percentage of defense business to total revenues varies widely from firm to firm. When government sales are taken to represent military consumption,[19] the dependency of private industry on the military establishment is striking. The volume of this business for some important electronics producers in 1964 is indicated in Table 1.

In the late 1950's, with a far less intense mobilization effort than today, a Department of Defense official estimated that "Over 50 percent of the output of the entire electronics industry is currently involved in the military effort and at least 60 percent of all electronic engineers in the country are now engaged in some degree of work on military programs." [20]

[18] *Standard & Poor's Industry Surveys, Electronic-Electrical Basis Analysis, Oct. 14, 1965* (vol. 133, no. 4P, sec. I), p. 312.

[19] In the fiscal year 1966, the sales of the electronics industry to the Government totaled $9.06 billions. Of this, $7.35 billions were DOD purchases, $1.6 billions expenditures of the National Aeronautics and Space Administration (NASA) and $110 millions, purchases by the Federal Aviation Industry. NASA's work, it should be added, moves in the twilight zone between military and nonmilitary activity. *Electronic Industries Yearbook* (Washington, D.C.: Electronic Industries Association, Marketing Division, 1965).

[20] Statement of Mr. Paul Goldsborough, Special Assistant to the Assistant Secretary of Defense, in *Spectrum Allocation*, Hearings before a subcommittee on the

TABLE 1 1964 Revenues of Leading Electronics Companies and Percentage Represented by Government Sales
In millions of dollars

Industry	*Total Revenues*	*Percentage of government sales to total*
General Electric	4,941	19%
IBM	3,239	10
Westinghouse	2,271	20 [1]
RCA	1,797	25
Sperry Rand [2]	1,248	40
Bendix [3]	742	64
Honeywell	667	32
TRW	553	46
Raytheon	454	85
Burroughs	390	11
Ling-Temco-Vought	323	92
Magnavox	227	21
General Precision Equipment	219	75
Emerson Electric [3]	219	12
Beckman Instruments	101	24

Source: Standard & Poor's Industry Surveys, Electronics-Electrical Basic Analysis, October 14, 1965 (vol. 133, no. 4P, sec. I), p. 312.

[1] Includes atomic energy product sales.

[2] Fiscal year ended March 31, 1965, 1964.

[3] Fiscal year ended September 30, 1964, 1963.

THE IMPACT OF RESEARCH AND DEVELOPMENT

A factor sometimes overlooked in the dynamics of the military-industrial alliance is the ability of the power-concentrate to continuously extend itself. This occurs as a natural consequence of the forces already in motion. Take for instance the matter of research and development. Receiving a great share of the funds appropriated for scientific inquiry,[21] Department of Defense contract researchers will produce, it is to be expected, a large portion of the new scientific and technical

Committee on Interstate and Foreign Commerce, House of Representatives, *Congressional Record*, 86th Cong., 1st Sess., June 8 and 9, 1959, p. 181.

[21] In the President's budget for fiscal year 1967, the military component of the research and development category amounted to well over 80 percent of the total amount requested. "R & D Funds Show Effects of a Tough Budget Year," *Science* 151, no. 3709 (1966): 425–428.

knowledge becoming available. One consequence of this pattern is that entirely new fields of study, as well as their practical application, become the exclusive preserves of the Armed Forces. The question naturally arises: Is this a custodianship in which a democratic society can have confidence? Military control of the discovery process automatically confers on the controller proprietary rights. When the security and survivability of the nation can also be invoked, an even tighter control is exerted. The knowledge sooner or later is applied practically and becomes functional in plants and equipment. At this point, economics takes over. The resultant facilities constitute the fixed costs that in themselves become a great inertial force, repulsing further efforts at change. Certainly this has characterized the scientific study of the radio spectrum to date. First, there is the advantage that discovery confers. The testimony of a former Administrator of the Federal Aviation Agency is instructive: ". . . As you expand the use of the spectrum, you do so in large blocks, so to speak. You don't eventually find a means of using a discrete frequency; you develop a technique of using a broad band of frequencies. Now if the experience of the future follows the experience of the past, it is going to follow that the Government is going to find ways and means of using the unusable parts of the spectrum. It follows that the agency of government that develops a means or a technique to use an unused portion of the spectrum will assume ownership thereof . . ." [22]

The "agency of government" that will be developing new portions of the spectrum, in all likelihood, already is the Department of Defense.

On another occasion, FCC Commissioner T. Craven told a congressional committee how the application of newly discovered technology quickly freezes the pattern and makes alternate arrangements extremely difficult, if not unthinkable: "Some time after World War II, when the problem (of unifying the control of governmental and private communications facilities) became acute, because during the war it was necessary for the military to utilize the then World War II technology to increase their communications systems, they found there were billions of dollars of investment that is very hard to undo. That is one of the major problems, as I see it, in spectrum management—what do you do with the invested capital?" [23]

[22] Testimony of General E. R. Quesada, Administrator, Federal Aviation Agency, in *Spectrum Allocation, op. cit.*, p. 198.

[23] Statement of FCC Commissioner T. A. M. Craven, *Space Communications*

In short, the mechanics are simple and automatic. Control of research enjoys an already-privileged position that is powerful enough to secure the research appropriations in the first place. The fruits of discovery further strengthen the existing power structure and, when applied practically, the material investment becomes a new obstacle to further change and flexibility.

Intolerable conditions in a changing world are defying American efforts at stabilization. The possibilities of social revolution across the globe are interpreted by American business as so many threats to its own existence and expansion. At the same time they are presented to the American public as a danger to the national security. Annual defense appropriations have risen to where they begin to approach the levels of all-out spending in World War II. These huge expenditures offer a large and secure outlet to some of the nation's most powerful businesses, producing goods and services (of broadcasting) in the most technologically advanced sectors of industry. The mutual reinforcement that the military and the communications industry power concentrates offer each other is strengthened additionally by their deep penetration into the highest levels of the governmental bureaucracy. Their extraordinary positions of authority are yet further advanced by control over the most sensitive and influential of the 20th century's power mechanisms. They dominate the nation's informational apparatus and its mass communications. In this setting of almost total electronic omnipotence, challenges to the direction and thrust of American policy, domestic and international, need desperately to find new channels for expression.

---

and Allocation of Radio Spectrum, 1961, Hearings before the Communications Subcommittee of the Committee on Commerce, Senate, 87th Cong., 1st Sess. in Space Communications, and S. J. Res. 32, Aug. 1, 23, 24, 1961, Washington, D.C.

7 ☆ SCIENCE AND THE UNIVERSITIES IN THE MILITARY-INDUSTRIAL COMPLEX

THE WAR AND ITS EFFECTS: THE MILITARY–INDUSTRIAL–ACADEMIC COMPLEX

J. William Fulbright

Mr. FULBRIGHT. Mr. President, today I resume my comments on the Vietnamese war and its far-ranging effects. In the first half of my statement I questioned the assumption on which the American war policy is based and suggested what seem to me to be the principal causes of the deep and widening division among the American people. Today I shall point to some of the destructive effects of the war upon our domestic life—to the growing militarization of the economy and the universities, to the deepening crisis of poverty and race, and to the underlying question of America's concept of herself, either as a traditional world empire as we seem to be becoming, or as an example of creative democracy, as we have traditionally regarded ourselves.

THE MILITARY-INDUSTRIAL-ACADEMIC COMPLEX

While young dissenters plead for resurrection of the American promise, their elders continue to subvert it. As if it were something to be

Congressional Record, 90th Cong., 1st Sess., December 13, 1967, vol. 113, pt. 27, pp. 36181–36184.

very proud of, it was announced not long ago that the war in Vietnam had created a million new jobs in the United States. Our country is becoming conditioned to permanent conflict. More and more our economy, our Government, and our universities are adapting themselves to the requirements of continuing war—total war, limited war, and cold war. The struggle against militarism into which we were drawn 26 years ago has become permanent, and for the sake of conducting it, we are making ourselves into a militarized society.

I do not think the military-industrial complex is the conspiratorial invention of a band of "merchants of death." One almost wishes that it were, because conspiracies can be exposed and dealt with. But the components of the new American militarism are too diverse, independent, and complex for it to be the product of a centrally directed conspiracy. It is rather the inevitable result of the creation of a huge, permanent military establishment, whose needs have given rise to a vast private defense industry tied to the Armed Forces by a natural bond of common interest. As the largest producer of goods and services in the United States, the industries and businesses that fill military orders will in the coming fiscal year pour some $45 billion into over 5,000 cities and towns where over 8 million Americans, counting members of the Armed Forces, comprising approximately 10 percent of the labor force, will earn their living from defense spending. Together all these industries and employees, drawing their income from the $75 billion defense budget, form a giant concentration of socialism in our otherwise free enterprise economy.

Unplanned though it was, this complex has become a major political force. It is the result rather than the cause of American military involvements around the world; but, composed as it is of a vast number of citizens—not tycoons or "merchants of death" but ordinary, good American citizens—whose livelihood depends on defense production, the military-industrial complex has become an indirect force for the perpetuation of our global military commitments. This is not—and I emphasize "not"—because anyone favors war but because every one of us has a natural and proper desire to preserve the sources of his livelihood. For the defense worker this means preserving or obtaining some local factory or installation and obtaining new defense orders; for the labor union leader it means jobs for his members at abnormally high wages; for the politician it means preserving the good will of his constituents by helping them to get what they want. Every time a new program, such as Mr. McNamara's $5 billion "thin" antiballistic missile system, is introduced, a powerful new constituency is created—a constituency that will strive mightily to protect the new program and, in the case of the ABM, turn the "thin" system into a "thick" one, a movement already underway according to reports in the press. The constituency-building process is further advanced by the perspicacity of Defense officials and contractors in locating installations and plants in the districts of influential key Members of Congress.

In this natural way generals, industrialists, businessmen, labor leaders, workers, and politicians have joined together a military-industrial complex—a complex which, for all the inadvertency of its creation and the innocent intentions of its participants, has nonetheless become a powerful new force for the perpetuation of foreign military commitments, for the introduction and expansion of expensive weapons systems, and, as a result, for the militarization of large segments of our national life. Most interest groups are counterbalanced by other interest groups, but the defense complex is so much larger than any other that there is no effective counterweight to it except concern as to its impact on the part of some of our citizens and a few of our leaders, none of whom have material incentive to offer.

The universities might have formed an effective counterweight to the military-industrial complex by strengthening their emphasis on the traditional values of our democracy, but many of our leading universities have instead joined the monolith, adding greatly to its power and influence. Disappointing though it is, the adherence of the professors is not greatly surprising. No less than businessmen, workers, and politicians, professors like money and influence. Having traditionally been deprived of both, they have welcomed the contracts and consultantships offered by the Military Establishment.

The great majority of American professors are still teaching students and engaging in scholarly research, but some of the most famous of our academicians have set such activities aside in order to serve their government, especially those parts of the government which are primarily concerned with war.

The bonds between the Government and the universities are no more the results of a conspiracy than those between Government and business. They are an arrangement of convenience, providing the Government with politically usable knowledge and the universities with badly needed funds. Most of these funds go to large institutions which need them less than some smaller and less well-known ones, but they do on the whole make a contribution to higher learning, a contribution, however, which is purchased at a high price.

That price is the surrender of independence, the neglect of teaching, and the distortion of scholarship. A university which has become accustomed to the inflow of government contract funds is likely to emphasize activities which will attract those funds. These, unfortunately, do not include teaching undergraduates and the kind of scholarship which, though it may contribute to the sum of human knowledge and to man's understanding of himself, is not salable to the Defense Department or the CIA. As Clark Kerr, former president of the University of California, expressed it: "The real problem is not one of Federal control but of Federal influence. A Federal agency offers a project. The university need not accept, but as a practical matter, it usually does. . . . Out of this reality have followed many of the consequences of Federal aid for the universities; and they have been substantial. That they are subtle, slowly cumulative and gentlemanly makes them all the more potent." [1]

From what one hears the process of acquiring Government contracts is not always passive and gentlemanly.

"One of the dismal sights in American higher education"—writes Robert M. Rosenzweig, associate dean of the Stanford University graduate division—

> is that of administrators scrambling for contracts for work which does not emerge from the research or teaching interests of their faculty. The result of this unseemly enterprise is bound to be a faculty coerced or seduced into secondary lines of interest, or a frantic effort to secure nonfaculty personnel to meet the contractual obligations. Among the most puzzling aspects of such arrangements is the fact that Government agencies have permitted and even encouraged them. Not only are they harmful to the universities—which is not, of course, the Government's prime concern—but they insure that the Government will not get what it is presumably buying; namely, the intellectual and technical resources of the academic community. It is simply a bad bargain all the way around.[2]

[1] Clark Kerr, *The Uses of the University* (Cambridge: Harvard University Press, 1964), pp. 57–58.

[2] Quoted in Walter Adams and Adrian Jaffe, *Government, the Universities, and International Affairs: A Crisis in Identity*, Special Report Prepared for the U.S. Advisory Commission on International Educational and Cultural Affairs, 90th Cong., 1st Sess., House Document No. 120 (Washington: U.S. Government Printing Office, 1967), pp. 5–6.

Commenting on these tendencies, a special report on government, the universities and international affairs, prepared for the U.S. Advisory Commission on International Educational and Cultural Affairs, points out that—"The eagerness of university administrations to undertake stylized, Government-financed projects has caused a decline in self-generated commitments to scholarly pursuits, has produced baneful effects on the academic mission of our universities, and has, in addition, brought forward some bitter complaints from the disappointed clients." [3]

Among the baneful effects of the Government-university contract system the most damaging and corrupting are the neglect of the university's most important purpose, which is the education of its students, and the taking into the Government camp of scholars, especially those in the social sciences, who ought to be acting as responsible and independent critics of their Government's policies. The corrupting process is a subtle one: no one needs to censor, threaten, or give orders to contract scholars; without a word of warning or advice being uttered, it is simply understood that lucrative contracts are awarded not to those who question their Government's policies but to those who provide the Government with the tools and techniques it desires. The effect, in the words of the report to the Advisory Commission on International Education, is—"To suggest the possibility to a world—never adverse to prejudice—that academic honesty is no less marketable than a box of detergent on the grocery shelf." [4]

The formation of a military-industrial complex, for all its baneful consequences, is the result of great numbers of people engaging in more or less normal commercial activities. The adherence of the universities, though no more the result of a plan or conspiracy, nonetheless involves something else: the neglect and if carried far enough the betrayal, of the university's fundamental reason for existence, which is the advancement of man's search for truth and happiness. It is for this purpose, and this purpose alone, that universities receive—and should receive—the community's support in the form of grants, loans and tax exemptions.

When the university turns away from its central purpose and makes itself an appendage to the Government, concerning itself with techniques rather than purposes, with expedients rather than ideals, dis-

[3] *Ibid.*, p. 6.
[4] *Ibid.*, p. 8.

pensing conventional orthodoxy rather than new ideas, it is not only failing to meet its responsibilities to its students; it is betraying a public trust.

This betrayal is most keenly felt by the students, partly because it is they who are being denied the services of those who ought to be their teachers, they to whom knowledge is being dispensed wholesale in cavernous lecture halls, they who must wait weeks for brief audiences with important professors whose time is taken up by travel and research connected with Government contracts. For all these reasons the students feel themselves betrayed, but it is doubtful that any of these is the basic cause of the angry rebellions which have broken out on so many campuses.

It seems more likely that the basic cause of the great trouble in our universities is the student's discovery of corruption in the one place, besides perhaps the churches, which might have been supposed to be immune from the corruptions of our age. Having seen their country's traditional values degraded in the effort to attribute moral purpose to an immoral war, having seen their country's leaders caught in inconsistencies which are politely referred to as a "credibility gap," they now see their universities—the last citadels of moral and intellectual integrity—lending themselves to ulterior and expedient ends, and betraying their own fundamental purpose, which, in James Bryce's words, is to "reflect the spirit of the times without yielding to it."

8 ☆ LABOR AND THE MILITARY-INDUSTRIAL COMPLEX

THE INTERNATIONAL ROLE OF THE AFL–CIO

George Meany

MR. CHAIRMAN: I wish to express my appreciation for this opportunity to appear before the Senate Foreign Relations Committee and to clarify the role of the AFL–CIO internationally. I also appear to describe the work of the American Institute for Free Labor Development [AIFLD] in Latin America since its effectiveness was challenged at a hearing of this Committee on July 14, 1969, according to UPI press reports published throughout the United States and Latin America, which I quote:

> Chairman J. William Fulbright of the Senate Foreign Relations Committee suggested today that funds for an AFL–CIO labor institute in Latin America had been "the price we paid" for President George Meany's support of the U.S. policy in Vietnam.
>
> Fulbright said he hoped the Nixon Administration would review the program, for which U.S. Government auditors could find "no specific conclusions on the relative success."
>
> AID administrator John A. Hannah said he would look into it.
>
> Fulbright said the program had involved close to $20 million since its inception. It included Alliance for Progress funds, channeled into the American Institute for Free Labor Development with the stated purpose of strengthening the democratic trade union leadership in Latin America.

Statement before the Senate Foreign Relations Committee, August 1, 1969.

The new aid bill contains $1 million for the Institute during the coming year. It is administered by the AFL–CIO.

"I have wondered if this represented the price we paid for Mr. Meany's support in Vietnam," Fulbright said. "He was a stalwart supporter of the previous administration policies, but I should not think the new administration would feel indebted to him."

On that occasion, Secretary of State Rogers was asked a question by the Chairman concerning funds allocated to the AIFLD under its contract with the Agency for International Development. He said, "Is this the price we pay them to support us in Vietnam?" According to the transcript of the Committee hearing at that session, the Chairman also quoted from a letter dated May 20, 1968, addressed to him, signed by Mr. Elmer B. Staats, Comptroller General of the United States, which he read as follows: ". . . We are not able during our review to reach any specific conclusion on the relative success of the institute as an instrument for achieving U.S. foreign policy objectives in the labor sector. . . ." Based upon this sentence from the Staats' letter and two newspaper articles which he subsequently inserted into the Record, the Chairman concluded that there is "considerable doubt about the effectiveness" of the AIFLD work in Latin America. Further, according to the transcript, the Chairman indicated that in a number of countries the AIFLD labor institutes have been closed down by the host country for meddling in internal politics.

It is interesting to note that Chairman Fulbright read only the opening sentence of a paragraph from the Staats' letter that attempted to evaluate the work of the Institute.

I would like to read into the Record the full evaluation, the complete paragraph of GAO Comptroller Staats' letter from which that sentence was taken: ". . . We were not able during our review to reach any specific conclusion on the relative success of the institute as an instrument for achieving U.S. foreign policy objectives in the labor sector. *We agree that* (emphasis mine) the institute represents a realistic and imaginative approach to some of the major problems of the Western Hemisphere. For example, it provides a means whereby the workers of Latin America can participate in the Alliance for Progress and become more active in the economic and social progress of their countries . . ."

To us it is most incomprehensible that the Chairman of this Committee in effect took a sentence out of context from a paragraph in the

GAO letter which was obviously intended to be quite complimentary of the AIFLD, giving it credit for having "a realistic and imaginative approach" and "providing a means whereby the workers can participate in the Alliance for Progress."

As to the statement that some in-country institutes had been closed down by the host countries, I wish to state very clearly and simply that this is not true. The AIFLD has never been closed down in any country anywhere. I state categorically that the AIFLD, which is now operating in more than 20 countries and territories in the Western Hemisphere, has been specifically invited by the workers in the trade union movement in each of these countries. We are proud of our long-standing fraternal relationships with these workers.

The AFL–CIO has always insisted on a deep sense of fiscal responsibility and we expect and welcome the continued scrutiny by the General Accounting Office and the Agency for International Development. This is as it should be especially because we are aware that we are using public funds under contract. Our policy has always been one of complete and total cooperation with both of these agencies of government. Moreover, I want to assure each and every member of this Committee that we welcome criticism. We are learning as we go on with our work in this comparatively new field. But we do not equate unfounded and carping accusations with constructive criticism.

We are thoroughly familiar with the report made by the GAO to this Committee in May, 1968, which was included in a Committee print of the Senate Foreign Relations Committee's Subcommittee on American Republics Affairs entitled, "Survey of the Alliance for Progress Labor Policies and Programs." We were assured by Senator Wayne Morse, the then Chairman of the Subcommittee, that this report, prepared by a Mr. Robert H. Dockery, was still *only a staff report despite the fact that it appeared in Committee Print*. We did note, of course, the disclaimer in the introduction to the report which stated that it did not express the official view of the Subcommittee. Nevertheless, it was released to the public, picked up by unfriendly news media throughout the world and made to appear as an attack by the Senate Subcommittee on the AIFLD.

In a letter of August 5, 1968, to Senator Morse, I stated that the AIFLD has submitted a memorandum concerning the GAO report, which you will find on page 80 of the Committee Print. I also pointed out that the Subcommittee report "contains quite a number of inaccuracies," that "the author made little attempt to make a balanced assessment" and further that "the document reflects preconceived and biased viewpoints without any foundation in fact."

In view of the unfounded assertions and conclusions of that report, we had requested that the Subcommittee on American Republics Affairs issue as a Committee Print my letter of August 5, 1968 to Senator Morse, which included the AIFLD analysis of the "Dockery Report" and also to include in such Committee Print the AIFLD response to an extensive Subcommittee questionnaire regarding AIFLD activities dated July 25, 1967. Since Communist and other extremist elements throughout the world continue to utilize this biased anti-labor report of the Subcommittee as part of their incessant propaganda against the efforts of our country to improve the lot of the working man under the Alliance for Progress, we reiterate this request. I am sure this Committee, in the interest of fairness, will honor our request that our reply be issued as a Committee Print.

We had an agreement with Senator Morse that, soon after the elections last November, a special meeting of the Subcommittee would be held, giving us the opportunity to set forth our viewpoints regarding the Dockery Report. However, the Subcommittee hearing was never held because the Senator became involved in a vote recount in Oregon and other matters. Nevertheless, the Senator was kind enough to include our answers in the Congressional Record.

At this point, I would like to submit our replies to the aforementioned Subcommittee questionnaire of July 25, 1967, my letter to Senator Morse of August 5, 1968, and the entire Dockery Report, including the GAO report, as a part of the Record of this hearing. In addition, I would also like to put into the Record the reply of Senator Morse to my letter of August 5, 1968 in which Senator Morse agreed to schedule a public hearing by the Subcommittee in which myself and other spokesmen of the AFL–CIO could present their views to the Subcommittee. This public hearing, promised by Senator Morse on this matter, has not been held to date.

It is a gratuitous insult to the American labor movement to accuse us of receiving a payoff for supporting the foreign policy of any administration. We are indeed proud of our support of the U.S. government during World War II, during the Korean War and during the war that is now taking place in Vietnam. Our official attitude regarding Vietnam was first made known in a resolution which was adopted by the then American Federation of Labor Executive Council as long ago as May, 1954. I ask that a copy of this resolution be placed in the Record. [Insert A] Then as now, our solution to the Vietnam situation called for a peaceful settlement through free elections. We further proposed to the Senate Foreign Relations Committee and the Administration in 1954 that the following measures, amongst others, be adopted: 1. that there should be a special session of the United Nations General Assembly mobilizing world support for ending the war in Indochina, safeguarding its national independence and territorial integrity and helping in its reconstruction; 2. that the special session of the U.N. General Assembly should insist on the full application of the principle of free elections in Indochina; and 3. that within the provisions of the U.N. Charter a regional defense organization should be established to build a Pacific Alliance for Peace and Freedom.

It is my opinion that the fundamental issues of national independence and territorial integrity are as valid today as in 1954.

Our involvement with Latin America stems from 1916 when the American Federation of Labor joined with Latin American Labor leaders to found the Pan American Federation of Labor. After World War II we expanded significantly our activities throughout the world, including Latin America where we helped to establish the first Inter-American Conference of Workers. In 1951, we also helped to establish the Inter-American Regional Organization of Workers which exists actively to this day, and is known as the ORIT.

In August 1960, when we came to a full realization as to what happened to the Cuban workers and the entire Cuban people under Castro, the AFL–CIO appropriated $20 thousand for the purpose of studying the establishment of a mechanism through which we could help to strengthen the free labor unions of Latin America and develop trade union leadership. This led to the creation of the AIFLD, during the Eisenhower Administration and long before the establishment of the Alliance for Progress.

We did not then and do not now want our Latin American trade union brothers to pattern their unions after our organizations in the United States.

We do expect and hope, however, that they will build unions which are strong, independent, representative of the workers and capable, through their own efforts, of improving the conditions of the workers, and making a contribution to the economic development of their own countries.

Throughout the years we had always wanted to see Latin American trade unionists and workers build a more effective labor movement. We hoped we could assist them to make significant contributions of their own to the economic and social development of their own countries.

Now, you might ask, "Why do we have this interest? Why would American unions have an interest in the situations in Latin America, in the workers of Latin America?"

The AFL–CIO has always had an interest in workers in every part of the world. That is fraternal solidarity, humanitarianism in the best sense of the word. We have a stake in the freedom of workers everywhere. We have learned from experience that when workers in other countries lose their freedom where they are forced to submit to the yoke of a dictatorship or tyrannical government of any kind, their repression and enslavement constitute a grave threat to our own freedom. And of course, we have learned from the history of recent years that the very first to lose their freedoms are the workers. For these reasons, AFL–CIO international activities have always been extensive so that in addition to the AIFLD in Latin America, we sponsor institutes conducting a broad range of similar assistance in Africa and Asia. I would like to emphasize, Mr. Chairman, that we are not looking for or trying to recruit members for the AFL–CIO in any country of any of these continents.

In view of our extensive international activities, on which we spend about 20% of our income, it was only natural when we looked at Latin America, our closest neighbors in the trade union field, we felt that we had a responsibility as workers to workers—yes, a great humanitarian responsibility—to be of help. We also felt, as American citizens, that it was certainly in the interest of our country that free governments be achieved and maintained in the Western Hemisphere. Now I'm not going to tell you that we have never made mistakes or performed miracles. Latin America still has its great problems. For example, there is still too much money being spent for unnecessary military hardware in many countries and too little being spent on the welfare of the people. But we are trying to make a contribution to help the working people of these lands play a constructive role in building democratic societies through free trade unions.

The AFL–CIO Executive Council decided *unanimously* that we should bring enlightened American business into this institution on the theory that they should also have an interest in developing a friendly attitude towards the building of free societies in Latin America. They naturally want to do business there, and they certainly want to do business with countries that have viable economies. We feel that you cannot have a viable economy unless you have the positive participation of all segments of the society, especially the workers who are the most important element of production and consumption. So we went to American business, and we told them why we thought they should cooperate. We got a most encouraging response.

The result is that we have some outstanding American businessmen contributing to the work of the AIFLD including Peter Grace, our chairman, President of the W. R. Grace Company; Mr. William Hickey, President of the United Corporation; Mr. H. W. Balgooyen, Director of EBASCO Industries; Mr. Berent Friele, Senior Vice President, American International Association for Economic and Social Development; Mr. Juan Trippe, founder and for many years head of Pan American Airways; Mr. Henry Woodbridge of the True Temper Corporation, among others. We have several outstanding businessmen sitting on the Board of Trustees, headed by our Chairman, J. Peter Grace. It should be noted that in going to these businessmen, we told them quite frankly what we wanted to do; namely, to help strengthen free trade unions in Latin America.

At this point I would like to submit for the Record a list of the American corporations and individual businessmen who have contributed to the AIFLD. [Insert B]

The AFL–CIO feels that in our democratic society the voluntary organizations have a great role to play in influencing and molding the foreign relations of our country. This is our responsibility as citizens and trade unionists. While we welcome and appreciate the assistance AIFLD has received from our government through the A.I.D. in order to carry out our programs, we would also like to point out that contributions in excess of $2,300,000 have been made to our work in Latin America from the AFL–CIO and the listed corporations. In addition, the AFL–CIO and U.S. private investors have themselves committed $31 million for low-cost worker housing sponsored by AIFLD.

. . . In summary, I would like to remind the members of this Committee that our work in Latin America has been based upon the sincere feeling of fraternity and solidarity that exists between the workers of the U.S. and the workers to the South. We are there by invitation to carry on a program designed to help people develop a fuller and happier life without violating their culture and traditions. Frankly speaking, we vigorously oppose many of the military establishments that are now in power and we are saddened by the awful reality that the gap between the very rich and the very poor continues to grow. However, we think that we have taken the initiative in the area of strengthening free trade unions which will enable the Latin American workers to participate meaningfully in their own development.

I think we are on the right track, and I am proud of my part in it, and I resent any inference from any source that the government assistance given to us in carrying out this vital and important work is a payoff of any kind.

9 ☆ DEFENDERS OF THE COMPLEX

THE MEN, THE MACHINES, THE MAKERS

Paul Thayer

THANK YOU for that wonderful introduction. Actually, you made it sound like I couldn't hold a job.

I would like to say at the outset that it gives me great pleasure and pride to address this group this morning. Knowing as many aerospace writers as I do, I feel that we speak each other's language, and that's comforting for a change. I therefore feel secure that anything I have to say today will not be heavily diluted or blown out of proportion by "translation."

I don't intend to be especially cautious in my remarks today because my topic has been so widely discussed and so poorly stated by so many people with divergent views that it's high time for some top people in our business to step up to the subject and "tell it like it is."

My subject is, "The Men, The Machines, The Makers." We all realize that I could have said, "the Military-Industrial Complex." As a matter of fact, the Military-Industrial Complex is my topic but I want to address it in the three parts identified in the title.

Many of us have become deeply concerned by certain political leaders, university professors, authors and even a segment of the news media who have made some very loose statements about a very complex subject.

They appear to have a "complex" about a complex. This would not bother me except that lately so many of the speakers that address themselves to the subject leave the implication that this so-called complex is too big. Being big, it is therefore dangerous, and a threat

Keynote address to the 1969 Annual News Conference and Meeting of the Aviation/Space Writers Association, Dayton, Ohio, May 12, 1969.

whose influence is detrimental to the best interests of our country—Nonsense!

Now with regard to that part of my talk devoted to *The Men* I find some self-appointed experts strongly suggesting that the military—especially those recently retired with the equivalent rank of colonel or above—have joined the industrial complex in some unholy alliance to perpetuate the arms race and foster conflict.

Let me assure you that I am not on this platform as a spokesman for the military establishment of the United States of America. The Eisenhowers, the Marshalls, the Halseys, the Arnolds, the Pattons, the MacArthurs, the Wheelers, and the millions of other uniformed men, past and present, neither ask for, nor need, such support. Their conduct, their records and their dedication speak with sufficient clarity.

I also know from serving under, and working with, and working for, many of our national military leaders that they are too dedicated, and have too much character, to mount the public platform in order to refute the malicious charges being leveled against them and their retired members; they refuse to lend such loose talk that much dignity.

I can only sympathize with these fine men as they suffer in silence the insinuation that they have compromised the integrity for which they are renowned for the sake of a few dollars. It is so preposterous to me that it's almost laughable—if it weren't so serious—that pseudo-experts in our universities write whole books on this subject. They organize a research team, which practically anyone can do in a week's time, and plot the course of retired military officers. From this antiseptic collection of facts—seldom balanced by any personal experience in either the top echelons of industry or the military—they then draw the conclusion that retired military men who are employed by industry constitute, and I quote, "a most dangerous and shocking situation."

I can speak from personal experience that I have never met a general who wanted to go to war—and I can also say that I have never met one who backed away from a war he was dealt—and further, I can also say that I have never met one who deliberately planned to procure equipment that would not enhance his chances of winning a war.

The military man is dedicated to defend his country if it is threatened, but to imply that this would lead him to create an international crisis for personal advancement is absolute rot. Today in Viet Nam, as in all recent conflicts, the military man is merely following instructions. He is not, by any stretch of the imagination, operating outside of a set of constricting instructions set down by his civilian superiors.

Day and night, year in and year out, some lonely military sentinel mans the "crow's nest"; another man stands the "midnight watch" and yet another flies the "dawn patrol." This they don't do because they enjoy the taste of salt, the risk of darkness or the peril of a new military day. No, they do it because it has become their tradition; drawn from the Constitution, *"to ensure domestic tranquillity and to provide for the common defense."*

Now to slide into the second phase of my remarks—*"The Machines."* Public attacks are being leveled almost daily at our weapons systems. Some critics go back as far as the 1950s to disclose, with great fanfare, all the systems that were funded and found lacking. The costs of these systems are tabulated as proof of a tremendous and stupendous waste of funds on so-called military equipment blunders.

Reasonable men should be rational enough when examining complex weapons systems to understand that failures themselves in many cases serve the useful purpose of pointing the way to workable, efficient and economical systems later downstream.

If anyone would compare the total dollars spent on projects that have been cancelled before deployment against the total dollars expended in the procurement of weapons systems, they would find that the "blunders" represent a very small fraction of the total.

I certainly don't have to enumerate before this audience the staggering list of unprecedented first-class hardware we have built. It is worthwhile to mention that within the time span in question our magnificent come-from-behind space effort last Christmas orbited the first human beings around the moon. I might add, these human beings were the same so-called potentially corrupt military men and they piloted a vehicle produced by the "scandalous" American industrial complex.

I am not prepared to speculate on what might have happened had we not maintained a strong military posture to support our national objectives and policies during the 50s and 60s. I must assume though, that were we caught in a weakened state, our avowed enemies might well have seized the opportunity to hasten the demise of the democracy that Karl Marx was so certain would destroy itself without outside influence.

I wonder if those so critical of our military hardware would care to speculate whether Russia would have removed the missiles from

Cuba were it not for the overwhelming military force President Kennedy was able to concentrate, on such short notice, in our southern states.

In my view, world opinion is that we have not always been consistent in our foreign or domestic policies or actions. But, make no mistake, this same world opinion will readily admit that the American military/industrial might has been sufficient to rectify or neutralize any inadequacy caused by the other weaknesses inherent in our democratic form of government.

Now let's consider that portion of the American free enterprise system that I call the "*Weapons Makers*." Please don't let this fresh, new term throw you. You have heard it described more often as "war monger," "merchants of death" or again, the "Military-Industrial Complex."

It is rather difficult to define all that the United States military weapons makers are accused of except that we allegedly extract profits which are not earned from our defense budget and entice key military officers in retired and active status to assist us in this overall vicious scheme to dupe the public and work against the national interest.

We find strong indictments by normally responsible political figures such as: "the Military-Industrial Complex of this country is preparing its greatest coup, one that will make all previous robberies of the public purse seem like petty thievery." The same individual who made that statement also said "a vast complex of defense-oriented firms have made a fortune from supplying armaments to the U.S. government."

The allegations are so numerous that it is pointless to attempt to comment upon all of them so I will confine my reply, and directly, to the issues concerning the use of retired military personnel in defense-oriented industries and the alleged excess profits being made in the past ten years by the so-called defense contractor "fat cats."

It has been cited, again and again, that in the past ten years over 2,000 retired officers in the equivalent rank of colonel and above have taken positions with the 100 largest defense contractors in the United States. One of our leading political figures often repeats this fact; but he then goes on to say that he does not claim, or even suggest, that any conspiracy exists between the military men and the contractors. He also charges no general wrong-doing on the part of either group.

My only question then is, why was he so concerned that he had the statistics entered in the Congressional Record including:

a) Naming each of the contractors.
b) The number of high-ranking retired officers each employs.
c) A comparison of 1969 employment statistics with the 1958 employment statistics.
d) Listing the names of the officers with each of the 100 contractors by first, middle and last name.

Yet this same individual says, "we should eschew even the slightest suggestion of any conspiracy between the Pentagon on the one hand, and the companies who hire former employees on the other. There is not a scintilla of evidence that it exists." May I ask then—what is his point?

Next he reports "that this is a most dangerous and shocking situation and the trend does represent a distinct threat to the public interest." He then switches around in his conclusion to say that he is not charging that this is necessarily wrong but merely that it is true. He states that former high-ranking officers have personal friendships—which most people do not have—with those still at the Pentagon. But again, he charges no specific wrong-doing.

I become so confused when I wade through this vacillating good guy, bad guy, good guy harangue that I can only assume that the author hopes that his readers and listeners will charge the retired military officer with disloyalty and lack of dedication. He would like someone else to draw a conclusion that for some reason he does not quite want to do himself.

Recently from a speech by a high-ranking national political figure at a midwestern university, we see such shocking allegations as—"spawned by our global military involvements the Military-Industrial Complex has become a powerful force for the *perpetuation of these involvements.*" To this he added—"In armament as in other lines of work it is not the price received but the service rendered *that gives a profession its name.*" If that were not enough he then informed the students that the universities have been drawn primarily into military research in the physical and social sciences, becoming in the process, "*card-carrying*" (his phrase) members of the Military-Industrial Complex.

With respected public citizens, in high government positions, making public statements such as these on our campuses, it does not surprise me one iota that the existence of our Reserve Officer Training Corps is being threatened and that students rise up in militant protest against the efforts of American defense industries to recruit graduating students for employment.

I have not been ordained by the American industrial complex to act as a spokesman on their behalf. On my *own* behalf, since I am one of the Corporate Presidents whose company employs retired high-ranking military officers and is proud of it; and because we also deal in military hardware, I feel I am in a position to state my own case.

First, I wholeheartedly subscribe to the need of the freedom to use retired military talent in our defense industries today—and in the future. But, I do not consider this a one-way street. I also feel that competent civilians from defense industries, regardless of their company, should continue in the future as they have in the past, to fill responsible positions in the Department of Defense.

This exchange, in my opinion, has led to an increased ability by all categories of civilian and military personnel in arriving at sound conclusions in the complicated process of evaluating national-security threats, establishing defense requirements, assessing technical capabilities and maintaining a competitive environment in the procurement of military hardware.

Now, *if* we found that the 2,000-plus officers who work for defense contractors were all working for *one* contractor or even if they worked for only the top ten contractors, we might have cause for concern. But, since they are in fact distributed among 100 competing firms, it would be naive not to recognize that this establishes a highly competitive intracontractor environment.

If it is considered unreasonable or dangerous to have retired military men employed by defense industries we should then advance this argument to its logical conclusion. Let's prohibit any federally connected employee (hired, elected, or appointed) from holding a position with industry where he can put his demonstrated skill and dedication to work. Let's see that former Bureau of the Budget or Auditor General personnel cannot be employed by lending institutions or banks. Let's see that no member of the Federal Judiciary can serve as legal counsel for or against defense industries. Let's see that no member of the Department of Transportation can be employed by a rail, airplane, or automobile company.

Obviously, this is ridiculous but it is also equally ridiculous to give credence to the slander campaign currently being carried out against a selected number of individuals and a selected segment of American industry.

As to the charge that excess profits are being made by defense contractors, I would recommend that those who make this claim read the Defense Industry Profit Review for 1958–1967 (conducted by the Logistics Management Institute) and published last April the 14th.

This meticulous report concludes that commercial business is increasing at a ratio of 4 to 1 over defense business and is almost twice as profitable. Any comments?

In summary, I would like to go on record as stating unequivocally that I see absolutely no threat to the safety, the security, or the prosperity of this nation from the so-called Military-Industrial Complex. As a matter of fact, we would be in a very sorry situation without it. I would like to enter a plea that objective and respected American public figures step forward and make a knowledgeable analysis of this so-called national dilemma.

It's quite possible that this is the most complex business in the world. For one thing, we have so many people involved in our business that are outside of either the military or industry. There are countless people who involve themselves in the decision-making process, but who are very hard to find when mistakes are uncovered.

We deal at all times on the feather edge of technology. When the threat is certain we sometimes have to schedule inventions to satisfy a need. And, as everyone knows, in that kind of environment, mistakes are inevitable. The mix of military and industrial talent is a huge asset in helping to minimize mistakes.

If the people in the leadership of the country want the Military-Industrial Complex to assume a "fall-back" position in terms of meeting the potential threat with a low-technical risk, low-cost inventory of weapons, I can promise you we will make very few mistakes. But, I can also promise you that our defense posture will be less than satisfactory.

If the opponents of the Military-Industrial Complex are seeking praise and applause for such a proposal they are quite likely to get it. I only hope they note from which corner of the globe the loudest applause originates. Thank you.

NATIONAL SECURITY IN PERSPECTIVE: THE MILITARY-INDUSTRIAL COMPLEX

Mendel L. Rivers

The SPEAKER. Under a previous order of the House, the gentleman from South Carolina (Mr. RIVERS) is recognized for 60 minutes.

Mr. RIVERS. Mr. Speaker, the catch word of the hour is "military-industrial complex."

A national magazine quoted a Senator as saying that on the banquet circuit "one sure applause line is a condemnation of the growing influence of the military."

The amount of space in newspapers, in magazines, in columns, and in editorials devoted to the military-industrial complex in recent months is remarkable. There have been countless statements and studies and attacks of great fury by scientists, academicians, and politicians, including Members of both Houses of Congress. We are told that military advice is unreliable and has led us to disasters. We are told that the ordering of national priorities is askew and that military spending should be vastly curtailed so that spending for welfare, urban problems, and other domestic needs can be greatly expanded. And we are treated to dark hints or even outright allegations of vast conspiracy between military leaders and giant industrial concerns.

The tendency to emotionalize on the issue is very strong. I believe the origins of these emotions are sometimes understandable. But the

Congressional Record, 91st Cong., 1st Sess., June 12, 1969, vol. 115, no. 97, pp. H4765–H4771.

most erudite terminology often buries remarkable inconsistencies and hides a deep emotional bias. And unjust statements which impugn innocent people are made by intelligent men who should know better.

I would like to look at the subject as dispassionately as I can. I would like to look at facts and realities, eschewing the leverage of hindsight and asking only that my points be considered in the real world in which we live rather than in the world as some would like it to be.

I believe some comment is required from me because of the responsibilities the House has imposed upon me as chairman of the Armed Services Committee. I would have it clearly understood that I feel no compunction to defend the defense industry; and our military men, who cannot always speak for themselves, could, I am sure, find a better defender than I. But I am deeply concerned about the picture that is being given to the American people of our governmental process, our defense needs, and—what is worse—the reality of the world we live in.

OUR TRADITION OF ANTIMILITARISM

The men who founded the United States feared militarism as they feared all unwarranted accumulations of power, and their earliest concerns were contained in provisions in the Constitution against infringing the right of the citizen to keep and bear arms and against the quartering of troops in a home without the consent of the owner. These were the second and third amendments to the Constitution. In our formative years in school, all of us learned these Bill of Rights provisions and the basic anti-militarism of the Founding Fathers has remained a feature of our national character.

Our first President, who was our first soldier-President, warned us "to avoid the necessity of those overblown military establishments which, under any form of government, are not auspicious to liberty and which are to be regarded as particularly hostile to republican liberty."

Through all periods of our history up until the last 20 years, we have neglected and disparaged our military forces except in time of war.

A feature of this antimilitarism has been the tendency to blame wars on economic causes or, more specifically, on the munitions makers. Many of us, for example, remember the antiwar plays of the

1930's that came as a reaction to World War I and that pictured the makers of munitions as evil, scheming men who fomented war for huge profits. Those plays were often good theater, but they showed a childish understanding of international politics.

All the wars in our history up to and including World War II, and to some extent including Korea, have required a hurried refurbishing of our military power both in terms of our weapons arsenal and our military leadership.

Over the last 25 years we have been in a kind of situation almost entirely new in historical terms—called, for want of a better word, "cold war." It has required the keeping of a vast defense force in a state of high readiness for an unknown length of time—for the one simple reason that the reality of warfare has changed so that a future global conflict would allow no warning time and no period for preparation. This is a kind of situation that calls for a greater demand on our national resources, and that calls for bringing the military into the mainstream of American life.

I would suggest to you that it is a psychological situation with which, as a nation, we have not yet learned to live.

A series of frustrations have combined to bring a new wave of the old antimilitarism to a head: Vietnam, the humiliation of the *Pueblo*, high taxes, anxiety over unsolved domestic problems, headlines about spectacular cost overruns on defense contracts, the siren call of disarmament negotiations. The frustration has found a convenient focal point in the "military-industrial complex."

As the words feed on themselves, the charges get stronger and stronger and the complex gets all-embracing. The academic world is added because of military research. Some papers have added the labor unions—and, of course, politicians have to be included in any roasting. So we have the "military-industrial-educational-political-labor union complex." We have just about everybody in there but the Boy Scouts.

Let us look at some of the charges—and then look at some facts.

Is it true that defense keeps taking an ever-increasing portion of our national wealth and taking more and more of our Federal budget? Are weapons costs spiraling out of sight?

Are profits of defense industries getting bigger all the time?

Is it national defense expenditures that prevent us from solving our domestic problems?

What about the constant charges of self-interest on the part of Congressmen? It is said that the Armed Services Committee members represent the districts with big defense contracts, that Congressmen vote for defense bills because of defense industry in their districts and are afraid to oppose defense bills because of the economic effect of defense spending in their districts. Is all this confirmed by facts?

It is said that the military failed in Vietnam and has got us overcommitted around the globe. And it is said that the Russians are ready for negotiations and that this country is the cause of the arms race and of the failure to negotiate.

Is our great strength unnecessary? Is that what General Eisenhower warned us about in his famous speech?

Is there, indeed, a conspiracy between the generals and the kings of big industry?

THE CONSPIRATORIAL THEORY

In 1945, Gen. George C. Marshall said: "We finish each bloody war with a feeling of acute revulsion against the savage form of human behavior. And yet on each occasion we confuse military preparedness with the causes of war and then drift almost deliberately into another catastrophe."

Americans are understandably fatigued with requirements of national security, and they have understandably a fierce desire to solve domestic problems. Because they cannot see and cannot strike at the totalitarian forces that have created the uneasy world we live in, some of our people tend to start blaming what they can see—our military and those who work for the military—for creating this world. But the facts are that our military power and the industry that serves it are in response to the international realities of the years since World War II—not the other way around. Because of our strength, we have been able to deter global war and we have still, for all its imperfections, a free society. We have not solved all its problems. But we retain the capacity to solve those problems, the capacity to act to create human betterment and preserve individual freedom.

The citizen in the Communist half of the world does not have that capacity or anybody to exercise that capacity for him. One of the most essential things about dissent in America—that some people seem to forget—is simply the right to voice it. In Russia they have no such rights. You do not hear of students taking over the office of the president of the University of Moscow. And you do not hear of scientists in Russia complaining about arms development. But you do hear, if you will listen, about writers being thrown in jail for the mildest forms of criticism of the government.

And we hear Milovan Djilas, the former Vice President of Yugoslavia, a tough and remarkable man and one of the most informed writers about conditions within the Communist orbit, making this forecast about the eventual control of the Soviet Union by military men: "The party apparatus and the secret police will be under the control of the army. The dominant role of the militarists in public life will be unconcealed and frankly accepted."

Suppose we did not have a huge industrial complex to supply the equipment and arms for our military forces. Without such an industry to provide the armament of modern war, the weapons, and sophisticated equipment, our military forces would be useless and our only hope would be that the Russians and Chinese would take a benign attitude toward our country.

The alternative would be to have all of the arms production handled by the Government with all of the industrial plants owned and operated by the Government. It would mean in effect virtually the elimination of the free enterprise system and a bureaucracy that would make present-day Washington look like a ghost town.

We have to get over our national guilt complex at having kept the world free. This is what we have done with our military might. And with our Marshall plan, our billions in foreign aid, our help to underdeveloped nations.

The greatest libel against military leadership and the leaders of our big defense industries is that there is somehow a vast conspiracy taking place, a dark collusion to determine policy and subvert the elected leadership of the government. It is the theory that led one journal to refer to the military-industrial complex as an all-embracing conglomeration.

The author and former presidential aid Douglass Cater, whose liberal credentials are impeccable, and who was one of the first to write in some detail about the military-industrial complex—or what he calls the subgovernment of defense—has this to say about the conspiratorial theory:

It would be wrong to regard the subgovernment of defense as a secret conspiracy of malefactors. The greater problem arises because of its wide array of competing factions—because of the ever shifting coalitions of politicians, pressure groups, and military professionals striving to assert dominancy for a service, a doctrine, or a weapon. The fact that defense has become a gargantuan governmental activity does not automatically bring increased risk of a military cabal capable of seizing power. On the contrary, the job of running anything as complicated as the modern defense establishment makes such seizure probably less likely than in the past. The missile cum nuclear warhead does not facilitate the staging of a coup d'Etat; nor is there convincing evidence that the man in uniform is less disposed to civilian government than is the man in mufti. The wise and the fanatical exist in both ranks.

There is little use in taking a doom-and-gloom view of "the warfare state" since the need for large-scale military preparedness during the foreseeable future is likely to continue. Too much of the literature on the subject—including Eisenhower's vague farewell admonition—begs the question of how to maintain military power while dealing with the political power that accompanies it.

Mr. Cater's book correctly states the truth about power in Washington—that it is diffused. It can still be made subject to our historic system of checks and balances.

Now let us look closer at that famous Eisenhower statement:

THE EISENHOWER STATEMENT

There is quoted at us over and over again from President Eisenhower's farewell radio and TV broadcast the following paragraphs: "In the councils of government, we must guard against the acquisition of unwarranted influence, whether sought or unsought, by the military-industrial complex. The potential for the disastrous rise of misplaced power exists and will persist. We must never let the weight of this combination endanger our liberties or democratic processes. We should take nothing for granted. Only an alert and knowledgeable citizenry can compel the proper meshing of the huge industrial and military machinery of defense with our peaceful methods and goals, so that security and liberty may prosper together."

What is not quoted are the other things President Eisenhower said in that same farewell address—including his clear statement that our

Military Establishment is "an inevitable necessity of our time." While saying that the conjunction of "an immense military establishment and large arms industry is new in the American experience," General Eisenhower stated, "we recognize the imperative need for this development." He further said: "A vital element in keeping the peace is our Military Establishment. Our arms must be mighty, ready for instant action, so that no potential aggressor may be tempted to risk his own destruction."

He also explained why a large defense industry was a necessary ingredient of our time: "We can no longer risk emergency improvisation of national defense: we have been compelled to create a permanent armaments industry of vast proportions."

And we must not forget that President Eisenhower warned—again in the same speech: "In holding scientific research and discovery in respect, as we should, we must also be alert to the equal and opposite danger that public policy could itself become the captive of a scientific-technological elite."

Finally, General Eisenhower in his farewell speech gave this warning which the critics of the military-industrial complex do not seem inclined to take to heart: "We face a hostile ideology—global in scope, atheistic in character, ruthless in purpose, and insidious in method. Unhappily the danger it poses promises to be of indefinite duration. To meet it successfully, there is called for, not so much the emotional and transitory sacrifices of crisis, but rather those which enable us to carry forward steadily, surely, and without complaint the burdens of a prolonged and complex struggle—with liberty the stake."

SPIRALING WEAPON COSTS AND SOARING PROFITS

Defense is enormously expensive, and the defense industry includes industrial giants which make substantial profit. And in anything as large and complex as defense procurement, examples come up from time to time of what can only be called terrible boo-boos. Mistakes are made—terrible mistakes. Our committee has been diligent in searching out and spotlighting these mistakes—on small procurements as well as large. And we are going to try to do an even better job in the future.

But the fact is that for all its size, defense today gets almost exactly the same share of U.S. output that it got a decade ago. The defense budget for the year ending June 30 is 8.8 percent of total U.S. goods and services and 43 percent of all Government outlays. In 1960, military costs were 47 percent of our Federal spending and 8.7 percent of total U.S. goods and services. Thus, spending on defense, contrary to popular belief, has maintained a consistent ratio to gross national product.

Another point to consider is that $29 billion of this year's defense budget is soaked up due to the Vietnam involvement. That leaves $49 billion for all other military needs. With the rise in payroll and other costs, this represents less actual buying power for defense needs—including costly weapons systems—than the Armed Forces had with a budget of $43 billion in 1960.

Contrary to popular belief, the majority of the defense budget is not poured out to the defense industry for hardware. More than half of all defense dollars go for personnel and operating costs. Military personnel costs this year are around $23 billion. Another $22 billion goes to operation and maintenance, including paying of Defense Department civilians. And another $7.5 billion goes for research and development, including the financing of research in some 350 colleges and universities and other nonprofit institutions.

Of the $78 billion budget, about $33 billion of it is spent buying arms and equipment from the so-called industrial complex.

You might be interested to know that on the whole the percentage of profit on defense business has tended downward over the last 10 years.

The public picture that is sometimes painted of ever-spiraling costs and ever-spiraling profits is not correct. An independent organization, the Logistics Management Institute, recently completed an extensive study entitled "Defense Industries Profit Review." The report contains extensive statistical material on the defense contracts for the 10-year period 1958 through 1967 and makes comparisons of the defense industry profits with profits of defense firms in their commercial business and profits by nondefense industries.

Among the interesting findings in this study are the following:

First. The average defense business profit as a percentage of total capital investment tended downward for the first 7 years of the study period and remained level for the last 3 years. Since Fiscal Year 1962, the percentage of profit on defense business was actually less than the percentage of profit on nondefense business.

In addition, it was found that average defense profit declined more than 25 percent over the 10-year period. Average profit of commercial firms increased during the same 10-year period.

Second. Defense industries which had the highest percentage of profit did not enjoy profits as high as the most profitable commercial firms.

Third. Commercial markets have expanded more rapidly than the defense markets.

For some 40 companies surveyed, all of which did at least $25 million annually in defense sales, defense business increased about 50 percent between 1958 and 1967. Commercial sales for the same companies rose almost 200 percent in the same period. For nondefense companies, sales increased more than 110 percent.

Fourth. Over the 10-year period defense business profit as a percentage of sales declined more than 20 percent. Among the conclusions drawn in the LMI study was that the reduction in the profit-to-sales ratio in defense business is due largely to the increased use of competition in defense procurement.

Even in the face of these statistics, it is still a conclusion of L. MENDEL RIVERS that competitive procurement is not used nearly as much as it could be in the Pentagon.

In pointing out the lower percentage of profits on defense business, I certainly would not wish to overstate the case. There are advantages to defense business—Government financing for research and development, use of Government facilities, progress payments, and cost reimbursements which considerably reduce the risks for industries, though the use of these incentives varies widely from industry-to-industry and from contract-to-contract.

There have been some reductions in the use of such Government financial support, and perhaps there should be further reductions.

There have been problems, and there is plenty of room for improvement. But weapons costs are not taking an ever-increasing share of our resources.

Finally, should a defense contractor realize excessive profits from his defense business, Congress has very prudently provided for this contingency, the Renegotiation Board, which was created in 1951, and has the responsibility to recapture excessive profits derived by contractors and subcontractors in connection with Government procurement.

Every defense contractor who does a substantial amount of business with the Department of Defense during any fiscal year must file a report with the Renegotiation Board. This report and related information accumulated by the Board enables the Government to ensure against unconscionable profits in defense industry.

This then places this entire matter of excessive profits in industry in proper perspective.

CONGRESS: THE ALLEGATION OF SELF-INTEREST

The catch-phrase is often extended to read "military-industrial-congressional complex." My district has been called a microcosm of the military-industrial complex. Charleston happens to be a great, natural warm-water port. It was made that way by God—who, I presume, is not a captive of the military-industrial complex. But I am not alone in being assailed. There is continual criticism that "members champion defense systems out of self-interest," and that Congressmen win reelection by their success in winning defense contracts for their constituents. One commentator typified this feeling when he said, "It takes a brave legislator to vote against funds that mean jobs for some of his own constituents." This is part of old folklore about the Congress. I think even the Members of the House will be surprised to find the extent to which it is not true.

In general, it is charged that the members of the Armed Services Committee represent districts dependent on the military industrial complex and get fat contracts for their districts in exchange for supporting unneeded weapons.

To begin with, the idea that the Armed Services Committee members represent the fat-cat districts is simply not true. I had an analysis prepared for fiscal year 1968 prime contracts of $1 million or more by congressional districts. The analysis compared members of the Armed Services Committee with House Members as a whole as regards number of prime contracts.

It showed that we have 10 members on the committee in the top quarter of House Members, 13 in the second quarter, nine in the next to the lowest quarter, and seven members in the lowest quarter. In other words, the membership of the committee almost exactly reflects the membership of the House in terms of the relative number of prime contracts in their districts. So, it can be fairly said that the Armed Services Committee is not weighted in favor of the so-called military-industrial complex.

In addition, of the top 38 Members of the House in terms of amount of defense contracts in their district, only three of them are members of the Armed Services Committee. You might be interested to know that I am not one of those three. There are 122 districts which receive more prime contracts than my own First District of South Carolina. It might also interest you to know that of the top 10 Democrats on the committee, none of them are in the top quarter, and only two of them are in the next to top quarter.

Now, as to the votes of Members of the House as a whole, an analysis was made on four votes—the procurement authorization and defense appropriations bills for fiscal year 1968 and fiscal year 1969.

There are 38 congressional districts that had no prime defense contracts. On the fiscal year 1968 defense authorization bill, none of these 38 voted against the bill. There were only three votes cast against the fiscal year 1968 bill, one being that of a Member who ranked in the next to top quarter and two by Members who ranked in the third quarter in defense contracts.

On the fiscal year 1969 authorization bill, there were 15 negative votes cast. Of these, two were Members whose districts received no contract awards. But of the other 13 negative votes, two were by Congressmen whose districts were in the top seven in terms of prime contracts, while three others were among the top 72 districts. The other negative votes ranged the entire spectrum.

On the 1969 appropriation bill, seven votes were cast in opposition. One of these was by a Congressman whose district received no prime contracts, while another was by a Congressman whose district ranked No. 7 in the amount of contract awards. The other negative votes ranged the entire spectrum.

In summary, it can be said that there is no correlation between the voting patterns of Congressmen and contracts made to defense industries within their districts.

It is important to note that this is true both for the men who support military authorization and appropriation bills and for those who oppose them.

The inconsistency of the criticism of Congress for its alleged role in the military-industrial complex is something to behold. If we authorize weapons systems and other expenditures, we are castigated as lackeys and handmaidens of the military-industrial complex. But, of course, if we criticize a Defense Secretary's program, then we are enemies of economy. Recently, in an article that criticized the Congress for the swollen expenditures within the Pentagon, I found that one of the sins blamed on Congress was that the Defense Department Public Affairs Office budget was three times as large as that of the State Department Public Affairs Office. I just want to say that if any Member of Congress wants to introduce a motion to cut the budget of the Defense Department Public Affairs Office by two-thirds, he will have my wholehearted support.

If it were not for its harmful implications, there is much in the current wave of criticism that would cause a Member of Congress to laugh.

For instance, I read in a newspaper a short time ago that there is a new skepticism in Congress about the explanations given of the programs by the minions of the Pentagon. I have got news for you—I have had that skepticism for years. I had it back in the days when, as the papers tell us, it was not at all popular.

It amuses me vastly to hear people say that in the past the Congress has been too unquestionably ready to accept anything that the Pentagon said. It amuses me when I reflect on the kind of criticism we received, particularly in the press, when at any time during the last 8 years we questioned the decisions or the programs of the Secretary of Defense. The kindest word applied to us was "irresponsible." We were always wrong and the Secretary of Defense was always right.

In one article attacking the military-industrial-congressional complex, I saw the TFX listed as one of the prime examples of misjudgment and waste and boondoggle by the military-industrial complex perpetrated with the acquiescence of Congress. I do not have to tell anybody in the House the kind of abuse that Members of Congress were subjected to when they questioned the decision of the Secretary of Defense concerning the TFX. And you might reflect that the Secretary of Defense forced the development of the common plane over strenuous military objections and, with the help of two other Defense civilians, overruled four military source selection boards in awarding the contract.

THE THEORY OF NATIONAL PRIORITIES

The argument is made that while protecting our national security externally we are decaying internally. The mayor of New York City, Mr. Lindsay, expressed this point very dramatically when he said: "We are in danger of spending billions for the ABM and other weaponry to defend a shell of society which died of neglect."

And here again one can see a cause for concern. We do have grave domestic problems, and they must be met if our Nation is to continue.

The military-industrial complex, however, is ceaselessly attacked on the grounds that it is taking the money that would otherwise go to meet domestic requirements.

The point is made that if billions could be cut from the defense budget—the estimates I have heard run as high as $35 billion—we could then pour that money into welfare and other domestic programs. The point is also made that our best minds are engaged in military work while they should be involved in domestic problems. Finally, the argument goes that crushing military costs have deprived cities and State of tax base. It is said that either the Federal Government should pour a large portion of its tax dollars back into municipalities or reduce Federal tax so that State and municipalities will be able to raise their taxes—and better meet their responsibilities for cleaning up cities, attacking pollution, improving education, and so on.

The concern of people who make these arguments is, as I said, understandable. Their reasoning, however, is based, quite simply, on conditions contrary to fact.

To begin with, the assumption is made of a constant Federal dollar: It is assumed that if a certain amount of those dollars are not spent for defense—if $5 billion or so were saved by canceling a certain weapons development—that a corresponding amount would be spent on welfare programs.

Now, the interesting thing is that in the first place this assumes that budgetary restraints have in the past prevented Congress from spending what it wanted to spend on welfare programs. This simply is not true. Quite obviously, the lack of Federal funds has not prevented the Government from spending on welfare. We have appropriated billions for various welfare programs for a good number of years, even though in many of those years the appropriations were part of a deficit budget. If Congress wants to put more money into domestic programs of one kind or another, it will do so—even when the money is not there. And, in addition, if it wants to do so badly enough, it can provide additional taxing to finance the program.

But let us consider the most naive part of the basic assumption—that is, if the defense budget is reduced by billions of dollars, the money will be transferred to welfare or other domestic programs. Do you really think that would happen? Do you really think that is what the majority of the Members of Congress want to happen? Is that what you think a majority of the American people would want to happen?

If the Vietnam war were ended and much of the $25 to $30 billion that war is costing annually were no longer needed in Southeast Asia, what would be the first thing the Congress would do? I think all of you know clearly the answer: It would eliminate the surtax. There would even be calls for greater tax reduction. There would be a strenuous attempt in Congress—entirely understandable—to have, for a change, a balanced budget.

The fact is that it is a fallacy to assume there is a constant budget dollar. The decisions both of Congress and the administration on domestic and welfare programs are made primarily on philosophical and not on economic grounds.

Finally, as you reduce Federal taxes somewhat, do you think the State and municipal officials would jump in and quickly increase local taxes to spend more money on schools and welfare improvement programs? Do you think that is what the majority of the citizens would want? Many of you have served on local and State governing bodies, and I think you have an idea of the enthusiasm with which tax increases at the local level are greeted.

Finally, it is a libel against the defense industry of this country to charge that it is the antithesis of social reform or the enemy of efforts to solve domestic problems. The defense industry and some of the associated "think" factories have been turning their systems management techniques to the solving of major domestic problems. The aerospace industry in California is making an effort to help with California's water and transportation problems.

I am aware that there are difficulties to be ironed out in turning this industrial talent toward the domestic scene—adjustments to be made in profit expectation, the relationship between research and development fees as compared with hardware sales, and the inaction of various local governments. But if our great defense and space problems are solvable, these difficulties are solvable.

The industrial know-how which supports our military forces provides a vital national resource which can help in all types of problems, ranging from education to housing, water and air pollution, and transportation.

I might add that the military services themselves have developed dramatic training and learning techniques which have proved and will prove of substantial value to other segments of our society.

The military services have successfully educated and given useful industrial skills to men from all sections of the country whom civilian society has discarded as unteachable and unusable. There is no reason why the military training techniques cannot be used by civilian agencies.

The Constitution of the United States charges the Congress with providing for the common defense and insuring domestic tranquillity. It has always been a requirement to pursue these responsibilities simultaneously, and there is such a requirement now. It is just plain silly to say that one can only be achieved at the expense of the other.

THE RESPONSIBILITY FOR VIETNAM

We all know that what is contributing most to the current debate on national purpose and national resources is the bitter sense of frustration because of the war in Vietnam. The enormous and unpredicted costs, together with the sense of futility, have created social and economic pressures that have been directed toward almost all defense programs. The failure in Vietnam, if such it is, is not basically a military failure but a civilian one. It is the failure of the approach to the war to bring forth the kind of response from the North Vietnamese that was predicted. That basic approach was decided upon by civilians, and all of the changes in the strategy were dictated by civilians and even some of the tactical maneuvers, always the province of military leaders in the past, were controlled by civilians. They were controlled neither by military men, nor industrialists, nor their supposed friends in Congress, but by the highest civilians in the executive branch.

I would not minimize the fact that there have been mistakes, bad decisions, and sometimes bad advice from military leaders. But the fact is that most of the decisions for which the military is presently being criticized were made by civilians. They were made most often by political leaders and often for political purposes.

In Vietnam we may never know if the generals were right. It is too late now, perhaps, to go the road of an all-out effort for victory, as I believe they recommend. But if what has happened has led to bitter disillusionment and uncertainty, the decision to do it this way was made by civilians—both the decision to get involved in the first place and the decision to follow a policy of gradual escalation. This is the first and only time the gradual escalation approach has been used for war; it goes against the grain of traditional military thinking. It may be that another approach would have had worse results. But in any case, the gradual escalation approach taken—the decision in 1965 against mobilization and for a "guns and butter" approach, the decision to expand bombing gradually, to commit forces piecemeal, to control each bombing target at the highest political level—and you know the address of the house where that level is—was a civilian decision.

Did you know that pilots in Vietnam were given seven pages of instructions on what to bomb and what not to bomb and how? And did you know that pilots had to get each target approved in Washington before they could attack it? Do you know that if they missed a target they could not return to it the next day but had to get it approved again in Washington?

The abandonment of the ancient principles of warfare, the announcement that we would not seek a military victory, the decision to modify the goals as we went along, and the false predictions of how things were going—these were almost entirely the work of civilians. If you believe we should never have gotten involved in the first place, then you must agree that a greater role must be played by Congress in the future.

THE CONTRADICTIONS OF THE CRITICS

Nothing confirms the emotional bias of those who rail against the military-industrial complex so much as the contradictions in the postures they assume. The people who cry out against the complex and the supposed militarism in our society are invariably the proponents of an all-volunteer Army and critics of the draft. But at the same time they are invariably against the ROTC and against a strong Reserve. Needless to say, they would send up a hue and cry if somebody proposes tripling the size of West Point, but if we are to have neither the draft nor ROTC, I wonder where these people think the officer leaders for our Armed Forces are to come from.

The people who want a volunteer Army are doing their utmost to prevent the recruitment of same.

As Secretary Laird recently told our committee in relation to the forcing of military recruiters off college campuses: "You can't have a volunteer force if people are prohibited from recruiting volunteers."

It is, of course, inconsistent to complain about too much military influence and at the same time attempt to deny the Armed Forces the opportunity of having officers from various great universities throughout the country rather than just from military schools. It would be logical for those who fear militarism to want to bring the military into the mainstream of American life, and particularly to want to infuse into the Armed Forces young men from our great universities who have broad cultural and liberal educations. Presumably that would be the best way to insure the maintenance of a respect for democratic institutions in our Armed Forces and to avoid the overemphasis on militarism.

But the same people who call for a volunteer Armed Forces are doing their utmost to alienate and isolate military people.

The simple fact is that we have accomplished in our time the feat of having both an efficient and an extraordinarily democratic Army. The training cycle rate in our Army today is fantastic. We take in and discharge around 800,000 men a year. The approach is not ideal either from a cost or efficiency standpoint. But it does make for a democratic Army.

We are also told that through the subterfuge of research contracts the military departments are having too great an influence in our colleges and universities.

It is really hilarious to pick up the daily newspaper and read on the first page about student revolts and sit-ins and file riflings and such at various universities and then to turn to the editorial page and read about the serious problem of too much military influence at colleges.

The military influence, if there were such, would seem to carry with it a leaning toward order, a respect for authority, or—at the very least—a propensity to defend buildings under siege.

POWER AND THE GENERALS

An effective military force is absolutely necessary for our survival for the foreseeable future—and such requires generals who think like generals. But it is untrue and unfair to say that such implies the threat of a military takeover. There is not a hint of the coup psychology among real-life military men in our country. Our officer corps has a splendid record of avoiding political ties.

If anything, the members of the military services are less materialistic than their civilian counterparts.

Our constitutional tradition of civilian control of the military is safe—as long as civilians, including civilians in Congress, do their job. The danger is not that generals will grab the power, but that the civilian leadership will default on it. The most difficult task of controlling defense spending and industrial influence is a civilian job. It depends on the judgment and the toughness of civilian leaders.

If you consider the point at length, you come back again and again to the conclusion that a fuller part has to be played in the decision-making process in the one place where, constitutionally, the people most directly exert their influence—and that is the Congress of the United States.

THE POWER OF FALSE RHETORIC ABOUT THINGS WHICH ARE TRUE

We are all aware that the rhetoric of a speaker or a group may obscure the truth as well as embellish it, and we are all aware that the understanding of a problem is colored by the way it is presented to people and by what might be a natural emotional bias. The wish, as it were, is often father of the thought.

But I have noticed over the years a similar phenomenon that takes place in public debate and, particularly, in the press. That is that ideas presented over and over again become accepted as true, particularly when presented with a catchy phrase on which to hang a thought. Ideas wrapped in a key word become almost a part of the language and are repeated over and over in newspapers and columns to imply a certain set of facts without any bother to examine the original basis for the idea to see if it is, indeed, valid. In this way things become accepted as true which, in point of fact, are not true.

For example, if enough academicians and editorialists make reference to the desire of the Soviets for negotiations, it seems to become an accepted fact in the intellectual community that the Soviets do, in fact, desire such negotiations and in time this leads to the conclusion that the failure to start negotiations is our fault rather than the Soviets'. In point of fact, of course, efforts for disarmament negotiations by this country have been rebuffed in the past by the Soviets.

As another example, the word "detente" was used so often in the press and in lectures in recent years that people seemed to have come to the belief that the character of the Soviet leadership has somehow magnificently changed. This kind of departure from reality must be reviewed against the fact that the only difference between the Russian reaction in Czechoslovakia last year and the Russian reaction in Hungary in 1956 is that in Czechoslovakia there was less provocation and, therefore, less requirement for the use of Soviet military force. There was no change in the readiness to use force—or in the reason for its use—to suppress an effort by people for greater freedom.

The Secretary of State recently said that the events in Czechoslovakia have not in any way altered the possibility of nuclear arms negotiations with the Russians. I recognize that that may be true, but I hope it has at least reminded the Secretary that in dealing with the Soviets he is not negotiating with the Bobbsey twins at Sunnybrook Farm (sic).

THE ILLUSION OF THE NEW RUSSIA

The outcry about the military-industrial complex is, as I said, a collocation of seemingly related but actually quite independent factors.

One of these is the age-old attraction of disarmament. Since the days of the Kellogg-Briand Pact, the idea of throwing away weapons and outlawing war has appealed to peace-loving Americans.

In its present rather sophisticated stage, the key words are "destabilization" and "arms limiting negotiations." Nobody really seriously expects the great powers to disarm any more, but great credence is given to the idea of, as it is generally stated, "halting the arms race." The theory is that both the Soviets and the United States now have the power to actually destroy the other and this is the best deterrent of war. Anything that tends to increase one side's capacity to survive an attack or to launch a first strike attack without suffering unacceptable retaliation is "destabilizing," since it increases the likelihood of a first strike or an accidental firing starting a war and since it calls for effort at countermeasures by the other side. So, we should negotiate an agreement not to develop any more nuclear weapons, either offensive or defensive.

We hear frequently of late that there is real chance for arms limitation negotiations with the Russians, and by extension it is, therefore, assumed that the Soviets are ready to limit arms production. With the possible exception of Talleyrand at the Congress of Vienna, I know of no cases in history where anybody won at the negotiations table what they were not able to defend on the battlefield. However, the word "negotiation" has great charm for many people today.

The Secretary of State has announced that he hoped to get talks with the Russians started soon. However, I have seen no concrete evidence that the Russians are interested in stopping the development of advance weapons systems—except by the United States. But public statements assuming Russian interest in negotiations jump quickly from that point to the idea that the United States is somehow responsible for preventing negotiations and must take a first step in getting arms limitations talk started.

Recently I read a widely circulated article in a scientific journal on the arms race. The article said that reducing the uncertainty about an adversary's intentions and capabilities is an essential condition to curtailing the arms race. Discussing ways to reduce uncertainty, the author said: "There is unilateral disclosure. In the case of the U.S. there has been a conscious effort to inform both the American public and the Russian leadership of the rationale for many American decisions regarding strategic systems and, to the extent consistent with security, of U.S. capabilities. This has been done particularly through the release by the Secretary of Defense of an annual 'posture' statement, a practice that, it is hoped, will be continued by the U.S. and will be emulated someday by the U.S.S.R. This would be in the interest of both countries."

Now, the remarkable thing in this paragraph is that it concedes the United States is making efforts to disclose its capabilities and intentions most clearly to the Russians so that there will be no misunderstanding. In point of fact, the annual posture statement by the Defense Secretary has been a feature of our Defense reviews for more than a decade. The posture statements have gone to great length and detail, sometimes running into hundreds of pages. The author vaguely hopes that the Russians will emulate us someday, but he seems somehow undisturbed that they have not done so up to now and includes no criticism of their intentions and posture because of that fact.

Yet the main burden of the article is that we have to take steps to stop the arms race, that we have to stop development of ABM and the MIRV—multiple independently targetable reentry vehicle—that we have to take steps, possibly by unilateral restraint, to stop new arms development that may be destabilizing.

Little thought is given to what happens to our position if the Russians continue weapons development after we stop.

For example, the author says deployment of a U.S. ABM "seems certain to have an effect on Russian planners, who may push for development of their own MIRV systems." I have news for him—the Russians are vigorously pushing their own MIRV development already.

The simple truth is that most discussions fail to recognize the basic fact that the Russians have done far more to create an arms race than we have. They acted first to develop ICBM's. They developed a bomb as large as 60 megatons, although we have never developed bombs of anywhere near that size. They developed a fractional orbital bombardment system—FOBS—a destabilizing weapon if I ever heard of one, since it is essentially a first strike weapon. They have not only developed, but have deployed, an ABM system, although of limited capability, and they have continued to try to improve and update this system. And they are proceeding with MIRV development.

The curious reasoning of those who are attracted by the illusion of the new Russia was illustrated exceptionally well by Vice Adm. Hyman G. Rickover—who is no darling of either the military or the industrial community—in stating his support for the ABM as a non-provocative weapon. He said: "The Russians have been singularly silent in this respect; the outcry has come mostly from those in this country who habitually apply a double standard when adjudging military developments in the U.S. and the U.S.S.R. One must ask how can our defensive capability be considered provocative, while theirs is not?"

If the Soviets are, indeed, prepared to enter negotiations, it will be for one reason—because they believe they have caught up or passed the United States and want to use negotiations as a device to freeze U.S. strength at present levels.

The idea that the beginning of negotiations is the end of the problem is not facing the facts. The negotiations process is a difficult task at best. And I have not heard even the supposition that the Russians would halt weapons development while the negotiations are in progress.

But those who call for negotiations invariably call for this country to cease its own weapons development pending the outcome of the negotiations. It is easy to see that the Russians could draw out the negotiations process for months or years—just as they have in the past—and during the negotiations continue to increase their weapons arsenal while the United States stood still.

I think it would surprise everybody if Russia agreed to inspection—even after an arms-limiting agreement were signed.

There is little hope of the Russians ever doing so because it is an example of the truth that goes to the heart of the relationship between the two countries. Theirs is a closed society and ours is an open society; ours is a country of free men and theirs is not.

Hand in hand with the illusion of a Soviet desire for arms limitation and an end to weapons development is the idea that the Soviet regime is more peaceful and more moderate in world affairs.

We are told that the nature of communism is no longer monolithic, that it is going through an evolution into better things.

I do not know if it is monolithic in its structure, but I know that it is paleolithic in its concerns for human freedom.

The Soviet actions in the Middle East show it to be as much committed to violence and unscrupulous measures to gain power as any Russian regime in history. In recent years there has been an attempt of intellectuals in Russia to speak out more and to take a greater part in determining Russian life. The result has been, of course, the jailing of artists and scholars, and senseless attacks against Jewish authors in the Soviet Union.

It is remarkable the degree to which some seemingly intelligent men can delude themselves on these points. In a letter to a newspaper, the British author Graham Greene remarked that he would much rather live in the Soviet Union than in the United States. The principal purpose of his letter was to say that he was giving the royalties from the sale of his books in Russia—which he could not get out of Russia anyhow—to the defense of two Russian writers on trial in Moscow. The reason for their trial was that they had criticized the state. Subsequently, they were convicted and are now in prison. Mr. Greene, a writer, would rather live in that society than ours.

Finally, what has all this got to do with the military-industrial complex? The answer, of course, is "nothing." No Members of the House or Senate would suggest for a minute that any major defense contractor would take steps, publicly or clandestinely, to prevent arms limitations negotiations with the Russians. No Member of the House or Senate would suggest that any of these major contractors would take any steps to prevent the carrying forward of negotiations concerning the Vietnam war or to prevent the President from bringing that war to an end. And I know of no Member of Congress who would allege that any defense contractor made an effort to get us into the war in Vietnam. Yet the pressures for arms negotiations or ending the war are frequently coupled with an attack on these industrial forces.

MILITARY INFLUENCE, FOREIGN POLICY, AND THE CONGRESS

In conclusion, where does the responsibility for policy lie? Where is the safeguard against unwarranted power?

Frequently, mention is made of the number of American bases and troops overseas and the number of countries in which we maintain a military presence, and this is generally stated in a way that implies both a criticism of the military and an overreaching influence of the military in our national decision-making processes.

It may be that we have overextended ourselves around the globe and overcommitted ourselves. I am inclined to think that to at least some extent we have. I am inclined to think that there are areas of the world we should stay out of. I would certainly agree with anybody who says that many of our allies could take a greater portion of the burden of military security in their own bailiwick and that some of our forces could be brought back. I am deeply concerned, as other Members of Congress are concerned, about our balance-of-payments problem and our gold reserves. And finally, I am convinced that we are committed, by bilateral and multilateral agreements, to more tasks around the world than we could always fulfill. A Special Subcommittee on National Security Policy found last year that our forces were not always adequate for the contingencies they were designed to face, that there had been inadequate coordination between commitments and resources made available, and that our planning for certain military contingencies—including various future contingencies in Vietnam—was inadequate.

I am convinced that a lot more thought has to be given to these problems and a lot better coordination achieved among the various branches of Government.

But the main truth to be recognized is that this military presence in foreign areas, this military response, took place as a result of foreign policy commitments decided by the President and the Congress. I think one might even say with some justification that foreign policy actions and foreign involvements which get the most bitter complaint are those which are decided by the civilian political leadership without a decision by Congress, or at least without adequate debate and study prior to acquiescence by Congress.

I was interested to see the majority leader of the Senate say recently that civilian authority was remiss for initiating foreign policy which resulted, in the end, in major military commitments.

Recently in one of the local papers I saw a Member of this body quoted as saying: "It is high time we got back to what the Founding Fathers had in mind."

I could not agree with him more. And what the Founding Fathers had in mind was for the Congress to perform an active role in decisionmaking—foreign policy decisionmaking and military policy decisionmaking.

If Congress carries out its constitutional role without shirking, without passing the cup, there will be no need to worry about overreaching power in the hands of the military-industrial complex or any other complex.

The Congress of the United States is the forum where the voice of the people can be brought to bear on policy decisions. And it is by assertion of its responsibility by the Congress—and only in the assertion of its responsibilities by the Congress—that there will be assured the separation of power and diffusion of power which is the one sure safeguard against the disastrous rise of misplaced power. If the Congress does its job, then security and liberty can prosper together.

A GRIMMER VIEW OF THE WORLD

Dean Acheson

You told me, Senator Proxmire, that you thought my views would be somewhat different from those hitherto expressed before this Committee. You may remember that some years ago Joe Alsop, who is an old friend, said that my views on affairs might be described by a line from Coleridge's Kubla Khan, "Ancestral voices prophesying war."

I have taken a rather grimmer view of the world around us than many who have appeared before you, and I shall probably continue to do so today.

I would like to make four points. The first one is that in the more than 70 years during which I have been dimly conscious of the world around me, I have been strongly impressed that the Congress throughout this entire time has underspent rather than overspent on the defense of the United States.

Secondly, during this time the Congress and the people of the United States have been greatly distracted from considering the real problems they have to face by witch hunts and cliches, all of which have taken their minds off the point.

Third, the old world which many of us still consider normal has completely disappeared. In former times we could count on time and distance as safety factors. That situation has vanished, probably forever. The development has not been due to some correctible error of judgment and practice on our part. The determining factors are the

Testimony before the Joint Economic Committee, Subcommittee on Economy in Government, 91st Cong., 1st Sess., June 11, 1969, pp. 618–628.

disintegration of the Europe-centered world, the establishment of a great power base for revolutionary purposes with universal ambitions, and the dynamism of technology. From here on, as far ahead as one can imagine, the nation will continuously be in the front line, and coping with adversary forces will be an unrelenting requirement. The war in Europe and the war in Asia have utterly destroyed the great empires upon which the nineteenth century world order and all its precepts and all its ideas were founded. They have gone entirely. Every one. And out of it have emerged two of the great powers confronting one another with diametrically opposed ideas, ambitions, influences, and purposes. The possibility of compromise is only that referred to by Mr. Churchill when he spoke of a balance of terror which makes possible co-existence. This is the basis on which we live and it is a vast mistake to believe that it is anything else.

The fourth point which I wish to make to you today is that as we add to, maintain, and protect our power, we do not in any way diminish the possibility of an agreement with the Soviet Union. In fact, we strengthen it. I mean that combination of population, resources, technology, and will which enables a people to have an impact beyond their own boundaries. That is what I mean by power.

The idea that the Soviet Union will negotiate with us in the sense in which we use that term is quite untrue. I am a Connecticut Yankee and my conception of negotiation is a David Harum type of negotiation and deal. You have a horse and I want to buy it. We are both trying to accomplish a common result. You wish to get as much out of me as you can. I wish to pay as little as possible. Somewhere between those two desires we have a negotiation and make a deal and perhaps I get the horse. That is not the Russian conception at all. The Russian conception of negotiation is the carrying on of war by other means. It is the converse of Clausewitz, who talked about war as carrying on diplomacy by other means.

Therefore, as we strengthen ourselves, we bring about that calculation of forces by the Russians which induces them to make a deal. They are not moved by argument, nor by exhortation, nor by considerations of morality. They are moved only when their calculations lead them to believe that it is more advantageous to make a deal than not to do so.

I do not claim to have had more experience than any other American in negotiating with the Russians. Obviously, my old and dear friend, Averell Harriman, has had more than I have, and some others have too. But I am no slouch in this field. I have had a good deal and my experience has been that negotiating with the Russians is not a delicate or difficult art at all. Sir William Hayter has said that it is like putting a coin in an old-fashioned penny-in-the-slot machine. Sometimes you got what you wanted, but usually not. Sometimes you got nothing at all. It helped from time to time to shake the machine and sometimes to kick it, but it never helped to argue with it.

This has been my experience in negotiating with the Russians as I shall exemplify if you wish me to in these hearings.

It is the duty of the Congress, of course, to appropriate the funds of the United States for the constitutional purposes which are enjoined upon you in the Constitution. It is the duty of the President to be your constitutional advisor in the matter and to recommend to you what he believes is good for the nation. While his is a recommendation only, it is an important one; a recommendation which one disregards at one's peril, and in doing so assumes responsibility which requires very careful thought. But it is your prerogative, your duty, your right, and therefore I am addressing myself to the problem which confronts you now.

Let me go back to point one and talk a little bit about the fact that the Congress has steadily underspent for the defense of the United States. I see no basis for the notion that we tend to overdo the military aspects. To the contrary, the nation has repeatedly neglected to provide a military basis to match its policy or to cope with aggressive forces. We tried unilateral arms reduction in the inter-war period. We got Pearl Harbor. We reverted to habit after World War II. We got the Korean war. With respect to military power, I do not share the worries of those who discern and deplore dangers of too much. We had a temporary advantage in ratios of available military resources at the time of the Cuban missile crisis. Some would have called it a redundancy. That margin was not a surplus. It provided the basis on which President Kennedy was able to bring off an acceptable outcome.

Among almost my earliest memories—I should think when I was probably six or seven years old—were the discussions which went on in our house in Middletown, Connecticut, about the shocking state of our armed forces in the war with Spain. It was not that there was much doubt or difficulty about the military engagements. It was not that our armaments were all pretty primitive and too few, but that we had practically no medical corps in the Army at all. The whole conception and provision for sanitation was almost nonexistent. And the very heavy toll of deaths which we had in that war came from the gross neglect of the health of the troops which we had brought into the field.

I think perhaps Congressman Bolling has heard, as I have heard, from Cordell Hull what it was like to be in the Army during the Spanish War. It put quite a strain on Cordell Hull's Tennessee vocabulary to give his opinion of those who had provided for the care of the Army.

General Marshall used to drill into me the vast importance of maintaining a mean of preparedness in armaments at all times and not to raise it to terrific heights during times of trouble and then scrap the whole thing and go down to almost zero between crises. We have always been unprepared for conflict. Our wars as a result have lasted too long. The casualties have been too high.

Many of you will remember our situation in 1914 to 1917. During that time the chances of our being drawn into the European War were tremendously high. As a bookmaker, one would have given odds that we would have become entangled in that war before it would be over, and yet we took almost no steps to prepare for it. After that we allowed what we had done to sink into disuse.

From 1933 to 1939 it was pretty clear that there was going to be trouble in Europe and that we were going to be drawn into it. Yet again the Government of the United States did all too little to prepare for trouble. The President, as well as the Congress, was at fault for this neglect. What little was done amounted to virtually nothing when measured against the requirements imposed by the war which overtook us.

Developments not only in Europe but also in the Pacific area, as you will recall, converged to bring on that war, and so I am going to shift the focus of my recollections to that latter area.

I have a great respect for the late Charles Evans Hughes, both as an Associate Justice of the Supreme Court and as Chief Justice of the United States. I think his reputation in the judicial field far outshines his record as Secretary of State. It was in 1922, at the time of his guidance of the State Department, that the United States led the way in bringing about a set of interlocked treaties focusing on limitation of naval armaments and on strategic stabilization in the Pacific. I shall not recall all their intricacies. Taken as a whole, they were, I believe, the most improvident treaties entered into by the United States in its long history. By their effect, the northwest Pacific was turned over to Japanese domination. The United States yielded the right to fortify any of the islands under its control in the western Pacific. We ended up in a position where we were utterly powerless to do anything about Japanese aggression in the northern part of the western Pacific. Our improvidence regarding defense matters, more than anything else in my estimation, led the Japanese to their fateful calculation that an attack on Pearl Harbor would pay off in an irreversible victory.

Such strength as the United States commanded was preponderantly in the naval arm. The bulk of our naval strength was in the Pacific. It was concentrated in and around Pearl Harbor in expectation that, in that position, the fleet would deter any Japanese move southward to the Strait of Malacca and thence into the Indian Ocean. In the Japanese estimate, Germany then was on the verge of inflicting a determinative defeat on the Soviet Union, whereupon Britain would be in such extremity that she would have to submit on whatever terms the Germans would grant. Germany would be triumphant in Europe, and her aggrandized potential in the Atlantic would place the United States in great danger. Germany, in this estimate, would also be in position to push her dominion eastward over a vast expanse.

The Japanese expected, by doing in the United States fleet at Pearl Harbor, to make this country helpless to move against the Axis in either direction. The Japanese then would be left free not only to clean up in China but also to establish an impregnable position in the Malay Barrier and, moving beyond it, to carry their dominion into the Indian Ocean area, rather than letting Germany become the sole heir to that area.

The calculation proved wrong in several particulars, but we should never forget how important a factor the meagerness of our preparations was in inviting danger or how close a call we had in the months following Pearl Harbor.

In retrospect we can see how a measure of luck helped us through that war. One element of luck was the extreme stupidity of the Germans in attacking the Soviet Union. That action was difficult to understand. It was a case of overweening ambition and excessive confidence induced by earlier successes. A more realistic strategy on the Germans' part might have had results much worse for us.

A second item of luck for us was the Germans' vast folly in declaring war on the United States after Pearl Harbor. That really brought all our nation together, unified into a colossal effort that enabled us to turn our power, as it developed, first on the German position in Europe and then against Japan to end that war victoriously in both theaters. The Germans could easily have left us to divert all our strength against the Japanese, thus giving themselves plenty of time and opportunity to clean up on Europe without the possibility of any intervention from us, but they did not.

The third lucky break was the development of the nuclear weapon. Such a revolutionary change in the nature of warfare does not happen very often.

I refer again to our neglect of forces in the period leading up to war—one of the circumstances which led the Japanese into their great miscalculation. We found ourselves with scant margins for strategic choices. With conditions as they were, the decision to make the primary military effort against the Germans was the best that could be done, but it resulted in a vast disadvantage to us in the Asian Theater. By the time we were able to turn our attention to Asia, it was too late to do very much in building up Chiang Kai-shek into a viable force on the Asian continent.

After 1945 we proceeded with a unilateral disarmament. Our conventional forces practically disappeared. We made a unique offer to negotiate with the Russians, the British, the French, and all the leading states in the United Nations about the international control of this great new force, atomic energy. I myself worked on the plan which we laid before the UN and all the time it seemed to me that the chances were almost nil that the Russians would join in any such negotiation. Our intelligence was clear that they were already at work on a weapon of their own. Any knowledge of the Russian temperament would have led anyone to believe that they would not rest upon international agreements, but they would insist that they must have a power equal to the power of the strongest nation in the world.

However, we went ahead, both disarming and negotiating until, when I became Secretary of State, the budget for defense for the fiscal year 1951 was down to $14.5 billion. This, I may say, terrified me, then the President, and finally the Secretary of Defense. We had two working parties set to work in which the task of both chairmanships fell to me. One was State-Defense organization which reviewed the entire foreign policy and military policy of the United States. Its work resulted in a national security paper called NSC 68 which is still classified and which has laid the foundation of both our foreign and military policy ever since.

The second dealt with the question of what to do about a hydrogen bomb. Scientific opinion was divided. Some scientists believed that the hydrogen atom could be split and that a hydrogen weapon of much greater force than the atom bomb could be made. Others said it was impossible.

Almost everything that was said in the discussion which followed has been said about the ABM before Committees of Congress in recent hearings. Hardly a new idea has been brought out to any of you. The same curious transformations happen now as happened then. The scientists to a large extent ceased to be scientists and tried to discourse as moralists and political scientists. They talked then about the wickedness of going forward to find out whether one could make an even more terrible weapon than the atom bomb.

Then, as now, laymen could have no scientific opinion whether the weapon could be made or not. It was futile for me to try to understand that aspect of the problem. I listened to one scientist in favor of it; he seemed persuasive. Then I would listen to one against it, and he also seemed persuasive. I knew nothing about the basic physical considerations involved. We knew however, that the Russians were going forward with work along these lines. It seemed absolute folly for us to deny ourselves knowledge of this sort when the Russians were developing such knowledge and to forego capacity to produce in this field, dreadful as it might be, thus permitting the Russians to have a monopoly of that capacity.

It came about that eventually, in November of 1952, we had a test of a thermonuclear device. Less than a year later the Russians announced and then tested a fully developed hydrogen bomb. They were ahead of us in weapon development, not behind us. Any idea that our venture into this field was what had stimulated the Russians to enter it was substantially refuted. It was not until March 1954 that we produced a hydrogen bomb.

After 1946 we continued our own disarming, as I said. The result was the war in Korea, which was again the obvious result of a calculation that we could not and would not undertake to propose a move in so remote an area even though it was an area over which we were at the very time exercising responsibility. Korea gave the recommendations of NSC 68 life and importance and led the Congress to support a great rearmament of the United States. It also quickened our efforts on the thermonuclear weapon.

I have mentioned this long sequence of events to show that every time we relax our efforts in the defense field, we regret it, and that by increasing our efforts and maintaining a solid and prudent stance, we do not discourage or impair negotiation with anybody.

One of our failings as a people I think is a preoccupation with witches. For some among us it is hard to get accustomed to the new circumstances. The temptation is to take the old situation as normal, to regard the huge expense and unremitting danger as aberrant, and to blame malign or heedless forces within our own establishment. Identify them, expose their machinations, cut down their powers, and lo the difficulties will be abated. So goes the argument, in a succession of faddish versions.

A version in vogue in the thirties cast the munitions industry as the malefactor. A few overzealous weapon merchants were supposed to have woven an evil spell over the nation. In the fifties, a handful of faithless persons at the center of policy-making were supposed to have manipulated the world to disparage our interests and undercut our security. The current substitute for serious thought is a cliche about a military industrial complex. Our involvements abroad, alleged to impede great strides in domestic improvement, are portrayed as something put over on a gullible nation by an excess of professional zeal at the Pentagon coupled with overactive entrepreneurship in industry.

In the 'twenties and 'thirties we had two witches—bankers and munition makers—as malefactors. Mr. Nye took care of the munition makers by passing legislation which made it almost impossible to help the allies in the early part of the Second World War. And you remember the outstanding episode in getting control of the bankers was when somebody put a midget on Mr. J. P. Morgan's lap and had him photographed at a congressional hearing. That was the mood of reformist activity of those days.

After the Second World War we had the contribution of the first Senator McCarthy in running down internal subversives. This was a time when I had perhaps my greatest prominence in the press as the well-known communist who was at the head of a group of communists in the State Department.

In 1969 the witch has changed and is now the military-industrial complex. This I find the strangest one of all. As most of the other witches were not known certainly to be communists, I cannot imagine that anybody on this Committee could take seriously the thought that such great people as General Marshall or Joe Collins or Hoyt Vandenberg or General Bradley or Admiral Forrest Sherman or Admiral Allen Kirk would be engaged in a conspiracy to waste the funds and money of the United States uselessly. And today their counterparts are equally incapable of such action. I should hope that that foolish cliché will be dropped for good.

What I decry is the effort to portray marginal problems as centrally important. It was probably a good idea to regulate the munitions industry in the thirties. It was folly to try to put American strategy into a straitjacket in the Neutrality Acts. Tighter security regulations were in order in the fifties. What was reprehensible was the attempt to exploit the situation as a lever for overthrowing due process and subverting our pattern of constitutional authority. Intensified rigor in congressional review of defense appropriations may well be appropriate now. What I wish to warn against—and I do so with all the emphasis at my command—is any effort to use the attendant issues as an excuse for tampering with defense and foreign policies which rise from external necessities and are vital to national existence.

Coming to my third point, the power of the United States alone blocks the Sino-Soviet ambitions in this world. They may fall out between themselves, they may have difficulties, they may fight with one another in a minor way, but on one matter they are completely and wholly agreed. The United States is the enemy.

It is our power which stands in the way of their ambitions and they have no doubt about that at all. We, as I said earlier, are alone at this pinnacle of power. There is an idea which has been given some currency by Mr. Walter Lippmann that it is our commitments which have outrun our capabilities. This is exactly backwards. Our capabilities are attempts to get aid in carrying out our responsibilities. Commitments have not created the difficulty. The difficulty is created by the outside world. For example, the NATO Treaty seeks to hold together the countries in Europe which, if held together, would deny their resources to the Soviet Union and make some of our problems more manageable. If they are not held together, if they are not under an umbrella of the United States, they can very easily be put under Soviet direction, and then our difficulties would be very great.

The same thing is true with the major treaties in the Pacific. Not all treaties are sensible. I thought that the Dulles treaties in the Far East and in the Middle East were a mistake. I thought there we did not need to have any commitment of any kind and we could draw no strength from them at all. I was much more in favor of having treaties among the Asian countries with the rest of us backing up the ones who got into trouble if they did get into trouble. But the moment we, Britain, and others got into CENTO and SEATO, it seemed to me that we alienated rather than encouraged support. However, this is a matter of not major importance here. As I said before, the dominating fact is that our power alone can protect the amplitude of the free world which makes our free life possible. In isolation, in a Fortress America, we could not have the kind of a country we have. We simply could not. And it is to our advantage, it is essential to our survival, that there should be a spacious area of freedom in the world.

It is in this setting that you approach your great task of deciding whether or not you think it wise as a priority matter to allot the resources necessary to go forward with the President's recommendation about the ABM.

How would one sensibly go about performing this duty? As I said a moment ago, when I had it to perform in connection with the H-bomb, I did my best to understand the technical arguments which were going on, but I felt that really that was not my province. These matters had been discussed and recommendation had been made by people who were charged with knowing more about them than I know or understand. It seemed to me that in making the choice one had to choose between the responsibility one took by going forward and the responsibility one took by standing still. I felt in the case of the thermonuclear bomb, with what I knew about the world, that the proper responsibility for me to take was to say go forward. Let us know as much about thermonuclear phenomena as anybody in the world. Let us take the chance of avoiding the necessary and finding ourselves in a very dangerous predicament.

So it seemed to me that the simpler part of my duty was to accept the recommendation and go forward with it.

If you analyze the problem further, you must have in mind the size of it. A great deal of talk by opponents of this proposal, both in the Armed Services Committee, the Foreign Relations Committee, and your Committee, gives one the impression that this is a vast program of such tremendous dimensions that it really forces a choice between a constructive domestic program and this. That just is not true at all. It is not remotely true. The dimensions of this problem have been exaggerated out of all sense of reality. It just is not that sort of a problem.

The *Washington Post* sometime ago published an interesting little chart which gave the spending by the United States on non-defense and defense from 1965, which is the real start of the Vietnamese war. One sees from it that non-defense spending has not only increased but has continued to be substantially ahead of defense spending. For instance, the budget for the current fiscal year, non-defense is $106 billion and for defense is $80 billion. As I look at the world, those magnitudes do not seem a disproportionate allocation of our resources. The part of the defense budget involved in the ABM program is $8 billion over a period of five years. If you add in the research and development costs, you get $11 billion. That is not a vast bet.

Suppose the expenditure is not made, and suppose the choice turns out wrong. The consequences could be disastrous. Turn the proposition around. Say to yourself that, to be on the safe side, we had better go ahead. Then suppose that the proponents of the ABM turn out to be wrong and that this weapon will not do all that they say it will do. Has anything disastrous happened? Have you wrecked the United States? Have you ruined the internal economy? Certainly not. What you may well have discovered is that the other side is not doing any better than we. Therefore, the danger is not so great as the military thought it would be.

The bets seem to me wholly different in kind and quality. The responsibilities seem to be wholly different. To reject ABM may mean terrible trouble. To go ahead with it cannot mean terrible trouble. It may indeed bring great assurance. If you lose the whole investment, it is not a very serious loss.

Will going ahead minimize the chances of having a negotiation with the Russians? I can assure you that this is not so. Not because I set myself up as the wisest man in the world but because a good deal of experience has led me to believe what I started out by saying. The Russian conception of negotiation is based on what they call the calculation of forces.

Let me illustrate this by two experiences. The first one concerns the blockade of Berlin. The Russians began the blockade of Berlin to frustrate the attempt of the allies to reconstruct Europe. What we were all trying to do was, first of all, to restore physically through the Marshall Plan our allies and a defeated Germany, and, having done that, to create some kind of a government capable of governing Germany, which would cease to be a menace to its neighbors.

What the Russians decided was that they were going to keep Germany divided. They would rather have complete control of East Germany than partial control of all Germany. So they started a series of actions against our actions which finally led to the blockade of Berlin.

At this point, there were several discussions as to what should be done. Some said, "We have the nuclear weapon and can use it to frighten the Russians." Only a few of us knew how few were the nuclear weapons we had. They were not a frightening number. Furthermore, the only way we could then use these weapons was to drop them from aircraft. And the Russians were in Germany, and we were likely to do more damage to Germany than we would do to the Russians. So this did not seem to be a wise response.

What did we do? We undertook a counter blockade. That is, we isolated East Germany from Europe and the West. As time went on, that measure hurt the Russians a great deal more than their blockade was hurting our side—particularly when we got the airlift going and it turned out to be such a signal success. The Russians did not wish to push the situation to a military confrontation because we had not only a few nuclear weapons, which would have been unhappy for them at home, but also some local forces which would have been difficult for them to deal with on the ground.

Time went on through 1948. Early in 1949, shortly after I became Secretary, a newspaperman asked Stalin some questions, which he answered. It seemed to me and my colleagues odd that Stalin would answer these questions because they were not of immediate importance and they did not say much that had not been said before. In discussing them we decided that this looked like a signal that the Russians were ready to quit if they could make a deal. So I got Phil Jessup, who was then at the United Nations, to see Malik and say that he had been interested in Stalin's answers to these questions and wondered whether there was anything more behind them than met the eye. Malik said, "Of course, well, I don't know. I haven't got the faintest idea." Phil said, "If you hear anything, let me know, will you?" He said, "Sure." Two or three weeks later Malik passed Jessup in the hall and said, "Oh, by the way, in answer to your question, there is a good deal more behind it than meets the eye." Phil said, "Fine. And would you want to tell me what it is?" Malik said, "You didn't ask me that before. I will try to find out again."

We had a secret negotiation known only to Jessup, Chip Bohlen, myself, and the President. Nobody else. Nobody telephoned. Nobody telegraphed. Nobody wrote. Everybody got on an airplane or a train and went back and forth to New York. This was done at the UN. Finally, Malik said to Phil Jessup, "I have word that we will call off the blockade if you call off the counter blockade, call off the creation of a West German State, and call a meeting of foreign ministers." And we said that the first two could be a deal. We said we would not call off forming a West German State because that could not be achieved until the autumn anyway. It was then only spring. We would go ahead and have a meeting of foreign ministers as soon as the blockade was lifted. If we could solve the whole German problem, we would not go ahead. If we could not, we would go ahead with West Germany.

After a great deal of groaning and grunting the Russians agreed to the deal.

This is what I was referring to when I quoted Sir William Hayter. There is nothing delicate about dealing with Moscow. You don't have to wear dark glasses and rubbers and creep around, you know.

The other matter was the ending of the Korean War. After MacArthur's unwise attempt to go to the Yalu River against his instructions, and our defeat in Korea, we thought of various things to do next. It seemed to us that we were drifting more and more into a really major confrontation which might involve the Russians in the Far East. We had finally stabilized the Korean front and dismissed General MacArthur. General Ridgway had created the Kansas line and this was holding strongly against all attempts by the Chinese to break it, but there were possibilities that the Russian Air Force might intervene, or they might land some troops. If this happened we were in for it as this would be World War III. We wanted to be sure that everybody understood everybody else's attitude. I suggested to George Kennan that he write a note to Malik and say that he would like to come up and have a chat, not having seen him for a long time. Malik suggested that Kennan meet him at his place on Long Island.

So he did. Kennan pointed out the way things were going; we were on a collision course here which we did not desire. They would be crazy to desire it because it would be a Chinese gain and not a Russian gain if it came off. But inevitably, if matters were pushed to the point of an attack, we would all end up in war. And we warned them that this had an end which they had better think over.

The answer came back that we quite misunderstood them. They did not want to push hostilities and believed that there should be an armistice. Malik made a public speech and presented this view on a UN radio program.

We had an awful time with the Chinese and the North Koreans after that for two years, but the Russian part of it was very, very simple. It was just a matter of putting to them a proposition which they could take or leave. They took it. They did what they could, and they stepped out.

The idea has been expressed that if we take the step proposed here it is going to make negotiations much more difficult. It is not going to make it any more difficult. Any negotiation will be difficult to start with. All the problems are very difficult. They are not made any more difficult by adding to our defense. I doubt emphatically that some great transformation of relations with the Soviet Union is about to move us from an era of confrontation to a phase of negotiation. We have been negotiating with the Soviet Union all along. We shall be involved in confrontation into an indeterminate future. The two go hand-in-hand in the Soviet view, and perforce we must see the matter in that perspective. The Soviet Union will come into agreement with us only in the measure that it discerns advantage in doing so and detriment in doing otherwise. I certainly do not oppose such negotiations. I am merely warning against the notion that the Soviet Union is on the verge of a conversion to tractability and accommodation.

This ABM proposal is a defensive action. The Russians realize that quite as well as the free world or anybody else does. They are working on it themselves. They are deeply into it. They know what it will do, and their whole purpose is to take out an incoming weapon. They may use it to take out a weapon before it is incoming, in which case it becomes an offensive weapon, but they know that what we are proposing is to meet what they might send against us.

This does not raise any problems with them. They are not children. They are not frightened. They are not easily scared. And if ABM works out and if it is true, as I believe it has been testified before either to your committee or another, that this operation as proposed can protect the Minutemen as they exist, and if the Russian attempt is increased, the defense can be increased at a lower cost than the offense. It does not add to the problem. It simplifies the problem.

I have come, Mr. Chairman, at your urging, to give you what wisdom I have summed up in these four points. If I had the responsibility, which is laid upon you, I would accept the recommendation of my constitutional advisor and go forward with it, confident that if it turns out to be good advice, we have greatly benefited the country. If it turns out to be unworkable, we at least shall know it is unworkable and we shall know also that what the other fellow is doing is unworkable, we will have a parity of knowledge and we will not have wasted the nation's resources in finding out.

THE CIVILIAN COMPLEX

Barry Goldwater

Mr. President: As a member of the Senate Armed Services Committee and as a member of the Senate Preparedness Subcommittee, I am greatly interested in the growing preoccupation of some groups and individuals these days with the so-called military-industrial complex in the United States. Indeed, if I were a psychologist, I might be tempted to the conclusion that the left wing in American politics has developed a "complex over a complex."

Judging from the view expressed by many of our public officials and commentators, the so-called military-industrial complex would seem to be responsible for almost all of the world's evils. Certainly a determined effort is under way to place at its doorstep almost full responsibility for the unfortunate war in Vietnam and the high cost of American defense.

We further find great attention being paid to the number of former military officers who have gone to work for defense-related industry. It has been shown with considerable flourish and head-shaking that some 2,000 former members of the United States Armed Services now are employed by companies that do business with the Defense Department. This revelation seemed to imply some kind of an unholy but non-specific alliance on the part of industry and one-time military officers to cheat and defraud the American taxpayer.

In presenting information on former military men employed by defense industries to the Senate on March 24, the gentleman from Wisconsin, Senator Proxmire, was careful to say that he was not charg-

Congressional Record, 91st Cong., 1st Sess., April 15, 1969, vol. 115, pp. S3719–S3721.

ing any general wrongdoing on anybody's part and that he had found no evidence that any conspiracy exists. He seemed most concerned about a condition he described as "the old school tie" and the fact that many former high-ranking officers working in defense industry still retain personal friendships with some men still in the services. He accurately observed that "there is a continuing community of interest between the military, on one hand, and these industries on the other."

Now, Mr. President, I don't see how anyone could deny either the fact that friendships continue or that a community of interest exists between the military and the people who supply them with the tools of their trade.

Consequently, I am quite mystified to understand why this situation strikes the gentleman from Wisconsin as—and I use his exact words—"most dangerous and shocking." I am sure that the gentleman would agree that former members of Congress now working for industries that do business with the United States Government still retain friendships with present members of the House and Senate. I am also sure that he would agree that former government officials now employed by companies doing business with the government retain "old school tie" relationships with friends they made while in the government and with friends still working in the government. This situation even exists, I believe, with some officials who once worked for government regulatory agencies and now are employed by industries which are being regulated. But apparently the critics of the military-industrial complex do not find situations like this shocking or dangerous.

Mr. President, .perhaps the "old school tie" is more binding if it happens to be the khaki-colored type worn by military men. Critics of the military seem to think so.

And in this connection I would like to point out the figure of 2,000-plus retired military officers working for defense-related industries is impressive only when it is permitted to stand by itself and without the proper explanation. These 2,000 officers are employed by 100 of the largest corporations in the world. They are employed by industries which do many billions of dollars worth of business every year. And these 2,000 former military men are only a very small fraction of the tens of thousands of employees who work for these 100 industries. What's more, they represent only a small portion of the military officers who have been retired. I am informed by the Pentagon that the number of former military officers receiving retired pay as of June, 1968 totaled 232,892. I also discovered that since the end of World War II some 36,800 officers in the highest grades (colonels and above) have been retired. A total of 21,484 were retired between the years 1961 and 1968.

Mr. President, I believe these figures make it amply clear that high-ranking military officers are not rushing into retirement at the beckoning of defense contractors.

Be that as it may, I believe it is long past time when these questions relating fundamentally to the defense of this nation should be placed in their proper perspective. Let us take the military-industrial complex and examine it closely. What it amounts to is that we have a big military establishment, and we have a big industrial plant which helps to supply that establishment. This apparently constitutes a "complex." If so, I certainly can find nothing to criticize but much to be thankful for in its existence. Ask yourselves, for example, why we have a large, expensive military establishment and why we have a large and capable defense industry. The answer is simply this: We have huge worldwide responsibilities. We face tremendous worldwide challenges. In short, we urgently require both a big defense establishment and a big industrial capacity. Both are essential to our safety and to the preservation of freedom in a world fraught with totalitarian aggression.

Merely because our huge responsibilities necessitate the existence of a military-industrial complex does not automatically make that complex something we must fear or feel ashamed of. You might consider where we would be in any negotiations which might be entered into with the Soviet Union if we did not have a big military backed by a big industrial complex to support our arguments. You might wonder how we could possibly pretend to be interested in the freedom of smaller nations if the only military-industrial complex in the world was possessed by Communist Russia or Communist China.

Mr. President, in many respects I am reminded of the problem which confronted our nation in the early days of World War II. The madman Hitler was running rampant. Freedom was being trampled throughout all of Europe. Suddenly the United States found itself forced to fill the role of the "arsenal of democracy." This nation had to start from scratch and finally out-produce the combined efforts of the Axis powers. And we had to do it quickly. The very existence of freedom in the world as we knew it in the early 1940's depended on it. And how did we perform this miracle? Well, I'll tell you that we performed it with the help of an industrial giant called an integrated steel industry. Although this industry and others like it performed miracles of production at a time when the chips were down all over the world, it still was the subject of long and harassing investigation after the war because of its "bigness." Incredible as it seems, the very size of an industry which enabled us to defeat the Fascist armies and remain free became the reason for investigation by liberals in the Congress during the immediate postwar period.

We never, Mr. President, seem to understand that size is not necessarily an evil. When the Russian Sputnik went up, this nation was deeply concerned. And that concern had to do with our inability at that time to duplicate the Soviet feat. Now that we have the industrial capacity to equal the Russians in space or in matters related to defense, there seems to be a nationwide effort to make us feel guilty.

What would the critics of the military-industrial complex have us do? Would they have us ignore the fact that progress occurs in the field of national defense as well as in the field of social sciences? Do they want us to turn back the clock, disband our military establishment and do away with our defense-related industrial capacity? Mr. President, do these critics of what they term a military-industrial complex really want us to default on our worldwide responsibilities, turn our backs on aggression and slavery and develop a national policy of selfish isolation?

Rather than deploring the existence of a military-industrial complex, I say we should thank heavens for it. That complex gives us our protective shield. It is the bubble under which our nation thrives and prospers. It is the armor which is unfortunately required in a world divided.

For all those who rant and rave about the military-industrial complex, I ask this question: What would you replace it with?

What's more, I believe it is fair to inquire whether the name presently applied is inclusive enough. Consider the large number of scientists who contributed all of the fundamental research necessary to develop and build nuclear weapons and other products of today's defense industries. Viewing this, shouldn't we call it the "scientific-military-industrial complex"? By the same token, don't forget the amount of research that has gone on in our colleges and universities in support of our defense-related projects. Maybe we should call it an "education-scientific-military-industrial complex." Then, of course, the vast financing that goes into this effort certainly makes the economic community an integral part of any such complex. Now we have a name that runs like this: "An economic-educational-scientific-military-industrial complex."

What we are talking about, Mr. President, is an undertaking which grew up from necessity. It is the product of American initiative, incentive and genius responding to a huge global challenge. It is perhaps the most effective and efficient complex ever built to fill a worldwide function. Its ultimate aim is peace in our time regardless of the aggressive, militaristic image which the left wing is attempting to give it.

Mr. President, I don't find the employment of military officers by 100 of the largest companies in this nation alarming or menacing. Many of those officers were technically trained to provide special services, many of which are required by the companies involved. And I hasten to point out that these same companies employ other free Americans, some of them former Senators, some of them former Congressmen, some of them former civilian employees of the government. It is my contention that a retired military officer is a private citizen. He has a right to seek employment wherever he can. It is only natural that he should look to sources of employment which involve matters he was trained to work in. The fact that he once was an Army officer and the company he works for does business with the Army does not automatically insure an undesirable relationship from the public viewpoint. I would like to say that anyone who has evidence of wrongdoing, of deliberate and unlawful favoritism in the dealings which involve defense industries and former military officers should come forth and make the circumstances clear. I say that anyone who has evidence that a conspiracy exists between the Pentagon on one hand and former military officers on the other should say so and produce evidence to back it up. I say that anyone who charges that a "military elite" is at work trying to turn the United States into an aggressive nation should stop dealing in generalities and come forward with names, specific dates, meeting place locations, and all the rest of the kind of data it takes to back up such a charge.

So far, Mr. President, I have yet to hear of any specific case of wrongdoing involving former military officers working for companies that do business with the Pentagon. In fact, I believe the record will show that the largest single cloud ever to hang over the so-called military-industrial complex stemmed from decisions made by civilian officers in the Department of Defense. I am, of course, speaking about the incredible circumstances surrounding the awarding of the largest defense contract in the history of the world to a company whose bid had been rejected by nearly all the military specialists and evaluation boards in the Pentagon. The contract was the multi-billion dollar TFX contract which former Defense Secretary Robert McNamara, former Navy Secretary Fred Korth and former Undersecretary of Defense Roswell Gilpatrick jammed down the throats of the Navy and Air Force.

This was undoubtedly the costliest fumble in American history. It has never been properly dealt with and I suggest to those, especially those in this body, who are sincerely interested in the dangers of a military-industrial complex becoming too powerful in this nation that a full investigation be launched into all aspects of the TFX–F111 fiasco. I would recommend that the activities of all present and former military and civilian officials involved in the awarding of the TFX contract be examined. I find it highly interesting, by the way, that one of those most directly involved in this questionable decision—Mr. Gilpatrick—is now part of the panel of experts being consulted by a member of the United States Senate in connection with his compaign to defeat the deployment of a missile defense in this country.

Mr. President, I hope I shall be fully understood in this respect. If there is wrongdoing, whether of a conflict of interest nature or something else, in our defense establishment I want it investigated and stopped and the guilty parties punished. And this goes for wrong-doing by anyone concerned, whether he be a military man, a former military man, a defense industry executive or a civilian officer of the government. I feel that this is our true concern. Maybe the hugeness of the system which we are now compelled to maintain does lend itself to improprieties. If so, let us concern ourselves with such improprieties and find means to deal with them legislatively. This is the constructive way to proceed. It does no good for us to gaze with awe on the tremendous increase in defense expenditures with which the McNamara Era saddled us and then pretend that denunciation of a military-industrial complex will somehow make it all right.

In the attacks on the military also you will find repeated reference to a speech once made by former President Eisenhower.

But I would remind you that when Dwight Eisenhower mentioned the possibility of unwarranted influence being acquired by such a complex, he had some other profound things to say. I want to quote one passage in particular. He said and I quote, "We face a hostile ideology—global in scope, atheistic in character, ruthless in purpose and insidious in method. Unhappily the danger it poses promises to be of indefinite duration. To meet it successfully, there is call for, not so much the emotional and transitory sacrifices of crisis, but rather those which enable us to carry forward steadily, surely, and without complaint the burdens of a prolonged and complex struggle—with liberty the stake. Only thus shall we remain, despite every provocation, on our charted course toward permanent peace and human betterment. . . . A vital element in keeping the peace is our military establishment. Our arms must be mighty, ready for instant action, so that no potential aggressor may be tempted to risk his own destruction."

As I have pointed out, many of the problems that are being encountered in the area of national defense today stem not so much from a military-industrial complex as they do from the mistakes and miscalculations of a "civilian complex" or perhaps I should say a "civilian-computer complex." My reference here, of course, is to the Pentagon hierarchy of young civilians (often referred to as the "whiz kids") which was erected during the McNamara era in the questionable name of "cost effectiveness." And this complex, Mr. President, was built in some measure to shut out the military voice in a large area of defense policy decision-making.

I suggest that the military-industrial complex is not the all-powerful structure that our liberal friends would have us believe. Certainly nobody can deny that this combination took a drubbing at the hands of Mr. McNamara and his civilian cadres during the past eight years.

If the military-industrial complex had been as strong and as cohesive as its critics would have us believe, it is entirely possible this nation and its taxpayers would not today be facing the need for rebuilding the defenses of freedom. I have already mentioned one example. The TFX decision which has proven to be such a costly fiasco was made by the civilian complex against the advice of experienced military men.

If the military-industrial complex had been the irresistible giant its critics describe, we would certainly today be better equipped. We would undoubtedly have a nuclear-powered navy adequate to the challenge presented by Soviet naval might. We would certainly have in the air—and not just on a drawing board—a manned, carry-on bomber. We would never have encountered the kind of shortages which cropped up in every area of the military as a result of the demands from Vietnam. There would have been no shortage of military helicopters. There would have been no shortage of trained helicopter pilots. There would have been no need to use outdated and faulty equipment. No concern ever would have arisen over whether our supply of bombs was sufficient to the task in Southeast Asia.

In conclusion, Mr. President, I want to point out that a very strong case can be made for the need for *a more powerful* military-industrial complex than we have had during the past eight years. At the very least, I wish to say that the employment practices of industries doing business with the Pentagon—practices which lead them to hire the most knowledgeable men to do their work—are no cause for shock. Nor are these practices dangerous to the American people.

I have great faith in the civilian leaders of our government and of our military services. I have no desire to see the voice of the military become all-powerful or even dominant in our national affairs. But I do believe that the military viewpoint must always be heard in the highest councils of our government in all matters directly affecting the protection and security of our nation.

ON CRITICS OF THE MILITARY

Richard M. Nixon

DERISION OF MILITARISM

However, I must warn you that in the years to come you may hear your commitment to America's responsibility in the world derided as a form of militarism.

It is important that you recognize that strawman issue for what it is, the outward sign of a desire by some to turn America inward—and to have America turn away from greatness.

I am not speaking about those responsible critics who reveal waste and inefficiency in our defense establishment, who demand clear answers on procurement problems, who want to make sure a new weapons system will truly add to our defense.

On the contrary, you should be in the vanguard of that movement. Nor do I speak of those with sharp eyes and sharp pencils who are examining our post-Vietnam planning with other pressing national priorities in mind. I count myself as one of those.

But as your Commander in Chief, I want to relay to you as future officers of our armed forces some of my thoughts on these great issues of national moment.

I worked closely with President Eisenhower for eight years. I know what he meant when he said "we must guard against the acquisition of unwarranted influence, whether sought or unsought, by the military-industrial complex."

Excerpts from the President's speech at the Air Force Academy, *New York Times,* June 5, 1969, p. 30.

Many people conveniently forget that he followed that warning with another. "We must also be alert to the equal and opposite danger that public policy could itself become the captive of a scientific-technological elite."

And we sometimes forget that, in that same farewell address, President Eisenhower spoke of the need for national security. He said a vital element in keeping the peace is our military establishment. Our arms must be mighty, ready for instant action, so that no potential aggressor may be tempted to risk his own destruction.

And I say to you, my fellow Americans, let us never forget those wise words of one of America's greatest leaders.

NEVER A "SACRED COW"

The American defense establishment should never be a sacred cow. But on the other hand, the American military should never be anybody's scapegoat.

America's wealth is enormous, but it is not limitless. Every dollar available in the Federal Government has been taken from the American people in taxes. And a responsible government has a duty to be prudent when it spends the people's money.

There is no more justification for wasting money on unnecessary military hardware than there is for wasting it on unwarranted social programs.

And there can be no question that we should not spend unnecessarily for defense. But we must also not confuse our priorities.

The question, I submit, in defense spending is a very simple one. How much is necessary? The President of the United States is the man charged with making that judgment.

After a complete review of our foreign and defense policies, I have submitted requests to the Congress for military appropriations. Some of these are admittedly controversial. These requests represent the minimum I believe essential for the United States to meet its current and long-range obligations to itself and the free world.

MILITARY EXPENDITURES

I have asked only for those programs and those expenditures that I believe are necessary to guarantee the security of this country and to honor our obligations. And I will bear the responsibility for those judgments.

I do not consider my recommendations infallible. But if I have made a mistake, I pray that it is on the side of too much and not too little.

If we do too much, it will cost us our money. If we do too little, it may cost us our lives.

Mistakes in military policy today can be irretrievable. Time lost in this age of science can never be regained. America had months in order to prepare and to catch up in order to wage World War I. We had months and even years in order to catch up so that we could play a role in winning World War II.

When a war can be decided in 20 minutes, the nation that is behind will have no time to catch up. And I say, let America never fall behind in maintaining the defenses necessary for the strength of this nation.

I have no choice in my decisions but to come down on the side of security because history has dealt harshly with those nations who have taken the other course.

CREDO FOR DEFENDERS

And so in that spirit for the members of this graduating class, let me offer this credo for the defenders of our nation:

—I believe that we must balance our need for survival of the nation with our need for survival as a people. Americans—soldiers and civilians—must remember that defense is not an end in itself; it is a way of holding fast to the deepest values known to civilized man.

—I believe that our defense establishment will remain the servant of our national policy of bringing about peace in the world, and that those in any way connected with the military must scrupulously avoid even the appearance of becoming the master of that policy.

—I believe that every man in uniform is a citizen first and a serviceman second, and that we must resist any attempt to isolate or separate the defenders from the defended. So you can see that in this regard, those who agitate for the removal of the R.O.T.C. from college campuses only contribute to an unwanted militarism.

—I believe that the basis for decisions on defense spending must be "what do we need for our security" and not "what will this mean for business and employment." The Defense Department must never be considered as a modern W.P.A. There are far better ways for Government to help ensure a sound prosperity and high employment.

—I feel that moderation has a moral significance only in those who have another choice. The weak can only plead; magnanimity and restraint gain moral meaning coming from the strong.

—I believe that defense decisions must be made on the hard realities of the offensive capabilities of our potential adversaries, and not on the fervent hopes about their intentions. With Thomas Jefferson, we can prefer "the flatteries of hope" to the gloom of despair, but we cannot survive in the real world if we plan our defense in a dream world.

—I believe we must take risks for peace—but calculated risks, not foolish risks. We shall not trade our defenses for a disarming smile or charming words. We are prepared for new initiatives in the control of arms, in the context of other specific moves to reduce tensions around the world.

—I believe that America is not going to become a garrison state, or a welfare state, or a police state simply because the American people will defend our values from those forces, external or internal, that would challenge or erode them.

—And I believe this above all: That this nation shall continue to be a source of world leadership, a source of freedom's strength, in creating a just world order that will bring an end to war.

10 ☆ OTHER CRITICS OF THE COMPLEX

THE MILITARY–INDUSTRIAL COMPLEX EIGHT YEARS LATER

George S. McGovern

IN HIS FAREWELL ADDRESS to the nation, President Eisenhower delivered what must be regarded as the most significant and obviously the most quoted words of his administration. Calling attention to the vast technological and scientific revolution in modern warfare, Mr. Eisenhower said that while the United States had no significant arms industry before World War II, we would no longer rely on emergency improvisations. Thus we have created, he said, "a permanent armaments industry of vast proportions." Then the older soldier President delivered his oft-quoted but perhaps not fully comprehended warning. [See pp. 31–32.] As Jack Raymond, the able *New York Times* reporter who covered Pentagon affairs during and after the Eisenhower years, wrote:

> Eisenhower's concern over the "complex" was based to a considerable extent on military spending pressures on his budget. At the height of a particularly aggravating dispute over the respective merits of Army and Air Force antiaircraft weapons, he declared that "obviously political and financial considerations" rather than "strict military needs" were influencing the weapons debate. And on another occasion, when asked whether he would be willing to allocate more money for defense if the nation could, as his critics insisted, afford it, he replied heatedly, "I would not." Anyone "with any sense," he said, knew that if military spending were not restrained, the country would become a "garrison state."

Speech before the Annual Hanukkah Dinner, Yeshiva University, Waldorf Astoria, New York City, December 8, 1968.

Reflecting afterward on his experiences, Eisenhower confirmed his "uneasiness about the effect on the nation of tremendous peacetime military expenditures." He complained in his memoirs, "The military services, traditionally concerned with 100 percent security, are rarely satisfied with the amounts allocated to them, out of an even generous budget." As for private industries, they were spurred by the desire for profits and created "powerful lobbies to argue for even larger munitions expenditures." Regarding political influence, he added, "Each community in which a manufacturing plant or a military installation is located profits from the money spent and jobs created in the area."

The Eisenhower warning was delivered as President-elect John F. Kennedy was about to assume office. President Kennedy had campaigned on the necessity of closing what he was led to believe was a dangerous "missile gap." He doubtless profited politically from the missile scare and the criticism which General Maxwell Taylor and others had directed at the Eisenhower defense policies. Although the new President soon discovered that the missile gap was a myth, tensions stemming from Cuba, Southeast Asia and Berlin combined with the desire to build a broadened military competence led the Kennedy administration to increase the last Eisenhower defense budget by $10 billion.

Under the Johnson administration, the war in Vietnam and other defense outlays have added still another $30 billion.

Mr. Nixon takes office with a military budget of more than $82 billion in the current year—$40 billion above the budget that led to President Eisenhower's warning eight years ago. The $82 billion now being spent directly on military items represents 56% of the total federal budget. This does not include such war-related expenditures as veterans' affairs and the interest on our war debts which would raise the total to $107 billion, or 72% of the federal budget. By comparison, all of our expenditures for health, education and welfare come to only $17.2 billion—11 per cent of the total budget. Yet, in the recent campaign Mr. Nixon spoke of the need to increase military and space outlays including the deployment of a costly anti-ballistic missile system and other new weapons—while reducing non-military portions of the budget. One can hear in Washington these days from well-informed sources that even if the war in Vietnam is ended, the military budget will climb to over $100 billion in the next four years. Certainly, both the cost and the influence of the military complex will continue to mount unless the new administration and the Congress exercise more prudence than we have seen in the past.

The most serious internal threat facing the United States on the eve of the new Nixon administration is the mounting influence of the military-industrial complex of which Mr. Eisenhower warned. A central question facing the new administration and the American people will be whether we use the $30 billion now being squandered in Vietnam to improve the quality of our society, or permit it to be gobbled up by the military for a new string of gadgets and adventures such as the ill-advised anti-ballistic missile system.

The big military-aerospace contractors and their allies in the Pentagon and the Congress are already preparing to divert the billions now going to Vietnam into the production of sophisticated new planes, missiles and other armaments.

Mr. Bernard Nossiter of the *Washington Post* has brilliantly reported the fantastic projections of the major military contractors in an article in today's *Washington Post* that I would like to nominate as the most valuable public affairs reporting of 1968.

Listen to Mr. Nossiter's conclusions after a close look at our biggest military suppliers:

> The shrewd and skillful men who direct large, sophisticated defense firms look forward to a post-Vietnam world filled with military and space business.
>
> For them, the war's end means no uncomfortable conversion to alien civilian markets. Quite the contrary, and with no discoverable exception, they expect handsome increases in the complex planes and missiles, rich in electronics, that are the heart of their business.
>
> The view these firms take of their future has political significance. Some government officials and economists have been suggesting that the major aerospace companies are capable and ready to use their considerable managerial skills and engineering expertise to solve a broad array of pressing social problems. No less an authority than Defense Secretary Clark Clifford recently said: "We now have a military-industrial team with unique resources of experience, engineering talent, management and problem solving capacities, a team that must be used to help find the answers to complex domestic problems as it has found the answers to complex weapons systems. These answers can be put to good use by our cities and our states, by our schools, by large and small business alike." This kind of thinking raises hopes that the aerospace industry's ability and interest in domestic areas will supplant its concern with defense dollars. So, the argument runs, there need be no fear that the industrial wing of what has been called the "mili-

tary-industrial complex" will remain a continuing source of pressure for ever-expanding arms budgets.

However, an extended survey of industry leaders in Dallas, Fort Worth, San Diego and Los Angeles—the heartland of the aerospace world—offers little support for this view. The great defense contractors display only a marginal interest in work outside their accustomed military-space sphere, devote only a fraction of their resources to it, and, for the foreseeable future, see no economic reason to change their ways.

Edward LeFevre, who heads the Washington office of General Dynamics—the nation's largest arms contractor, puts it this way: "Basically, we're a big systems builder for military weapons. Over 90 per cent of our business is military. We're in that business to stay."

A high official in the Arms Control and Disarmament Agency who asked Mr. Nossiter to keep his name in confidence, said: "I'm not sanguine about any reductions in military spending, especially since the election. We are now at the edge of a precipice where we can escalate sharply. The industry thinks that agreements to limit arms are unlikely and will go all out to realize their expectations. We are at the threshold of another round in the arms race, just as we were eight years ago when we went all out for long-range missiles." Ling-Temco-Vought, the nation's eighth biggest military supplier, headed by the currently celebrated James J. Ling, expects its arms sales to more than double in the next five years with 80% of its business coming from the Pentagon and the Space agency.

A study compiled last year by the Electronics Industries Association, entitled "The Post-Vietnam Defense and Space Environment" concludes that arms control agreements "during the next decade are unlikely," the "likelihood of limited war will increase" and "thus for the electronic firms, the outlook is good in spite of (the end of hostilities in) Vietnam."

In Mr. Nossiter's words:

These forecasts govern the planning of aerospace firms and provide them with a rationale for promoting their views and wares. To an undetermined extent, the companies can be expected to use their influence to make their prophecies self-fulfilling. By no mean coincidence, their views of the world outlook usually coincide with conditions that would maximize their military orders.

The companies are understandably guarded in talking about the effect of more immediate political changes on their future. But they leave little doubt that an important source of their optimism lies in the departure of Defense Secretary Robert McNamara and the election of Richard Nixon.

"People are pressing for new programs more intensely than ever," says W. Paul Thayer, the quiet ex-test pilot who runs Ling's LTV Aerospace. "With McNamara stepping out, that was the turning point."

J. Leland Atwood, the low-keyed president and chief executive officer of North American Rockwell, an aviation designer for nearly 40 years, employs the cautious euphemisms of many modern corporate executives. "All of Mr. Nixon's statements on weapons and space are very positive," he says. "I think he has a little more awareness of these things than some people we've seen in the White House."

Samuel F. Downer, the financial vice president for LTV Aerospace, covers the walls of his sparkling new Dallas apartment with his own paintings and is proudest of a cityscape that looks west on New York's Wall Street ("because it's all there, the flag, the church and money"). For the energetic Downer, the postwar world must be bolstered with military orders.

"It's basic," he says. "Its selling appeal is defense of the home. This is one of the greatest appeals the politicians have to adjusting the system. If you're the President and you need a control factor in the economy, and you need to sell this factor, you can't sell Harlem and Watts but you can sell self-preservation, a new environment. We're going to increase defense budgets as long as those bastards in Russia are ahead of us. The American people understand this."

Richard E. Adams, the plain-spoken engineer who directs advanced projects for the Fort Worth division of General Dynamics, producer of the controversial F–111 fighter-bomber, also talks of the domestic political realities that favor expanding military business. In any conflict between increased spending on social programs and spending on defense, he says: "We know where the power is (on Capitol Hill and among the Executive Departments). There's going to be a lot of defense business and we're going to get our share of it."

These political estimates, global and domestic, are carefully translated by each company into dollar terms, new weapons systems and the amounts that will be spent for them. There is a standard industry view here and it runs like this:

Vietnam is eating up about $22 billion a year of the $80 billion defense outlay (the war's cost is actually about $6 billion more but this sum would be spent on repositioning American forces elsewhere if they were not in Vietnam). Only $2 billion of the Vietnam budget, however, buys the advanced weapons that the aerospace crowd makes. Thus, the war's end will do little damage to these companies: "We are little impacted by the cessation of hostilities." Military payrolls and makers of uniforms, artillery shells, C-rations and the like will bear the brunt of any cutback.

Thus, the end of hostilities opens up great new opportunities for sophisticated munitions makers. They and their Pentagon colleagues will press for bigger research and development budgets, an outlay guaranteed to produce new designs that military men could find irresistible. Several new weapons already designed will be ordered for extensive production. The VFX, a new Navy fighter-bomber; the VSX, an anti-submarine plane and the AMSA or Advanced Manned Strategic Aircraft, a new bomber, all fall in this category.

Over and above these items, each worth several billion dollars, are those on the Pentagon's "wish list" as it is known in the trade. It comprises more fighter wings; a V/STOL, or Vertical/Short Takeoff and Landing, transport; thickening the "thin" anti-ballistic-missile system so that it supposedly could shoot down Russian as well as Chinese nuclear missiles; a new fleet of submarines armed with missiles. Also, a new intercontinental ballistic missile for the Air Force; new light attack aircraft; a new series of interceptor planes and a new generation of MIRV, the Multiple Independently Targeted Re-entry Vehicle, a missile with several warheads, each capable of being electronically guided to a different target.

Looking at this shopping list, some knowledgeable Pentagon officials see post-Vietnam defense budgets conceivably rising to $100 billion a year in dollars of present purchasing power.

The aerospace executives are more modest. They think defense budgets will fall by $5 to $10 billion after the war, but then begin to grow at some constant percentage of an expanding gross national product. Space budgets, it is thought, will be held on their current plateau a bit longer, but in time will gently start climbing again, too.

None of this, however, detracts from the central theme: The great aerospace firms have a strong appetite for military business. They look forward to expanding, not contracting, their sales in this sphere.

One of the shrewdest and most important civilian officials at the Pentagon also sees the initiating process as a seamless web. "Pressures to spend more are going to be there," he says. In part, they come from the industry selling new weapons ideas, he thinks, "and in part from the military here. Each (military) guy has his own piece, tactical, anti-submarine, strategic. Each guy gets where he is by pushing his own particular thing. Don't forget, too, part of it is based on the perception of needs by people in Congress."

This, then, is the present prospect: powerful industrial giants eagerly pressing for more military business, Pentagon defense planners eager to get on with new weapons production, Congressmen whose districts profit directly from the anticipated contracts, and millions of Americans from the blue collar aircraft worker to the university physicist drawing their pay checks from the production of arms. About to take over the White House is a new President whose campaign left little doubt of his inclination to support the ABM and other costly arms spending while tightening up on expenditures for civilian purposes. This is the military-industrial complex of 1969.

Posed in opposition to this formidable challenge are the sobering warnings of the Kerner Commission reminding us that unless we set about the reconstruction of our cities—better housing, better schools, and more job training and job opportunities—we will confront a two-society nation exploding in bitterness, crime and violence.

More recently we have the thoughtful report of the Brookings Institution, "Agenda for the Nation," calling for an immediate end to the war in Vietnam and a major reduction in defense spending to not more than $50 billion in order to channel resources and energies into the reconstruction of our society. This report representing the thinking of 18 of our nation's best scholars, calls upon us to recognize that the day of the superpowers is over and that we must devise a foreign policy and a set of domestic priorities based less on military power and more on the quality of our society.

Nearly six years ago, as a freshman Senator, I called for a new criteria of national security based on the recognition that American power and influence in the world is based more on the excellence of our political, social and moral ideals than upon the size of our nuclear stockpile. I suggested that with a capacity to blow up the world many times over, we ought to reduce our military budget with the guidance of an Economic Conversion Commission designed to convert excess military competence to civilian construction. I close my first six-year term in the Senate and begin a second term with the same proposal.

I leave you tonight with this question: Will we permit our country and our posture in the world to fall increasingly under the sway of the military-industrial complex, or will we demonstrate the wisdom and the wit to realize that we will lose the American dream if we continue to pursue the illusion of security through arms?

Before we make that choice, let us recall the words of Virgil: "Easy is the descent to Hell; night and day the gates stand open; but to reclimb the slope and escape to the outer air, this indeed, is a task."

DIMENSIONS OF SECURITY

J. William Fulbright

MR. MANSFIELD. Mr. President, the chairman of the Committee on Foreign Relations, Senator FULBRIGHT, delivered a speech to the National War College on May 19, entitled "Dimensions of Security."

The student body at the National War College is one of the most distinguished and able in the United States. Speaking to that audience provided a good occasion for the chairman of the Foreign Relations Committee to convey to that group some of the deep concern some of us feel in the Senate about the direction of our foreign policy and its relation to our military posture.

There is little I can add to the remarks which Senator FULBRIGHT made, but I would like to emphasize that the speech as reported in the press may imply that the chairman of the committee has not been sympathetic and understanding and admiring of the conduct of American soldiers in the field. This simply is not true. Senator FULBRIGHT said: "The courage and endurance of our fighting men command the respect of all Americans; the fault in our war policy lies not with them but with the political decisions which committed them to an impossible task."

Mr. President, I ask unanimous consent that the remarks of Senator FULBRIGHT be inserted in the RECORD at this point.

There being no objection, the speech was ordered to be printed in the RECORD, as follows:

Congressional Record, 91st Cong., 1st Sess., May 20, 1969, vol. 115, no. 82, pp. S5393–S5395.

DIMENSIONS OF SECURITY

In the old Western movies there was a standard climax in which the villain emerged from his hideout shielded behind the captive heroine and snarling: "Shoot me and the girl dies!" I perceive in this old melodrama a kind of analogue to my own relations with the military. In these years of criticizing our war policy in Vietnam, I have thought a number of times that I had my fellow politicians in the executive branch concerned—intellectually, that is—only to have them burst out of their hideout shielded behind the military in the role of the heroine, and snarling: "Shoot me and the girl dies!"

I am tired—as I expect you may be—of seeing the military used as a hostage for policies made by civilian officials. I am tired of having my criticism of the war in Vietnam interpreted as an attack on our soldiers in the field. In fact it is no such thing. The courage and endurance of our fighting men command the respect of all Americans; the fault in our war policy lies not with them but with the political decisions which committed them to an impossible task. We have been trying to defeat a nationalist insurgency on behalf of a government which has shown itself incapable of inspiring either the support of its people or the fighting spirit of its army. For reasons having nothing to do with the fighting abilities of our GI's or the leadership qualities of their officers, that task has been found impossible—not in the sense that it is beyond our military means but because it is beyond any military means that we have been morally and politically willing to employ.

Some of us have perhaps not been as aware as we should of the anguish that Vietnam has involved for our professional soldiers. In the two world wars, and even the Korean War, our armed forces were bolstered by stalwart allies and strong public support at home. Both of these are lacking in Vietnam: our client is a weak reed and the American people are divided and demoralized. These, I am well aware, are heavy psychological burdens for an army facing a resourceful and tenacious enemy.

In addition, there is the specter of having to settle for something less than victory, perhaps even something less than a standoff. That would be a new experience for American soldiers, whose morale has been built not only on their unbroken history of success but on their "can-do" spirit in the face of any challenge. That spirit has served the American people well but it also contains a pitfall: it can lead an army to misjudge its prospects, by gauging them more on the basis of its own elan than a cold appreciation of the facts of the situation.

We politicians have a different standard. In our dealings with each other victories are rare; standoffs are routine; and sometimes we get beaten. Quite obviously soldiers cannot conduct wars by the pliant standards of parliamentarianism. But there is value in the experience of settling for less than you had hoped for, of trimming your sails, and carefully distinguishing between what you can do and what you cannot do. More than a few wars have been lost—I think of France in 1870 and Germany in 1914—in part because soldiers told their civilian chiefs that they could do more than it turned out they could do. And more than once in history a peace has been lost because politicians persuaded themselves that they could do more than it turned out they could do. In this connection, it occurs to me that few Presidential advisers, military or civilian, ever served their country and President better than General Ridgway did when he advised President Eisenhower in 1954, not that we could not intervene and win in Indochina, but that we could not do it at reasonable cost, or to any useful end. I think it is a great misfortune that there were no such persuasive "no-men" serving the Johnson Administration in 1964.

Mistakes are not liquidated with glory, and Vietnam, I believe, has been a mistake. At such time and by whatever means this war is ended, we are all likely to emerge somewhat sobered. There will be little for any of us to be proud of—except for the soldiers who fought so hard in so unpromising a cause. I stress this point to you as soldiers not only because I believe it to be true but, frankly, because I have had the fear that, out of an exaggerated feeling of our own responsibility for the stalemate in Vietnam, some of our military leaders have been professing an unwarranted optimism about the war, thereby encouraging its continuation.

THE DILEMMA OF ENDS AND MEANS

Having emphasized as clearly as I know how that I have no criticism to make of military *men*, or their performance in Vietnam, I turn now to the influence in our affairs that I *do* criticize: not the military but *militarism*, and its effects upon American life. I do not propose to be-labor you with a discourse on the military-industrial-labor-university complex. I expect you have heard something about it already—more perhaps than you have cared to hear. Nor do I propose to recite the list of our foreign installations and the names of the countries to which we have committed ourselves militarily by one means or another. I propose instead to suggest some of the ways in which our far-flung military commitments are bringing about profound changes in the character of our society and government—changes which are slowly undermining democratic procedure and values, and which, taken together, have set us on the path toward authoritarian government.

My theme is the relationship of ends to means, the connection between the objective of our foreign relations and the nature of the policies we pursue. The ultimate test of any foreign policy is not its short-term tactical success but its effectiveness in defending the basic values of the society. When a policy becomes incompatible with, or subversive of, those values, it is a bad policy, regardless of its technical or tactical effectiveness. I think we would all agree that the central, commanding goal of American foreign policy is the preservation of constitutional government in a free society. My apprehension is that we are subverting that goal by the very means chosen to defend it.

Confronted in the last generation with a series of challenges from dynamic totalitarian powers, we have felt ourselves compelled, gradually and inadvertently, to imitate some of the methods of our adversaries, seeking to fight fire with fire. I do not share the view that American fears of Soviet and Chinese aggressiveness have been uniformly paranoiac, although I think there have been a fair number of instances of that. My point is that the very objective we pursue—the preservation of a free society—proscribes certain kinds of policies to us even though they might be the most tactically expedient. We cannot, without doing to ourselves the very injury that we seek to secure ourselves against from foreign adversaries, pursue policies which rely primarily on the threat or use of force, because policies of force are inevitably disruptive of democratic values. Alexis de Tocqueville, that wisest of observers of American democracy, put it this way: "War does not always give democratic societies over to military government, but it must invariably and immeasurably increase the powers of civil government; it must almost automatically concentrate the direction of all men and the control of all things in the hands of the government. If that does not lead to despotism by sudden violence, it leads men gently in that direction by their habits. All those who seek to destroy the freedom of the democratic nations must know that war is the surest and shortest means to accomplish this. That is the very first axiom of their science." [1]

For more than a decade out of the last three we have been engaged in large-scale warfare, and for the rest of that period we have been engaged in the cold war and in ever more costly preparations for war. In the wake of our disappointment with the United Nations in the forties, we have taken it upon ourselves to preserve order and stability in much of the world, purporting to do on our own the things that Wilson and Roosevelt hoped to accomplish through world organization but never dreamed of America doing on its own. As I have said, I am not one of those who believe that these vast commitments were taken on out of delusion or the conscious lust for power. The threat, though exaggerated and distorted in some instances, has been real enough in others, but in either case the effect has been the same for our internal life. War, and the chronic threat of war, have been carrying us, "gently" by our "habits," toward despotism.

The dilemma involved in all this for a soldier must be a particularly agonizing one. It must sound as though he is being asked to fight with one hand behind his back, accepting limits upon his own stock in trade of which his adversary is free. And that is exactly what you, as soldiers, are being asked to do. You are asked to conceive of security in a dimension broader than that of your own trade. You are asked to conceive of security in terms of ends as well as means, in terms of the procedures and values of a free society as well as the most efficient means of thwarting an adversary.

There are times, to be sure, when a threat may seem so great and imminent as to warrant the circumvention of democratic procedure. There are times when war is thrust upon you. But there are times when a threat turns out in retrospect to have been less ominous than it seemed; there are times when we have some choice in the matter of war and peace. Psychologists tell us that our perceptions are only partly reflections of the real world; the other part is determined by our own expectations. I think that we have perceived more menace in the world around us than is actually there. I believe that we have had more choice than we have known. Korea was perhaps forced upon us; Vietnam was not. Pearl Harbor left us with no choice; the incident in the Gulf of

[1] Alexis de Tocqueville, *Democracy in America* (New York: Harper and Row, 1966), vol. 2, chap. 22, p. 625.

Tonkin left us with ample choice. The Cuban missile crisis may have warranted unusual procedures; the Bay of Pigs and the Dominican Republic patently did not.

Because of the kind of country we are, we cannot, except in the most exceptional circumstances, allow foreign policy to take priority over domestic and constitutional requirements. Given a choice between the use of force and less certain but peaceful methods, it is in our interests to take a chance on the latter. Given a choice between efficient emergency procedures and cumbersome democratic ones, it is in our interests to gamble on the latter—in full consciousness of the possibility that our democratic procedures may cost us embarrassment or worse in our foreign policy.

It is quite beside the point to contend, as some of the advocates of the anti-ballistic missile contend, that it is safer to "err on the side of security," because security is involved on both sides of the argument. One has to do with the security of *means*, the other with the security of *ends*.

For three decades we have been erring on the side of the security of means. The consequences of that error are only now coming clearly into view. I should like to suggest what some of these consequences have been—economic, political and moral—and how they have undermined our security in its broader dimension.

THE PRICE OF EMPIRE

Every nation has a double identity: it is both a *power* engaged in foreign relations and a *society* serving the interests of its citizens. As a *power* the nation draws upon but does not replenish its people's economic, political and moral resources. The replenishment of wealth—in this broader than economic sense—is a function of domestic life, of the nation as a society. In the last three decades the United States has been heavily preoccupied with its role as the world's greatest power, to the neglect of its societal responsibilities, and at incalculable cost to our national security. The economic cost is reflected in the disparity of almost ten to one between federal military expenditures since World War II and regular national budgetary expenditures for education, welfare, health and housing. The political cost is reflected in the steady concentration of power in the hands of the national executive, in a long-term trend toward authoritarian government. The moral cost is reflected in the unhappiness of the American people, most particularly in the angry alienation of our youth.

Speaking first of the economics of our global role: I have been told many times that in terms of our gross national product, we can well afford to do the things that need to be done at home without reducing our activities abroad. The answer to that assertion is that we are *not* in fact rebuilding our cities; we are not overcoming poverty and building schools and houses on anything approaching a scale commensurate with the need; nor are we effectively combating crime, pollution, and urban and suburban ugliness.

Even if the economic resources were there, the psychological resources are not. The war in Vietnam has drained off not only money but political energy and leadership, and public receptiveness to reform. The war has totally altered the atmosphere of a few years ago, when hopes and confidence were high and the American people seemed willing to embark upon an era of social reform. An excellent start was made with the landmark legislation of 1964 and 1965, but Vietnam cut that short, dividing the country and the Congress, and inciting dissent and disorder. These in turn have given rise to a middle class reaction based on the fear of violence and anarchy. The result is an atmosphere uncongenial to reform, urgently needed though it is. Until the war in Vietnam is ended, there can be no prospect of the nation's more sober and generous instincts reasserting themselves, no prospect of a renewal of the nation's strength at its vital domestic source.

Having promised not to lecture you on the military-industrial-labor-academic complex, I confine myself to this one observation: With military expenditures providing the livelihood of some 10 percent of our work force; with 22 thousand major corporate defense contractors and another 100 thousand subcontractors; with defense plants or installations located in 363 of the 435 Congressional districts; with the Department of Defense spending $7.5 billion on research and development this year, making it the largest consumer of research output in the nation—millions of Americans whose only interest is in making a decent living have acquired a vested interest in an economy geared to war. These benefits, once obtained, are not easily parted with. Every new weapons system or military installation soon acquires a constituency—a process which is aided and abetted by the perspicacity with which Pentagon officials award lucrative contracts and establish new plants and installations in the districts of influential Members of Congress. I have not the slightest doubt that, if the anti-ballistic missile is deployed, it will soon acquire its own powerful constituency, and then we will be saddled with it—for reasons wholly independent of its ostensible military utility.

According to current intelligence calculations, made in terms of equivalent real purchasing power, the Russians are spending only three-fourths as much as we are on defense. Nonetheless, we are told, they threaten to pull ahead of us in strategic weapons and we must be prepared to counter that threat. I do not understand why they should be getting so much more for their money than we are. Perhaps the fault lies in inferior American efficiency—a disconcerting thought. Perhaps it lies in the lack of legislative oversight of the defense budget comparable in rigor and thoroughness to that exercised over the much smaller budgets of the other departments.

Be that as it may, by any standard the amounts spent on defense have become staggeringly disproportionate to the rest of the economy. It fills me with dismay when Department of Defense officials suggest that, as part of a "grand design" for strategic policy, we may be forced to "win" an arms race with the Russians by relying on our superior resources to spend them into bankruptcy. Such a strategy puts me in mind of the practice among the Indians of the Pacific northwest known as the "potlatch." Starting as a rivalry in gift-giving for the sake of prestige, the practice degenerated, as the tribes became wealthier, into competitive orgies of waste and destruction. An anthropologist describes it as follows:

> No longer did the potlatch serve its traditional functions of redistributing wealth, validating rank, and making valued alliances. The wealth of these new rich seemed limitless, more than they could ever consume at a potlatch. So they instead destroyed vast amounts of wealth before the horrified eyes of the guests, as well as the other contenders, to dramatize the extent of their holdings. Fortunes were tossed into potlatch fires; canoes were destroyed; captives were killed. The competing claimants had no alternatives but to destroy even more property at *their* potlatches.
>
> A contender for rank ultimately found himself in a position whereby the only way he could humiliate a wealthy rival was to destroy one of the precious coppers—a kind of bank note representing vast wealth. The act

was equivalent to wiping out all the debts owed to him. It was an incredible price to pay, but the man who made such a dramatic gesture no doubt rose meteorically in rank.[2]

Quite as inevitably as if it were deliberate, our imperial role in the world has generated a trend toward authoritarian government.

Vested by the Constitution *exclusively* in the Congress, the power to initiate war has now passed under the virtually exclusive control of the executive. The "dog of war," which Jefferson thought had been tightly leashed to the legislature, has now passed under the virtually exclusive control of the executive. The President's powers as commander-in-chief, which Hamilton defined as "nothing more than the supreme command and direction of the military and naval forces," are now interpreted as conferring upon the President full constitutional power to commit the armed forces to conflict without the consent of Congress. On the one hand it is asserted that the initiation of an all-out nuclear war could not possibly await Congressional authorization; on the other hand it is contended that limited wars are inappropriate for Congressional action. There being, to the best of my knowledge, no other kinds of war besides "limited" and "unlimited," it would seem that the Congressional war power has been effectively nullified.

The treaty power of the Senate has also been effectively usurped. Once regarded as the only constitutional means of making a significant foreign commitment, while executive agreements were confined to matters of routine or triviality, the treaty has now been reduced to only one of a number of methods of entering binding foreign engagements. In current usage the term "commitment" is used to refer to engagements deriving sometimes from treaties but more often from executive agreements and even simple, sometimes casual declarations.

Thailand provides an interesting illustration. Under the SEATO Treaty the United States has only two specific obligations to Thailand: to act "in accordance with its constitutional processes in the event that Thailand is overtly attacked," and to "consult immediately" with the other SEATO allies should Thailand be threatened by subversion. But the presence of 50 thousand American troops in Thailand, assigned there by the executive acting entirely on its own authority, creates a *de facto* commitment going far beyond the SEATO Treaty. In addition,

[2] Peter Farb, *Man's Rise to Civilization as Shown by the Indians of North America from Primeval Times to the Coming of the Industrial State* (New York: E. P. Dutton and Co., 1968), pp. 150, 151.

on March 6, 1962, former Secretary of State Dean Rusk and Thai Foreign Minister Thanat Khoman issued a joint declaration in which Secretary Rusk expressed "the firm intention of the United States to aid Thailand, its ally and historic friend, in resisting Communist aggression and subversion." This, obviously, goes far beyond the SEATO Treaty.

An even more striking illustration of the upgrading of a limited agreement into a *de facto* military obligation is provided by the series of agreements negotiated over the last sixteen years for the maintenance of bases in Spain. Initiated under an executive agreement in 1953, the bases agreement was significantly upgraded by a joint declaration issued by Secretary Rusk and Spanish Foreign Minister Castiella in 1963 asserting that a "threat to either country" would be the occasion for each to "take such action as it may consider appropriate within the framework of its constitutional processes." In strict constitutional law, this agreement, whose phrasing closely resembles that of our multilateral security treaties, would be binding on no one except for Mr. Rusk himself; in fact it is what might be called the "Functional equivalent" of a treaty ratified by the Senate. Acknowledging even more explicitly the extent of our *de facto* commitment to Spain, General Wheeler, acting under instructions from Secretary Rusk, provided Spanish military authorities in 1968 with a secret memorandum asserting that the presence of American armed forces in Spain constituted a more significant security guarantee than would a written agreement.

Quite aside from questions of the merit or desirability of these commitments, the means by which they were incurred must be a matter of great concern to anyone who is concerned with the integrity of our constitutional processes. For at least thirty years powers over our foreign relations have been flowing into the hands of the executive. So far has this process advanced that, in the recently expressed view of the Committee on Foreign Relations, "it is no longer accurate to characterize our government, in matters of foreign relations, as one of separated powers checked and balanced against each other." [3] To a limited extent this constitutional imbalance has come about as the result of executive usurpation; to a greater extent it has been caused by the failure of Congress to meet its responsibilities and defend its prerogatives in the

[3] *National Commitments,* Report of the Committee on Foreign Relations on S. Res. 85, Senate, 91st Cong., 1st Sess. (Washington, D.C.: U.S. Government Printing Office, 1969), p. 7.

field of foreign relations; but most of all it has been the result of chronic warfare and crisis, of that all but inevitable concentration of powers in time of emergency of which Alexis de Tocqueville took notice over a century ago.

Under circumstances of continuing threat to the national security, it is hardly surprising that the military itself should have become an active, and largely unregulated, participant in the policy making process. Bringing to bear a degree of discipline, unanimity and strength of conviction seldom found among civilian officials, the able and energetic men who fill the top ranks of the armed services have acquired an influence disproportionate to their numbers on the nation's security policy. The Department of Defense itself has become a vigorous partisan in our politics, exerting great influence on the President, on the military committees of Congress, on the "think tanks" and universities to which it parcels out lucrative research contracts, and on public opinion. I was, quite frankly, disturbed to learn some weeks ago that the Department of the Army actually planned a national publicity campaign, involving exhibits and planted magazine articles to be solicited from civilian scientists, in order to "sell" the ABM to the American public and to counteract the criticisms of Congressmen and the scientific community.

Again, let me emphasize that the danger I perceive here is not military men but *militarism.* Applying the same principle to the executive as a whole, the danger of executive dominance over our foreign relations has nothing to do with the wisdom or lack of it of individual officials. A threat to democracy arises from *any* great concentration of unregulated power. I would no more want unregulated power to be wielded by the Congress than by the executive or the military—not even by the Senate Committee on Foreign Relations. The principle is an old and familiar one, and is just as valid today as it was when Jefferson expressed it in the simple maxim: "Whatever power in any government is independent, is absolute also."

In recent months the Senate has shown a growing awareness of the need for restoring a degree of constitutional balance in the making of our foreign policy. To a great extent this new attitude has been reflected in the debate on the anti-ballistic missile and a general disposition to bring the military budget under the same scrutiny that has always been applied to the budgets of the civilian agencies. In addition, the Senate is about to debate a "national commitments" resolution, the essential purpose of which is to remind the Congress of its constitutional responsibilities both for the making of treaties and the initiation of war.

These, I believe, are hopeful and necessary steps, but in the long run it is unlikely that constitutional government can be preserved solely by the vigorous exercise of legislative authority. No matter what safeguards of attitude and procedure we employ, a foreign policy of chronic warfare and intervention has its own irreversible dynamic, and that is toward authoritarian government. A democracy simply cannot allow foreign policy to become an end in itself, or anything more than an instrument toward the central, dominating goal of securing democratic values within our own society. I would indeed lay it down as a fairly confident prediction that, if American democracy is destroyed within the next generation, it will not be destroyed by the Russians or the Chinese but by ourselves, by the very means we use to defend it. That is why it seems to me so urgent for us to change the emphasis of our policy, from the security of means to the security of ends.

Finally, I would like to say a word about the moral price of our imperial role in the world. The success of a foreign policy, as we have been discovering, depends not only on the availability of military and economic resources but, at least as much, upon the support given it by our people. As we have also been discovering, that support cannot be gained solely by eloquent entreaty, much less by the devices of public relations. In the long run it can only be secured by devising policies which are broadly consistent with the national character and traditional values of the society, and these—products of the total national experience—are beyond the reach of even the most effective modern techniques of political manipulation.

History did not prepare the American people for the kind of role we are now playing in the world. From the time of the framing of the Constitution to the two world wars our experience and values—if not our uniform practice—conditioned us not for the unilateral exercise of power but for the placing of limits upon it. Perhaps it was a vanity but we supposed that we could be an example for the world—an example of rationality and restraint. We supposed, as Woodrow Wilson put it, that a rational world order could be created embodying "not a balance of power but a community of power; not organized rivalries, but an organized common peace."

Our practice has not lived up to that ideal but, from the earliest days of the Republic, the ideal has retained its hold upon us, and every time we have acted inconsistently with it—not just in Vietnam but every time—a hue and cry of opposition has arisen. When the United States invaded Mexico, two former Presidents and one future President [4] denounced the war as violating American principles. The senior of them, John Quincy Adams, is said even to have expressed the hope that General Taylor's officers would resign and his men desert.[5] When the United States fought a war with Spain and then suppressed the patriotic resistance to American rule of the Philippines, the ranks of opposition were swelled with two former Presidents, Harrison and Cleveland, with Senators and Congressmen including the Speaker of the House of Representatives, and with such distinguished individuals as Andrew Carnegie and Samuel Gompers.

The dilemma of contemporary American foreign policy is that, while becoming the most powerful nation ever to have existed on the earth, the American people have also carried forward their historical mistrust of power and their commitment to the imposition of restraints upon it.[6] That dilemma came to literal and symbolic fulfillment in the year 1945 when two powerful new forces came into the world. One was the bomb at Hiroshima, representing a quantum leap to a new dimension of undisciplined power. The other was the United Nations Charter, representing the most significant effort ever made toward the restraint and control of national power. Both were American inventions, one the product of our laboratories, the other the product of our national experience. Incongruous though they are, these are America's legacies to the modern world: the one manifested in Vietnam and the nuclear arms race, the other in the hope that these may yet be brought under control.

The incongruity between our old values and our new unilateral power has greatly troubled the American people. It has much to do, I suspect, with the current student rebellion. Like a human body reacting against a transplanted organ, our body politic is reacting against the alien values which, in the name of security, have been grafted

[4] John Quincy Adams, Martin van Buren, and Abraham Lincoln.

[5] Charles A. Barker, "Another American Dilemma," *Virginia Quarterly Review* (Spring 1969), pp. 239–240.

[6] The theme here developed, the dilemma posed by American power as against the commitment to an equality of rights in a community of world power, is adapted from an article by Professor Charles A. Barker of the Department of History of Johns Hopkins University, *ibid.*, pp. 230–252.

upon it. We cannot—and dare not—divest ourselves of power, but we have a choice as to how we will use it. We can try to ride out the current convulsion in our society and adapt ourselves to a new role as the world's nuclear vigilante. Or we can try to adapt our power to our traditional values, never allowing it to become more than a means toward domestic, societal ends, while seeking every opportunity to discipline it within an international community.

We cannot resolve this dilemma by choosing to "err on the side of security," because security is the argument for both sides. The real question is: which represents the more promising approach to security in its broader dimension?

11 ☆ THE FUTURE OF THE MILITARY-INDUSTRIAL COMPLEX

CAN MILITARY SPENDING BE CONTROLLED?

Jonathan B. Bingham

NINETEEN SIXTY-NINE may be remembered as the year Americans woke up to the importance of an issue that was to be a dominant one in the 1970s. The question of Viet Nam still had the emotional clout. The great ABM debate still captured most of the headlines. But more and more people were beginning to see that bigger and more permanent than both of these was the question of whether America's military spending could be brought under more rational control. In the winter of 1969 it became increasingly clear that we had to find a way to re-orient our national priorities so that imperative human needs on the home front were not always being shunted aside because of the claims of "national security." No longer could it be successfully argued that we could afford the needed amounts of "guns *and* butter." A difficult choice—or at least choices—had to be made, and would have to be made repeatedly, for many years to come.

The issue of military spending is more than just newly discerned; it is in fact new in its dimensions. For the first time in history, each of two great antagonists has the power to destroy the other and security depends almost entirely on the gruesome theory of "mutually assured destruction." At the same time, the satisfaction of basic human needs has become more of an imperative than ever before if we are to survive as a society, because today for the first time those needs *can* be met and the people, including the poor, know it.

Foreign Affairs 48, no. 1 (October 1969): 51–66. Reprinted by special permission from *Foreign Affairs*, October 1969.

I

Until World War II Americans generally had been suspicious of "standing armies" and had been inclined to keep the armed forces on meager rations, except in time of actual war. Even the experience of World War II itself did not change this feeling. Right after V–J Day the cry was "Bring the boys home!" and, with a sigh of relief, America demobilized. But only two years later, with the growing threat from the Soviet Union becoming apparent, with Britain's withdrawal from Greece and the enunciation of the Truman Doctrine, the tide of military spending turned and has been flooding ever since. It surged during the Korean War, subsided briefly, and then continued to mount.

The figures tell a vivid story: in 1948 the defense budget was $11.8 billion; for 1969–70 the budget submitted to Congress was about $80 billion, representing an increase of 680 percent. Allowing for inflation, the increase in constant dollars is 345 percent. This is more than twice the percentage rise in the GNP.

Since 1961, it is true, federal spending for domestic needs has increased faster than defense spending. Programs inaugurated in the progressive 89th Congress, including medicare and medicaid, aid to education and the expanded war on poverty, have made heavy demands on the federal treasury. And, for the years 1963, 1964 and 1965 and again for 1969 and 1970 (estimated) the percentage growth in military spending was actually fractionally smaller than the growth in GNP.

As we look ahead, however, the picture is bleak. Not only are the pressures for a steeper rate of increase in the defense budget intense, but also we are beginning to have a new and clearer conception of the dimensions of our home-front needs. The Kerner Commission report was an electric shock to the conscience of America. By any standard, the amounts required for substantial improvements in our social programs are large: for example, a 35 percent increase in Social Security benefits would cost about $13 billion. An educational assistance program to equalize per-pupil expenditures in all states at the level of New York would cost $19 billion per year. A mass transit improvement program equivalent to half the federal highway aid program would run about $2 billion annually. Everyone wants to move away from the present welfare system, but any move in the direction of a guaranteed minimum income, or negative income tax, is bound to be expensive: for a reasonably comprehensive program, the net cost would be at least $20 billion a year. A federal housing program geared to meet the country's needs is bound to run well into the billions. And so it goes.

For a while it was hoped that, if only the Viet Nam war could be ended, enough resources could be made available to ease the strain. But Charles Schultze, former Budget Director, and others have exploded that myth. Proceeding on the assumption that an end to the Viet Nam war might produce savings of about $20 billion annually after two years, these experts point out that within two to three years after that these savings would be more than wiped out by normal increases in the defense budget, including pay increases and spending on weapons systems already approved. Assuming continued economic growth produces annual increases in federal revenues of $15 billion, Schultze estimates that about half of this will be drained off by built-in increases on the civilian side, so that five years from now we can expect to have only about a $7–$8 billion a year increment to meet the competing demands for (*a*) the kind of massive domestic programs the Kerner Commission called for, (*b*) stepped-up demands for military spending, (*c*) tax relief. Schultze's figures were based on the admittedly arbitrary assumption that tax levels, aside from the surcharge, would remain the same. But the demand for tax relief is intense, as Congressional action this past summer clearly showed. If tax levels are in fact reduced, and if the factors making for military spending are not brought under better control than they have been in the past, the entire "fiscal dividend" could be drained off without leaving any room at all for home-front programs.

II

The pressures from within the Pentagon for increased expenditures are enormous. They stem in part from traditional and still acute competition among the military services. In part, they are the natural result of increasing technologies; each new generation of weapons means greater complexity and sophistication, and the expense seems to rise by geometric rather than arithmetic progression. Thus, during the Korean War the standard fighter plane, the F86, cost about $300,000; today the standard Navy F4 costs about $3 million, and the Navy wants to move to the F14, estimated to cost some $14 million. The existence of a new technology seems to compel a new weapons system based on that technology; some of my ablest colleagues in the Congress believe that this process is inevitable with respect to MIRV, for example, and cannot be arrested by arms-limitation agreements or in any other way.

To the experts in the Pentagon, the fear of what the other side may be doing is ever present. It is natural for the military man to try to achieve absolute security against any contingency that may arise, even though intellectually he may recognize that absolute security is unattainable. He is trained and paid to think this way. Thus the military services will always and inevitably want more than they have. Their appetites are insatiable. And the industrial concerns that are ready and eager to undertake the required contracts will encourage them. In upstate New York, for example, one hears that anybody connected with General Electric is "of course" for the ABM. The effect of all this may be sinister, but the motives are not.

The real trouble comes when those civilians in government who are supposed to see to it that the military's appetite is restrained are not capable of performing that function because they have come to share the military point of view. Although the top civilians in the Pentagon are most exposed to the generals and admirals, it is by no means inevitable that they should be dominated by them. In Robert McNamara the Joint Chiefs of Staff had a tough boss who exercised a great deal of independent judgment, based on extensive and intensive review and analysis carried out by civilians under his control. Secretary Laird, too, has insisted on cutbacks.

Above the Secretary of Defense, the next level of review is that of the President. To exercise this responsibility he must of necessity rely on the Bureau of the Budget. But for years the BOB review of defense requests has not been nearly as tough or effective as it should have been. For one thing, the Bureau has had too few examiners. For another, with regard to the Pentagon, the BOB has not had the authority as it does in the case of all other departments, to decide on the dollar amounts of the requests going to Congress, subject to an appeal to the President by the department head. For the Department of Defense, the reverse has been true: the Secretary has had the authority to decide on the requests, subject to an appeal to the President by the Budget Director (and McNamara once boasted that he never lost such an argument).

A third limitation on the Budget Bureau, according to former director Schultze, has been that it was too much concerned with details; it did not get into the Pentagon's planning process early enough to raise questions about the fundamental assumptions and strategy which determined the order of magnitude of defense spending. Thus, according to Schultze, there was never sufficient attention or debate within the Executive Branch about the so-called "2½ war" concept underlying U.S. planning, *i.e.* the assumption that the United States had to be prepared to carry on simultaneously a land war in Europe, a land war in Asia (presumably against Communist China) and a brushfire war elsewhere.

In the past the influence of the BOB, so great in other areas, has been overshadowed in the military area by the Pentagon on the one hand and the Congress on the other. The present Budget Director, Robert P. Mayo, has indicated an inclination to change this. He says, for example, that from now on the appeal procedure will be the same for all departments. And the President has said that he will back Mayo against Laird, if disagreements arise. But it is yet too early to tell how Mayo will fare. Even if he has the full backing of the President, he may run into trouble on Capitol Hill.

All too often, the dominant members of the Congressional committees having responsibility in this area—the Armed Services Committees and Appropriations subcommittees having jurisdiction over defense and "military construction"—come to share the point of view of the military. Chairman Mendel Rivers of the House Armed Services Committee is a conspicuous example. So many defense installations have been located in his district that fears have been expressed that the city of Charleston might sink under their weight. His belief in military solutions to international problems has been well illustrated by his unleash-the-military position on Viet Nam. A sizable majority of his committee tends to share the Chairman's point of view. Civilian DOD officials associated with McNamara and Clifford report that, in hearings before the Rivers committee, they were vigorously challenged to defend, not the size of DOD requests, but the reductions they had made in the requests of the Joint Chiefs. For FY 1967 and 1968, the Committee actually increased the Pentagon's requests for procurement and RDT&E (Research, Development, Test and Evaluation) by a total of $1,325,200,000. At the same time, Rivers and a majority of his associates are conservative and intensely economy-minded when it comes to social problems on the home front.

The makeup of the defense appropriations subcommittees is similar. In both the Senate and the House, the top four Democratic members of the appropriations subcommittees on defense are southern conservatives. Until his appointment as Secretary of Defense, Mr. Laird was a prominent member of the House subcommittee. The Chairman of the House subcommittee on military construction, Mr. Sikes of Florida, was until last year a Major-General in the Reserves and a board member of the National Rifle Association.

Although these committees have held extensive hearings on the Pentagon's requests for authorizations and appropriations, the chairmen typically exercise tight control. Usually the only witnesses called, except for fellow members of Congress, have been from the Pentagon. (In the recent ABM hearings, adverse witnesses were heard at the insistence of anti-ABM committee members, but this was unusual.) Those members of the committees who have chosen to challenge Pentagon requests have had to rely on their own resources to pursue their inquiries effectively. They are not considered a "minority" in the traditional sense (this term applies only to the minority party) and no committee staff is assigned to them.

Once brought before the membership of the Senate or the House, the committee recommendations used to sail through, until 1969, with a minimum of meaningful discussion. The proposals for defense authorizations or appropriations were invariably presented as "essential," never as "desirable," much less as "of marginal value." The committee reports were full of military jargon and rarely related the specific requests to particular policy objectives. As for the hearing records, they were technical, voluminous and suffered from extensive deletions of testimony for reasons of security.

Typically, those few members who sought to raise questions or objections were treated either with scorn as uninformed, or with anger as unpatriotic. There was no debate about the fundamental assumptions underlying the military requests (such as the "2½ war" concept, the existence of which was unknown to most Congressmen until this year) and very little discussion of the pros and cons of proposed force levels or weapons systems. What talk did take place was replete with such clichés as "better too much than too little," "you can't measure lives with dollars," etc.

At no point in the Congressional process was there an opportunity for comparing the domestic needs of the nation with its external needs.

Priority for the requirements of national security was assumed, not debated. A double standard was consistently applied: what was said to be needed for survival against dangers from abroad, we would do; what was said to be needed for survival against dangers from within, we would consider.

III

In spite of the enormous influence of what one liberal Congressman has called the "military-industrial-Congressional complex," we as a nation have the tools to solve the problems of military spending, if we can find the will to use them.

First of all, and fundamentally, the structure of civilian control in the federal establishment was solidly built by the Founding Fathers and stands intact today; the dangers of a military takeover seem remote. Even freshmen Congressmen who cut little swath in the Capitol are sometimes surprised by the deference with which they are treated by bemedaled officers. The deference may be wholly superficial, but it represents a sturdy tradition.

Second, the climate for action to give reality to the principles of civilian supremacy is at least temporarily favorable. The myth of the military's infallibility in matters supposedly within its competence has been thoroughly exploded in Viet Nam, in terms both of consistent over-optimism and of obvious over-reliance on what military power could do. The military have been further embarrassed by the poor planning evident in the *Pueblo* case, the lack of discretion or foresight, or both, in having nerve gas stored all over the lot, and the just plain bungling displayed in the sinking of a submarine at its dock. Another factor has been the revelation of fantastic overruns in anticipated contract costs, as in the case of the C5A.

The increasing skepticism toward the peremptory demands of the military has been accompanied by a growing realization of the size and urgency of our domestic needs and by a widespread awareness that some hard choices would have to be made. Stimulated by the ABM debates, a number of private organizations have started to focus public attention on the overall problem of military vs. domestic spending. For example, a group of businessmen have formed a Fund for New Priorities in America which sponsored two well-publicized conferences on the subject in Washington, with members of Congress, scientists, economists and others taking part.

Similarly, on Capitol Hill more and more members have been getting educated on the issue of priorities. The Democratic Study Group, comprising the liberal majority of the Democratic House membership, has organized a task force to look simultaneously at foreign policy and defense policy issues, and has arranged seminars and circulated fact sheets on various aspects of the subject. Another informal organization, in this case bipartisan and bicameral, known as Members of Congress for Peace Through Law, has also in 1969 focused for the first time on the military-spending problem: under Senator Hatfield's chairmanship, a subcommittee of the organization has produced and released a series of responsible recommendations for cutbacks in procurement authorizations totaling some $3.1 billion. Even within the Armed Services Committees themselves, substantial minorities are beginning to challenge the military's recommendations on a number of programs.

The close votes on Safeguard in the Senate on August 6 were significant, less for the result than for the narrowness of the Administration's victory. The precedent that major new military programs will not go unchallenged was firmly established. Shortly after the ABM vote, Secretary Laird was compelled to accept a restrictive amendment on CBW (Chemical and Biological Warfare) funds, and an amendment authorizing General Accounting Office audit of major Pentagon contracts was also adopted. All concerned were agreed that a kind of uprising was on against the military.

The Pentagon has obviously not been insensitive to these developments. Under pressure from Congressional critics, and influenced also by the need for containing inflationary trends, the Nixon Administration has announced various cutbacks. Some of these represent deferrals of expenditure, but a pet project of the Air Force, the Manned Orbiting Laboratory, long considered by skeptics to be an unnecessary duplication of NASA activities, was cancelled altogether by the Nixon Administration. The controversial Cheyenne helicopter was also dropped.

In August, Secretary Laird announced further economy measures, mostly involving conventional forces. These cuts would reduce spending in FY 1970 by $1.5 billion, over and above the reductions of $1.1 billion announced earlier; and he said an additional cutback of $1.5 billion was on the way. He grumbled at the Congress and warned that the cuts would weaken our "defense readiness," but it was the action that was important.

So the tide that has been flooding so long is at last showing signs of being contained. But sporadic, impetuous and grudging measures will not be enough. An effective and durable flood-control system will be required.

IV

Like others who have addressed this topic, I have often stressed the urgent need for "new priorities." The expression is perhaps acceptable as a shorthand way of saying that in the future we must be less generous toward the military than we have been and less stingy about meeting our home-front needs. But the word "priorities" can be misleading if it implies a system of making budgetary decisions on the basis of constant comparisons between national security needs and domestic needs. Such comparisons must indeed be made, but this can be done only at certain points in the review process and by a few people. Obviously, for example, Defense Department officials cannot be expected to be familiar with specific domestic needs, yet the task of bringing military spending under responsible civilian control must begin in the Pentagon.

What can and should be required of the civilians in the Pentagon is a tough, "show me" attitude toward the requests of the brass, an attitude based on awareness that total security is unattainable but will always be sought by the military, and that federal spending for military purposes must be severely limited in the light of other acute needs. The civilian heads of the DOD should make sure that they are provided with the arguments against military spending proposals, as well as the arguments for.

Secretary McNamara did set up, through an Office of Systems Analysis and extensive use of bright, aggressive civilians, a method of providing for himself an independent, hard-boiled review of the Joint Chiefs' requests. The brass resented the "whiz kids" and reportedly has brought intense pressure on Secretary Laird to rely more on the judgment of the military and to weaken the process of civilian review. The indications are that Laird is giving way to this pressure, both by reducing the authority of civilian offices and by appointing to some key posts men who are even more military-minded than the generals and admirals. (Reflecting the changes in the Pentagon's Office of International Security Affairs, or "little State Department," a current Washington *bon mot* reports the following exchange: First liberal: "The influence of Pentagon civilians on arms-control decisions has been reduced." Second liberal: "Thank God!")

In recent months a number of former Pentagon officials have expressed their concern about the present trend, drawing upon their experience to illustrate the need for subjecting the requests of the military to searching analysis by truly civilian minds. An illustrative case was the following: In a presentation with regard to relative Soviet and U.S. strength in submarines, the Navy deducted from effective U.S. strength X percent for those vessels that would have to be in home port at any given time. When asked by one of the "whiz kids" what percentage had been deducted from the Soviet strength figure for the same reason, the answer was that no deduction had been made; the incredible excuse was that "we don't know what their lay-up percentage is."

An even more vital reason for civilian analysis, starting within the Pentagon, is that non-military judgments are needed with regard to the probabilities of enemy action, or, to use a controversial word, with regard to the probable *intentions* of a potential enemy. According to standard military doctrine, the safest course is to assess only the capabilities, not the intentions, of the enemy. Yet the doctrine is not in fact, and cannot be, strictly applied. The whole theory of mutual deterrence rests on the conclusion that the other side's capabilities will not be used if destruction is sure to follow. The degree to which nation A responds to nation B as a threat depends very heavily on A's assessment of B's intentions. For example, not even the most chauvinistic nationalist will argue that the United States should be prepared to cope militarily with a combined attack upon the United States by all the other nations of the world; and Canadian defense planners are hardly likely to look solely at U.S. capabilities in judging whether Canada is safe from a U.S. attack.

In spite of all their stress on capabilities, the generals and the admirals are clearly very much influenced by what they regard as the Soviets' aggressive intentions. But any consideration of Soviet intentions must involve a host of factors—political, psychological, historical, geopolitical, etc.—with respect to which the military may well be less expert than well-trained civilians.

Two major cases in point are the controversies about Safeguard and the MIRV. In these areas, questions such as the following are obviously pertinent: What will be the effect of U.S. decisions on Soviet attitudes toward the SALT talks, and on the likelihood of success of these talks? Is it reasonable to suppose the Soviets want to achieve a first-strike capability against us, or to appear to want to do so (in the light of our probable response)? Obviously, to answer questions such as these, the military have no exclusive expertise, if indeed they have any expertise at all. Hence, they must accept the fact that their civilian boss, the Secretary of Defense, must have the benefit of civilian analysts and advisers.

Before the DOD's requests are submitted to the Congress, the President must also scrutinize the specifics. He, as well as the Congress, should be furnished, not only with the figures, but with full information about underlying assumptions and rationale. The detailed posture statement issued annually by the DOD since McNamara's day is essential for this purpose, and requested expenditures should be precisely related to it. A comparable annual posture statement by the State Department, reviewing U.S. commitments and policies, would be an invaluable supplement. In addition, the President, and eventually the Congress, should be provided with the future financial implications of proposed expenditures. Innocuous research and development acorns have a tendency to grow into giant oaks of weapons systems.

In rendering judgments on all this material, the President, of course, has to rely heavily on his staff. Obviously his adviser on national security affairs can touch only the major problems, such as force levels for the Army, the size of the Navy and strategic-weapons questions. This puts a heavy burden on the Budget Director and his staff; they cannot be restricted to the traditional question of whether X dollars is too much to spend on Y purpose, but must also be concerned with whether Y is needed at all or whether the job could not be done effectively and at less expense with Z. The Budget Bureau should be instructed to be just as tough in reviewing DOD requests as in the case of all other departments and should be in a position to see that the President does not have to say yes or no to a particular proposal but is presented with alternatives. The President also has available to him, and should use, the National Security Council and its staff. This is another way that expert civilian judgments can be brought to bear.

When the Executive Branch requests finally go to Capitol Hill, they will continue to be examined in the first instance by the Armed Services Committees and Appropriations subcommittees. Ideally, the makeup and the power structure of these committees should be drastically changed so as to make them more representative of, and responsive to, the Congress as a whole. The chairmen should be legislators who are in accord with the main thrust of their party's policies, at home and abroad, as set forth, for example, in the party platform. The membership should reflect, more or less, the same urban-rural and North-South ratios as the House or Senate as a whole. At least a few representatives of ghetto areas should be included. To my mind, the most constructive change of all would be to limit the terms of members on these committees to four or six years, thus avoiding the buddy-buddy relationship toward the military that too often builds up over time.

While admittedly such drastic changes as these are not precisely imminent, they are perfectly feasible. On the House side, for example, the Democratic members, acting in caucus, by majority vote, have ample authority to accomplish these changes with respect to the present chairmen and the Democratic members of the committees. No concurrence by the Senate or by the Republican members of the House would be required. All that is needed is for the majority of the House Democrats to have the will to do what is needed. And if their constituents got angry enough to demand a modification of the strict seniority rule, they would find the will.

Failing such a fundamental revamping, a minimum change—one for which there really should be no opposition—would be to afford basic privileges to the minority voices on these committees, those members who are increasingly demonstrating a healthy skepticism toward the demands of the military. These members need expert staffs if they are to do the kind of probing questioning of DOD witnesses that is required. They also should have the right to arrange for their own witnesses to appear before the committees, thus assuring that points of view other than the Pentagon's are heard. Under most committee rules, such protections as these are usually afforded the members of the minority party. But most Republicans on the defense committees are at least as military-minded as the senior Democrats. Hence, if these committees are to have the benefit of an effective "loyal opposition," party lines must be disregarded.

There is another whole area of activity where the Congress has a major role to play in controlling military spending. This year's revelations of sloppy and wasteful procurement methods by the Pentagon, coupled with attempted concealment of the facts, call for strengthened and systematized Congressional oversight. Individuals like Senator William Proxmire and Congressman William Moorhead have performed yeoman and courageous service, but one gets the feeling that only the top of the iceberg has been revealed. In addition to the Armed Services and Appropriations Committees, the two Government Operations Committees have a major role to play here, and a subcommittee of the Joint Economic Committee has also made a contribution. Highly trained staff is available in the Government Accounting Office, if only the Congress would make more use of them. Too often the redoubtable GAO has been put on the trail only of the relatively piddling overspending of departments and agencies less powerful than the Pentagon.

V

The task of assuring a hard-boiled review of military spending requests is a relatively simple one if we have the will to undertake it. The problem of setting up a system of national priorities as between military and home-front requirements is much more difficult, both conceptually and organizationally.

Conceptually, the difficulty stems from the absence of a common standard for measuring relative urgencies. It's a case of apples and oranges. Subjectively, I have no difficulty in concluding that we ought to spend $2 billion in building two hundred community colleges rather than one additional nuclear carrier with appropriate escort vessels. But how does one compare the needs analytically?

Organizationally, the problem of making specific decisions on particular military requests in the light of specific needs in our cities, suburbs or countryside seems insoluble. For one thing the competing demands are virtually unlimited: in deciding whether the defense establishment should not be trimmed of X billion dollars worth of bureaucratic fat (some expert observers regard this as the number one problem), which home-front shortage do you look at—housing, daycare centers, hospitals, subways? For another, most decision-makers, whether in the Executive Branch or the Congress, simply cannot have the expertise in all fields that would permit such multi-faceted judgments to be made.

The best that can be done, I believe, is to compare overall expenditures and to arrive at a reasonable allocation of federal revenues as between military and domestic needs. Although the judgment will necessarily be largely subjective, it should not be made in an arbitrary *a priori* way; it can be made intelligently only with a basic knowledge of the specific components that make up the request totals on each side of the ledger.

On the Executive Branch side this is clearly a job which only the President, with the assistance of his immediate staff, including the Budget Director, can do. He can turn to his Council of Economic Advisers, particularly with regard to total federal expenditures; he can invite his Cabinet to debate the urgency of competing demands. Some have suggested that he ought to have a special advisory group, possibly a Council on National Priorities, to assist him, but ultimately the decision will be his.

On Capitol Hill, there is today no machinery for reviewing the President's proposed allocation of resources as between defense and home-front needs. Theoretically, the Appropriations Committees could do so, but they function almost entirely through subcommittees with special interests. I believe the best solution would be for the Congress to establish a special joint committee to review, in the first instance, the President's spending requests in terms of the broad allocations to various national purposes. This committee should include members from the various committees concerned so that the competing demands could be intelligently debated. Broad allocations confirming or modifying the President's recommendations would then be communicated to the Members of Congress and the substantive committees. These would not be inflexible but would serve as guidelines, subject to later adjustment. Failing the establishment of a new joint committee for this purpose, the present Joint Economic Committee could undertake the task. That committee, which has an exceptionally able membership and a fine staff, has already been doing extremely useful work in the field of military spending.

To facilitate this kind of Congressional review of overall allocations —or priorities—the President could usefully divide his budget into two parts. One would cover home-front needs. The other would include, not just military expenditures, but also other programs concerned with the nation's responsibilities vis-à-vis the rest of the world—support of the United Nations, foreign aid, the Peace Corps and other international activities. These activities could then be judged in a truer perspective than they are now. Foreign-aid programs, for example, should not have to compete for funds with domestic programs. (One liberal Member of Congress has been saying, understandably: "Not one dime for foreign aid until we start doing what we ought to be doing in the ghettos.") They should rather be judged as against other "external" needs. By a curious twist, the power of the Pentagon could be mobilized in this way for the benefit of international activities that are less popular than straight-out defense programs but are equally essential for national security and the preservation of world peace.

Obviously, there would be problems of classification involved in breaking down the budget into "external" and "internal" sectors, but these would be relatively minor. And the gain in terms of clarity of thinking—seeing the problems in perspective—would be considerable.

VI

What would be a reasonable target for reductions in the FY 1970 and future defense budgets?

Without specifying where the cuts should be made, various groups, such as Walter Reuther's UAW, have suggested $10 billion. Though this is not likely to be achieved, it is not a "way-out" figure. One former Pentagon official, Robert S. Benson, has proposed a number of cuts totaling $9 billion, and a former colleague of his has estimated that $7 billion a year could be saved through improved procurement practices alone. *Fortune* magazine has listed possible savings amounting to $17 billion by 1972, even assuming deployment of Safeguard and MIRV. Although the cutbacks in procurement proposed by the Hatfield subcommittee of the Peace Through Law group amount to only $3.1 billion, some of them might save very large sums if carried through into later years. For example, indefinite deferral of AMSA (Advanced Manned Strategic Aircraft) would save only $80 million this year, but the eventual saving might well be $10 billion. Similarly, a decision not to deploy Safeguard would have saved about $700 million this year, but the ultimate saving might amount to tens of billions, especially if one assumes that deployment of Safeguard may well lead to larger, more elaborate ABM systems later on.

Other areas which call out for cuts include CBW (Chemical and Biological Warfare) preparations; the beginning of a sophisticated new antiaircraft system, complete with "lookdown" radar, designed to cope with a Soviet bomber threat which does not yet exist; development of new aircraft types; and the so-called FDL (fast-deployment logistic ship), which many regard as intended for future Dominican Republic-type incidents. A minimum immediate target, especially in view of Laird's announcement, would be to keep non-Viet Nam expenditures from growing (apart from pay increases and other built-in factors).

For the longer run, achievement of really big savings will require basic decisions involving substantial cutbacks in conventional forces. A reduction of one million, or less than a third, in the number of Americans in uniform would save on the order of $10 billion a year. A decision to abandon the notion that we have to be prepared to fight an extended war at sea with the Soviet Union could save a good part of a projected $30 billion for fleet modernization, plus billions of dollars annually in naval operations and maintenance costs.

It is, in my judgment, literally impossible to overstate the importance of the SALT talks. If restrictions on the deployment of ABM and MIRV can be agreed upon, not only will tens of billions be saved eventually in the construction, procurement and operation of these systems, but the indirect effect is likely to be such a lessening of tensions as to make possible major reductions in conventional forces. If the talks fail, the opposite will be true, and America will continue to be deprived of the better life for all that is now within reach.

Neither in the Executive Branch nor in the Congress does there yet appear to be the sense of overwhelming urgency about the SALT talks that there ought to be. Too often the emphasis is on the difficulties and the risks of arms-limitation agreements, with little or no mention of the calamitous consequences and danger of allowing a new arms race and tension to escalate together.

Until recently Americans generally have been content to let their officials carry the awesome responsibility for making decisions in these areas. Where national security is concerned, John Q. Citizen has tended to say, "Poppa knows best." But there are growing numbers of people, especially among the young and the disadvantaged, who insist on making known their feelings about the road the United States should take. Hopefully, this tendency will spread.

THE BUDGET PROCESS

Robert P. Mayo et al.

THE BUDGET PROCESS

Budget making is a continuous process of interchange among the President, the executive agencies, and the Congress. This interaction is the budget process, and that is why everybody says that we are in the middle. Shortly after one budget is sent to the printer, work begins on the next. Agency and Bureau of the Budget staff continually evaluate programs, identify relevant policy issues, and reconsider budget projections. In evaluating programs special attention is given to possible modifications and innovations in programs, to alternative program plans, and to the benefits and costs of each.

The formal launching pad of the budget process is the spring planning preview, which usually begins in May and ends in July. We are currently, therefore, in the midst of our spring preview for fiscal 1971. The purpose of the spring preview is to permit the Bureau to identify and examine systematically prospective major program issues, possible alternatives, and budget impacts. Overemphasis on program details is avoided to permit concentration on issues of major importance.

The spring preview involved: A review of the economic outlook in broad aggregate terms to help develop fiscal policy guidelines, and this is terribly important; an examination of major Federal programs in terms of benefits and costs; an evaluation of the likely long-range impact of emerging issues; the development of specific planning guidelines to aid agencies in preparing budget requests.

Testimony before the Joint Economic Committee, Subcommittee on Economy in Government, 91st Cong., 1st Sess., June 12, 1969, pp. 666–672.

The planning guidelines are the principal product of the spring preview.

The budget is put together in the fall and winter and is transmitted to the Congress in January. During the period of budget preparation, individual agency budgets are formulated and then are subjected to the budget review process. Simultaneously, the economic outlook is reevaluated as are the fiscal policy guidelines developed during the spring preview. These guidelines, which are revised as conditions require, provide the constraints on the budget totals.

Agency budget requests begin to come in during September and are reviewed thoroughly by the Bureau's budget examiners. After discussions with agency representatives to obtain a better understanding of each agency's policies and budget proposals, the requests are "marked up" to reflect the recommendations of the examiners to the Budget Director.

In November and December, the Director meets daily with Budget Bureau staff to review in depth each agency's requests and the Bureau staff's recommendations. Shortly after each meeting, the "mark" the Director plans to recommend to the President for the relevant agency or program is made known to the agency. Previously, the Director will have discussed with the President the principal issues to be considered for each major agency and the recommendations that the President can expect to receive from the Director. In making his recommendations, the Director is mindful of the constraint on the budget total and the overall fiscal policy developed earlier.

There will be occasional appeals—and they may be more than occasional—to the Director by agency heads. In a few cases, the Director may modify his decisions. In other cases, the Director will not modify his decision and the agency head may appeal to the President. In any case, the Director discusses his recommendations and agency issues with the President. The President may, of course, modify either the Director's recommendations or those of an agency head. When all issues are resolved executive branch preparation of the budget is concluded. The budget document is then sent to the Congress, and the congressional review process begins.

BUREAU OF THE BUDGET REVIEW OF THE DEFENSE BUDGET

I know you are particularly interested today, gentlemen, in the Bureau's review of the Defense budget. As in the case of all other agencies, the Bureau's review of the Defense budget for any fiscal year begins immediately following submission to the Congress of the President's budget for the prior year. During the late winter and spring, our examiners devote a great deal of effort to probing the major issues and problems in their assigned areas.

First, the examiners become intimately familiar with the underlying factors that determine the upcoming Defense budget proposals. These proposals represent an evaluation of the threats, existing and potential, to the Nation and its international commitments. In turn, this evaluation determines the missions our forces are expected to perform. Our examiners must look into alternative strategies, relevant forces and weapons systems, and the available technological, productive, and financial resources at our command. In addition to depth of understanding, Bureau staff are expected to recommend other viable alternatives if such are not already under consideration.

Our analysts acquire knowledge about their program by reviewing literally hundreds of reports produced at all levels of the Defense organization; by meeting and working with key personnel in the Office of the Secretary of Defense, the services and the Defense agencies, other concerned agencies, and outside the Department; and by visiting military installations and contractor facilities. Information and understanding are obviously essential to independent and responsible analysis and I stress both of those words.

The actual preparation of the 1971 Defense budget will officially begin with the establishment this summer of a planning guideline by the Bureau of the Budget based on a review of principal program plans and issues. Early in October, budget submissions will come to the Office of the Secretary of Defense from the three military departments, the Defense agencies, the Office of the Secretary of Defense staff, and others, including the Office of the Joint Chiefs of Staff. These estimates must be consistent with the currently approved 5-year defense program, which summarizes the projected force, manpower, and budget requirements for the currently approved defense programs. The

5-year defense program is not, of course, binding on the President, the Bureau of the Budget or even more so the Congress. Nonetheless, the internal Department of Defense review process provides adequate opportunity for considering different judgments on military necessity.

Following the submission of estimates by the Military Departments and Defense agencies, Bureau of the Budget staff and the staff of the Office of the Secretary of Defense will conduct a thorough and detailed review of all submissions. Force requirements to be supported, plans for deployment, proposed levels of operations, procurement quantities and costs, personnel strengths, production lead-time factors, and other details will be intensely examined. By combining resources—in joint hearings with the services, for example—Bureau and Office of the Secretary of Defense analysts can cover more ground in greater detail with less duplication of effort than would otherwise be the case. During this review, the Bureau of the Budget examiners must have access to all materials available to their Defense counterparts—plus the products of the Bureau's own investigations. In addition, Bureau staff will be in a position to offer alternatives at the staff level and to assure that these alternatives receive appropriate attention early in the review.

The review will culminate within the Department of Defense with a series of 400 to 500 program/budget education documents. Each document addresses a separate budget issue and consists of a concise description of the issue, a statement of the internal Department of Defense cost estimate, and a discussion of possible alternatives, as well as a brief description of the rationale for each alternative offered.

When the Secretary has chosen either the service submission or one of the alternatives, this choice is recorded on the program/budget decision document. Together, the Service estimates, or selected alternatives, constitute the Defense budget to be transmitted to the Bureau.

While the Secretary is making choice from among the alternatives, Bureau staff will be discussing with the Budget Director the implications of the possible choices, particularly in those areas of major financial consequence or where Bureau staff are in disagreement with a chosen or likely Defense position.

Next, a budget mark, reflecting the Director's review and his recommendations for Defense, will be transmitted to the Secretary of Defense. Discussions will be held with the Secretary to review any appeals that he judges to be warranted. On any issue that may remain in dispute, the Secretary has the same right—and, indeed, responsibility—of appeal to the President as any other agency head.

After review and final "mark up" by the President, the Defense part of the budget is prepared for incorporation into the budget document to be transmitted to the Congress in January.

FUTURE DIRECTIONS

Let me turn to the future for a few moments, Mr. Chairman.

The Federal budget reflects the Nation's priorities as perceived by the President and modified by the Congress. Be that as it may, sweeping reductions in individual elements of the budget do not often occur from one budget to the next. The momentum of ongoing programs—powered by existing laws and international commitments—is too great.

President Nixon knew the strength of this momentum when he took office in January. He had been around the track. He became aware of it even more keenly when he began the difficult task of bringing Federal outlays under control and of trying to shift the course of Federal programs toward his administration's objectives. He is currently supporting fully our searching review of both our defense and international programs and our domestic policies.

The President has enunciated several high-priority goals toward which recommendations stemming from this review will be directed. These goals include—a return to relatively stable prices, maintenance of high level employment, an early, honorable peace in Vietnam, adequate provision for our national security, finding solutions to urgent domestic problems, and stepping up our battle against crime.

The proper definition of the first two goals provides primary guidance for allocating resources between the private sector and the Federal sector. The last four goals set priorities for allocating resources within the Federal sector. And obviously I am talking at the moment only about the expenditure side of the budget, not the receipts side.

International commitments—Our national defense outlays—which account for about 40 percent of total outlays—are closely related to our international commitments. Unless there is a reduction in these commitments, we should not expect drastic reductions in spending for these programs. Assistant Secretary Moot suggested in his testimony before

attempt to satisfy the Nation's emerging needs to the extent possible, whether for defense or for other purposes. We will exert extreme care in evaluating these needs and the way in which they are financed, whether by subordinating less important Federal programs—civilian or military—or by levying taxes that would divert resources from less important private uses.

CONCLUSION

Early in his administration, President Nixon directed that a thorough review be made of all Federal programs—military as well as nonmilitary. The first phase of that review was concluded when revised budget estimates for fiscal year 1970 were published in mid-April. As indicated earlier, we are continuing to evaluate those estimates. In establishing priorities for the fiscal 1971 budget, we are taking a hard look at the military budget and its relationship to other national priorities, with a heavy reliance on continuing program evaluation.

The Bureau of the Budget, through the review process described earlier, has the opportunity to make independent recommendations to the President—indeed the responsibility to make such recommendations—on the Defense Department budget. The Department, of course, has the right to appeal those recommendations, similar to other agencies.

The magnitude of the Defense budget is largely a function of the existing and potential threats to the Nation and its international commitments. To be sure, alternative budgets are possible, given these commitments; it is possible to procure more or less forces, depending on the assessment of risks, strengths of allies, and the number and kind of contingencies we want to face. Also, as this committee has stressed, the level of the Defense budget depends on the efficiency and management control we exert in acquiring equipment and supplies. But, while we will—as must—insist upon efficient procurement to reduce costs, considerably lower defense costs will be obtained only if we reduce our international commitments significantly. Such a decision can be made only by the President, with the consent of the Congress.

THE PEOPLE VERSUS THE PENTAGON

George S. McGovern, Gaylord Nelson, George Brown, Jr., Phillip Burton, John Conyers, Jr., Don Edwards, Donald M. Fraser, Robert W. Kastenmeier, Benjamin S. Rosenthal, William F. Ryan

On March 28, 1969, two separate but ironically related events occurred which insistently pointed to the most urgent public issue of our time: the role of the military-industrial establishment in the United States.

The first event of that day was the death of Dwight David Eisenhower, himself a hero of the American military heritage. As a departing President he had startled the nation with his Farewell Address, in which he warned of a military establishment supported by an immense arms industry which "has the potential for a disastrous rise of misplaced power." Eight years later his words take on new import—after at least 500 billion dollars sunk in military expenditures, a disastrous war in Vietnam, a senseless intervention in the Dominican Republic, more than forty-two treaty commitments to as many countries to intervene "in case of aggression"—all this while acute poverty and distress persist within the United States itself.

These misplaced priorities were the setting for the other event of

The Progressive 33, no. 6 (June 1969): 5–8. The ten authors of this introductory essay are the Senators and Representatives who initiated the Congressional Conference on the Military Budget and National Priorities. Their comments were prepared especially for this issue of *The Progressive* and were not part of the Conference proceedings. The Editors. Reprinted by permission from the June, 1969, issue of *The Progressive*.

March 28, the Congressional Conference on the Military Budget and National Priorities, which brought together former Government leaders, foreign policy scholars, experts on weapons technology, economists, Senators and Representatives to investigate the actual enormity of that "misplaced power" of which President Eisenhower warned.

We initiated the Conference in the conviction that Congressional control of military policy must be reasserted and that the level of Congressional analysis of these critical issues can be raised through a greater intimacy between the legislative branch and the intellectual community. Our purpose was to articulate the basic issues of the militarization of American society for the general public as well as for Congress, and to examine concrete proposals for restoring democratic control over the military budget. The substance of our discussions is included in the pages which follow, but two principal themes should be underscored.

The first is the nature of the national security bureaucracy itself. It is composed of the Armed Services, the Central Intelligence Agency, the National Security Agency, the Atomic Energy Commission, and other bodies provided for in the National Security Act of 1947, and it is closely linked to the aerospace and armaments industry, segments of the labor movement, and a new middle class of scientists, engineers, businessmen, and universities with defense research contracts. This complex is not a conspiracy; it is an enormous, self-perpetuating institutional organism. It receives such a disproportionate amount of Federal funds that there is no effective counterbalance to it, and such decisions as those on Vietnam and ABM are generated from institutional momentum rather than conscious policy decisions.

Second, to reassert control over this enormous bureaucracy we must undertake a new look at our own role in the world, assess the nature of our own social, economic, and political institutions, and redetermine our national priorities. Without such a public debate, we will be unable to translate public anxieties into political realities and forge a new political will to reverse our present priorities.

We hope this Conference will be a forerunner of a debate that will be taken up by local organizations, political clubs, university groups, and every individual man and woman who cares about the society in which he lives. There is a fundamental decision to be made by all of us, and that is how we want our tax dollar to be spent. We are heavily taxed by Federal, state, and local levies. Even with added sales taxes, gasoline taxes, surtaxes, not enough money is generated to provide for such necessary services as schools, public transportation, parks, pollution control. The pattern is nationwide.

The urgency of our concern is underscored by the critical juncture at which we stand in the development of nuclear weapons. The reason we called for the postponement of ABM deployment, a moratorium on testing of MIRV (multiple individually-targetable re-entry vehicle), and immediate commencement of strategic arms talks with the Soviet Union is that the time for such talks may soon pass the point of no return. Because of the impossibility of detecting the number of warheads inside the deployed missiles we will reach a stage in a few months when neither nation will be able to accept a limitation on its strategic force. The Soviet Union has been pressing for such talks, and we have been putting them off while we complete testing.

A profound indication of the acceleration of the arms race is the fact that our own military strategists are presently engaged in a debate to shift the basic question of defense policy from preventing nuclear war to surviving it.

Unless we act decisively within the next few months, the opportunities for maintaining any kind of security in the next decade may be almost nonexistent. The bureaucratic momentum of the defense establishment, with its parochial view of the world, is projecting decisions that are contrary to the needs of the nation and to the well-being of mankind.

The staggering costs of this proposed arms spiral cannot be measured accurately in dollars or in percentage of Gross National Product. The proper measures are in "opportunities foregone": funding the Manned Orbiting Laboratories, or providing Upward Bound summer courses for 600,000 ghetto students who have college potential; permitting excessive contractor costs to go unchecked, or providing Head Start education for 2,250,000 additional children plus enough school lunches to feed twenty million children for a whole year; spending this year's Safeguard funds, or training 510,000 more hard-core unemployed.

In the decade from 1959 to 1968, direct defense outlays of the United States came to more than $551 billion. This is twice the amount spent for new private and public housing in the same decade, and nearly twice as much as Federal, state, and local governments allocated to education. In 1967 alone, a conservative estimate of military-related spending was $100 billion. This was more than all Federal, state, and local expenditures on health, hospitals, education, old age benefits, welfare, unemployment, and agriculture.

This order of priorities prevails at a time when twenty million Americans live in dilapidated, rat-infested housing while the building industry cannot even keep up with the population increase and is in fact declining in productivity; when there are at least ten million victims of malnutrition and untold thousands of children with permanent brain damage because of insufficient food; when there are close to forty million people living in poverty with little access to medical or welfare care; while millions of children are doomed to lives of misery and poverty because of inadequate or non-existent school facilities.

The degree of economic damage done each year by the massive allocation of resources to military spending has been noted by such economists as Kenneth Boulding, who points out that by reducing "domestic consumption by about fifteen per cent and by diverting the growth resource into the rat hole of competitive weapons systems, or even space technology, it unquestionably diminishes the rate of growth by as much as two per cent per annum."

Unlike investments in education or in new factories, expenditures for missiles add nothing to the nation's productive capacity, although they do generate income for a certain segment of the population. Other costs are just as great, although less easily quantified. Civilian businesses suffer because they cannot match the salaries offered by subsidized defense firms; scientists and engineers are trapped into doing research that is contrary to life-serving causes; a new class of business executive arises—men who know little about marketing or cost controls, but who know how to negotiate effectively with Government officials.

The most striking evidence of the decay of our society is that we have sought to meet the local crises of race and poverty by increasing militarization—by training more than 400,000 National Guardsmen and police in local riot control. The pervasive use of military means to solve our social and political problems is the most alarming indication of the emptiness of other conflict-resolving institutions.

In many other subtle ways individual values and ideals have been eroded. We are slowly becoming conditioned to the acceptance of regimentation, wiretapping, snooping, and spying by large national and internal-security related agencies. In many communities the existence of large defense installations has retarded necessary social reform by reinforcing prevailing patterns of segregation and economic rigidity. In industry the military have taken over fundamental business decisions, even necessitating security clearances for business executives.

Eventually we must recognize that the factors which determine our massive military budget are to be found less abroad than they are here at home. The reason we are able to move a wounded Marine from the jungles of Vietnam to the finest medical care in minutes, yet cannot do the same for a sick child on the Mississippi delta or on an Indian reservation, is very much bound up in our image of ourselves.

Being the greatest power in the world carries not only political and economic implications, but psychological elements which many of us have not yet truthfully faced. We do a great deal to buttress that image of power. Other sacrifices we find harder to make. We are six per cent of the world's population using more than sixty per cent of its goods and developed resources. We are convinced that the American way of life is the best in the world, that American management and enterprise are the best in the world, and that capitalism is the best tool for development. The result is that our foreign policy is not dictated as much by external threats, as we would like to think, but is an extension of our own economic, political, and social institutions.

The questions we must ask ourselves are not who are the Russians, or what are the Chinese or Vietnamese about, but who and what are Americans? If anti-Communism is all we can agree on as a national credo, we will never be able to break the psychosis of force and destruction which is the American tragedy.

Our national priorities were set out in the Constitution. Somehow we have forgotten them. The priorities of our forefathers were "to form a more perfect union, establish justice, ensure domestic tranquillity, and to provide for the common defense." Our first task is to reinterpret these great goals in light of the realities of the Twentieth Century and the dawn of the Twenty-first Century.

"To form a more perfect union" is to end the racism and discrimination that have long permeated American life. "Our society is moving toward two societies, one white, one black—separate and unequal." The extraordinary Kerner Commission Report on Civil Disorders outlines the decisive deepening of the racial division of our country. To continue on our present course can only lead to the fragmentation of America into increasingly violent and repressive factions and to the ultimate destruction of basic democratic values. Despite all our talk of strength and wealth and power, we are a weak and divided society.

To form a more perfect union is surely our first task.

"To establish justice" is to end the exploitation of the poor and the weak and to make our legal system one that will insure we are governed by laws and not by men.

At a time when we have equated justice with law and order, it is important that we take a look at the "crime" in our society. The crime we talk about in America is crime in the streets. What about the crime of a society which would shoot a sixteen-year-old for looting a television set but think nothing of hungry children in a land of surplus food? What is not talked about is the crime of a society with dual standards of justice, where property is protected at any price while the costs of extortion, price-fixing, rake-offs, restraint of trade through duress or threat, blackmail, and consumer frauds are either ignored or passed on to the citizen in the form of higher prices. Organized crime drains the body politic of an estimated $22 billion per year. This crime does not appear in the statistics, but it underlies the moral fabric of our society and gives a hypocritical ring to cries for law and order. The real issue is justice.

"To ensure domestic tranquillity" is to redefine the difficult yet essential role of the police in contemporary society; to assist them in becoming more effective and creative servants of a pluralistic society; and to make sure that their role is not reduced to that of mere agents of a local power structure. The continued training of police and National Guardsmen in military techniques will not eliminate the economic and social failures which generate discord and disruption.

In the next five years twenty million Americans will leave the rural poverty in which they no longer can eke out a livelihood and migrate to cities which cannot house, feed, educate, or employ them. Massive disorder will be the inevitable result.

In the next few years millions of students will rebel against institutions which allow them no real responsibility, offer them careers they find abhorrent, and send them off to die for wars in which they cannot believe. They will disrupt the only segment of society over which they have any control—schools and universities.

The police and National Guard can quell riots. They cannot bring tranquillity. "There is no more urgent task than to break down the walls of isolation which surround our local police," warned the President's Commission on Law Enforcement. Our police are isolated from the society they serve, and the redefining and reorganization of our entire system of law enforcement—police, courts, and correctional apparatus—are essential to ensuring domestic stability and tranquillity.

"*To provide for the common defense*" means in the nuclear age to find new ways of leading in international cooperation, of building international institutions which can provide effective arms control and disarmament. The common defense does not require maintaining an American force for every conceivable contingency, however remote, nor does it require an endless arms race of nuclear and thermonuclear weapons which, if used, would destroy exactly what we are trying to protect.

One nuclear exchange between the United States and the Soviet Union would claim at least 120 million American lives. To offer up a percentage of our population as a human sacrifice is not to provide for the common defense.

The current strategic plans of our armed forces do not meet their Constitutional obligations as historically defined. To provide for defense in the nuclear age is to formulate and carry through a policy aimed at a stable peace. It means, at this point in time, a moratorium on further testing, no further ABM deployment, and successful arms limitation and disarmament agreements with the Soviet Union and other nations. A policy consciously directed towards creation of a stable peace which allows for profound change in the third world must now be fashioned to provide for the common defense of the United States.

How can we reassert the realities of our national priorities? It is clear that President Nixon will be no more able to control military spending than were Presidents Johnson or Kennedy. The size of our national security institutions precludes any partisan responsibility. The most urgent challenge confronting the Congress today is to reassert control of the military bureaucracy and the policy decisions it has preempted.

This can be accomplished only by effective Congressional leadership backed by a broadly based, informed, and concerned public constituency. In recent years the military budget and weapons policies have been determined by the Pentagon and the Armed Services Committees without critical evaluation by the Congress or the public. Last year the House Armed Services Committee held months of hearings on the military budget, but of hundreds of witnesses only two were not employees of the Pentagon.

The size and complexity of the military budget make effective review almost impossible once the appropriations measures reach the floor of either House. This year some of our colleagues will attempt to impose a ceiling on the military budget, a ceiling of $50 billion, which would match the Soviet Union's military budget plus an additional twenty per cent. An attempt will be made to analyze the budget on a line-item basis which would permit us to explore the policies underlying the equipment for which we are asked to vote. If we are asked, for example, to vote millions of dollars for high speed troop transport, we should ask whether or not we want to be able to move troops around the world to various trouble spots at a moment's notice, and if we do, why? Our policies should determine our weapons and not vice versa.

This Conference reflects a new depth and awareness in the public mood which for the first time seems ready to translate concern into effective action. It is our hope that the Conference itself will serve as a catalyst to develop similar debates across the country which will allow us to assert our role as legislators for programs of the future rather than speechmakers on the problems of our past.

THE MILITARY BUDGET AND NATIONAL ECONOMIC PRIORITIES

Charles L. Schultze

THE COMMITTEE'S DECISION to hold hearings on the military budget and national economic priorities is not only welcome but timely. Over the next several years, the Executive and the Congress will be faced with a series of basic decisions on military programs and weapons systems, whose outcome will largely determine not only the nation's security and its military posture, but also the resources available to meet urgent domestic needs. It would be most unfortunate if those decisions were made piecemeal, without reference to their effect on nonmilitary goals and priorities. Moreover, any one year's decisions on military programs —and, in fact, on many elements of the civilian budget—cast long, and usually wedge-shaped shadows into the future. Their costs in the initial budget year are often only a small fraction of the costs incurred in succeeding years.

For these reasons there are two major prerequisites to informed discussion and decision about military budgets: First, the benefits and costs of proposed military programs cannot be viewed in isolation. They must be related to and measured against those other national priorities, which, in the context of limited resources, their adoption must necessarily sacrifice. Second, the analysis of priorities must be placed

Testimony before the Joint Economic Committee, Subcommittee on Economy in Government, 91st Cong., 1st Sess., June 3, 1969, pp. 57–70.

Note: The views expressed in this paper are those of the author and do not necessarily represent the views of the trustees, the officers, or other staff members of the Brookings Institution.

in a longer-term context than the annual budget, since annual decisions —particularly with respect to large military forces or weapons systems —usually involve the use of scarce national resources, and therefore affect other national priorities, well into the future.

I might also add, parenthetically, that a review of military budgets in the context of a long-run evaluation of national priorities can directly serve the interests of national security itself. In the past year there has sprung up a widespread skepticism about the need, effectiveness, and efficiency of many components of the defense budget. This is a healthy development. But it must be harnessed and focused. In particular it must not be allowed to become a "knee-jerk" reaction, such that any proposed new military program is automatically attacked as unneeded or ineffective. We still live in a dangerous world. Effective and efficient provisions for the national security should rightfully be given a high priority. I believe that a proper balancing of military and civilian programs can best be achieved by a careful and *explicit* public discussion and evaluation of relative priorities in a long-term budgetary context. Neither the extreme which automatically stamps approval on anything carrying the national security label, nor its opposite which views any and all military spending as an unwarranted waste of national resources, has much to recommend it as a responsible attitude.

In this context I should like to discuss with the Committee three major aspects of the problem of national priorities:

a five-year summary projection of federal budgetary resources and the major claims on those resources;

a more detailed examination of the basic factors which are likely to determine the military component of those budget claims;

finally, some tentative suggestions for improving the process by which defense budget decisions are made, designed particularly to bring into play an explicit consideration and balancing of national priorities, both military and civilian.

THE BUDGETARY FRAMEWORK

By definition, the concept of "priorities" involves the problem of choice. If, as a nation, we could have everything we wanted, if there were no constraints on achieving our goals, the problem of priorities would not arise. But once we recognize that we face limits or constraints, that we cannot simultaneously satisfy all the legitimate objectives which we might set for ourselves, then the necessity for *choice* arises.

There are various kinds of constraints. There is probably some limit to the public "energy" of a nation. Psychologically, the nation and its leaders cannot enthusiastically pursue a very large number of energy-consuming goals at the same time. The psychic cost is too high. Sometimes we face limits imposed by the scarcity of very specific resources. What we can do quickly, for example, to improve the availability of high quality medical care is limited in the short run by the scarcity of trained medical personnel. But the most pervasive limit to the achievement of our goals, even in a wealthy country like the United States, is the general availability of productive resources. If the economy is producing at full employment, additions to public spending require subtractions from private spending—and vice versa.

From the point of view of public spending, the practical constraints we face are even tighter than this. I think it is a safe political prediction that during the next five years or so, and particularly once a settlement in Vietnam is reached, federal tax rates are unlikely to be raised. Reforms may, and should, occur. But the overall yield of the system is unlikely to be increased. If this judgment is correct, then the limits of budgetary resources available are given by the revenue yield of the existing tax system—a yield which will, of course, grow as the economy grows. And even those who believe that the needs of the public sector are so urgent as to warrant an increase in federal tax rates are likely to agree that an examination of long-term budgetary prospects should at least start with a projection of revenue yields under current tax laws.

Assuming for purposes of projection an initial constraint imposed by existing tax laws, it is then possible to determine roughly how large the budgetary resources available to the nation will be over the next five years for expanding existing high-priority public programs, for creating new ones, for sharing revenues with the states or for reducing federal taxes. The magnitude of the budgetary resources available for these purposes—the "fiscal dividend"—will depend on four basic factors:

the growth in federal revenues yielded by a *growing economy;*

the budgetary savings which could be realized from a *cease-fire and troop withdrawal in Vietnam.*

(These two factors, of course, *add* to fiscal dividend available for the purposes listed above. The next two *reduce* the fiscal dividend.)

The "built-in" or "automatic" increase in *civilian expenditures* which accompanies growing population and income. (This expenditure growth must be deducted before arriving at the net budgetary resources available for discretionary use.)

The probable increase in *non-Vietnam military expenditures* implicit in currently approved military programs and postures. (This increase must also be deducted in reaching the net fiscal dividend which can be devoted to domestic needs. Needless to say, of course, changes in military programs, policies, and force levels can affect this total.)

The net result of these four factors—the revenue yield from economic growth, the savings from a Vietnam ceasefire, the built-in growth of civilian expenditures, and the probable growth of the non-Vietnam military budget—measures the fiscal dividend available for meeting domestic needs.

Let me summarize the likely magnitude of each of these four budgetary elements five years from now. More precisely, I will attempt to project them from fiscal 1969 to fiscal 1974.

If we assume that economic growth continues at a healthy but not excessive pace, and that—optimistically perhaps—the annual rate of inflation is gradually scaled down from the current 4½ percent to a more tolerable 2 percent, *federal revenues should grow each year by $15 to $18 billion.* This is, of course, a cumulative growth, so that by the end of five years federal revenues should be about $85 billion higher than they are now. It is highly likely, however, that once the war in Vietnam is over, or substantially scaled down, the present 10 per cent surcharge will be allowed to expire. The yield of the surcharge five years from now would be some $15 billion. This must therefore be subtracted from the $85 billion revenue increase, leaving a net $70 billion growth in federal revenue between now and fiscal 1974.

A second potential addition to budgetary resources is the expenditure saving which could be realized upon a *Vietnam ceasefire and troop withdrawal* and a return to the pre-Vietnam level of armed forces. The current budget estimates the cost of U.S. military operations in Vietnam at about $26 billion. As I have pointed out elsewhere, however, this figure overstates somewhat the *additional* costs we are incurring in Vietnam. Even if our naval task forces were not deployed in the Gulf of Tonkin, they would be steaming on practice missions somewhere else. Hence some of the costs of those forces would be incurred even in the absence of fighting in Vietnam. Similarly, our B–52 squadrons, if not engaged in bombing missions, would be operating on training exercises. And the same is true for other activities. As best I can judge, the truly incremental, or additional, costs of Vietnam—which would disappear if a ceasefire and a return to pre-Vietnam force levels occurred—amount to about $20 billion. These savings would not, of course, be available the day after a ceasefire occurred, but would gradually be realized as withdrawal and demobilization occurred.

Within perhaps 18 months to two years after a ceasefire, this $20 billion in budgetary savings would be available to add to the $70 billion net growth in budget revenues—a total gross addition of $90 billion to resources available for other public purposes.

From this $90 billion, we must, however, make several deductions before arriving at a net fiscal dividend freely available for domestic use.

We can expect a fairly significant built-in growth in federal civilian expenditures over the next five years. As the GI's come home from Vietnam, educational expenditures under the GI bill of rights will naturally increase. Even if interest rates rise no further, the roll-over of older debt into new issues will increase interest payments. Expenditures under the Medicaid program will rise, although at a slower pace than in the last few years. A larger population and income almost automatically lead to higher public expenditures in many areas: more people visit national parks and the Park Service's outlays grow; more tax returns are filed and the Internal Revenue Service must expand to handle them; as airplane travel increases, federal expenditures on air traffic safety and control rise; and so on down the list. Social security benefits will almost certainly rise sharply if past practice is followed under which the Congress tends to raise benefit levels more or less in line with payroll revenues. For all of these reasons, I believe one must allow for a "built-in" growth of federal expenditures by some $35 billion over the next five years. Subtracting this $35 billion from the $90 billion additional resources calculated above leaves $55 billion for the fiscal dividend.

But yet another deduction must be made. Barring major changes in defense policies, military spending for *non-Vietnam* purposes will surely rise significantly over the next five years. There are five major factors working towards an increase in military expenditures.

1. *Military and civilian pay increases.* There are now 3½ million men in the Armed Forces. In addition some 1.3 million civilian employees, about 45 percent of the federal total, work for the Department of Defense. As wages and salaries in the private sector of the economy rise, the pay scales of these military and civilian employees of the Defense Department must also be raised. The military and civilian pay raise scheduled for this coming July 1 will add some $2.3 billion to the Defense budget. If we assume, conservatively, that in succeeding years private wage and salary increases average 4 to 4½ percent per year, the payroll costs of the Pentagon will rise by about $1½ billion each year.

2. *The future expenditure consequences of already approved weapons systems.* A large number of new and complex weapons systems have been approved as part of our defense posture, the bulk of the spending on which has not yet occurred.[1] Some major examples are:

the Minuteman III missile, with MIRVs, cost, $4½ billion;

the Poseidon missile, with MIRVs, cost, including conversion of 31 Polaris subs, $5½ to $6½ billion;

the Safeguard ABM system, with a currently estimated cost, including nuclear warheads, of some $8 billion, plus hundreds of millions per year in operating costs;

the F–14 Navy fighter plane in three versions; the 1970 posture statement indicates that the entire F–4 force of the Navy and Marine Corps may be replaced by the F–14. If so, the total investment and operational cost of this system over a 10-year period should be well in excess of $20 billion;

a new F–15 air-to-air combat fighter for the Air Force;

three nuclear attack carriers at a currently estimated cost of $525 to $540 million each;

62 new naval escort vessels, at an investment cost of nearly $5 billion;

a number of new amphibious assault ships;

[1] For most of the systems listed below, the decision to procure the item has already been made. In a few cases, such as the Navy's VSX anti-submarine plane, procurement has not yet been approved, but development is well along, and official statements of Defense Department officials have already indicated that the system is most likely to be approved.

a new Navy anti-submarine plane, the VSX, at a cost of $2 to $2½ billion;

a new continental air-defense system, including a complex "look-down" radar and an extensive modification program for the current F–106 interceptor.

These do not exhaust the list of new weapons systems already a part of the approved defense posture. But they do give some idea of the magnitude of the expenditures involved.

3. *Cost escalation.* The weapons systems costs given for each of the systems listed above represent current estimates. But, as this Committee is well aware, past experience indicates that final costs of complex military hardware systems almost always exceed original estimates.

A study of missile systems in the 1950's and early 1960's revealed that the average unit cost of missiles was 3.2 times the original estimates.

The nuclear carrier Nimitz, now under construction, was estimated in 1967 to cost $440 million. One year later the estimate was raised to $536 million. No new estimates have been released, but given the rapidly rising cost of shipbuilding, it is almost certain that this latter figure will be exceeded.

In January 1968 the Defense Department proposed a plan for building 68 naval escort vessels at a total cost of $3 billion. In January 1969 the estimated costs of that program had risen to $5 billion.

The cost of modernizing the carrier Midway was originally given as $88 million, and the work was scheduled to be completed in 24 months. In January 1969 the cost estimate was doubled, to $178 million, and the time estimate also doubled, to 48 months.

The Air Force's manned orbiting laboratory (the MOL) was originally announced by President Johnson at a cost of $1.5 billion. The latest estimate was $3 billion.

In many cases the rising unit costs of these systems force re-evaluation of the program and a reduction in the number purchased. The F–111 program is a classic case in point. Consequently the *aggregate* costs of the procurement budget do not rise by the same percentage as the inflation in *unit* costs. Nevertheless, cost escalation does tend to drive the total military budget upward.

4. *Weapons systems under development, advocated by the Joint Chiefs of Staff, but not yet approved for deployment.* In addition to weapons systems already approved, there are a large number of sys-

tems, currently under development, which are being advocated for deployment by the Joint Chiefs. Among these items are:

The AMSA (advanced manned strategic aircraft) is a supersonic intercontinental bomber designed as a follow-on to the B–52. President Johnson's proposed 1970 budget requested $77 million for advanced development. Secretary Laird proposed an additional $23 million to shorten design time and start full-scale engineering development. This $10 million will be supplemented by $35 million of carryover funds. The investment costs of the AMSA, if procurement decision is made, are difficult to estimate, but it is hard to see how they could be less than $10 billion.

The new main battle tank is now in production engineering. Depending on the number purchased, a procurement decision will involve investment costs of $1 to $1½ billion.

A new advanced strategic missile in super-hard silos is being advocated by the Air Force.

A new attack aircraft, the AX, is under development for the Air Force.

The Navy is proposing a major shipbuilding and reconversion program to replace or modernize large numbers of its older vessels.

A new continental air-defense interceptor, the F–12, is being advocated by the Air Force.

A new underwater strategic missile system (the ULMS) is under development for the Navy.

In the normal course of events, not all of these new systems will be adopted in the next five years. But, in the normal course of events, some will be.

5. *Mutual escalation of the strategic arms race.* The United States is currently planning to equip its Minuteman III and Poseidon missiles with multiple independently targeted reentry vehicles (MIRVs). MIRV testing has been underway for some time. The original purpose of MIRV was as a hedge against the development of a large-scale Soviet ABM system, in order to preserve our second-strike retaliatory capability in the face of such Soviet development. Recently, however, Pentagon officials have indicated that we are designing into our MIRVs the accuracy needed to destroy enemy missile sites—an accuracy much greater than needed to preserve the city-destroying capability of a retaliatory force. Secretary of Defense Laird, in recent testimony before the Armed Services Committee, for example, asked

for additional funds to "improve significantly the accuracy of the Poseidon missile, thus enhancing its effectiveness against hard targets."

Putting MIRVs with hard-target killing capabilities on Poseidon alone will equip the U.S. strategic forces with 4000 to 5000 missile-destroying warheads. Viewed from Soviet eyes the United States appears to be acquiring the capability of knocking out the Soviet land-based missile force in a first strike. It might be argued that the difficulties of attaining a hard-target killing capability on our MIRVs are so great that the objective will not be realized for many years, if ever. But without attempting to evaluate this observation, let me point out that what counts in the arms race is the Soviet reactions to our announcement. And, like our own conservative planners, the Soviets must assume that we will attain our objectives.

The United States has announced that in answer to the 200 Soviet 22–9s—which may be expanded and MIRVed into 800 to 1000 hard-target warheads—it will build an ABM system. What must the Soviet reaction be when faced with the potential of 4000 to 5000 hard-target killers on Poseidon alone? As they respond—perhaps with an even larger submarine missile force than now planned, or by developing mobile land-based missiles—we may be forced into still another round of strategic arms building. This may not occur. But its likelihood should not be completely discounted.

I have seen several arguments as to why a new round in the strategic arms race will not be touched off by current U.S. policy. I think they are dubious at best. One argument notes that the U.S. development of MIRV and ABM is being made against a "greater-than-expected" threat—i.e., a Soviet threat larger than current intelligence estimates project. Hence, runs the argument, should the Soviets respond to our new developments, this response has already been taken into account in the "greater-than-expected" threat against which we are currently building. Consequently, we would not have to respond ourselves with a still further strategic arms buildup. But this misses the very nature of "greater-than-expected" threat planning. Once the Soviets proceed to deploy a force which approaches the *current* "greater-than-expected" threat, then by definition a *new* "greater-than-expected" threat is generated, and additional strategic arms expenditures are undertaken to meet it. This is the heart of the dynamics of a strategic arms race.

Another argument is often used to discount the mutual escalation threat posed by MIRV. Multiple warheads, it is argued, make an effective large-area ABM practically impossible to attain. Hence, deployment of MIRV destroys the rationale for a large-scale, city defense, ABM. So long as MIRVs do not have the accuracy to destroy enemy missiles on the ground, this argument might indeed have some validity. But once they acquire hard-target killing capability—or the Soviets think they have such capability—they are no longer simply a means of penetrating ABM's and preserving a second-strike retaliatory force; they provide, in the eyes of the enemy, a first-strike capability, against which he must respond.

Given these various factors tending to drive up the cost of the non-Vietnam components of the military budget, by how much are annual defense expenditures, outside of Vietnam, likely to rise over the next five years? Obviously, there is no pat answer to this question. Any projection must be highly tentative. But assuming the increase in civilian and military pay mentioned earlier, calculating the annual costs of the approved weapons systems listed above, and allowing for only modest cost escalation in individual systems, it seems likely that on these three grounds alone non-Vietnam military expenditures by 1974 will be almost $20 billion higher than they are in fiscal 1969. They will, in other words, almost fully absorb the savings realizable from a cessation of hostilities in Vietnam. And this calculation leaves *out* of account the possibility of more than modest cost escalation, the adoption of large new systems like the AMSA, and a further round of strategic arms escalation.

I might note that the 1970 defense budget—even after the reductions announced by Secretary Laird—already incorporates the first round of this increase. From fiscal 1969 to fiscal 1970, the *non-Vietnam* part of the defense budget will rise by $5½ to $6 billion, after allocating to it the Pentagon's share of the forthcoming military and civilian pay raise. In one year, almost 30 percent of this $20 billion rise will apparently take place.

Starting out with an additional $70 billion in federal revenues over the next five years, plus a $20 billion saving from a ceasefire in Vietnam, we earlier calculated a $90 billion gross increase in federal budgetary resources. From this we subtracted the $35 billion growth of "built-in" civilian expenditures, and now we must further subtract a $20 billion rise in non-Vietnam military outlays, leaving a net fiscal dividend in fiscal 1974 of something in the order of $35 billion, available for discretionary use in meeting high priority public needs or additional tax cuts. That $35 billion, in turn, is itself subject to further reduction should major new weapons systems be approved or should another round in the strategic arms race take place.

Let me make it clear, of course, that there is nothing inevitable about this projection of military expenditures. Some of the weapons systems I listed are in early stages of procurement. Other areas in the military budget can be analyzed, reviewed, and, if warranted, reduced as a budgetary offset to the new systems. Hopefully, disarmament negotiations, if held quickly, may prevent mutual strategic escalation. My projection assumes that no changes in basic policies, postures, and force levels occur. It is obviously the whole purpose of these hearings to examine that assumption, in the context of other national priorities.

THE BASIC FACTORS BEHIND RISING MILITARY BUDGETS

While the budget projection summarized above discusses some of the specific weapons systems which are likely to cause the defense budget to expand sharply in the next five years, it does not address itself to the underlying forces which threaten to produce this outcome. In the first half of the 1960s the military budget ran at about $50 billion per year. With those funds not only were U.S. strategic and conventional forces maintained, they were sharply improved in both quantity and quality. Both land- and sea-based missile forces were rapidly increased. Similarly dramatic increases in the general purpose forces were undertaken. Fourteen Army divisions, undermanned, trained primarily for tactical nuclear war, and short of combat consumables were expanded to over 16⅓ divisions, most of them fully manned. Equipment and logistic supply lines were sharply increased. The 16 tactical air wings were expanded to 21. Sea-lift and air-lift capability were radically improved.

In short, on $50 billion per year in the early 1960s, it appeared to be possible to buy not only the maintenance of a given military capability, but a sharp increase in that capability. By the early 1970s, taking into account general price inflation in the economy plus military and civilian pay increases, it would take $63 to $65 billion to maintain the same purchasing power as $50 billion in 1965. Yet, as I have indicated earlier, even on conservative assumptions the non-Vietnam military budget is likely to approach $80 billion by fiscal 1974—$15 to $17 billion more than the amount needed to duplicate the general purchasing power the pre-Vietnam budget had—a budget which already was providing significant increases in military strength. Why this escalation? What forces are at work?

While there are a number of reasons for this increase, I would suggest that four are particularly important.

First, the impact of modern technology on the strategic nuclear forces. During most of the 1960s the primary goal of our strategic nuclear forces was the preservation of an "assured destruction capacity"—the ability to absorb an enemy's first strike and retaliate devastatingly on his homeland. In turn this capability provided nuclear deterrence against a potential aggressor. In general this could be described as a stable situation, in part because of the technology involved. To mount a first strike, an aggressor would have to be assured that he could knock out all—or substantially all—of his opponent's missiles. Since missiles did not have 100 percent reliability and accuracy for this task, more than one attacking missile would have to be targeted on the enemy missile force. For every missile added by the "defender," the attacker would have to add more than one. Hence, it was easy to show that first-strike capability could not be attained, since the opposing side could counter and maintain his second-strike capability at a less-than-equal cost. And, of course, the existence of mobile submarine launched missiles made the stability of the system even greater.

But the development of MIRV and more critically the development of guidance systems which are designed to make them accurate enough to "kill" enemy missiles on the ground changes this balance. Now a single attacking missile, with multiple warheads, can theoretically take out several enemy missiles. The advantage to the first attacker rises sharply. Strategic planners on both sides, projecting these developments into the future, react sharply in terms of the danger they perceive their own forces to be facing. Add to this the development of ABM, which—however initially deployed—raises fears in the minds of enemy planners that it can be extended to protect cities against his submarine launched missiles, and escalation of the strategic arms race becomes increasingly likely.

The impact of changing technology on strategic arms budgets, therefore, is one of the driving forces which changes the prospects of post-Vietnam military expenditures from what they might have seemed several years ago.

The second major factor in driving arms budgets up is the propensity of military planners to prepare against almost every conceivable contingency or risk. And this applies both to force-level planning and to the design of individual weapons systems. Forces are built to cover possible, but very remote, contingencies. Individual weapons systems are crowded with electronic equipment and built with capabilities for dealing with a very wide range of possible situations, including some highly unlikely ones.

If military technology were standing still, this propensity to cover remote contingencies might lead to a large military budget, but not to a rapidly expanding one. As technology continually advances, however, two developments occur: (1) As we learn about new technology, we project it forward into the Soviet arsenal, thereby creating new potential contingencies to be covered by our own forces; (2) The new technology raises the possibility of designing weapons systems to guard against contingencies which it had not been possible to protect against previously.

Continually advancing technology and the risk aversion of military planners, therefore, combine to produce ever more complex and expensive weapons systems and ever more contingencies to guard against. Let me give some examples.

According to Dr. John S. Foster, Jr., Deputy Director of Defense Research and Engineering in testimony before the Senate Armed Service Committee last year, the Poseidon missile system was originally designed to penetrate the Soviet TALLINN system—a system originally thought to be a widespread ABM defense. When this system turned out to be an anti-aircraft system, the deployment decision on the Poseidon was not revised. Rather it was continued as a hedge against a number of other possible Soviet developments, including in Dr. Foster's words the possibility that "the Minuteman force could be threatened by either rapid deployment of the current Soviet SS–9 or by MIRVing their existing missiles and improving accuracy."

Once the Soviets began to deploy the SS–9 in apparently larger numbers than earlier estimated, however, this gave rise to the decision to deploy a "Safeguard" ABM defense of Minutemen sites.

In short the sequence went like this: (1) The Poseidon deployment decision was made against a threat which never materialized; (2) despite the disappearance of the threat against which it was designed, the Poseidon was continued, presumably as a hedge against other potential threats, including faster-than-expected Soviet deployment of the SS–9; (3) but now a decision has been made to hedge against the SS–9 by building a "hard-point" ABM—so we are presumably building the Poseidon as a hedge against a number of possible Soviet threats, including the SS–9, and then building a hedge on top of that; (4) finally, new technology has made it possible to design a hard-target killing accuracy into the Poseidon—an accuracy not needed to preserve our second strike capability against either the SS–9 or a Soviet ABM. The technology is available—why not use it! Yet the existence of that capability may well force a major Soviet response.

Another example of hedging against remote threats is the currently planned program of improvements in our continental air-defense system. The existing SAGE system cost $18 billion to install but is apparently not very effective against low-altitude bomber attack. Although the Soviets have no sizable intercontinental bomber threat, the decision has been made to go ahead with major investments in a new air-defense system. The major reasons given for this decision are these: to deter the Soviets from deciding to reverse their long-standing policy and develop a new bomber; to guard against one-way Kamikaze-type attacks by Soviet medium-range bombers; and to protect those of our missiles which would be withheld in a retaliatory strike. There is admittedly no direct threat to be covered. But a number of more remote threats are covered. And since we cannot defend our cities against Soviet missiles, it gives small comfort to have them protected against, as yet, non-existing bombers or Kamikaze attacks.

Another case in point is the new F–14 Navy aircraft. Both the F–111B and its successor, the initial version of the F–14, were designed to stand off from the carrier fleet and, with the complex Phoenix air-to-air missile, defend the fleet from a Soviet supersonic bomber plus missile threat, in the context of a major Soviet attack against our carrier forces. But as the Senate Defense Preparedness Subcommittee noted last year, this threat is "either limited or does not exist." Or as Chairman Mahon of the House Appropriations Committee noted, "The bomber threat against the fleet, as you know, has been predicted by Navy officials for some time. It has not, of course, developed to date."

The problem of what contingencies and risks are to be guarded against goes to the very heart of priority analysis. Primarily what we buy in the military budget is an attempt to protect the nation and its vital interests abroad from the danger and risks posed by hostile forces. We seek either to deter the hostile force from ever undertaking the particular action or, if worst comes to worst, to ward off the action when it does occur. Similarly, in designing particular weapons systems, the degree of complexity and the performance requirements built into the systems depends in part on an evaluation of the various kinds of contingencies which the weapon is expected to face. Now there are almost an unlimited number of "threats" which can be conceived. The likelihood of their occurrence, however, ranges from a significant possibility to a very remote contingency. Moreover, the size of the forces and complexity of the weapons systems needed to guard against a particular set of threats depends upon whether the threats materialize simultaneously or not. If they do not occur simultaneously, then very often forces developed to meet one contingency can be deployed against another. But the probability of two or more remote contingencies occurring simultaneously is obviously even lower than either taken separately.

Clearly we cannot prepare against every conceivable contingency. Even with a defense budget twice the present $80 billion, we could not do that. The real question of priorities involves the balance to be struck between attempting to buy protection against the more remote contingencies and using those funds for domestic purposes. In any given case, this is not a judgment which can be assisted by drawing up dogmatic rules in advance. And since it is a question of balancing priorities, it is not a question which can be answered solely on military grounds or with military expertise alone—although such expertise must form an essential component of the decision process.

For what it is worth, it is my own judgment that we generally have tended in the postwar period to tip the balance too strongly in favor of spending large sums in attempting to cover a wide range of remote contingencies. And, as I have pointed out, this tendency—combined with the relentless ability of modern technology to create new contingencies and new systems to combat them—threatens to produce sizable increases in the defense budget.

A third important factor which is responsible for driving up the size of defense budgets is "modernization inflation." [2] The weapons systems we now buy are vastly more costly than those we bought 10

[2] This is the term used by Malcolm Hoag.

or 20 years ago. The F–111A and the F–14A, for example, will cost 10 to 20 times what a tactical aircraft cost at the time of Korea. A small part of this increase is due to general inflation. But by far the largest part is due to the growing complexity and advanced performance of the weapons. In the case of tactical aircraft, speed, range, bombload, accuracy of fire, loiter time, ability to locate targets, and other characteristics are many times greater than models one or two decades older. The same kinds of performance comparison can be drawn between modern missile destroyers and their older counterparts, and between modern carriers and their predecessors. We pay sharply increased costs to obtain sharply increased performance. Yet seldom if ever is this advance in "quality" used to justify a reduction in the *number* of planes or carriers or destroyers or tanks. If bomb-carrying capacity and lethal effectiveness is doubled or tripled, then presumably a smaller number of new planes can do the same job as a larger number of old planes. But the numbers generally stay the same or increase. As a consequence, modernization inflation primarily causes a net increase in military budgets rather than providing—at least partially—a reasoned basis for maintaining military effectiveness while reducing the level of forces.

In some cases, of course—for example, Soviet fighter aircraft—rising enemy capabilities may reduce the possibility of substituting quality for quantity. But the same kind of argument is hard to adduce for such weapons as carriers or attack bombers.

The fourth, and perhaps most important, reason for increasing military budgets is the fact that some of the most fundamental decisions which determine the size of these budgets are seldom subjected to outside review and only occasionally discussed and debated in the public arena. This problem is most acute in the case of the budget for the nation's general purpose forces. The fundamental assumptions and objectives of the strategic nuclear forces are more generally known and debated. But the assumptions, objectives, and concepts underlying the general purpose forces—which even in peacetime take up 60 percent of the defense budget—are scarcely known and discussed by the Congress and the public. Congress does examine and debate the wisdom and effectiveness of particular weapons systems—the TFX, the C–5A, etc. But choices of weapons systems form only a part of the complex of decisions which determine the budget for our general purpose forces.

Those decisions can conveniently be classified into four types:

1. What are the nation's *commitments* around the world? While our strategic nuclear forces are primarily designed to deter a direct attack on the United States, our general purpose forces have their primary justification in terms of protecting U.S. interests in other parts of the world. At the present time, we have commitments of one kind or another to help defend some 40-odd nations around the world—19 of them on the periphery of the Soviet-Eastern European bloc and Communist China. Almost all of these commitments were made quite some time ago, but they are still in force. Unless we wish to rely solely on "massive retaliation" as a means of fulfilling our commitments, they do pose a fundamental "raison d'etre" for general purpose forces of some size.

2. Granted the existence of these commitments, against what sort of *contingencies* or *threats* do we build our peacetime forces? A number of examples will help illustrate this aspect of decision making:

> Pre-Vietnam (and, barring changes in policy, presumably *post*-Vietnam), our general purpose forces were built to fight *simultaneously* a NATO war, a Red Chinese attack in Southeast Asia, and to handle a minor problem in the Western Hemisphere, as in the Dominican Republic. Obviously the forces-in-being would not be sufficient, without further mobilization, to complete each of these tasks. But they were planned to handle simultaneously all of the three threats long enough to enable mobilization to take place if that should prove necessary.
>
> The Navy is designed, among other tasks, to be capable of handling an all-out, nonnuclear, protracted war at sea with the Soviet Union.

The incremental costs of maintaining in-being a force to meet the Chinese attack contingency probably amount to about $5 billion per year. When in 1965 the nation decided to begin Federal aid to elementary and secondary education—which has subsequently been budgeted at less than $2 billion a year—a major national debate took place. To the best of my knowledge, there was no public comment or debate about the "Chinese contingency" decision. Yet the decision was not classified—it was publicly stated in the unclassified version of the Secretary of Defense's annual posture statement several years running. This is not to say that the decision was necessarily wrong. Rather, I want to stress that it has a very major impact on the defense budget yet was not, so far as I know, debated or discussed by the Congress.

This lack of debate cannot be laid at the door of the Pentagon, since the information was made available in the defense posture statement.

3. Granted the commitments and contingencies, what *force levels* are needed to meet those contingencies, and how are they to be based and deployed?

The Navy, for example, has 15 attack carrier task forces. The carrier forces are designed not merely to provide quick response, surge capability for air power, but to remain continually on station during a conflict. As a consequence, because of rotation, overhaul, crew-leave, and other considerations, one carrier on station generally requires two off-station as back-up. Thus for *five* carriers on station, we have *ten* back-up carriers. (The "on-station" to "back-up" ratio depends on the distance of the station from the carriers' base. The 2/1 is an average ratio.)

The pre-Vietnam Army comprised 16⅓ active divisions with eight ready-reserve divisions. The 16⅓ division force is supported by a planned 23 tactical air wing (only 21 were in-being pre-Vietnam).

The Navy has eight antisubmarine carrier task forces.

Defense plans call for a fast amphibious assault capability, sufficient to land one division/air wing in the Pacific and ⅔ division/air wing in the Atlantic.

The force levels needed to meet our contingencies are, of course, significantly affected by the military decisions and capabilities of our allies. The U.S. situation in NATO, for example, is strongly affected by whether or not the divisions of our NATO allies are equipped with the combat consumables and rapid fire-power weapons enabling them to conduct a prolonged conventional war.

4. With what *weapons systems* should the forces be equipped? Such questions as nuclear versus conventional power for carrier and carrier escorts, the F–111B versus the F–14, the extent to which the F–14 replaces all the navy's F–4's, must, of course, be decided.

Let me hasten to point out that there is no *inexorable logic* tying one set of decisions in this litany to another. Do not think that once a decision has been made on commitments, that the appropriate contingencies we must prepare against are obvious and need no outside review; or that once we have stipulated the contingencies, that the necessary force levels are automatically determined and can be left solely to the military for decision; or that once force levels are given, decisions about appropriate weapons systems can be dismissed as self-evident. There is a great deal of slippage and room for judgment and priority debate in the connection between any two steps in the process.

Some examples might help:

There is no magic relationship between the decision to build for a "2½ war" contingency (NATO war, Red Chinese attack, and Western Hemisphere trouble) and the fact that the Navy has 15 attack carrier task forces. In the Washington Naval Disarmament Treaty of 1921, the U.S. Navy was allotted 15 capital ships. All during the 1920s and 1930s, the Navy had 15 battleships. Since 1951 (with temporary exception of a few years during the Korean war) it has had 15 attack carriers, the "modern" capital ship.[3] Missions and "contingencies" have changed sharply over the last 45 years. But this particular force level has not.

If one assumed, for example, that the Navy's carrier force should provide "surge" support to achieve quick air cover and tactical bombardment during an engagement and then turned the job over to the tactical Air Force, the two-to-one ratio of back-up carriers to on-station carriers would not have to be maintained and the total force level could be reduced, even with the same contingencies. The wisdom or lack of wisdom in such a change would depend both upon a host of technical factors and upon a priority decision—does the additional "continuation" capability as opposed to "surge" capability buy advantages worth the resources devoted to it, on the order of $300 to $400 million per year in operating and replacement costs per carrier task force?

Similar questions arise in other areas. Does the 16⅔ division Army peacetime force need 23 tactical air wings for support, or could it operate with the Marines' one-to-one ratio between air wings and divisions? Granted the 15 carrier task forces, must all of their F–4s be replaced by F–14s, as the Navy is apparently planning?

In short there is a logical order of decisions—commitments to contingencies to force levels to weapons systems—but the links between them are by no means inflexible and require continuing review and oversight.

As I mentioned earlier, I am impressed by the fact that the Congress tends to concentrate primarily upon debate about weapons systems to

[3] This observation is reported by Desmond P. Wilson, "Evolution of the Attack Aircraft Carrier: A Case Study in Technology and Strategy," Ph.D. dissertation, M.I.T., February 1966.

the exclusion of the other important elements of the general purpose component of the defense budget. Many of the elements involved in military budget decision-making cannot, of course, be made subject to specific legislation—I find it hard to see how the Congress could, or should, legislate the particular contingencies against which the peacetime forces should be built. But the Congress is the nation's principal forum in which public debate can be focused on the basic priorities and choices facing the country. It can, if the proper information is available and the proper institutional framework created, critically but responsibly examine and debate *all* of the basic assumptions and concepts which underlie the military budget. And it can do so in the context of comparing priorities. The Congress can explicitly discuss whether the particular risks which a billion dollar force level or weapons systems proposal is designed to cover are serious enough in comparison with a billion dollars worth of resources devoted to domestic needs to warrant going ahead. By so doing, the Congress as a whole can create the kind of understanding and political climate in which its own Armed Services and Appropriations Committees, the President, his Budget Bureau, and his Secretary of Defense can effectively review and control the military budget.

This brings me to my next point. The size and rapid increase in the defense budget is often blamed on the military-industrial complex. Sometimes it is also blamed on the fact that the Budget Bureau uses different procedures in reviewing the military budget than it does in the case of other agencies.

The uniformed Armed Services and large defense contractors clearly exist. Of necessity, and in fact quite rightly, they have views about and interests in military budget decisions. Yet I do not believe that the "problem" of military budgets is primarily attributable to the so-called military-industrial "complex." If defense contractors were all as disinterested in enlarging sales as local transit magnates, if retired military officers all went into selling soap and TV sets instead of missiles, if the Washington offices of defense contractors all were moved to the West Coast, if all this happened and nothing else, then I do not believe the military budget would be sharply lower than it now is. Primarily we have large military budgets because the American people, in the cold war environment of the nineteen fifties and sixties, have pretty much been willing to buy anything carrying the label "Needed for National Security." The political climate has, until recently, been such that, on fundamental matters, it was exceedingly difficult to challenge military judgments, and still avoid the stigma of playing fast and loose with the national security.

This is not a reflection on military officers as such. As a group they are well above average in competence and dedication. But in the interests of a balanced view of national priorities we need to get ourselves into a position where political leaders can view the expert recommendations of the military with the same independent judgment, decent respect, and healthy skepticism that they view the budgetary recommendations of such other experts as the Commissioner of Education, Surgeon General, and the Federal Manpower Administration.

I think the same approach can be taken with respect to the procedures used by the Budget Bureau to review the Budget of the Defense Department. In all other cases, agency budget requests are submitted to the Bureau, which reviews the budgets and then makes its own recommendations to the President subject to appeal by the agency head to the President. In the case of the Defense budget, the staff of the Budget Bureau and the staff of the Secretary of Defense jointly review the budget requests of the individual armed services. The staffs make recommendations to their respective superiors. The Secretary of Defense and the Budget Director then meet to iron out differences of view. The Secretary of Defense then submits his budget request to the President, and the Budget Director has the right of carrying to the President any remaining areas of disagreement he thinks warrant Presidential review.

Given the complexity of the Defense budget and a Secretary of Defense with a genuine interest in economy, efficiency, and effectiveness, this procedure has many advantages. It probably tends to provide the Budget Director with better information on the program issues than he gets from other Departments. I think the procedure might perhaps be strengthened if the Budget Director and the Secretary of Defense *jointly* submitted the budget recommendation to the President, noting any differences of view.

But essentially, this procedural matter is of relatively modest importance. The Budget Bureau can effectively dig into and review what the President wants it to review under this procedure or many others. It can raise questions of budgetary priorities—questioning, for example, the worth of building forces against a particular set of contingencies on grounds of higher priority domestic needs—when and only when the President feels that *he* can effectively question military judgments on those grounds.

In my view, therefore, the issues of the military-industrial complex and of budget review procedures are important. But they are far less important than the basic issue of public attitudes, public understanding, and the need to generate an informed discussion about the fundamentals of the military budget in the context of national priorities.

With this in mind, let me suggest a few tentative proposals for improving public understanding and putting the military budget in a priorities framework.

TENTATIVE PROPOSALS FOR IMPROVING MILITARY BUDGET DECISIONS

The proposals I have in mind are addressed primarily to the Congress. As I noted earlier, many of the basic assumptions and concepts which determine the size of the military budget do not lend themselves, in the first instance, to direct legislative actions. But the Congress has another historic function—focusing public understanding and debate on important national concerns as a means of creating the framework within which both the Congress and the President can take the necessary specific actions. It is to this second function that my proposals are addressed.

As you know, each year for the last eight years the Secretary of Defense has submitted to the Congress an annual *posture statement.* This statement contains a wealth of information and analysis and lays out most of the basic assumptions and concepts on which the military budget request is based. But, as I pointed out earlier, one of the most fundamental determinants of the military budget, particularly the general purpose forces, is the set of overseas commitments in which we have undertaken to defend other nations. Yet the Secretary of State submits no annual posture statement covering his area of responsibility and concern. Because of this lack of a State Department posture statement, the Defense posture statement each year has devoted its lengthy opening sections to a review of the foreign policy situation.

Recommendation 1. The Secretary of State should submit to the Congress each year a posture statement. This statement should, at a minimum, outline the overseas commitments of the United States, review their contribution or lack of contribution to the nation's vital interests, indicate how these commitments are being affected and are likely to be affected by developments in the international situation, and relate these commitments and interests to the military posture of the United States.

The Defense posture statement itself could be much more useful to the Congress and the nation if two important sets of additional information were supplied:

Recommendation 2. The Defense posture statement should incorporate a five-year projection of the future expenditure consequences of current and proposed military force levels, weapons procurement, etc. This need not, and should not, be an attempt to forecast *future* decisions. But it should contain, in effect, the five-year budgetary consequences of past decisions and of those proposed in the current budget request. And not only should this sum be given in total, but it should be broken into meaningful components.

One of the major problems in priority analysis is the fact that the first year's expenditures on the procurement of new weapons systems is very small. Hence it is quite possible in any one year for the Congress to authorize and appropriate, in sum, a relatively small amount for several new systems which, two to five years in the future, use up a very large amount of budgetary resources.

All sorts of technical details need to be worked out if this proposal is to be useful. What is a "decision" about a weapons system? The Defense Department plans, for example, call for three nuclear carriers to be built. Procurement funds have been requested for only two so far. Should the cost of the third be included in the projection? But with a little goodwill on both sides, these questions could be ironed out. Let me also note that I am aware that the Congress—relying on past experience with cost escalation—may want to increase the official projections of many weapons systems costs in order to get a more accurate idea of the overall total.

Recommendation 3. The Defense posture statement should include more cost data on relevant components of forces and weapons systems. What is the annual cost of the forces we maintain in peacetime against the contingency of a Chinese attack in South East Asia? What is the systems cost of constructing and operating a naval attack carrier task force? What is the cost of buying and maintaining one tactical air-wing? What is the annual cost of operating each of the Navy's eight anti-submarine warfare carriers? These are precisely the kinds of information needed to make possible a rational and responsible debate about the military budget in the context of national priorities.

Given this information, it seems to me that the Congress could organize itself to use it effectively. To that end, very tentatively I would suggest the following recommendations:

Recommendation 4. An appropriate institution should be created within the Congress to review and analyze the two posture statements in the context of broad national priorities, and an annual report on the two statements should be issued by the Congress.

I use the peculiar terms "an appropriate institution" because I am not familiar enough with either Congressional practices or Congressional politics to specify its title more closely. Whether this institution should be a new Joint Committee, an existing Joint Committee, a Select Committee, an *ad hoc* merging of several Committees, or some other form, I do not know. But I can specify what I believe should be the characteristics of such an institution:

It should review the basic factors on which the military budget is based, in the context of a long-term projection of budgetary resources and national priorities.

It should have, as one part of its membership, Senators and Congressmen chiefly concerned with domestic affairs, to assert the claims of domestic needs.

It should not concern itself primarily with the technical details of weapons systems, procurement practices and the like; while these are very important, they are the province of other Committees. It is the "national priorities" of the military budget which should be the essence of the new institution's charter.

Above all, it should have a top flight, highly qualified staff. The matters involved do require final solution by the judgment of political leaders, but in the complex areas with which the new institution would deal, its deliberations must be supported by outstanding, full-time, professional staff work.

The institution I have described would have no legislative responsibilities. But I do not believe that makes it any less important. After all, the Joint Economic Committee has no legislative mandate. Yet in the past twenty-two years, its activities have immeasurably increased the quality and sophistication of public debate and of Congressional actions on matters of economic affairs and fiscal policy. Should an institution such as I have described be created, I would only hope that twenty-two years from now it could look back on an equally productive life.

APPENDIX

WORLD MILITARY EXPENDITURES 1969

Source: U.S. Arms Control and Disarmament Agency, *World Military Expenditures 1969,* Publication 53 (Washington, D.C.: U.S. Government Printing Office, December 1969).

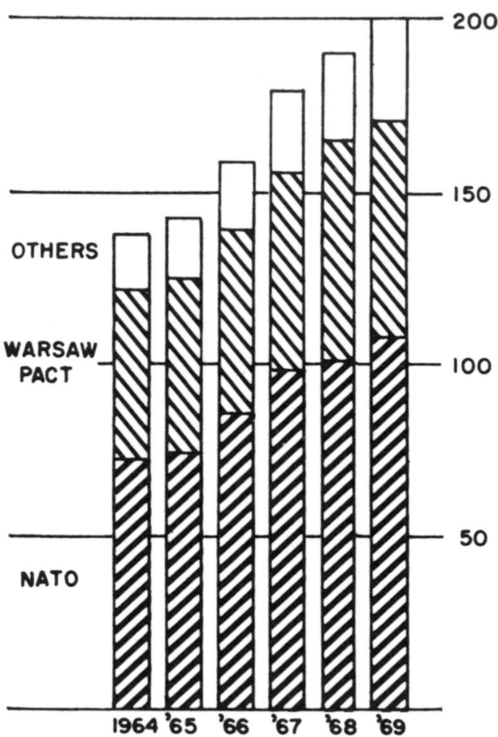

Military Expenditures (billion dollars)

	1964	*1965*	*1966*	*1967*	*1968 (Est.)*	*1969 (Est.)*
World	*139*	*143*	*160*	*181*	*191*	*200*
NATO	73	74	86	100	105	108
Warsaw Pact	49	51	54	57	60	63
Other	17	18	20	24	26	29

Military Expenditures and GNP in Constant Prices

(1964 = 100)

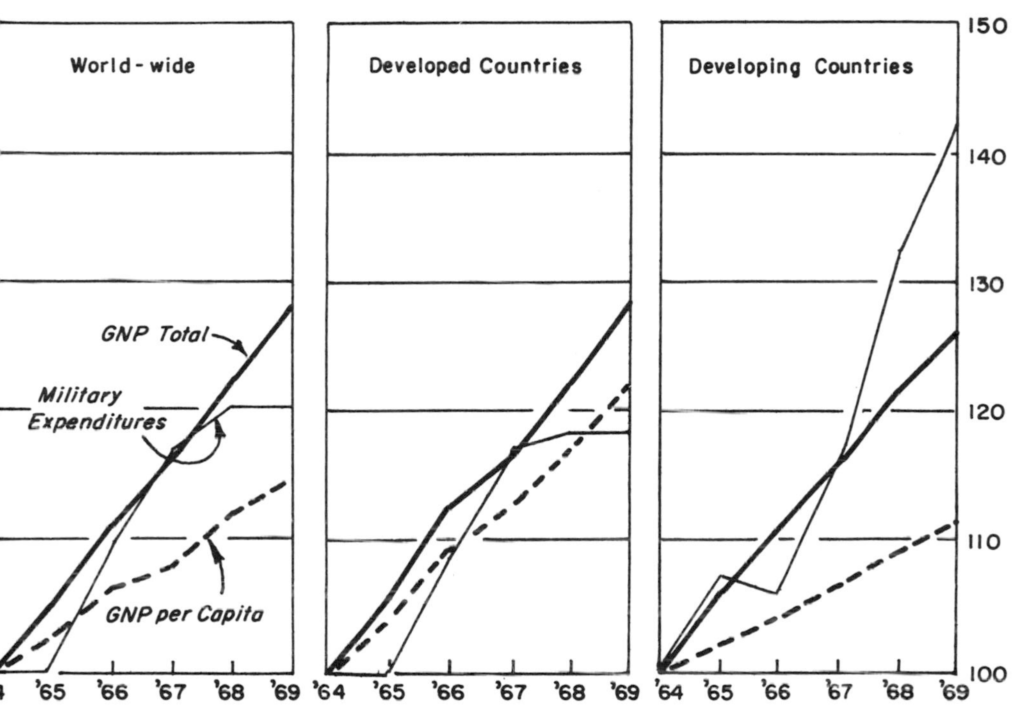

TABLE II.—MILITARY EXPENDITURES AND RELATED DATA: 1967

[Amounts in current dollars] [1]

Region, group, and country	Military expenditures (mil. dol.)	Gross national product (mil. dol.)	Relative burden: Military expenditure (% of GNP)	Relative burden: GNP (dollars per capita)	Other public expenditures: Public education [2] (mil. dol.)	Other public expenditures: Public health [3] (mil. dol.)	Foreign economic aid [4]: Received (mil. dol.)	Foreign economic aid [4]: Given (mil. dol.)	Armed forces: Armed forces (thous.)	Armed forces: Population (thous.)	Armed forces: Forces (per thous. pop.)
A. SUMMARY											
World total	180,682	2,481,743	[5] 7.3	722	127,869	59,803	7,244	8,079	21,576	3,434,967	6
Developed	160,364	2,054,440	7.8	2,151	114,677	54,131	——	7,927	10,314	955,113	11
Developing	20,318	427,303	4.8	172	13,192	5,672	7,244	107	11,262	2,479,854	5
North America*	77,301	850,900	9.1	3,875	46,566	19,622	——	4,341	3,503	219,559	16
Europe	83,187	1,111,700	[5] 7.5	1,553	62,859	34,713	491	3,169	7,996	715,662	11
Developed	80,357	1,044,000	7.7	1,733	61,197	33,776	——	3,111	6,445	602,424	11
Developing	2,830	67,700	4.2	598	1,662	937	491	58	1,551	113,238	14
Latin America**	2,468	110,039	2.2	433	3,195	1,921	1,291	——	944	254,200	4
Far East	10,950	244,686	4.5	203	9,487	1,609	1,235	424	6,268	1,206,977	5
Developed	1,076	115,660	.9	1,158	5,332	162	——	375	246	99,920	2
Developing	9,874	129,026	7.7	117	4,155	1,447	1,235	49	6,022	1,107,057	5
South Asia**	2,015	61,309	3.3	91	1,831	262	2,105	——	1,660	673,912	2
Near East**	2,440	27,687	8.8	310	1,240	680	320	——	737	89,202	8
Africa	1,061	44,622	2.4	171	1,576	464	1,297	——	375	260,978	1
Developed	370	13,080	2.8	698	467	39	——	——	27	18,733	1
Developing	691	31,542	2.2	130	1,109	425	1,297	——	348	242,245	1

World total	180,682	2,481,743	[5] 7.3	722	127,869	59,803	7,244	8,079	21,576	3,434,967	6
North America	77,301	850,900	9.1	3,875	46,566	19,662	—	4,341	3,503	219,559	16
United States	75,484	793,500	9.5	3,985	42,435	18,000	—	4,130	3,400	199,118	17
Canada	1,817	57,400	3.2	2,808	4,131	1,662	—	211	103	20,441	5
Europe	83,187	1,111,700	[5] 7.5	1,553	62,859	34,713	491	3,169	7,996	715,662	11
NATO, European	23,054	501,000	4.6	1,686	21,101	6,021	250	2,593	2,937	297,193	10
Belgium*	569	19,500	2.9	2,035	913	39	—	77	102	9,581	11
Denmark*	326	12,200	2.7	2,521	767	411	—	22	47	4,839	10
France*	5,856	115,900	5.1	2,323	4,219	394	—	873	520	49,890	10
Germany, West [6]*	5,349	121,000	4.4	2,097	4,235	1,561	—	634	460	57,699	8
Greece	313	7,000	4.5	803	164	50	37	—	159	8,716	18
Iceland*	—	600	—	3,000	22	8	NA	NA	—	200	—
Italy*	2,175	67,000	3.2	1,280	2,539	415	—	286	[7] 425	52,334	8
Luxembourg*	8	700	1.2	2,090	35	10	NA	NA	1	335	29
Netherlands*	884	22,700	3.9	1,802	1,435	†241	—	88	130	12,597	10
Norway*	294	8,300	3.5	2,193	470	139	—	11	35	3,784	9
Portugal	333	4,600	7.2	487	67	41	—	58	149	9,440	16
Turkey	511	10,600	4.8	324	313	121	214	—	480	32,710	15
United Kingdom*	6,436	110,900	5.8	2,014	5,922	2,961	—	542	429	55,068	8
NATO total	100,355	1,351,900	7.4	2,616	67,667	20,555	250	6,934	6,440	516,752	12
Warsaw Pact	57,070	512,600	[8] (7–8)	1,492	37,567	26,639	—	†456	4,267	335,601	13
Bulgaria	260	8,200	3.2	987	316	194	—		150	8,309	18
Czechoslovakia*	1,340	26,300	5.1	1,839	1,107	1,091	—		225	14,305	16
Germany, East*	890	28,800	3.1	1,780	1,236	†1,117	—		127	16,001	8
Hungary*	290	12,600	2.3	1,234	529	339	—	†116	102	10,212	10
Poland*	1,680	33,900	5.0	1,061	1,576	1,424	—		270	31,944	8
Romania*	610	18,800	3.2	975	923	600	—		173	19,287	9
Soviet Union*	52,000	384,000	[8] (8–9)	1,630	†31,880	21,874	—	†340	3,220	235,543	14
Other European	3,063	98,100	3.0	1,184	4,191	2,053	241	120	792	82,868	10
Albania	†69	†700	[9] 9.9	356	68	12	NA	—	38	1,965	19
Austria*	144	10,600	1.4	1,447	434	298	—	58	47	7,323	6
Finland*	148	7,100	2.1	1,522	434	234	NA	NA	[7] 45	4,664	10
Ireland*	39	3,200	1.2	1,104	131	36	NA	NA	10	2,899	3
Spain	948	26,900	3.0	837	371	†301	157	—	[7] 335	32,140	10
Sweden*	945	23,900	4.0	3,037	1,718	672	—	50	65	7,869	8
Switzerland*	374	16,000	2.3	2,645	672	282	—	13	12	6,050	2
Yugoslavia*	396	9,700	4.1	487	363	218	84	—	240	19,958	12

See footnotes at end of table.

TABLE II.—MILITARY EXPENDITURES AND RELATED DATA: 1967—Continued

[Amounts in current dollars][1]

Region, group, and country	Military expenditures	Gross national product	Relative burden		Other public expenditures				Armed forces		
			Military expenditure	GNP	Public education [2]	Public health [3]	Foreign economic aid [4]		Armed forces	Population	Forces
							Received	Given			
	(mil. dol.)	(mil. dol.)	(% of GNP)	(dollars per capita)	(mil. dol.)	(mil. dol.)	(mil. dol.)	(mil. dol.)	(thous.)	(thous.)	(per thous. pop.)
B. BY COUNTRY—Continued											
Latin America	2,468	110,039	2.1	433	3,195	1,921	1,291	—	944	254,200	4
Argentina	271	14,945	1.8	649	752	42	85	—	[7] 144	23,031	6
Bolivia	15	712	2.3	164	27	†27	31	—	20	4,337	3
Brazil	940	29,743	3.2	347	276	†675	283	—	[7] 225	85,655	5
Chile	115	5,426	2.5	605	279	134	141	—	[7] 46	8,970	5
Colombia	85	5,534	1.7	288	136	43	146	—	[7] 55	19,191	3
Costa Rica	—	671	—	421	28	61	22	—	—	1,594	—
Cuba	†380	†5,400	[9] 7.0	622	302	†150	1	—	[7] 200	8,033	25
Dominican Republic	31	1,068	2.9	275	24	†24	67	—	19	3,889	5
Ecuador	27	1,350	2.0	249	31	14	34	—	17	5,429	3
El Salvador	10	882	1.2	286	25	12	16	—	6	3,082	19
Guatemala	16	1,416	1.2	288	28	11	21	—	9	4,913	2
Guyana	2	†230	[9] 1.0	338	11	6	NA	—	1	680	1
Haiti	7	300	2.4	65	4	3	3	—	5	4,581	1
Honduras	8	577	1.3	236	16	6	13	—	5	2,445	20
Jamaica	5	994	.5	530	26	16	24	—	2	1,876	1
Mexico	168	24,112	.7	528	596	265	161	—	70	45,671	2
Nicaragua	10	641	1.6	360	10	17	19	—	[7] 6	1,783	3
Panama	1	773	.1	582	25	13	24	—	—	1,329	—
Paraguay	10	477	2.0	221	7	2	22	—	13	2,161	6
Peru	134	3,974	3.4	321	191	70	80	—	50	12,385	4
Trinidad & Tobago	3	816	.3	808	23	18	5	—	1	1,030	1
Uruguay	28	1,483	1.8	533	55	†27	10	—	12	2,783	4
Venezuela	202	8,515	2.4	910	323	285	82	—	[7] 38	9,352	4
Far East	10,950	244,686	4.5	203	9,487	1,690	1,235	424	6,268	1,206,977	6
Burma	103	1,803	5.7	70	45	19	11	—	137	25,811	5
Cambodia	57	962	5.9	150	42	9	14	—	[7] 48	6,415	7
China, Mainland	†7,000	†85,000	[9] 8.2	108	†2,975	†1,148	—	†49	2,700	789,000	4
China, Republic of	415	3,602	11.5	263	103	9	92	—	[7] 600	13,700	44
Indonesia	[illegible]	[illegible]	[illegible]	[illegible]	[illegible]	[illegible]	[illegible]	[illegible]	[illegible]	[illegible]	[illegible]

Japan*	†1,076	115,660	[9] .9	1,158	5,332	†162	—	375	246	99,920	2
Korea, North	†600	†3,000	[9] 20.0	236	†93	†17	NA	—	368	12,700	29
Korea, Republic of	184	4,612	4.0	155	157	29	270	—	612	29,784	21
Laos	35	194	17.8	70	6	18	74	—	65	2,770	23
Malaysia	123	3,176	3.9	315	129	59	(‡)	—	[7] 44	10,071	4
Mongolia	†25	†500	[9] 5.0	427	†5	†1	NA	—	23	1,170	12
Philippines	108	6,519	1.7	188	188	34	127	—	[7] 47	34,656	1
Thailand	133	5,078	2.6	149	145	28	68	—	126	34,008	4
Vietnam, North	†500	†2,000	[9] 25.0	100	†136	†36	NA	—	447	20,100	22
Vietnam, Republic of	419	2,980	14.1	177	34	17	450	—	[7] 465	16,973	27
South Asia	2,015	61,309	3.3	91	1,831	262	2,105	—	1,660	673,912	2
Afghanistan	16	1,340	1.1	85	15	2	41	—	75	15,751	5
Ceylon	15	1,800	1.8	154	81	39	49	—	10	11,701	1
India	1,486	43,650	3.4	85	1,571	188	1,447	—	[7] 1,200	514,200	2
Nepal	6	794	.8	76	5	†10	14	—	15	10,500	1
Pakistan	492	13,725	3.6	113	159	23	553	—	360	121,760	3
Near East	2,440	27,687	8.8	310	1,240	680	320	—	737	89,202	8
Cyprus	9	469	1.9	764	12	4	6	—	1	614	2
Iran	418	7,495	5.6	285	184	113	82	—	180	26,284	7
Iraq	268	2,240	12.0	265	126	22	14	—	[7] 84	8,440	10
Israel	428	4,005	10.7	1,501	292	38	85	—	[7] 80	2,669	30
Jordan	77	575	13.4	286	22	4	50	—	50	2,013	25
Kuwait	55	1,860	6.4	3,577	64	35	12	—	6	520	12
Lebanon	40	1,700	2.4	633	42	15	8	—	12	2,685	4
Saudi Arabia	341	2,000	17.1	444	146	†45	−12	—	[7] 54	4,500	12
Syrian Arab Republic	†125	1,130	11.1	203	50	66	20	—	[7] 64	5,570	11
Yemen	†13	†520	[9] 2.5	104	3	†44	2	—	6	5,000	1
United Arab Republic	666	5,693	11.7	184	299	†294	51	—	[7] 200	30,907	6

See footnotes at end of table.

TABLE II.—MILITARY EXPENDITURES AND RELATED DATA: 1967—Continued

[Amounts in current dollars] [1]

Region, group, and country	Military expenditures	Gross national product	Relative burden: Military expenditure	Relative burden: GNP	Other public expenditures: Public education [2]	Other public expenditures: Public health [3]	Foreign economic aid [4]: Received	Foreign economic aid [4]: Given	Armed forces: Armed forces	Armed forces: Population	Armed forces: Forces
	(mil. dol.)	(mil. dol.)	(% of GNP)	(dollars per capita)	(mil. dol.)	(mil. dol.)	(mil. dol.)	(mil. dol.)	(thous.)	(thous.)	(per thous. pop.)
B. BY COUNTRY—Continued											
Africa	1,061	44,622	2.4	171	1,576	464	1,297	—	375	260,968	1
Algeria	100	3,000	3.3	242	144	†12	103	—	58	12,380	5
Cameroon	18	775	2.4	142	19	10	41	—	[7]6	5,470	1
Central African Republic	†3	†190	[9]1.6	130	7	†3	21	—	1	1,459	2
Chad	†8	†270	[9]3.0	79	9	3	21	—	1	3,410	(‡)
Congo, Brazzaville	†6	†125	[9]4.8	145	4	†2	22	—	2	860	2
Congo, Kinshasa	37	1,332	2.7	80	48	†24	96	—	31	16,585	2
Dahomey	4	†180	[9]2.2	72	8	†5	20	—	2	2,505	1
Ethiopia	37	1,551	[9]2.4	66	22	†48	32	—	43	23,457	2
Gabon	†3	†180	1.7	380	12	5	15	—	1	473	2
Ghana	39	1,734	2.3	213	70	3	72	—	15	8,143	2
Guinea	14	310	4.5	83	17	†7	11	—	5	3,735	1
Ivory Coast	17	1,071	1.6	267	51	†8	41	—	4	4,010	1
Kenya	15	1,181	1.3	119	47	†20	61	—	3	9,928	(‡)
Liberia	3	240	1.3	216	6	3	45	—	4	1,110	4
Libya	30	1,580	1.9	909	51	†3	4	—	8	1,738	5
Malagasy Republic	12	730	1.7	118	44	12	47	—	4	6,200	1
Malawi	2	217	.8	52	12	3	30	—	1	4,150	(‡)
Mali	5	333	1.5	70	18	9	18	—	4	4,760	1
Mauritania	†6	†155	[9]3.9	141	9	2	9	—	1	1,100	1
Morocco	75	2,660	2.8	188	101	†28	76	—	[7]58	14,140	4
Niger	†3	†280	[9]1.1	79	5	†8	59	—	1	3,546	(‡)
Nigeria	89	5,340	1.7	107	117	†85	84	—	20	50,055	(‡)
Rhodesia, South	19	1,074	1.8	237	20	14	−4	—	4	4,530	1
Senegal	†15	790	[9]1.9	215	28	†8	52	—	5	3,670	1
Sierra Leone	3	380	.8	156	13	†5	8	—	2	2,439	1
Somali Republic	8	132	6.1	50	2	3	16	—	8	2,645	3
South Africa, Republic*	370	13,080	2.8	698	467	†39	NA	—	27	18,733	1
Sudan	†50	1,554	[9]3.2	108	61	†30	21	—	18	14,355	1
Tanzania	12	[10]858	1.4	[10]73	28	8	37	—	4	12,173	(‡)
Togo	3	205	1.3	119	4	2	16	—	1	1,724	1
Tunisia	14	954	1.5	209	49	20	110	—	[7]23	4,560	5
Uganda	15	734	2.0	93	19	†15	22	—	6	7,934	1
Upper Volta	†5	253	[9]2.0	50	6	4	20	—	1	5,054	(‡)
Zambia	21	1,174	1.8	297	58	12	70	—	3	3,947	1

Oceania	1,260	30,800	4.1	2,128	1,115	492	——	145	93	14,477	6
Australia*	1,155	25,200	4.6	2,145	890	290	——	145	80	11,751	7
New Zealand*	105	5,600	1.9	2,054	225	202	——	NA	13	2,726	5

*Developed countries. **Developing countries. NA Not available. †Rough ACDA estimate. ‡Less than one-half unit. ——None or not applicable.

[1] For most countries, conversion into U.S. dollars is at official par value exchange rates as rounded by AID (see Notes on Data).

[2] Estimates for 1967 based on data for 1966 or earlier (see Notes on Data).

[3] Most entries are estimates for 1967 based on data for earlier years; some entries are rough projections (see Notes on Data).

[4] Economic aid given by communist countries is included in the world total of aid received but is not distributed by individual recipient countries or regions.

[5] Military expenditures and GNP are not fully comparable due to the use of different dollar conversion rates for the two variables in the Warsaw Pact countries (see footnote 8). Using the more valid ratios shown for these countries in parentheses, the ratio for the world would be 6 to 7 percent and for Europe, 5 to 6 percent.

[6] Includes West Berlin.

[7] Includes paramilitary as well as regular forces.

[8] The implied relationship between dollar amounts of GNP and military expenditures (or other variable) is not entirely valid for Warsaw Pact countries due to the use of noncomparable conversion rates for particular sectors. Military expenditures as a percent of GNP would be about as shown in parentheses when measured in national currencies and at factor cost rather than at market prices.

[9] Since either or both military expenditures and GNP estimates are approximations, the resulting ratio should be viewed with particular caution.

[10] Tanganyika only.

TABLE V.—RANKING OF MAJOR COUNTRIES ACCORDING TO GNP AND MILITARY EXPENDITURES: 1967

[Amounts in current dollars]

	Gross national product				Military expenditures			
	Total		Per capita		Total		Per capita	
	Rank	Billion dollars	Rank	Dollars	Rank	Billion dollars	Rank	Dollars
United States*	1	793.5	1	3,985	1	75.5	1	379
Soviet Union*	2	384.0	19	1,630	2	52.0	2	221
West Germany	3	121.0	11	2,097	6	5.3	10	93
France*	4	115.9	8	2,323	4	5.9	5	117
Japan	5	115.7	25	1,158	13	1.1	58	11
United Kingdom*	6	110.9	15	2,014	5	6.4	7	117
Mainland China*	7	85.0	97	108	3	7.0	62	9
Italy	8	67.0	23	1,280	7	2.2	21	42
Canada	9	57.3	5	2,803	8	1.8	11	89
India	10	43.7	105	85	10	1.5	89	3
Poland	11	33.9	27	1,061	9	1.7	18	53
Brazil	12	29.7	53	347	15	.9	56	11
East Germany	13	28.8	18	1,780	18	.8	18	56
Spain	14	26.9	32	837	17	.8	34	25
Czechoslovakia	15	26.3	16	1,839	11	1.3	9	94
Australia	16	25.2	10	2,145	12	1.2	8	87
Mexico	17	24.1	44	528	45	.2	78	4
Sweden	18	23.9	3	3,037	14	.9	4	120
Netherlands	19	22.7	17	1,802	16	.9	14	70
Belgium	20	19.5	14	2,035	22	.6	17	59
Romania	21	18.8	29	975	20	.6	29	32
Switzerland	22	16.0	6	2,645	31	.4	16	62
Argentina	23	14.9	37	649	39	.3	55	9
Pakistan	24	13.7	96	113	25	.5	77	4
South Africa	25	13.1	36	698	32	.4	38	20
Hungary	26	12.6	24	1,234	42	.2	33	28
Denmark	27	12.2	7	2,521	36	.3	15	62
Turkey	28	10.6	55	324	23	.5	48	16
Austria	29	10.6	22	1,447	47	.1	44	20
Yugoslavia	30	9.7	46	487	30	.4	43	20

*Denotes country possessing nuclear weapons.

Note.—All value data in this table are from table II; see also notes to that table for explanation of data on Communist countries.

BIBLIOGRAPHY

BOOKS

Adler-Karlson, Gunnar. *Western Economic Warfare, 1947–1967*. Stockholm: University of Stockholm, 1968.

Armacost, Michael H. *The Politics of Weapons Innovation: The Thor-Jupiter Controversy*. New York: Columbia University Press, 1969.

Baldwin, William L. *The Structure of the Defense Market, 1955–1964*. Durham, N.C.: Duke University Press, 1967.

Baran, Paul A., and Paul M. Sweezy. *Monopoly Capital*. New York: Monthly Review Press, 1966.

Barnet, Richard J. *The Economy of Death*. New York: Atheneum, 1969.

Benoit, Emile, and Kenneth E. Boulding, eds. *Disarmament and the Economy*. New York: Harper and Row, 1963.

Bolton, Roger E. *Defense Purchases and Regional Growth*. Washington, D.C.: The Brookings Institution, 1966.

Clayton, James L. "Defense Spending: Key to California's Growth." In Davis B. Bobrow, ed. *Components of Defense Policy*. Chicago: Rand McNally, 1965.

Clayton, James L., ed. *The Economic Impact of the Cold War*. New York: Harcourt, Brace and World, 1970.

Coffin, Tristram. *The Passion of the Hawks: Militarism in Modern America*. New York: Macmillan, 1964.

Committee on the Economic Impact of Defense and Disarmament, *Report of the Committee*, July, 1965. Washington, D.C.: U.S. Government Printing Office, 1965.

Cook, Fred J. *The Warfare State*. New York: Macmillan, 1962.

Duscha, Julius. *Arms, Money, and Politics*. New York: Ives Washburn, 1964.

Hammond, Paul Y. *Organizing for Defense*. Princeton, N.J.: Princeton University Press, 1961.

Hitch, Charles J., and Roland N. McKean. *The Economics of Defense in the Nuclear Age*. Cambridge, Mass.: Harvard University Press, 1960.

Hoopes, Townsend. *The Limits of Intervention*. New York: McKay, 1969.

Horowitz, David, ed. *Corporations and the Cold War*. New York: Monthly Review Press, 1969.

Javits, Jacob K., Charles J. Hitch, and Arthur F. Burns. *The Defense Sector and the American Economy*. New York: New York University Press, 1968.

Kolko, Gabriel. *The Politics of War*. New York: Random House, 1969.

Lapp, Ralph E. *The Weapons Culture*. New York: W. W. Norton, 1968.

Lens, Sidney. *The Military-Industrial Complex*. Philadelphia: United Church Press, 1970.

Leontief, Wassily W., and Marvin Hoffenberg. "Input-Output Analysis of Disarmament Impacts." In Emile Benoit and Kenneth E. Boulding, eds. *Disarmament and the Economy*. New York: Harper and Row, 1963.

Logistics Management Institute. *Defense Industry Profit Review, 1958–1967*. Washington, D.C.: L.M.I., 1968.

Lyons, Gene M., and Louis Morton. *Schools for Strategy: Education and Research in National Security Affairs*. New York: Praeger, 1965.

Mansfield, Edwin, ed. *Defense, Science, and Public Policy*. New York: W. W. Norton and Company, 1968.

Marzani, Carl, and Victor Perlo. *Dollars and Sense of Disarmament*. New York: Marzani and Munsell, 1960.

McGaffin, William, and Erwin Knoll. *Scandal in the Pentagon*. Greenwich, Conn.: Fawcett, 1969.

McKean, Roland N., ed. *Issues in Defense Economics*. New York: National Bureau of Economic Research, 1967.

Melman, Seymour. *Our Depleted Society*. New York: Holt, Rinehart, and Winston, 1965.

Mills, C. Wright. *The Power Elite*. New York: Oxford University Press, 1956.

Mollenhoff, Clark R. *The Pentagon: Politics, Profits, and Plunder*. New York: G. P. Putnam's Sons, 1967.

Nieburg, H. L. *In the Name of Science*. Chicago: Quadrangle Books, 1966.

Noel-Baker, Philip. *The Private Manufacture of Arms*. London: Victor Gollancz, 1937.

Peck, Merton J., and Frederic M. Scherer. *The Weapons Acquisition Process: An Economic Analysis*. Boston: Division of Research, Graduate School of Business Administration, Harvard University, 1962.

Perlo, Victor. *Militarism and Industry*. New York: International Publishers, 1963.

Proxmire, William. *Report from Wasteland: America's Military-Industrial Complex*. New York: Praeger, 1970.

Raymond, Jack. *Power at the Pentagon*. New York: Harper and Row, 1964.

Scherer, Frederic M. *The Weapons Acquisition Process: Economic Incentives*. Boston: Division of Research, Graduate School of Business Administration, Harvard University, 1964.

Schiller, Herbert I. *Mass Communications and American Empire*. New York: Augustus M. Kelley, 1969.

Smith, Bruce L. R. *The Rand Corporation*. Cambridge, Mass.: Harvard University Press, 1966.

Steel, Ronald. *Pax Americana*. New York: Viking, 1967.

Stockfish, J. A., ed. *Planning and Forecasting in the Defense Industries.* Belmont, Calif.: Wadsworth, 1962.

Stockholm International Peace Research Institute. *SIPRI Yearbook of Armaments and Disarmaments 1968/69.* Stockholm: SIPRI, 1969.

Swomley, John M., Jr. *The Military Establishment.* Boston: Beacon Press, 1964.

Swomley, John M., Jr. "The Military-Industrial Alliance." In Houghton, Neal D., ed. *Struggle Against History: United States Foreign Policy in an Age of Revolution.* New York: Simon and Schuster, 1968.

Thayer, George. *The War Business.* New York: Simon and Schuster, 1969.

Weidenbaum, Murray L. *The Modern Public Sector.* New York: Basic Books, 1969.

PERIODICALS

Adams, Walter. "The Military-Industrial Complex and the New Industrial State." *American Economic Review* 58, no. 2 (1968): 652–665.

Barro, Stephen M. "The Economic Impact of Space Expenditures." *Business Horizon* 10, no. 2 (1967): 71–80.

Brown, Seyom. "Southern California's Precarious One-Crop Economy." *The Reporter* 22, no. 1 (1960): 25–28.

Burkhead, Jesse. "Vietnam and the Great Income Reshuffle." *Challenge* 15, no. 5 (1967): 12–13, 35–37.

Cameron, Juan. "The Case for Cutting Defense Spending." *Fortune* 80, no. 2 (1969): 69–73, 160–162.

Demaree, Allan T. "Defense Profits: The Hidden Issue." *Fortune* 80, no. 2 (1969): 82–83, 128, 131.

Dibble, Vernon K. "The Garrison Society." *New University Thought* 5 (special issue, 1966–67): 106–115.

Galbraith, John Kenneth. "The Big Defense Firms Are Really Public Firms and Should Be Nationalized." *New York Times Magazine,* November 16, 1969, pp. 50 ff.

———. "The Cold War and the Corporations." *Progressive* 31, no. 7 (1967): 14–18.

———. "How to Control the Military." *Harper's* 238, no. 1429 (1969): 31–46.

Goldwater, Barry. "Is There a Complex About the Complex?" *Armed Forces Management* (May, 1969), pp. 36–38.

Gray, Charles H., and Glenn W. Gregory. "Military Spending and Senate Voting: A Correlational Study." *Journal of Peace Research* 5, no. 1 (1968): 44–54.

Greenberg, Edward. "Employment Impacts of Defense Expenditures and Obligations." *Review of Economics and Statistics* 49, no. 2 (1967): 186–198.

Halverson, Guy. "The Military-Industrial Complex." *Christian Science Monitor,* March 21, 1969 through June 27, 1969 (15-part series published each Friday).

Heinl, Colonel R. D., Jr. "His Recall Never Came." *Armed Forces Journal* 108, no. 32 (1969): 27.

Hersh, Seymour M. "The Great ABM Pork Barrel." *War/Peace Report* (January, 1968), pp. 3–9, 19.

Heuse, Carl, Jr. "The Aerospace/Defense Complex." *Challenge* 13, no. 5 (1965): 32–35.

Kaufman, Richard F. "As Eisenhower Was Saying . . . 'We Must Guard Against Unwarranted Influence by the Military-Industrial Complex.'" *New York Times Magazine*, June 22, 1969, pp. 10–11, 68–72.

———. "The 80-Billion-Dollar Defense System," *Information Please Almanac, 1970.*

Koistinen, Paul A. C. "The Industrial-Military Complex in Historical Perspective: The Interwar Years." *Journal of American History* 56, no. 4 (1970): 819–839.

Lall, Betty Goetz. "Arms Reduction Impact." *Bulletin of the Atomic Scientists* 22, no. 7 (1966): 41–44.

Leontief, Wassily, and Marvin Hoffenberg. "The Economic Effects of Disarmament." *Scientific American* 204, no. 4 (1961): 47–55.

Magdoff, Harry. "Militarism and Imperialism." *Monthly Review* 21, no. 9 (1970): 1–14.

McCarthy, Eugene J. "The Pursuit of Military Security–1: The Power of the Pentagon." *Saturday Review*, December 21, 1968, pp. 8–10, 44.

McGovern, George. "And Now That the American Dream Is Safely in the Hands of the Military-Industrial Complex, We Wake to a New Decade." *Esquire* 73, no. 6 (1969): 188, 324–326, 328.

Meyerson, Martin. "Price of Admission into the Defense Industry." *Harvard Business Review* 45, no. 4 (1967): 111–123.

"The Military: Servant or Master of Policy?" *Time*, April 11, 1969, pp. 20–26.

"The Military-Industrial Complex: A Problem for the Secretary of Defense." *Congressional Quarterly Weekly Report* 26, no. 21 (1968).

"Military-Industrial Complex: The Facts vs. the Fictions." *U.S. News and World Report* 66, no. 16 (1969): 60–63.

Nelson, Bryce. "Research Probe: Rickover Broadsides 'Military-Scientific Complex.'" *Science* 161 (August 2, 1968): 446–448.

Oliver, Richard P. "The Employment Effect of Defense Expenditures." *Monthly Labor Review* 90, no. 9 (1967): 9–16.

Phelan, William D., Jr. "The Complex Society Marches On." *Ripon Forum* 5, no. 1 (1969): 9–20.

Raymond, Jack. "Growing Threat of Our Military-Industrial Complex." *Harvard Business Review* 46, no. 3 (1968): 53–64.

Rukeyser, William S. "Where the Military Contracts Go." *Fortune* 80, no. 2 (1969): 74–75.

Shoup, David M. "The New American Militarism." *Atlantic* 223, no. 4 (1969): 51–56.

"Special Report: The Military-Industrial Complex: A Problem for the Secretary of Defense." *Congressional Quarterly Weekly Report,* no. 21, May 24, 1968.

Swomley, John M., Jr. "Domestic Economic Bases of the Cold War." *Christian Century* 85 (May 1, 1968): 581–585.

Weidenbaum, Murray L. "Arms and the American Economy: A Domestic Convergence Hypothesis." *American Economic Review* 58, no. 2 (1968): 428–437.

———. "Concentration and Competition in the Military Market." *Quarterly Review of Economics and Business* 8, no. 1 (1968): 7–17.

———. "The Defense Business: A Far Cry from Adam Smith." *Challenge* 14, no. 5 (1966): 35–37, 44.

———. "The Defense-Space Complex: Impact on Whom?" *Challenge* 13, no. 4 (1965): 43–46.

INDEX

Roster of Contributors

DEAN ACHESON Secretary of State in the Truman Administration

JONATHAN B. BINGHAM United States Congress, New York State

KENNETH E. BOULDING Professor of Economics, University of Colorado; Past President, American Economics Association

RICHARD B. DUBOFF Associate Professor of Economics, Bryn Mawr College, Pennsylvania

J. WILLIAM FULBRIGHT United States Senator, Arkansas

BARRY GOLDWATER United States Senator, Arizona

PAUL GOODMAN Author, *Growing Up Absurd, Like a Conquered Province, Five Years,* and *Hawkweed,* a collection of poems

CHARLES J. HITCH President, University of California; formerly, Assistant Secretary of Defense; also, Head of the Economics Division, The Rand Corporation

RALPH E. LAPP Formerly Assistant Director, Argonne National Laboratory

GEORGE MCGOVERN United States Senator, South Dakota

ROBERT P. MAYO Director of the Bureau of the Budget

GEORGE MEANY President, AFL–CIO

JOSEPH D. PHILLIPS Research Professor of Economics, University of Illinois

WILLIAM PROXMIRE United States Senator, Wisconsin

MENDEL L. RIVERS Chairman, House Armed Services Committee, United States House of Representatives

HERBERT I. SCHILLER Professor of Communications, University of California, San Diego

CHARLES L. SCHULTZE Senior Fellow, Brookings Institute; Professor of Economics, University of Maryland; formerly, Director of the Bureau of the Budget

GENERAL DAVID SHOUP Former Commandant, United States Marine Corps

PAUL THAYER President and Chief Executive Officer, LTV Aerospace Corporation

JEROME B. WIESNER Provost, Massachusetts Institute of Technology; formerly, Science Advisor to Presidents Kennedy and Johnson